THE AFRICAN AMERICAN
THEATRICAL BODY

Presenting an innovative approach to performance studies and literary history, Soyica Diggs Colbert argues for the centrality of black performance traditions to African American literature, including preaching, dancing, blues and gospel, and theater itself, showing how these performance traditions create the "performative ground" of African American literary texts. Across a century of literary production using the physical space of the theater and the discursive space of the page, W.E.B. Du Bois, Zora Neale Hurston, James Baldwin, August Wilson, and others deploy performances to resituate black people in time and space. The study examines African American plays past and present, including *A Raisin in the Sun*, *Blues for Mister Charlie*, and *Joe Turner's Come and Gone*, demonstrating how African American dramatists stage black performances in their plays as acts of recuperation and restoration, creating sites that have the potential to repair the damage caused by slavery and its aftermath.

SOYICA DIGGS COLBERT is an assistant professor of English at Dartmouth College. She has published articles on James Baldwin, Alice Childress, and August Wilson, and is currently working on a second book project entitled *Black Movements: Performance, Politics, and Migration.*

T0349753

THE AFRICAN AMERICAN THEATRICAL BODY

Reception, Performance, and the Stage

SOYICA DIGGS COLBERT

CAMBRIDGE
UNIVERSITY PRESS

Shaftesbury Road, Cambridge CB2 8EA, United Kingdom

One Liberty Plaza, 20th Floor, New York, NY 10006, USA

477 Williamstown Road, Port Melbourne, VIC 3207, Australia

314–321, 3rd Floor, Plot 3, Splendor Forum, Jasola District Centre, New Delhi – 110025, India

103 Penang Road, #05–06/07, Visioncrest Commercial, Singapore 238467

Cambridge University Press is part of Cambridge University Press & Assessment, a department of the University of Cambridge.

We share the University's mission to contribute to society through the pursuit of education, learning and research at the highest international levels of excellence.

www.cambridge.org
Information on this title: www.cambridge.org/9781009310581

© Soyica Diggs Colbert 2011

First published 2011
First paperback edition 2022

A catalogue record for this publication is available from the British Library

Library of Congress Cataloging-in-Publication data
Colbert, Soyica Diggs, 1979–
The African American theatrical body : reception, performance, and the stage / Soyica Diggs Colbert.
p. cm.
Includes bibliographical references and index.
ISBN 978-1-107-01438-1 (Hardback)
1. American literature–African American authors–History and criticism.
2. African Americans in literature. 1. Title.
PS153.N5C54 2011
812′.509896073–dc23

2011019696

ISBN 978-1-107-01438-1 Hardback
ISBN 978-1-009-31058-1 Paperback

To Rodger

Contents

Illustrations

ix

Acknowledgements

The thoughts that would become this book were first generated in my sophomore year at Georgetown University. As I prepared to write my final paper for my English Seminar, Amy Robinson gave me Hortense Spillers' "Mama's Baby, Papa's Maybe: An American Grammar Book." The following semester Angylen Mitchell, a true mentor in every sense of the word, told me to read Cheryl Wall's *Changing Our Own Words*. I read it and immediately flashed back to Spillers' essay and knew that I wanted to do "this" work. At the time, I had little idea what "this" was. But I knew a significant turn had taken place in my thinking. With Dr. Mitchell's encouragement and guidance and Kim Hall's generous advisement through the Minority Mentoring Program at Georgetown, I embarked on my journey as a scholar.

I have many people to thank for their support of my intellectual pursuits and for guidance in writing this book. From my days at Georgetown to the present I have had wonderful mentors who shepherd me. My dissertation committee went above and beyond the call of duty, always finding time to read my work, meet with me, and offer me professional and personal advice. Without the collective insight of Cheryl Wall, David Eng, and Elin Diamond this project would not have been possible. Thank you Cheryl for being an academic triple threat – an excellent scholar, mentor, and administrator. While wearing her various hats expertly, Cheryl found time to entertain and nurture my far-out ideas, help me carve out a field of study, and show me how to navigate the academy. Cheryl taught me how to see the big picture. I am indebted to you and hope that my work serves as a positive reflection of your legacy. David Eng demonstrated intellectual creativity, ingenuity, and precision. Alongside the stunning theoretical heft he brought to our orals meetings and chapter review sessions, he also showed me compassion and kindness with his characteristic charisma. Elin Diamond sparked my passion for drama. In my first year in graduate school, I read *Color Struck* in Elin's class and after reading my final paper she encouraged me to continue to write about drama. With an eye for the abstract and unlikely connection, Elin taught me to look beyond the obvious and even probable. Brent Hayes Edwards also served as a mentor and model of academic excellence. Several of the ideas in this book began as papers in his classes. I am grateful to Brent for his encyclopedic knowledge, generosity, and insight. Harry J. Elam, Jr. played an essential role in helping me to transform my dissertation into a book. Reading drafts, offering advice, and providing strategic insight, Harry helped me to develop a sense of the plays not just as texts but also as theatrical works. His expertise as a director, critic, and teacher and his generosity and accessibility as a mentor have sharpened my analysis of drama, theater, and performance. Thank you to Kimberly Benston, Jennifer Brody, Daphne Brooks, Harry J. Elam, Jr., Donald Pease, and Ivy Schweitzer for reading the manuscript in its entirety and giving me essential feedback. Thank you to my readers at Cambridge University Press and to my editors Victoria Cooper and Rebecca Taylor for your support. I am also indebted to Jennifer Brody, Abena Busia, Michele Elam, Koritha Mitchell, Paula Moya, Evie Shockley, Salamishah Tillet, and Harvey Young for their professional support. From Dartmouth, I thank Aimee Bahng, Colleen Boggs, Michael Chaney, Jonathan Crewe, George Edmondson, J. Martin Favor, Gretchen Gerzina, Alexandra Halasz, Thomas Luxon, Patricia McKee, Sam Vasquéz, Barbara Will, and Melissa Zeiger for their insight and feedback on my work.

Portions of Chapters 5 and 6 were published previously in different forms. Chapter 5 appeared in *Sonic Interventions*, ed. Sylvia Mieszkowski, Joy Smith, and Marijke de Valck (Amsterdam: Rodopi, 2007), 193–210; and Chapter 6 appeared in *New England Theatre Journal* 19.1 (2008), 45–60. I thank Rodopi and *New England Theatre Journal* for allowing me to reuse this material. I would not have been able to write this book without the generous support of the Woodrow Wilson Foundation, which enabled its completion. I am also grateful to the Robert W. Woodruff Library Fellowship and the Walter and Constance Burke Research Award for providing funding for the archival research that enhances this project, and the Dartmouth College Presidential Scholars Program that funded the research assistance of Graciela Pichardo. Thank you to the American Society of Theater Research for enabling the inclusion of images from *Blues for Mister Charlie* through the Brooks McNamara Publishing Subvention. In addition, the Stanford University Humanities Postdoctoral Fellowship gave me time to write the first draft of the manuscript. I am also grateful for the support of Dartmouth

Provost Berry Scherr, Associate Dean of Faculty Katharine Conley, and Chair of African and African American Studies Antonio Tillis.

I am blessed to be a part of several collectives that remind me of the power of community. Thank you to the members of my dissertation reading group, particularly Kelly Baker Josephs and Richard Mizelle. Thanks to the members of the Black Performance Theory Research Group and to the participants of the Futures of American Studies Institute. Perhaps most importantly, thank you to the members of the New England Black Scholars Collective who have sustained me and kept me sane through the long winters in New England. You remind me of why we do this work. With love and gratitude to Aliyyah Abdur-Rahman, Sandy Alexandre, Nicole Aljoe, Alisa Braithwaite, Kimberly Juanita Brown, Régine Jean-Charles, Stéphanie Larrieux, Monica White Ndounou, and Sam Vasquéz. From Georgetown I thank Crystal Brown, Heather Burrs, DaQuaan Carter, Deitra Wynn Scott, Woodrow Scott, George Stover, and Michelle Wallace-Soyinka. I am very lucky to have two close friends who have laughed with me, commiserated with me, encouraged me, talked through ideas with me, and reminded me of what is truly important. Thank you to Rosenny Fenton and Robert J. Patterson for your friendship.

Although my professional cultivation began at Georgetown, I owe my investment in education to the Brown Family. To my grandparents Harold Coblyn (now deceased) and Ruth Harris, I am grateful to have learned what love looks like in action from you. To my parents, R. Harrington and Joanne Diggs, thank you for your love, tireless support, encouragement, prayer, sacrifice, and guidance. In each stage of my life you have been a consistent source of support, thank you. Thanks to my brother Diallyo Diggs and nephew Diallyo Diggs II for laughter, encouragement, and insight. Thanks to my one and only sister Rakiya Diggs for being my best friend, my advocate, and my biggest cheerleader.

And finally I want to thank Rodger I. Colbert for helping me to do better. Thank you for your love, care, and patience as this project matured into a book. Rodger, I thank you for giving me time to write, ideas to consider, words to communicate, a shoulder to cry on, and a safe space to grow. This book is dedicated to you and all that you have done to make it possible.

SOYICA DIGGS COLBERT
Concord, NH

Overture: rites of reparation
Suzan-Lori Parks' The America Play

The black theatrical body is rendered flexible in Pulitzer Prize-winning playwright Suzan-Lori Parks' *The America Play*. *The America Play* stealthily appropriates national comportment by drawing attention to the artifice of the show that is US citizenship. Twisting, turning, holding, and slumping his body just so, the protagonist of *The America Play* unravels mimetic blackness and centuries of black theatricality, revealing how performance "highlights the *mechanics* of spectacle."[1] In order to disrupt the equivalence of blackness with display and thereby to interrupt the passing down of black theatricality from one generation to the next, the play troubles genealogy. The protagonist is a gravedigger who moonlights as an Abraham Lincoln impersonator and, upon his death, leaves a hole in the ground to his son Brazil. The hole left as Brazil's inheritance serves as the setting of the play and replicates another hole, the Great Hole of History, which is a historical theme park. The protagonist, also known as the Foundling Father, first encounters the Great Hole of History while honeymooning with his wife Lucy. A desire to recreate the Great Hole drives the Foundling Father to leave his family and to go west and dig a replica. Once transplanted, people begin to notice that the protagonist bears "a strong resemblance to Abraham Lincoln."[2] Although "diggin [is] his livelihood ... fakin [is] his callin," so the Foundling Father, whose name implies his lack of parentage, becomes an Abraham Lincoln impersonator (179). His protean nature bolsters ironically his presidential bona fides to the point where the Foundling Father suffers the same fate as Lincoln: a stray bullet kills him in the theater at the end of act 1, which is how, as Parks describes, "he digged the hole and the whole held him" (159).

In the play the hole accumulates several different meanings: it serves as the setting of the play, refers to graves and women's genitals, undermines a teleological view of history, functions as a locale for improvisation and creation, and recalls the trauma enacted when the Foundling Father leaves

Brazil and Lucy. Filled with ambiguity, riddled with doubling, and saturated with slippages, I argue that the hole also evokes two historical holes: the hole the bullet bored in President Abraham Lincoln's head and the one resulting from the trans-Atlantic slave trade that the Middle Passage symbolizes. Referencing the history of US chattel slavery, *The America Play* fills metaphorically the cavities related to the trade in human flesh with performances – faking and digging – which are two exemplary examples of reparative modes central to the black theater throughout the twentieth century. To clarify, I define performance – borrowing and intertwining Richard Schechner's and Ngugi wa Thiong'o's theories – as "restored" or "twice-behaved behavior" that "assumes an audience during its actualization."[3] While Schechner's often-cited definition does not explicitly require an audience, I assert the dynamics of reception to emphasize how reception functions as a critical part of the literary history of a play. African American dramatists direct the exertive force black performance produces to create rites of repair.

The combination of digging and faking metonymically represents black theatrical reparations, which are acts of redress and social justice. Faking becomes the motif through which Parks calls into question the certainty of the body as a signifier of the real. *The America Play* foregrounds this line of inquiry by having the Foundling Father refer to his beards, the shape of his body, his costume, and the wart on his face throughout the first act. In Brechtian fashion, he emphasizes the artifice of his physical properties and challenges the mimetic quality often associated with great acting. Unable to seamlessly impersonate Abraham Lincoln, the Foundling Father explains the illogic that "Some inaccuracies are good for business. Take the stovepipe hat! Never really worn indoors but people dont like their Lincoln hatless"; as he implies, patrons do not accept other inaccuracies (168). His comments raise the question of why audiences require some "inaccurate" details and disdain others, and may anticipate and arguably produce the desires of the live theater audience. In the Yale Repertory Theater production (1994), this comment would have drawn attention to any dissonance an audience member might have felt about a black actor, Reggie Montgomery, playing Lincoln.

The Yale Repertory Theater's production of the play sets a precedent for casting that the text supports even though the play never mentions race explicitly. Although Parks does not specify the race of the main character in *The America Play*, she gives him an occupation – digger – that rhymes with a familiar racial slur. Throughout Parks' oeuvre she uses punning and rhyming to impart meaning. Additionally the back cover of *The America*

Play and Other Works that the Theatre Communications Group (TCG) first published in 1995 features a black man elusively in profile dressed as Abraham Lincoln and standing in front of the American flag. The front cover depicts a disembodied Lincoln with the title of the collection superimposed on the signature stovepipe hat and Parks' name in red capital letters over the chest area of the suit, suggesting that by the time one finishes the collection, the engagement will fill the hole the founding father leaves with the foundling one. The back cover of the TCG volume responds to the visual call of the front cover, creating protocols for literary reception that mimic the engagement among actors and audiences encouraged in Parks' theater, whereby the drama manages the expectations of the audience through the references to patrons who find some historical inaccuracies troubling and others necessary. Until and perhaps even after the inauguration of President Barack Hussein Obama, Reggie Montgomery's physical characteristics seem at odds with the role he plays; "the U.S. president has traditionally stood for everything that blackness was not: commanding, legitimate, virtuous, white," according to Tavia Nyong'o.[4] Yet Montgomery and President Obama play it nonetheless. The Foundling Father's faking elucidates how the theater exemplifies a "real" that constantly slips and destabilizes bodies and thus race, which renders blackness a dubious guarantor of the real.[5] Even in a postmodern context, black bodies often represent the authentic and material. In the play, theater becomes a masterful exemplar of the malleability of the archive, even of the black body – a *sine qua non* of material evidence.[6]

The play continues to press the limits of material evidence, bolstering the interrogation of archives as complete chronicles of the past.[7] The hole in *The America Play* also represents the loss of narrative and the active process between writers and readers and actors and audiences that repeatedly attempts to fill the gaps. The active improvisational impulse marks distinctly the benefit of using the theatrical event as a model for practices of reading more generally. Just as each theatrical reproduction of *The America Play* results in an individual and shared experience, so too does each individual reading of the text, suggesting that all literary history should acknowledge how the event may alter the archive, the materiality of the play as text, and make an ephemeral yet necessary addition to literary histories. Keeping in mind the literary implications, the theater as a model for dynamics of reading has particular importance in terms of black studies. Loss remains a central concern to black historiography, in large part due to the nature of archives that rely solely on material evidence, evidence regarding the experiences of enslaved Africans in the

US that is in many instances irrecoverable. At the same time the legacy of slavery, as communicated through racial hierarchies, reduces black people to materiality – walking archives – reflecting the assumption that at one point the ancestor of a black person was literally property. Through manipulations of the relationships between actors and audiences, African American drama foregrounds the ideologically constituted nature of all bodies, making African American drama the perfect medium to untangle this snarled web of racial inheritances and, in Parks' words, to make history. She writes, "theatre is an incubator for the creation of historical events – and, as in the case of artificial insemination, the baby is no less human."[8]

Although the term is often associated with legal battles for material remuneration, *The African American Theatrical Body* uses "reparations" to signify acts of making history that result in "the symbolic reordering of the social and political hierarchy," as cultural critics Harry J. Elam, Jr. and Michele Elam put it.[9] For decades, black literary theorists have contemplated the ways black writers challenge existing historical narratives by inserting their voices and therefore remaking the very meaning of history. These important revisionary acts have been key to the development of black feminist thought. The act of revising, nevertheless, stands at a critical distance from the act of making. Revision is reactive while making is proactive. I do not offer this distinction to create a hierarchy, especially since revisionist histories provided the vantage point by which theorists might imagine the use of reparations as a term that describes the act of narrative. One such important study, the autumn 2005 issue of *Representations*, edited by Stephen Best and Saidiya Hartman on behalf of the Redress Project, specifies how and why the production of narrative qualifies as a historical act that imparts reparations. The issue focuses on trans-Atlantic slavery. Best and Hartman explain, "What is crucial for us … is the incompletion of abolition. We understand the particular character of slavery's violence to be ongoing and constitutive of the unfinished project of freedom."[10] Best and Hartman clarify that in their engagement with slave narratives they "are concerned neither with 'what happened then' nor with 'what is owed because of what happened then,' but rather with the contemporary predicament of freedom, with the melancholy recognition of foreseeable futures still tethered to this past."[11] The tie to the past, through the stories we tell, identities we live, or societies we build, creates an opportunity to not only "squarely engage the problem of 'futures'" but also actively and continually address history.[12]

Whereas Best and Hartman focus on the way narrative mobilizes politics that may advance the ongoing pursuit of freedom "on behalf of the slave (the stateless, the socially dead, and the disposable) in the political present," this book considers how symbolic reordering functions through narration, visual representation, and acoustic signification (speech, song, and music) to create historical events that demonstrate the political power of aesthetics. As the Elams cogently argue in "Blood Debt: Reparations in Langston Hughes's *Mulatto*," the symbolic function of the reparative act, or what they call "payback," does not limit its political potency but enhances it. They insist that history, as form of narration, is the living force of ideas, embodied in and daily enacted by people. "Thus social change can potentially occur through history itself."[13] Moreover, the constitutive force of history on individuals enables an active consideration of not only who we may become but also who we thought ourselves to be, a radical formation of self that advances liberation in the now and creates the conditions in which political change may occur in and through the body.

While the first act of *The America Play* establishes the characteristics of the hole as a site to be filled with acts of repair – faking and digging – the second act locates the restorative quality in the act of transfer. Act II takes place thirty years later and features Brazil and Lucy, searching for the Foundling Father's remains. The protagonist leaves detritus buried in the ground and his Lincoln act for Brazil to find. Lucy's persistent admonition, "DIG," punctuates Brazil's labor. As he digs, Brazil demonstrates the repertoire, a "nonarchival system of transfer," that his father left him.[14] Brazil explains:

(*Rest. Rest.*) On thuh day he claimed to be the 100th anniversary of the founding of our country the Father took the Son out into the yard. The Father threw himself down in front of the Son and bit into the dirt with his teeth. His eyes leaked. "This is how youll make your mark, Son" the Father said. The Son was only 2 then. "This is the Wail," the Father said. "There's money init," the Father said. The Son was only 2 then. Quiet. On what he claimed was the 101st anniversary the Father showed the Son "the Weep" "the Sob" and "the Moan." How to stand just so what to do with the hands and feet (to capitalize on what we in the business call "the Mourning Moment"). Formal stances the Fatherd picked up at the History Hole. The Son studied night and day. By candlelight. No one could best him. The money came pouring in. On the 102nd anniversary the Son was 5 and the Father taught him "the Gnash." The day after the Father left for out West. To seek his fortune. In the middle of dinnertime. The Son was eating his peas. (182)

The father leaves his son a physical and emotional hole and the mechanisms to capitalize on his losses. The Foundling Father's conspicuous enactment of mourning reconfigures the Great Hole of History – the

Middle Passage – from a negative site that affiliates black people – shared trauma binds together – into the wellspring of common practices that an individual may choose to repeat. While Parks' play focuses on a specific set of practices – faking and digging – these exemplify the general deconstructive impulse at the heart of all the performances explored in this book. With varied success, the performances beg audiences to sympathetically relate to and critically analyze the competing and conflicting interests that inspire Brazil's performance – the genuine trauma the loss of his father causes, the avaricious appetite that profitable mourning business produces, and the emotional pleasure created by crafting history in relationship to the person he will become.

In Parks' play blackness no longer solely corresponds to that which tragically marks the subject and binds him to a past he did not choose. Alternatively, blackness produces the potential for intergenerational profits as its performance passes from the Foundling Father to Brazil. Nevertheless, the profitability requires the sacrifice of the body; the tears the Father produces and Brazil may reproduce communicate the physical pain the performance induces, the Father throwing himself down and biting into the dirt. Notably, in Brazil's reenactment he may emphasize the theatricality of the display by mimicking his father's physical action or choose to resist that representation by standing still as he tells the story. If Brazil were to mimic the Lesser Known's actions, then the assertion "this is how youll make your mark" would pun on the word "mark," underscoring how performance manipulates actively the racially signified body. Glenda R. Carpio suggests, "Parks distinguishes the kind of mourning that her work dramatizes from the kind that the Faker teaches his son by insisting that her audience process rather than simply consume the mourning her plays enact."[15] I add to Carpio's cogently argued interpretation an acknowledgement of the director's choice or that of the actor, which creates the potential for Brazil to refuse his inheritance – to simply tell the story and not reenact mourning. Such a performance would take on a derisive tone. I point out the interpretive multiplicities in order to highlight the collaborative process at the heart of all literature and to locate collaboration as a site of political action. This multiplicity enables Parks' character to disavowingly embrace racialized inheritances. In this gesture he is not alone: an entire generation of artists has attempted to attenuate race's burden while mobilizing its productive power. One such artist, Glenn Ligon, coined the term "postblack" to demarcate art that refuses to be bound by a category, black art, which the artists found limiting. "It was characterized by artists who were adamant about not being labeled as 'black artists,' though their work was steeped, in fact deeply interested, in redefining notions of blackness."[16] Appropriating Ligon's concept, Brazil's narration has the potential to materialize a postblack performance that embraces the desire to shirk the burden of inheritance. Such a move endows agency upon the makers of black historiography, locating them behind the scholar's desk, on the stage, and in quotidian performances.

In staging a melodramatic scene of mourning at the replica of the Great Hole of History, the play reclaims that negative physical and psychic space, an apparent vacuum, and fills it with performance, noting "This is the Wail … There's money init." By emphasizing Brazil's inherited ability to stage mourning, Parks separates the black actor from his role. As a result, hypervisibility becomes a constitutive element of blackness that overdetermines black people's physical bodies and undermines their psychological, intellectual, and emotional lives. The stereotype that black people in the US intrinsically excel at singing and dancing, for example, stems from a long history of displaying not only black people but also people of color in the Americas more generally.[17] From the first enslaved Africans brought to US shores, uninhibited looking participates in the production of blackness. In the nineteenth century, blackface minstrelsy serves as one of the primary demarcations of the performative nature of blackness, which notably stands at a critical distance from black people. Audiences knew famous performers Bert Williams and George Walker for, among other things, performing in blackface. Seeing images of them may provoke the question why a black person would need to don black face paint? The addition of black face makeup on brown skin attests to the active construction of blackness that occurred on, but not in, their bodies.

Similarly, *The America Play* advances a model of bodily materialization through performance; however, it purposefully stages replicas and repetitions to demonstrate how those performances may shift over time and serve to manage and transform inheritances. The play calls attention to the ability to transform the history of black people's losses in the US through site-specific performances that must be repeated in order to facilitate an alternative manifestation of birthrights. Instead of only offering the burden of the Middle Passage, which the hole metaphorically represents, to Brazil as a legacy, the Foundling Father leaves mechanisms for his son to capitalize on those losses. In so doing, the play not only unsettles the relationship between black identity and loss but also reveals that white identity does not necessarily imply fullness. Additionally, *The America Play* deconstructs blackness' inherent theatrical nature, by depicting Brazil being taught to perform even as the Foundling Father highlights the monetary incentive for him to wail.[18] The potential for wailing in Brazil's description produces echoes throughout this book, resounding most forcefully in Chapters 2, 5 and 6.

While each chapter considers the co-option of putatively negative space, emphasizing African American drama's ability to intercede in material histories, by beginning with an Overture – a hole and a revelation – I set this book in a hole that twentieth-century black dramatists have transformed into a (w)hole à la Parks. Unlike Parks, I insert parentheses to mark the unfinished reparative project. The space – physical and psychic, geographical and affective – that black dramatists carved out in the twentieth century marks a central political and aesthetic innovation of the genre; the creation of space enables African American drama to render rites that continually redress the rupture the trans-Atlantic slave trade causes. Indeed, slavery in the Americas marks the beginning of this tale with a break that organizes the scenes of the drama that will unfold.[19] The geographical relationships and corporeal legacies of that rupture still regulate psychic, physical, economic, communal, and governmental relationships, and modes of looking, hearing, and feeling in the twentieth century and the contemporary moment. Each artistic period of the twentieth century, from the Post-Bellum, Pre-Harlem era (1877–1919) to the Post-Soul one (1978 to the present), reflects the strictures of the trans-Atlantic slave trade as a primal scene that, in opposition to the organizing principles of Sigmund Freud's tale of origins, enables plenitude.[20] Using the same principles that enable *The America Play* to produce a (w)hole, African American drama creates participatory sites on the page and stage that transform modes of hearing, seeing, and being, such that the trauma associated with Freud's rendering of the primal scene, from a different point of view, allows a historical lesson that dramatists then co-opt in the name of repairing historical damage that will not go away but that also does not have to live on in its current manifestation. This book considers the way African American dramatists flipped the epistemological script, transforming absence into ways of being present, homelessness into modes of finding a home, loss into mechanisms of mourning, and disenfranchisement into rites that render repairing.

More specifically, Parks demonstrates her notion of "Reconstructed Historicities," structuring the progress of *The America Play* with repetitions and reversals (163). Not only does the play call for Brazil to repeat his father's performance, but it also undermines the singular authority of historical narrative marked by specific dates and times. The play establishes the dates as "hearsay," which explains why Brazil remembers being two years old at the one hundredth anniversary and five years old at the one hundred and second (182). The slippages in Brazil's memory function as a part of the play's overall reworking of the past, which Parks introduces with the epigraph "in the beginning, *all the world was* America" (159). The epigraph has an oppositional relationship to the play, which foregrounds narratives that exceed national memory, the voice of the Foundling Father versus that of Lincoln. The reversals in Parks' canon, and African American drama more generally, enable black performers to continually manipulate subject and object positions.

Once *The America Play* establishes the mutability of history, it advances the importance of attending to the content of narratives. Take for example a line often repeated in the play that is also an example of chiasmus, "he digged the hole and the whole held him" (159). The line depicts a world turned upside down not only through the pun on (w)hole but also by foreshadowing that the Foundling Father's digging will result in his demise.[21] Through the transformation in the line and the play (from hole to whole) the Foundling Father shifts from agent of action (the subject of the sentence) to the object receiving the action. Marking a slippage between the written and the oral, the homophones function to denote the constructed nature of all historiography that factual evidence purportedly underpins.

The use of chiasmus is a fitting device to negotiate the relationship between historicity and the theater, which, as a form, reverses positions and allows for shifts in the status quo. Parks collapses the distance between historicity and the theater by deploying the same rhetorical strategy used in one of the most often-cited lines from *The Narrative of the Life of Frederick Douglass, an American Slave, Written by Himself.* In Frederick Douglass' 1845 autobiography, he details the brutality of the slave breaker, Mr. Covey, and remarks, "You have seen how a man was made a slave; you shall see how a slave was made a man."[22] In the *Narrative*, chiasmus communicates Douglass' movement in the opposite direction from the Foundling Father. Instead of becoming an object, Douglass becomes a subject – from slave to man. The critical difference between Douglass' assertion and the Foundling Father's prediction informs the shape of history that each figure may draw. In Douglass' autobiography, the development of the narrative follows the evolution of a great man in the tradition of other great men, demonstrating distinctively how the formerly enslaved man stands in for black people in the Americas in general.[23] His narrative attests to the humanity of enslaved Africans and advocates their freedom. The Foundling Father, conversely, is a black man playing Lincoln. His actions call the audience to reconsider a relationship between the legacy of Lincoln and black people. This reflexive and complicated relationship does not undermine the humanity the *Narrative* establishes; in fact it broadens the freedom sought in Douglass' autobiography through the transition from an empty hole to a full one – a (w)hole – that holds the Foundling Father by the end of the play. By revising Douglass through visual and spatial associations, Parks situates the theater as a potential space for birthing radical aesthetics and histories through performance.

When modified by the demarcation "black," performance becomes at once a mode of subjection and of objection. My purposeful use of chiasmus, referencing subjection as subordination and the act of becoming a subject, and objection as being rendered an object and resisting the dominant order, communicates the simultaneity of the revolutionary and black-minstrel-like characterizations expressed in William Wells Brown's *The Escape* (1858), the first published African American play.[24] Eleanor Traylor's essay "Two Afro-American Contributions to Dramatic Form" (1980) locates the source of all American theater in the minstrel show and the slave narrative.[25] Following Traylor's early study, Fred Moten designates black performance as a radical aesthetic tradition in his groundbreaking work *In the Break* (2003). *In the Break* revises Saidiya Hartman's pioneering *Scenes of Subjection* (1997), and in so doing enacts an ethical shift that recalibrates the value attributed to black life. As described in *The Narrative of the Life of Frederick Douglass*, both authors reference the brutal beating of an enslaved black woman to mark her as an object. In Chapter 2, I investigate the inaugural scene of Aunt Hester's objectification as depicted in Douglass' narrative, but alternatively turn here to the organizing grammar that Parks' play shares with the autobiography. I return to the scene of this crime via Suzan-Lori Parks' *The America Play* and argue that black drama destabilizes the temporality of the black radical tradition. African American drama often introduces familiar racial performances that have historically been associated with the objectification of black people (i.e., lynching or minstrel-inspired style) and then challenges those performances by creating sites that interrupt that objectification (for example, Chapter 5 analyzes the haunting quality of a lynching victim's voice). African American drama returns to the scenes of crimes to interrupt historical processes used to render black people objects and offers performance strategies that not only keep the dehumanizing force of objection at bay but also enable the performers and audiences to object by reconfiguring the historical order.

Through a theorization of this practice, I add repair to the aesthetic line Hartman and Moten delineate. Black performance not only perpetuates a radical tradition, it intervenes in the past not to undo or override it but to actively engage and abide with it in the present. My attention to temporality, the way African American dramatists literarily make history, seeks neither to disclaim the use of recuperation nor to substitute another model. Instead, I am emphasizing the reparative quality of performance that I locate in a theatrical context.

Parks' play presents Douglass as the Foundling Father of the African American literary tradition, reproducing the status of foundling and its relationship to national history in order to specify a literary genealogy.[26] If, as Hartman convincingly argues, the brutality of slavery created a primal scene reconstituted through quotidian expressions of "pleasure, paternalism, and property," Parks' reproduction of one of Douglass' organizing grammars calls forth "a disturbance that is neither unfamiliar nor unfamilial."[27] Parks ties the imagery of the patriarchal nation state to the false promise the moniker "Foundling Father" implies. Parks' "faux-father" denaturalizes the metaphor of national paternity through the depiction of Brazil's inheritance (184), presenting "an origin-less father of our country's history."[28] *The America Play* reproduces Douglass' status as a bastard in order to mark the continual negotiation and therefore malleability of what that position entails.[29] The use of names in the play addresses the historical refusal to recognize the resemblance between foundling and founding fathers, which not only reconfigures Douglass' place in the order of things, but also his common position as bastard and bearer of an alternative genealogy that enables "the African-American male [to] regain . . . an aspect of his own personhood – the 'power' of 'yes' to the 'female' within."[30] Through the figure of the origin-less father, Parks challenges the regulatory norms that materialize the body (sex, race, genealogy) in the service of whiteness, patriarchy, and heteronormativity, revealing an opportunity that the familial fractures formed in relation to the trans-Atlantic slave trade produced.

DEVELOPING A TRADITION OF REPAIR

The African American Theatrical Body examines a century of African American drama and theatrical production that draws on the social, cultural, political, and economic conditions surrounding each play's attempts to repair the losses and attenuate the haunting legacy of trans-Atlantic slavery and its racialized, gendered, and class-specific aftermath. I argue for the centrality to the African

American literary tradition of black performance traditions expressed in cakewalking, preaching, hustling, migrating, rituals (e.g., dancing the juba and making blood sacrifices), and singing of blues and gospel. These performance traditions create the 'performative ground' of African American literary texts. Using the physical space of the theater and the discursive one of the page, W.E.B. Du Bois, Zora Neale Hurston, Langston Hughes, Lorraine Hansberry, James Baldwin, Amiri Baraka, August Wilson, Suzan-Lori Parks, and Tarell Alvin McCraney deploy performances to resituate black people in time and space. I contend that throughout the twentieth century, African American dramatists stage black performances in their plays as acts of recuperation and restoration, creating sites that have the potential to repair the damage slavery and its aftermath cause.

Beginning with *the* African American play – an urtext of African American drama – Lorraine Hansberry's *A Raisin in the Sun* (1959), I challenge the notion that it stabilizes the idea of a black home and, conversely, situate the play within the history of migration narratives to emphasize how black performance operates as a form of psychic management in the face of displacement. Attending to black performance reveals historical repertoires (i.e., cakewalking or singing gospel music) that produce social, material, and cultural knowledge in multisensory registers. After establishing movement as fundamental to the sites black drama creates, on the page and in theatrical production, the book examines key moments of African Americans' displacement. It investigates the spatial dynamics that develop in relation to the trans-Atlantic slave trade, Jim Crow, the Civil Rights Movement, and Black Power Movement, and ends with a consideration of the spatial ambiguity of the Post-Soul era. During each of these periods, black dramatists devised modes of performance to manage the loss of physical space. The range of black performances this book examines, from the prototypical (the African American sermon) to the atypical (lynching), represents a broad diversity. Following Chapter 1, I organize the book chronologically to emphasize the different ways reparations function in African American drama throughout the twentieth century. The reparative acts transform from practices that claim histories in Chapters 2 and 3, which examine the first decades of the century, to social affirmations of the present in Chapters 4 and 5, which consider the mid-century, to ritual practices that imagine future histories in Chapters 6 and 7 and the Epilogue, which comment on the last decades of the twentieth century and the early twenty-first century. Viewing the drama as a tradition as opposed to individual plays exposes the development of systems of repair.

My selection of plays creates a canon of black drama that underscores the inventiveness, creativity, and resourcefulness expressed through black performance. *The African American Theatrical Body* demonstrates how African American drama provides a critical context to interpret black performance and how that intervention extends African American literary, theatrical, performance, and black studies by considering a non-cartographically specific model of cultural exchange. The model, nevertheless, depends on staging in a specific place, but the mutability of that site emphasizes the process, development, and movement of the ritual instead of particular coordinates on a map. Such flexibility calls attention to the live event as a part of an ongoing exchange between actors and audiences that actively challenges the limits of imagining any literary history within a closed geographic circuit.

This book emphasizes that African American drama extends African American literary and theatrical studies by inviting us to focus on how the object of inquiry, the play, continues to develop through multiple mechanisms of reception – in every publication and in every restaging of the drama. Each of the texts engages a widespread concern of its literary and historical period, such as colorism in *Color Struck*, a major concern during the Harlem Renaissance. At the same time in each chapter, I examine the drama alongside a written form (essay, song, poem, or novel) to demonstrate how drama augments our understanding of some of the most often-read texts in black studies. Yet African American drama stages rites of repair that strive toward audience engagement and therefore necessitate a particular understanding of the eventfulness of the theatrical production, an eventfulness that may exceed what can be captured in an archive. I use theatrical studies in conjunction with performance studies, since the intersection reveals how African American theater, like performance, relies on "the conjunction of reproduction and disappearance [which] is performance's condition of possibility, its ontology and its mode of production."[31]

REPETITION/REPRODUCTION

The double helix – repetition/reproduction – that forms the DNA of black expressive culture broadly, and drama specifically, insists that it must stay in motion. Repetition/reproduction creates a structure by which the repetition of performances may find fitting space to reproduce a scene and rework that scene's history. Black dramatists use the space of the theater to create an atmosphere that capitalizes on the political potential the perpetual nature of the dyad generates, which gives black dramatists and audiences an ongoing opportunity to redo the past. The dyad may also render other sites – the classroom, lecture hall, or conference – ripe for black performance and the opportunity to see the past differently. Black dramatists use the present to rethink the past and reorient the future. Black feminist studies strongly informs this model, which clarifies how the Middle Passage becomes a site of repair in Wilson's *Joe Turner's Come and Gone*, which I explore in Chapter 6, and more broadly how performance may transform other sites of trauma into generative primal scenes.

The repetition/reproduction dyad reconfigures repetition as a term central to performance theory, black studies, and black theater studies, by intertwining it with reproduction, a term that materializes the reparative practices key to black literary studies.[32] Repetition is the simultaneous reiteration and transformation of something we have seen before. According to Freud, it serves as one of the primary methods to solidify the ego and therefore raises the question of how previous performances communicate psychic legacies. Repetitions occur in cultural practices, language, and people's personal lives. Phrases repeat; ceremonies repeat; and actions repeat. Each time a black performance repeats, it reproduces the historical conditions that initiated it in a new context, enabling an engagement with and departure from sites of previous trauma. Through the theoretical musings of Suzan-Lori Parks, black theatrical criticism builds on Henry Louis Gates, Jr.'s formulation of signifying – repetition with a difference – with Parks' "rep and rev" (short for repetition and revision), which incorporates a temporal quality.[33] Parks' formulation folds revision into repetition and considers each repeated act as an opportunity to rethink the past. "Rep and rev" does not aim to theorize the literary tradition and therefore does not account for repetitions among texts. Nevertheless, Parks' notion of revision as historical intervention informs reproduction. At the same time, my term purposefully references African Americans' lack of reproductive freedom (their inability to decide the conditions in which biological reproduction would occur) in order to centralize the body in the repairing this book endeavors to perpetuate. My argument intersects with Gates', but, unlike Gates, I am interested in how performatives – saying that brings about doing[34] – materialize the body. As shown in my opening example, African American drama's uniqueness in terms of genre resides in its ability to demonstrate the constructed nature of the body, the last bastion of the real. Instead of dissipating, the question of the material versus the representational seems to have increased political potency in the digital age. Institutionally, the politics surrounding visual markers of race both undergird and threaten race-based identity categories that drove the development of ethnic studies in colleges and universities as well as the cultivation of community and political organizations. Decoupling blackness from the real enables a shift in how black people understand themselves in relation to each other, the past, and the future because it challenges the notion of race as a fixed entity.

Black performance pressures materiality in engaging with and redirecting the discursive regimes that seek to exclude it. As a result, repetition/reproduction challenges the individuality of Freud's theory of repetition to suggest its applicability to groups. The visual dynamic inherent in the classical renditions of psychic splitting, from Freud to Du Bois, has particular resonance with the manipulation of presence and absence at the heart of drama, theater, performance, and race theory. Although the psychic splitting at the heart of Freudian psychoanalysis asserts heterosexual difference as the only difference of any importance, some critics of ethnic studies have chosen to read against the grain of Freud's discourse, finding psychoanalysis to be a useful point of departure.[35] In "'All the Things You Could Be By Now, If Sigmund Freud's Wife Was Your Mother': Psychoanalysis and Race," Hortense Spillers positions race as psychoanalysis' uncanny other. She explains, "Freud could not 'see' his own connection to the 'race'/culture orbit, or could not theorize it, because the place of their elision marked the vantage point from which he spoke ... Perhaps we could argue that the 'race' matrix was the fundamental *interdiction* within the enabling discourse of founding psychoanalytic theory and practice itself."[36] The forbidden quality of race within Freudian psychoanalysis marks it as the enabling discourse that haunts psychic ruptures. The visual recognition of difference and corresponding psychic trauma reverberates in the black performances staged in African American theater. Moreover, the plays examined in this book challenge the physical signifiers of race by calling into question the psychic structures that underpin them and therefore also the very meanings attributed to race. To examine black performances in terms of reproduction is to move from ghostly memory to the introjection of history, from the incorporation of loss to the "work of mourning."[37]

RETRACING MY STEPS

Studying black performance, in the context of African American drama, as a literary and theatrical enterprise raises concerns with regard to source material, especially since this study attends to the movement of performances between genres and locations. The uneven distribution of critical attention that favors certain plays and dramatic periods over others, whether due to the notoriety of the artist as a playwright at the time of the performance or to the scale of the production, creates a hierarchy of value in the archive that *The African American Theatrical Body* works to dismantle.[38] Absence plagues performance studies as it characterizes ethnic studies.[39] In a historical moment when budget crises put particular pressure on the precarious position of interdisciplinary studies, this book foregrounds alternative ways of producing knowledge and begins with the assumption of the limits to evidence available in the archive. While theatrical and literary methodologies play an important role in my analysis, the chapters that follow foreground the dynamic, subversive, and elusive quality of black performance that may be captured in literary contexts – biographies, periodical reviews, playbills, footage, and ethnographic studies – but is often excluded from literary studies. The methodology foregrounds performance as moving through the repetition/reproduction dyad, which contextualizes, for example, the acerbic reviews of Langston Hughes' *Tambourines to Glory* as particular to time and place while the performance itself stays in motion.

The first chapter establishes a question: What happens to a dream deferred? The well-known query marks an existential crisis that the interrogative structure mediates. I argue that this structure establishes an epistemological framework central to African American drama as it introduces deferred dreaming as a problem that the remainder of the book takes up. The book does not speak to dreaming in a utopian sense. Rather, it considers the active psychic mechanisms that organize the symbolic world in such a way that the family Hansberry depicts must always fall short of obtaining its idealized state. American audiences continue to watch *A Raisin in the Sun* because it brushes up against a familiar desire, the American dream. But notably, the play does not unfold from a position of possibility but instead imagines the creativity impossibility engenders – a dream *deferred*. *A Raisin in the Sun* does not assume entitlement to the pursuit of happiness but instead asks what happens in the midst of the denial of such pursuit? Starting from a position of disentitlement, displacement, and alienation, the characters question the relationship between decolonization and American possibility and suggest that the tension created by the competing rhetoric of the American dream and black freedom struggles, nationally and internationally, continues to defer Hansberry's characters' achievement of the

American dream. Chapter 1 interrupts the chronological order of the chapters to draw attention to how Hansberry's drama depicts the unfinished business of African American drama.

The sense of perpetual deferment finds it historical nexus in the play discussed in Chapter 2. The state of deferred dreaming – a liminal space – coincides with the feeling of being outside of history that Du Bois' *The Star of Ethiopia* addresses. The pageant stages a history lesson that educates audiences about the limits and possibilities of history as a rubric that defines life and death. Du Bois' extravagant pageant depicts the political wrangling over Africa leading up to the trans-Atlantic slave trade, the trade, and its aftermath. Considering the importance of Du Bois' *The Souls of Black Folk* (1903), the second chapter analyzes the provocative dialectic between his 1903 work and his pageant. *The Star of Ethiopia* builds on the central assumptions that underpin Du Bois' description of double consciousness, by staging the visual dynamics that cohere in one of the most important social phenomena threatening African Americans at the turn of the twentieth century – lynching. The chapter explores why Du Bois chooses to depict a woman as the victim of lynching. By the end of the pageant, the same woman is resurrected and gives birth to revolution.

The third chapter questions how the reparative acts of historical recuperation central to Chapters 2 and 3 contend with the histories of groups of people that fall out of popularity, or ones that were never well liked at all. Chapter 3 considers the historical repetition of the cakewalk, a popular dance that Zora Neale Hurston reproduces in *Color Struck*. Although undoubtedly a dance known far and wide during the late nineteenth century and early twentieth century, by 1926 the cakewalk is no longer in vogue. Hurston's play takes place over a twenty-year period and therefore uses the dance as a metaphor for the simultaneous development and popularity of identity types depicted in the play and key to the Harlem Renaissance – the tragic mulatta and the New Negro. It analyzes the dangers that emerge when certain identities, like the New Negro, solicit the attention and desire of audiences and how such a dynamic informs making histories in the present.

Chapters 4 and 5 take up a different method of repair; instead of focusing on reclaiming history, they exhibit active resistance. Hughes' *Tambourines to Glory* offers modes of performance – preaching and singing gospel music – that work to counter the shame associated with blackness as degeneracy, deliberately opposing the mandate that developed in the first decades of the twentieth century that African Americans always behave with dignity. Specifically, the fourth chapter delves into the funk of life. *Tambourines to Glory* showcases the irreverent and aggressive practices of Tambourine Temple, founded on a street corner in Harlem, New York. The setting of and activities that take place in Tambourine Temple offer an alternative to the shame expressed in Richard Wright's *Native Son* (1940) and Ralph Ellison's *Invisible Man* (1952) and transform the spatial isolation of the underground world Ellison depicts. Instead of turning inward the anger and pain an alienating judgment produces, Hughes' play calls attention to how longstanding black religious practices act as modes of resistance and psychic forti- fication. *Tambourines to Glory* deflects the intrusive and judgmental gaze with a sly wink, which creates a transition from reparation as an act of claiming the past in Chapters 2 and 3 to forming the present in Chapters 4 and 5.

Similarly to Chapter 4, Chapter 5 analyzes the black pride that develops during the Civil Rights Movement as an active force that challenges the association of black men and boys with predators. Put another way, *Blues for Mister Charlie* demonstrates why subjects attribute pride to their physical appearances and danger to others' bodies. Through an examin- ation of the threat physical differences pose, Baldwin's play questions the social and historical circumstances that enable America's most famous lynching, that of Emmett Till. Writers, from Gwendolyn Brooks to Toni Morrison, reference Till's death, while historians associate Till's murder with the development of the Civil Rights Movement. Baldwin's play challenges readers and viewers to consider Till's murder as evidence of the violent cultural struggle in the US over black masculinity. The play depicts a character loosely based on Till to restructure the visual legacy of lynching by obscuring the protagonist's lynched body from view and focusing on the sound of his voice. Through the acoustic, the play destabilizes the evidentiary quality of the body, challenging the materiality of blackness.

In Chapters 2, 5, and 6, I examine bodies that transcend graves – individuals' and the mass oceanic burial plot of the millions lost at sea during the trans-Atlantic slave trade. Chapter 6 focuses on August Wil- son's dramatic rendering of the Middle Passage in *Joe Turner's Come and Gone* and considers it as a part of the escalation of artistic representations of slavery in the late 1970s and 1980s that the premier of *Roots* in 1977 and the publication of Toni Morrison's *Beloved* in 1987 mark. Using Baraka's *Slave Ship* (1969) as a literary precursor, I examine the historical landscape leading up to and including the late 1980s to decipher African American artists' motivations for an intensified examination of slavery. In particular, this chapter explores Wilson's impulse to reproduce the dynamics of the Middle Passage, asserting that the play calls for a form of reparation that transforms the theatrical space into a ritual one.

While Wilson's play attempts to create a communal environment in theatrical production, Parks' second Lincoln play, *Topdog/Underdog*, subjects its audience to a confidence game. All of the chapters in the book, including the Overture, emphasize how African American theater actively calls into question materiality (from the physical representation of the actors to the ostensibly fixed sets). The final chapter exemplifies that inquiry, arguing that nothing in *Topdog/Underdog* is as it appears. Performing as foils, the main characters named Lincoln and Booth participate in masquerade in order to con people out of their money. Parks' play reproduces the performance of hustling to demonstrate its generative qualities, which result from its centrality to American culture. In American literature from Melville's eponymous protagonist in *The Confidence Man* to Ellison's Rinehart in *Invisible Man*, writers connect the hustler figure to constructions of the US. The hustler serves as the antithesis of the self-made made man – Abraham Lincoln – that Parks' character Lincoln impersonates. The Janus-faced performance of Parks' Lincoln reflects the overarching ability of African American theater to make the past and future simultaneously. I extend my meditation on the temporal life of performance in the Epilogue and consider the voice of an emerging African American playwright, Tarell Alvin McCraney. African American drama demonstrates the stunning implications of black performance for the project of reparative historical reproductions. *The African American Theatrical Body* intertwines repetition with reproduction to emphasize the afterlife of all modes of performance and the perpetual opportunity for revisionary futures therein.

CHAPTER I

Repetition/reproduction: the DNA of black expressive culture

Lorraine Hansberry's A Raisin in the Sun

On February 25, 2008, *A Raisin in the Sun* (1959) proved the lasting appeal of explosive dreaming. Through the 2008 ABC made-for-television movie production, Lorraine Hansberry's classic American drama reclaimed the national spotlight, making the play accessible to a new generation of viewers. Directed by Kenny Leon and starring Sean Combs (Walter Lee Younger), Phylicia Rashad (Lena Younger also known as Mama), Audra McDonald (Ruth Younger), and Sanaa Lathan (Beneatha Younger), the ABC production marks another milestone in the noteworthy history of the play (Figure 1). In 1959, *A Raisin in the Sun* debuted on Broadway with Sidney Poitier and Ruby Dee as Walter Lee and Ruth. The first play produced on Broadway that an African American woman had written, *A Raisin in the Sun* was nominated for four Tony Awards and won the New York Drama Critics' Award, making Hansberry the first African American and woman to win the award. Hansberry's play became a film in 1961. Robert Nemiroff adapted the play into a musical, which ran on Broadway in 1973 and won a Tony Award. In 1989, the first made-for-television movie version of the play premiered starring Danny Glover as Walter Lee. *A Raisin in the Sun* returned to Broadway in 2004 featuring the same cast as the 2008 production.

In each revival and adaptation of the play, the audience participates in making meaning and making history. Those acts, however, do not occur in a vacuum. Instead, they reflect the material and performance remains of prior productions, including the originating performance of a role. Although the 2004 production garnered critical acclaim, including Tony Awards for Best Performance by a Leading Actress to Phylicia Rashad, the first African American woman to win in that category, and Best Revival of a Play, many critics questioned the casting of hip-hop mogul Sean Combs as Walter Lee. I agree with Richard Zoglin's assessment of the 2004 production in *Time*. He judges that Combs' "expressive – now sullen, now cocky, now bitterly mocking" performance functions well in the

Figure 1 Actors Sanaa Lathan, Phylicia Rashad, Sean 'P. Diddy' Combs, Audra McDonald, and Justin Martin in *A Raisin in the Sun* (ABC TVM), directed by Kenny Leon. Original airdate: February 25, 2008

comedic scenes, but does not "measure up ... in the big scenes."[1] Lacking indeed, Combs' at times ineffectual performance allowed a version of the play to emerge that differed significantly from the 1959 production. Combs' performance fell short particularly in comparison to that of Sidney Poitier. Poitier originated the role and through it emerged as a star. As Walter Lee, Poitier transformed the dynamic of the play from Mama's story to the son's drama. The less refined Combs left comparatively more room for the women characters to shine. The 2004 production captured the drama, desire, and emotional lives of Mama, Ruth, and Beneatha. In that light, the production that resulted from the decision to cast Combs as Walter Lee suffered with Combs' acting chops, or lack thereof, as much as it benefited from the opportunity provided for the actresses to shine.

Surrogation, according to Joseph Roach, is a process by which "culture reproduces and re-creates itself."[2] Combs' performance as Walter Lee "creates a deficit" in the ability to evoke the emotional pull that Poitier commanded; it serves, however, as a suitable alternative to Poitier's performance in that it initiates a loss Rashad, McDonald, and Lathan fill. The vacancies that Combs created were not only the boon of his co-stars but also ones Leon and his producers hoped to engender.[3] Leon maintains, in an interview conducted by the *Washington Informer*, that Combs "was very instrumental in creating the vision that I wanted for this production. He was committed to my vision to bring a new generation to the theater."[4] Combs' act of surrogation falls short of filling the vacancy Poitier's performance leaves, yet his performance attracts a new generation of theatergoers, translating a deficit into a gain. In that regard, Combs' act of surrogation garnered some monetary success.

Leon boasts that the play countered perceptions about African Americans on Broadway, specifically regarding the saleability of their work. Moreover, "the audience is multicultural and represents all ages. [And] it's in its seven[th] week as the highest gross."[5] Anna Deavere Smith concurs, describing the play's "hip hop-to-pearls audience that nightly spills out onto 45th Street."[6] Leon's choice to cast Combs serves as one example among others explored in this book of the purposeful constitution of black theatrical audiences. While such measures have garnered limited success, the methods used to cultivate audiences still merit consideration since they add a dynamic complication to questions regarding reception. Part of the critical work African American drama can do is to cultivate viewing audiences. African American drama, however, is not alone in its use of star power. As Marvin Carlson notes, "One need only look at the advertisements and advance publicity for the plays in any new season on Broadway to see the power of this dynamic at work."[7] Many viewers may have come to the theater to stargaze but they left with Hansberry's play.

Although Combs' celebrity served as a marketing tool for the 2004 production, *A Raisin in the Sun* is a classic American drama because it depicts the will to dream in the face of seemingly intractable social, familial, and cultural demands. The Youngers dare to desire more for their lives than only what the segregated South Side of Chicago has to offer them in the late 1950s. Their desire approximates a familiar American desire and therefore taps into an abiding aspect of US culture – the American Dream. Hansberry's representation of dreaming participates in mid-century American dramatic representations of possibility (e.g., *Death of a Salesman* and *The Glass Menagerie*), and challenges the accessibility of the American dream when represented as home ownership. Rather, Hansberry's freedom dreams require the Youngers' perpetual movement. In the play, Mama's dream of home ownership comes true when she purchases a house in Clybourne Park, but that accomplishment does not satiate her larger pursuit of freedom. Rather, her journey continues after the final curtain and in each subsequent production of the play. In their migration from the South Side of Chicago to Clybourne Park, the Youngers model a mode of performance that challenges the ability to satisfy the desire for freedom with the purchase of a home. The play offers movement as an alternative locus for the fulfillment of the Youngers' dreams.[8]

Depicted as dreams, the careers, identities, and relationships the Youngers desire reflect a psychic battlefield made visible through theatrical production. In the rundown apartment that serves as the setting, Mama recalls moving to Chicago as a young bride and all the dreams she shared with her husband. Now deceased, Big Walter has left her insurance money that will enable another move. Her children's desires for the future also depend on this inheritance. Walter Lee, Ruth, and Beneatha (Walter Lee's sister and Lena's daughter) dream of moving beyond the restrictions the crowded apartment imposes. Although the play only briefly references migration as relocation from one space to another, many of the characters' dreams require social migrations. Their hopes reflect the way migration may also mean movement from one state of being to another state of being. What I call migration, then, refers to actual and desired physical and psychological movement, for example, the development of Walter Lee's notions of manhood, Ruth's yearning for a home, Beneatha's desire to become a doctor, and Mama's projections onto her children and grandchild. The migrations animated in Hansberry's play stage psychic struggles, which inform communal histories and continue to play out over the long production history of the play.

The 2004 production of *A Raisin in the Sun* draws attention to the unfinished business of the play. Although evocative of the American dream, *A Raisin in the Sun* does not unfold from a position of possibility. Instead it imagines the creativity engendered by impossibility – a dream *deferred*. *A Raisin in the Sun* does not assert entitlement to the pursuit of happiness, but instead asks what happens in the midst of the denial of such pursuit. Beginning from a position of disentitlement, displacement, and alienation, the play questions the relationship between decolonization and American possibility and suggests that the tension created by the competing rhetoric of the American dream and black freedom struggles, nationally and internationally, continues to defer the American dream and begs for repeated productions of Hansberry's play. The play begins with an assumption of a dream deferred, as opposed to insistence on the ratification of the American dream as depicted in contemporary Anglo-American drama, for example in Arthur Miller's *Death of a Salesman* (1949). Deferred dreaming creates a perpetual state of recurrence that buffers the dreamer from the disappointment of postponement. At the same time, it inaugurates a sense of belatedness and urgency that results in insurgent action.

The persistent drive toward the elusive category of freedom informs, according to Leon, the longevity of the play and its timeliness. He explains, "This play is what all the politicians are saying in this election year [2008]: It's time for a change, and it's time for a dream."[9] The title of Hansberry's play borrows from Langston Hughes' poem "Harlem" (1951). The poem begins with the question, "What happens to a dream deferred?" After offering several answers, it concludes with a simile followed by a question, "Maybe it just sags / like a heavy load. / *Or does it explode?*"[10] In a gloss on Hansberry's title, Amiri Baraka noted the revolutionary nature of the play in a speech given at Georgetown University on April 16, 2008. Previously, in his essay "Sweet Lorraine," he associated the play with the freedom struggles of African Americans.[11] The potential for transformation, explosion, and change finds a suitable form in *A Raisin in the Sun*. Just as Hansberry's play exploded onto Broadway in 1959, a first in many ways, dreaming, a psychic action described in Hughes' poem, inserts itself in the social terrain through the imagery of rupture. Whereas Hughes' poem situates the potential for change in rhetorical questions – what happens to a dream deferred – Hansberry's play produces change through theatrical production.

The productions make history that mediates the deferment of the American dream by mobilizing black performance – in this chapter, migration.[12] The migrations referenced in *A Raisin in the Sun* (for example Mama and Big Walter's move to Chicago from the South and the Youngers' anticipated move to Clybourne Park) qualify as repeated behavior in the play and in the history of black people in the US who have suffered several forced or coerced migrations. Hansberry knew firsthand the dangers of migration and social integration. As a child she had almost been killed when her family attempted to integrate into a white neighborhood just on the border of the South Side. Hansberry recalls, "I was on the porch one day with my sister when a mob gathered. We went inside, and while we were in our living room, a brick came crashing through the window with such force it embedded itself in the opposite wall. I was the one the brick almost hit."[13] Hansberry's father fought back and filed suit in a case, *Hansberry* v. *Lee* (1940), in which the Supreme Court found in Hansberry's favor.

Hansberry's play mobilizes the force of black migration by interweaving it with the transformative quality of dreaming. As such, the play makes evident the ontology of black performance: repetition/reproduction. Repetition/reproduction describes the recurring nature of black performance and calls attention to its materiality. Drama is exemplary in its ability to demonstrate the repetition/reproduction double helix that forms the DNA of black expressive culture. The drama evokes black performances and offers multiple media for them to assume material form through their life in publication and production. As discussed in the Overture, the material remains, or lack thereof, of performance in general and black performance in particular, has been a contested topic in performance theory. As the repetition/reproduction dyad suggests, black performance occurs in tandem with the black body. Therefore, each act of black performance constitutes the black body. Black drama intervenes proactively in producing the materiality of the body not to reinforce its static dominance but to reveal its malleability. Through the intertwining of repetition/reproduction, black performance deconstructs black materiality and challenges the racialization of the body.

The repetition of performance in *A Raisin in the Sun* invokes some of the most recognizable modes of black performance, including blackface minstrelsy. For example, in act III Walter Lee must find a way to compensate for losing the portion of his father's life insurance money that his mother entrusted him to manage. He has a chance to regain some of the money by allowing the Clybourne Park Improvement Association to buy, at a loss, the house his mother purchased. The association is willing to buy the house at a loss in order to keep black people from moving into the neighborhood. As Walter describes calling Karl Linder, the representative of the association, he mimics the actions and language of a buffoonish Uncle Tom:

Maybe I'll just get down on my black knees . . . (*He does so; Ruth and Bennie and Mama watch him in frozen horror*) Captain, Mistuh, Bossman – (*Groveling and grinning and wringing his hands in a profoundly anguished imitation of the slow-witted movie stereotype*) A-hee-hee-hee! Oh, yassuh boss! Yasssssuh! Great White – (*Voice breaking, he forces himself to go on*) Father, just gi' ussen de money, fo' God's sake, and we's – we's ain't gwine come out deh and dirty up yo' white folks neighborhood.[14]

Walter Lee's performance draws on a recognizable stereotype of black subservience, lowering his body and using dialect in his speech; nevertheless, that performance is revised by the staging of Ruth, Beneatha, and Mama's horrified gazes. Their looks shift his performance: "*Voice breaking, he forces himself to go on.*" As Walter Lee continues, their vision of him doubles his vision of himself. In other words, his performance stages the psychic splitting fundamental to W.E.B. Du Bois' concept of double consciousness, which I discuss in greater detail in the next chapter. In *A Raisin in the Sun*, the eyes of the other looking in horror are not the gaze of white people, but Walter's family members. The transference of judgment from the white other described in *The Souls of Black Folk* to Walter Lee's mother and sister causes him to break down in tears and begin to wring his hands. Walter Lee internalizes their looks; he sees himself through their eyes and cannot stand the sight of what he sees.

Although Walter Lee contemplates denigrating himself, *Time* magazine, arrestingly but also predictably, located the repertoire from which he draws in the body of Claudia McNeil, the actress playing Mama. In a review of the 1961 film version, the writer derisively charges that McNeil, "worshiped by Broadway critics as an Earth mother, too often on the screen suggests a mean old man in a wig."[15] The imagery of an "Earth mother" activates stereotypes of black women's purportedly all-consuming ability to nurture and care for others, offering an abundance of resources that users might exploit just like the earth itself. The reviewer does not indicate the process by which McNeil transforms from a self-replenishing source of exploitation to an actress unable to even approximate the female gender. In the same review, the magazine describes Hansberry as a Mammy who sprinkles the film with "Mammy's own brand of brown sugar." In addition, the reviewer offers the off-handed compliment, "the strongest element in the picture is the Hansberry script, which has the towering merit of presenting the Negro not as a theatrical stereotype or a social problem, but as an all-too-human being. For the rest, the film is a charming, passionate, superior soap opera in blackface." As discussed in the Overture, well into the twentieth century black actors still had to contend with the association of blackness and theater with minstrelsy. While the actors in the 1961 film version do not wear blackface paint, their brown skin automatically situates them as recovering minstrelsy. The reviewer, whom Hansberry categorizes in her response to the review as a white supremacist, projects a repertoire of performance onto McNeil's body that the staging of the scene purposefully disrupts.[16]

The dynamic of the scene works against the association of a full-figured, dark-skinned, black woman with the role of Mammy, a disassociation further reinforced in the 2004 production through Rashad's star power and body type. Rashad, well known for her role as the quick-witted, book-smart, and sexy Claire Huxtable in the hit television sitcom *The Cosby Show*, reinvented Mama. In the repeated performance of the role, Rashad reproduces the black maternal figure in and through her body and in doing so transforms the imagined parameters of Mama's body. A sign of Rashad's brilliant acting abilities, her performance as Lena shared almost nothing with the role she played as Claire. Nevertheless, casting her as Mama calls forth a repertoire of black mothering that challenges the overworked legacy of the Mammy. In the final scene of act II, Mama learns that Walter Lee has lost the insurance money that she entrusted to him. The anguish that Rashad produces in the scene grips the audience. The next scene opens act III with Walter Lee's misguided attempt at redemption through his Uncle Tom performance. In this scene Walter Lee too must express anguish. Comparatively speaking, Rashad's ability to draw the audience into her character's pain highlights Combs' inability to do so minutes later. In the 2004 production, the associations marshaled through the star power of the cast foreground the dynamic complexity of Lena's character. The juxtaposition of the two scenes affirms *A Raisin in the Sun* as the women's play but it does not pin down what shape those black women take – it leaves that in motion.

BLACK INTERNATIONALISM IN THE SOUTH SIDE OF CHICAGO

A Raisin in the Sun depicts domestic and international freedom struggles. It presents struggles in the US for fair housing and in the international arena it references postcolonial movements in Africa. It anticipates the

Black Power Movement, which begins in 1965, as it calls attention to
the solidarity among black radical leaders in support of postcolonial
movements. The play stages the intersection of national movements for
black power and international cries against colonization across the body of
Beneatha Younger and through her relationship with Asagai, and as a
result demonstrates the insurgent energy of black power. In act I, scene 2,
Asagai presents Beneatha with a Nigerian robe. As he drapes her in the
fabric he comments on her beauty but teases that she has mutilated hair.
Beneatha, bothered by his comment, decides to cut off her straightened
hair, much to the surprise of her other suitor, George Murchison. George,
a bourgeois African American, who believes Beneatha's only asset is her
physical beauty, comes to pick her up for a date in the first scene of act II
to find her draped in the robes Asagai brought her and donning a head
wrap. After George reminds Beneatha, "we're going *to* the theatre – we're
not going to be *in* it," Beneatha ceremoniously removes her head wrap
to reveal her "*close-cropped and unstraightened*" hair (80). In the 1959
production of the play, Hansberry cut the reveal scene, to borrow from
reality television parlance, because the haircut Diana Sands, the actress
who invented Beneatha, received did not complement her face. The
inadequacy of Sands' haircut undermined the point of the scene, which
is to demonstrate the beauty of natural hair. The Afro signifies a rejection
of white standards of beauty and, correspondingly, cultural colonization.
The combination of Beneatha donning the robes Asagai brought her
from Nigeria and sporting a freshly cut Afro symbolically represents a
call for black internationalism. *A Raisin in the Sun* uses the visual quality
approximated on the page and realized on the stage to communicate the
movement of Beneatha's consciousness in relationship to the political
movements of black people in the world.

Through costuming, the play positions the US, and specifically the
South Side of Chicago, as a locale of black internationalism – a space in
which black people of different nationalities exchange customs, costumes,
and political points of view. Hansberry grew up with an uncle who taught
and studied African history at Howard University and in a household in
which Du Bois and Langston Hughes visited. She also worked with Paul
Robeson on his leftist newspaper, *Freedom*, which gave her an opportunity
to analyze liberation struggles in Africa. Hansberry's experience informed
her politics, which she expressed through the outfitting of her body.
According to Nina Simone, Hansberry "was truly dedicated: although
she loved beautiful things, she denied them to herself because they would
distract her from the struggle, which was her life. She wore no make-up

except lipstick, and had only five dresses. 'I'm pretty the way I am,' she'd say, 'I don't need lots of clothes.'"[17] In the same vein, the play references black freedom movements through the alterations it calls for in Beneatha's physical appearance, which transform her materiality – the length and texture of her hair. Calling attention to the discursive and political mandates that shape the body, the shift in appearance corresponds to the evolution of Beneatha's thoughts, and also points to a battle at the site of black women's bodies as to how others perceive them and how that determines the material conditions of their lives. To the extent that the black freedom struggles enable black women to gain additional control of their bodies, the play intercedes in the movement of those struggles.

Thus, the play uses the particular formal qualities of drama and theatrical production (costuming, dialogue, action, gesture, setting) to demonstrate what black performance adds to the shape of history, for example constitutive detours from the representation of black freedom struggles in the late 1950s and early 1960s as exclusively masculine. Beneatha's reveal demonstrates a black revolutionary impulse, even in the wake of the House Un-American Activities Committee's investigation of Hansberry's mentor Paul Robeson and others, as it anticipates a resurgence of that impulse in the Black Power Movement. As Robin D.G. Kelley asserts in *Freedom Dreams*, "Cold War repression did not stop the movement." "Inside the belly of the beast, black radical leaders began working actively in support of anticolonial movements."[18] The impulse of the black freedom movements surges throughout Hansberry's work. Although *A Raisin in the Sun* is set in Chicago, it participates in the anticolonial critique Hansberry makes in *Les Blancs* (completed posthumously by Robert Nemiroff) and recalls her coverage of the trial of Jomo Kenyatta in the pages of *Freedom*. *A Raisin in the Sun* provides a particular context in which to read Beneatha donning her Afro by also having her dress in Nigerian robes (Nigeria gained its independence from Great Britain in October 1960), which distinguishes the way in which the Afro functioned as a mode of subversive physical presentation in the everyday lives of African American women in the 1950s and 1960s and points to the particular work of African American theater in staging black people. Beneatha's appearance onstage, then, is a reappearance of anticolonial movements that shows the gendering of historical lines and the possibility of their bends, disruptions, breaks, routes, and reroutes.

In the same scene before Beneatha reveals her freshly cropped hair, Walter Lee actively remembers a mythical Africa (Figure 2). He enters the apartment and cries out "YEAH ... AND ETHIOPIA STRETCH

Figure 2 Actors Diana Sands, Sidney Poitier, and Ruby Dee in *A Raisin in the Sun* (1961), directed by Daniel Petrie

FORTH HER HANDS AGAIN!" (77). His assertion harnesses insurgency through a connection to Africa and the mythologizing of Psalm 68:31, which I discuss in detail in the next chapter. For a brief moment in an inebriated haze, Walter migrates from the confines of his apartment "back to the past" (Figure 3) (77). The play communicates his temporal transport through a shift in the lighting "to suggest the world of Walter's

Figure 3 Actors Ruby Dee, Ossie Davis, and Diana Sands in *A Raisin in the Sun* (Broadway, 1959–60), directed by Lloyd Richards

imagination" (79). He augments his invocation of Africa, asserting "Me and Jomo ... That's my man, Kenyatta" as he dances on a table (78). While his gaze toward the past images a reconstitution through a feminine line – according to Ivy Wilson his cry to Ethiopia constitutes "a plea for Mother Africa to rescue him" – his association with Kenyatta and the

freedom struggles in Kenya reincorporate him in a masculine model of
leadership that betrays him throughout the play.[19] Wilson argues that
Walter's reference to Kenyatta "translates his plight as a working-class
male in the United States with the colonial struggle in Kenya as one and
the same."[20] I agree that the scene collapses the complex geographical
specificity of black freedom struggles but would emphasize that the
imaginative play of the scene offers a performance strategy that tempers
the painful experience of Walter's daily life. In his performance, Walter
Lee delimits the pull of his material surroundings and finds some solace in
an imagined solidarity.

Besides emphasizing the implications of gender for the political
struggle for decolonization, the play also comments on the structure of
political movements. Asagai visits the Youngers to assist them in their
packing in anticipation of their move. He joyfully asserts, "I like the look
of packing crates! A household in preparation for a journey! ... Movement, progress ... It makes me think of Africa" (132). The notion of
progress underpins Asagai's assertions throughout this scene. Nevertheless, the play resists the notion of movement necessarily engendering
progress. When he arrives the family has just learned that, save what
Mama placed as a down payment on a house, Walter Lee lost all the
inheritance to a man, according to Beneatha, whom even Travis (Walter
Lee and Ruth's son) would not trust. The stage directions call for "*a sullen
light of gloom in the living room ... [Beneatha] sits looking off. We feel that
this is a mood struck perhaps an hour before, and it lingers now, full of the
empty sound of profound disappointment*" (131). Asagai enters the apartment
and questions Beneatha's outward expression of disappointment,
reasoning "isn't there something wrong in a house – in a world – where
all dreams, good or bad, must depend on the death of a man?" (135). Asagai
offers a model of futurity that does not depend on the individual but
considers the collective as citizens within a nation state, so that even if he
dies in the name of the postcolonial struggle in Nigeria, if the country
gains independence he would mark his death as a victory. His analogy
frames the individual and competing dreams of the Youngers as the true
tragedy of the play, not the loss of the money. He suggests a sense of
collectivity will result in a fuller realization of agency for all. Although
utopian, Asagai locates progress in struggle and not, for example, a
singular political change such as Nigeria achieving independence from
British rule. Such a political vision further dissociates 'home' from a
specific geographical location and begs for a consideration of the progressive politics that movement – of ideas, ideologies, and bodies – facilitates.

The ending of the play clarifies that, even though the Youngers band together and decide to move to Clybourne Park in spite of the fact that Walter Lee lost the money, they will face struggles that the integration of neighborhoods posed in the 1960s and 1970s. In act 1, scene 1, Walter Lee reports racially motivated unrest, saying "Set off another bomb yesterday." His comment emphasizes the commonplace of racial terror that Ruth's response, "Did they?" – "*rendered with maximum indifference*" – further magnifies (26). According to Stephen Meyer, the US Commission on Civil Rights "found that between 1956 and 1958, some 256 incidents of racial violence were reported, including Chicago's biggest race riot in years."[21] The palpable social unrest serves as a historical backdrop, quantifying the physical danger often associated with black migration in the US.

STAGING THE GREAT MIGRATION

A Raisin in the Sun engages with the history of the Great Migration, elucidates a psychic component of that history, and establishes the imagery of migration and movement as a performance that is fundamental to depictions of home in African American culture, literature, and drama. The negotiation of home and homelessness in African American literature from Harriet Jacobs' *Incidents in the Life of a Slave Girl* (1861) to August Wilson's *Joe Turner's Come and Gone* (1988) centralizes a larger concern about spatial authority. The precarious relationship the trans-Atlantic slave trade created for African Americans represents only one of its many tragic outcomes. This particular outcome, however, relates to the theater as a space that has the potential to mimic the feeling of a house, through the enfranchisement property rights create. Countering the statelessness produced by the Middle Passage and by the disenfranchisement that Jim Crow laws enacted, black theater artists in the US, from the Little Theatre Movement in the 1920s to the Black Arts Movement in the 1960s, developed theaters as communal spaces that situated black people in a certain place at a certain time. Resisting a perpetual sense of placelessness, theater can approximate the psychic reassurances of home by creating a safe space of belonging. The tiny apartment the Youngers occupy in *A Raisin in the Sun* revises the spatial dynamics of the garret that *Incidents in the Life of a Slave Girl* depicts, suggesting the potential to reorient physical dynamics and move to a space of less containment. *A Raisin in the Sun* communicates the intense pressure the Younger family feels to move beyond their material constraints by situating a migration narrative in an apartment. The living room calls attention to everything the migration fails to produce, most importantly financial opportunity. The setting does not merely act as the backdrop to the drama, but instead enables insights into the psychic implications of relocation. The living room exemplifies what the Youngers sought to gain and what they lost by moving north, as it establishes the conditions that necessitate the perpetuation of the family's desire to move from the South Side of Chicago to Clybourne Park, an opportunity enabled by the life insurance policy Big Walter leaves. To clarify, the migrations and their material evidence serve as signs, among others, of the Youngers' overwhelming desire to overcome the limitations of their material reality. Even as the apartment marked by cramped, suffocating conditions causes each adult to question his or her surroundings, the setting also serves as a reflection of each character's limitations, working to constitute who they are and believe themselves to be.

The South Side apartment in *A Raisin in the Sun* initially provided a degree of increased social freedom for Mama and Big Walter, the patriarch of the play. As their family grew and their opportunities did not, the apartment came to symbolize a dream deferred. Act 1, scene 2 depicts Beneatha and Mama spraying the apartment for roaches. The Youngers' living conditions reflect the fact that at the time African Americans were predominantly confined to black Chicago, which encompassed "a geographic area seven miles long and a mile and a half wide from 22nd to 63rd streets between Wentworth and Cottage Grove." As a result, "many of the dwelling units were overcrowded and poorly ventilated and lacked windows and private bathrooms."[22] In the opening scene of the play Walter Lee, Travis, and the Johnsons (the Youngers' neighbors), jockey for time in the bathroom they share. In another scene, when Ruth learns Mama is considering using Big Walter's life insurance money to buy a house, she rejoices in the prospect of leaving their apartment, which she calls a "rat trap." Mama responds:

(*Looking up at the words "rat trap" and then looking around and leaning back and sighing – in a suddenly reflective mood –*) "Rat trap" – yes, that's all it is. (*Smiling*) I remember just as well the day me and Big Walter moved in here. Hadn't been married but two weeks and wasn't planning on living here no more than a year. (*She shakes her head at the dissolved dream*) We was going to set away, little by little, don't you know, and buy a little place out in Morgan Park. We had even picked out the house. (*Chuckling a little*) Looks right dumpy today. But Lord, child, you should know all the dreams I had 'bout buying that house and fixing it up and making me a little garden in the back – (*She waits and stops smiling*) And didn't none of it happen. (44–45)

A Raisin in the Sun reproduces the dehumanizing feeling, also expressed in Wright's *Native Son*, of being trapped like a rat, even as the play illustrates how hope and necessity underpin migration. Consider the scripting of Mama's body as kinesthetic evidence of the dehumanizing effect of Walter Lee's performance; she moves from "*looking up*" with surprise to "*sighing*" with despair, from "*smiling*" with hope to "*shaking her head at the dissolved dream.*" Mama's movements emphasize her ambiguous relationship to a space she recognizes as a rat trap only after Ruth's designation. The living room as spatial metaphor for the psychic–social history of migration illustrates how the repetition of African Americans' mass movement in the United States, first from the South to the North and then from segregated urban centers outward into predominantly white communities and suburbs, required a balancing act of hope and necessity. The threat of lynching or other forms of systematic violence often motivated African Americans to move north in the early part of the twentieth century to survive. As illustrated in *Native Son* and *A Raisin in the Sun*, African Americans' migration and integration into urban centers in the 1940s and 1950s set the hope of attaining greater social space against the necessity of social freedom.

Besides acting as a symbolic reminder of the major narrative theme of the play, the Youngers' apartment represents loss of space as the condition, for some urban migrants, for resisting racial violence. In the stage directions, Hansberry indicates that "*a section of the room, for it is not really a room unto itself, though the landlord's lease would make it seem so, slopes backward to provide a small kitchen area*" (24). The tight layout of the Youngers' apartment emphasizes the crowded conditions. In *Packing Them In: An Archaeology of Environmental Racism in Chicago, 1865–1954*, Sylvia Hood Washington analyzes housing conditions on the South Side of Chicago during and following the Great Migration. She explains that real estate owners divided existing spaces to increase the occupancy in their buildings and meet the housing demand African Americans migrating to Chicago created. Often, the new structures "would have more than twice the number of occupants as the original structure."[23] While the Great Migration allowed many African Americans to escape the physical terror of the South, they also had to face the spatial restrictions of Jim Crow housing in the North. The Youngers' apartment accurately represents the results of the social history of the family's movement from the South to the North and their impending move to Clybourne Street in Clybourne Park, a predominantly white neighborhood. Seeing the fragmented apartment onstage calls attention to the sacrifices migration necessitates; in addition, watching the Youngers' combative interactions in the apartment demonstrates a set of psychic, social, and familial relationships emerging out of the history of migration.

The set for the 1959 Broadway production further evidences my assertion that the restricted setting of a stable domestic unit will not meet the Youngers' desire for home. The set consisted of an apartment building without a ceiling. Some might interpret the lack of a ceiling as a symbolic representation of the possibility of the American dream even within the confines of the Youngers' cramped apartment. Rather, I interpret it as evidence of the reproductive power of the stage to demonstrate the mutability of material history, since we engage with all material history through semiotics. Although places and bodies create a fantasy of the real, the stage has the capacity to reveal mutability in what we understand as a static apartment. As a result, what seems to be a dichotomous relationship between the archive and the repertoire is actually more malleable in African American theater through repetition/reproduction. In her important study, *The Archive and the Repertoire: Performing Cultural Memory in the Americas*, Diana Taylor makes clear that "Even though the relationship between the archive and the repertoire is not by definition antagonistic or oppositional, written documents have repeatedly announced the disappearance of the performance practices involved in mnemonic transmission. Writing has served as a strategy for repudiating and foreclosing the very embodiedness it claims to describe."[24] Taylor's study attends to an imperialistic dynamic that has profound implications for histories of African American performance. The archives that she discusses in the quote are supported by or in the furtherance of the state. To that material evidence I add the physical apparatus – stage, set, and props of the theater – arguing that the theater calls into being additional archives, which undermines the stability of all material evidence, including the body. As such, the archive itself is set in motion.

The apartment Mama and Big Walter find in Chicago does not achieve the fullness implied by "home." They must settle instead for what Toni Morrison calls a racial house. In "Home," Morrison uses domestic metaphors to elucidate her relationship to language. As she evaluated her writing, "It became increasingly clear how language both liberated and imprisoned me." Therefore, "it was important, at the least, to rebuild it [the racial house] so that it was not a windowless prison . . . from which no cry could be heard, but rather an open house, grounded, yet generous in its supply of windows and doors."[25] Morrison uses the "racial house" as a metaphor for the way racial politics limit the discursive power of language. In order to write, she had to accept certain linguistic restrictions. Morrison argues, "Home seems a suitable term because, first, it lets me make a radical distinction between the metaphor of house and the metaphor of home and helps me clarify my thoughts on racial construction."[26] Her use of the word "home" draws attention to the way *A Raisin in the Sun* uses domestic space to stand in for the multiplicity of losses Mama, and urban migrants similar to her, suffered moving to Chicago and then from the South Side to the suburbs. For Mama to address her psychic homelessness she must, to borrow and reorient an assertion David Eng makes, attempt "neither to reinforce nor to reify the hegemonic regimes of heterosexuality and whiteness that facilitate unimpeded access to home, citizenship, and membership in a social community."[27] For Mama, as well as for Morrison, forming a home requires an imaginative process. In *A Raisin in the Sun*, however, the fragile process almost crumbles under the weight of the material pressures her children exert.

Yet even as the imagery of the play references migration, the static setting serves to introduce theatergoers to a particular place, a dramatic representation of the South Side of Chicago. Although many Americans still remembered the dark, dismal, and dehumanizing space that Bigger Thomas and his family occupied in Richard Wright's *Native Son*, *A Raisin in the Sun* offered another dynamic representation of black Chicago and black families' living rooms.[28] Whereas aggressive rats typified the Thomas' kitchenette, the cramped Youngers' living room shines even as it sags under the same material pressure central to *Native Son*. Instead of festering like a pulsing sore, the living room shows signs of hope. The theme of relocation set against the living room emphasizes what is left behind in the act of migration.

It is through the setting of action that African American drama reveals the latent psychic and material histories embedded in black performance, in this case the performance of migration. The Youngers' movement reflects a condition of black life in the US that corresponds to the psychic dynamic of deferred dreaming. Through the staging (in the dramatic text and the theatrical production) of perpetual movement, African American drama creates mechanisms to analyze the psychic and material histories reproduced through black performances. Setting the migration narratives in the seeming stasis of the Youngers' apartment extends Freud's theorization of the psychic condition of repetition compulsion by demonstrating how it applies to black movement. Just as Freud depicts repetition compulsion as a practice that secures the psyche temporarily, hence the need to repeat the action, *A Raisin in the Sun* demonstrates the homeless status of African Americans through the necessity that three generations of the Younger family move to alleviate some of the psychic pressures their environments create – only to find, by the end of the play, that new challenges await the family in Clybourne Park.

Nevertheless, this book moves beyond Freud's theory of repetition through its analysis of reproduction. I engage and diverge from the primary theorizations of repetition, including Freud's analysis in *Beyond the Pleasure Principle* exemplified through his depiction of fort/da (gone/ there), by focusing on how African American performance challenges the given subject/object relationship at the heart of fort/da and considering how repetition stands in for the suppressed memory of not only individual but also collective histories, written and oral. In each act of repetition the actor creates a symbolic relationship to an object that stands in for the social relationship he or she attempts to rearrange. Freud describes the repetition of a game to explain the social strategies a child uses to negotiate his mother's leaving and return. Similar to the way a yo-yo functions, the game consists of a child sending his toy, which is attached to a string, away and then pulling it back. Unable to control his mother's flight and return, the game allows the young boy symbolic control over the emotion that his mother's departure produces. The toy comes to stand in for his mother, but it does not replace her. His mother always exists at a critical distance, representing a lost fullness that haunts the child and forces him to create a game to negotiate that loss. The game signifies psychic distress. Lacan comments on Freud's depiction of fort/da, explaining, "This reel is not the mother reduced to a little ball by some magical game worthy of the Jivaros – it is a small part of the subject that detaches itself from him while still remaining his, still retained."[29] Lacan presents a model making the reel an extension of the child. In an effort to conquer the disruptive split caused by his mother leaving, the child displaces part of himself onto his toy and subsequently controls that fragment. Nevertheless, the child's innovative act of reconciliation remains incomplete and separate from the pleasure he would experience if able to preempt the psychic tear the movement of his mother causes. As the child plays the game he iterates fort/da, which calls attention to the anxiety he feels over his mother leaving, even as it conceals the motivating source.

Analogously, in each repetition of a black performance, pleasurable and unpleasurable memories are reproduced as the performer splits off part of himself or herself in an attempt to negotiate the loss. Due to the historical objectification of black people in the Americas during slavery and in its aftermath, in black performance the performer is often the subject and object of a repetition that serves to manage latent psychic and social histories. As previously discussed, in act III Walter Lee threatens to perform a stereotypical role of subservience to facilitate the fantasy of Karl Linder, the white man who represents the association that is willing to buy back the Youngers' home in Clybourne Park at a loss to the association. In his rehearsal, Walter Lee teeters between assuming the role of a subject who will take financial responsibility for the mistake he made and becoming the potential object of Linder's fantasy. Beneatha calls Walter Lee a "toothless rat" following his dehumanizing rehearsal (144). The rat, a liminal figure throughout the play, functions to imply the complete erosion of Walter Lee's humanity and more broadly points to how black performance, whether intentionally or not, negotiates object and subject positions. When Walter Lee has the opportunity to stage his show, instead of following through with his planned performance, a performance that would yield him a sense of control even as it produced shame, he departs from his role as a groveling Negro and acts as a father, allowing him to seize a sense of psychic cohesion. Walter Lee explains to Linder with his son by his side and his wife, mother, and sister watching that "this is my son, and he makes the sixth generation our family in this country. And we have all thought about your offer ... And we have decided to move into our house because my father – my father – he earned it for us brick by brick" (148). Summoning the remains of his father in the house they will inhabit, Walter Lee manages the loss of the remainder of the inheritance by situating Travis as the beneficiary of his performance.

The repetitions of black performances serve as signs of absences in historical construction and therefore do not seek to exorcize the ghostly trace but incorporate it instead. Freud saw repetition as a problem, a symptom in need of a cure. In this book, repetition reflects an active strategy of recuperation, reincorporation, and even at times reproduction, as it points to social and historical problems. In that way, *The African American Theatrical Body* considers cultural repetitions as a "cure" unto themselves; a methodology that counters the hegemonic regimes that seek to deny the contributions of black people to modern culture. In African American drama and literature, the repetition/reproduction dyad – always in motion – resists oppression. The representations of cultural repetitions in African American drama and literature reveal how those cultural actions complicate Freud's formulation.

Precisely in response to the formative role repetition plays in black cultural production, the term has become a central concept of black literary and cultural studies. James Snead establishes repetition's ability to reinstate the scene of the crime, so to speak. One might extrapolate from Snead's point and posit an uncanny and unnatural quality to kinesthetic memory due to its tendency to disrupt the sequence of events. The restaging of the past in black drama, whether the execution of Lincoln in Parks' Lincoln plays, which I discuss in the Overture and Chapter 7, or the integration of white suburbs in *A Raisin in the Sun*, actively situates the performance in the historical order of things. The critical lens black drama provides reveals the repetition of black performance as a necessary disruption of historical narrative. As Walter Benjamin has argued, "To articulate the past historically does not mean to recognize it 'the way it really was.' It means to seize hold of a memory as it flashes up at a moment of danger."[30] The thing that erupts and causes disruption to the sequence of events constitutes them as it calls attention to the constitution of all history and the regulatory forces that linger before and after the interruption. Black drama creates a critical context to bear witness to historical events and the process of their construction.

Nevertheless, I realize blackness and black performance mean and do different things and therefore have no static meaning in *The African American Theatrical Body*. This book works in part to interpret the convoluted meaning of "black performance" across the twentieth century. In *Performing Blackness: Enactments of African-American Modernism*, which examines the Black Arts Movement, Kimberly Benston posits, "Blackness, far from being inextricable from the paradoxes of its articulation, finally transcends representation."[31] The slipperiness blackness produces through the "paradoxes of its articulation" accounts, I argue, for the way black performance exceeds historical narratives, as it points to gaps, holes, and lack in the story. Through its use of black performance, African American drama fills gaps by juxtaposing narrative with gestures, gazes, movements, music, and sounds. Drama and performance allow audiences to use their senses of sight, hearing, and smell to establish a visceral sense of history. In addition, there are aspects of history that cannot be captured in historical accounts and are better suited for the movement fundamental to performance.

DISLOCATING HOME

The perpetual movement at the heart of *A Raisin in the Sun* asserts the "*un*meaning of place" and builds on the dislocation of seemingly stable signifiers begun in the Overture.[32] Una Chaudhuri suggests that theater provides the opportunity to defeat what "Jacques Derrida has called 'the closure of representation,' a possibility offered by the theater more than by any other art because of its use of reality as a medium. If the real can be represented by the real itself, then representation does not have to settle for the limits and frames that constrict it in all the other media."[33] In African American theater, dramatists deploy reality in the service of a historical imperative that challenges the desire to domesticate the Youngers' drama, resisting an effort to assimilate deferred dreaming into the rubric of the American dream. African American drama constitutes theater as a master trope of the real in order to challenge the totalizing visibility projected onto black bodies and the limited visibility associated with black histories. Creating a double bind at the site of materiality, both modes of viewing limit black humanity and the subsequent quest for freedom that obtains therein. The Overture demonstrates how African American drama calls into question the materiality of the body and this chapter shows the ways *A Raisin in the Sun* destabilizes location.

By 1940 the dreams of safety, increased social freedom, and prosperity that motivated northern migration had given way to the economic turmoil of the Great Depression and its aftermath. According to Farah Jasmine Griffin, the urban landscape had become the "locus for producing and maintaining the negative effects of urbanization – fragmentation, disloca- tion, and material and spiritual impoverishment."[34] Refocusing the violent imagery *Native Son* conjures, the South Side takes on a more intimate, but nevertheless gloomy and impoverished quality in Gwendolyn Brooks' "Kitchenette Building" (1945). In Brooks' description of the kitchenette the "giddy sound" of dreams competes with the "strong" sound of "'rent,' 'feeding a wife,' 'satisfying a man'" and the odoriferous smell of "onion fumes ... fried potatoes / And yesterday's garbage ripening in the hall."[35] In the poem, dreams must battle immediate material demands. The confines of the kitchenettes in *Native Son* and "Kitchenette Building" intensify the palpable feeling of hopelessness. Hansberry shifts the social terrain slightly as she references Wright and Brooks.

In Hansberry's play, the feeling the setting of the play creates competes with the "giddy sound" of the dreams that Big Walter's life insurance policy enable. All of the individual battles coalesce around the family's struggle to leave its domestic space. In the Youngers' living room, the polish and neatness fight to overpower years of use. The furniture struggles for a second birth in an overcrowded apartment. The living room, which doubles as Travis' bedroom, contains one window, an adjoining kitchen, and three doors. One door leads to Walter Lee and

Ruth's bedroom, the second to Mama and Beneatha's bedroom, and the third to the hall containing the communal bathroom. In the stage directions, Hansberry describes how the weary, worn "*couch upholstery has to fight to show itself from under acres of crocheted doilies and couch covers which have themselves finally come to be more important than the upholstery*" (23). The stage directions enable the furniture to participate in the aggressive performance the characters enact, and call for a certain relationship among objects and actors. The stage directions also augment a feeling of struggle that permeates the play – Mama and Big Walter fight to migrate and then to provide a home for their family in the North, Walter Lee fights to become a 'successful American businessman,' Beneatha fights to become a doctor and establish her independence, and Ruth fights to secure the cohesion of her family as her own dreams slowly diminish before her eyes. The vying for control in any particular scene displaces the characters' larger desire to achieve psychic cohesion.

A Raisin in the Sun depicts the way migration transforms identities and identification by necessitating that the subject split off and leave part of the self as she moves on. Most often viewed as a generational conflict between Mama and Beneatha, the famous scene in which Beneatha questions the existence of God draws attention to how individuals seek to mediate their psychic losses. The conversation begins with Mama and Ruth playfully interrogating Beneatha about one of her suitors. Beneatha defends herself, asserting her financial independence, or at least her resistance to relying on a husband for financial security.

BENEATHA Get over it? What are you talking about, Ruth? Listen, I'm going to be a doctor. I'm not worried about who I'm going to marry yet – if I ever get married.
MAMA *and* RUTH *If*!
MAMA Now, Bennie –
BENEATHA Oh, I probably will . . . but first I'm going to be a doctor, and George, for one, still thinks that's pretty funny. I couldn't be bothered with that. I am going to be a doctor and everybody around here better understand that!
MAMA (*Kindly*) 'Course you going to be a doctor, honey, God willing.
BENEATHA (*Dryly*) God hasn't got a thing to do with it.
MAMA Beneatha – that just wasn't necessary. (51)

The conversation between Mama, Beneatha, and Ruth diverges into an existential debate that threatens all of the women. Both Mama's and

Beneatha's physical and psychic places in the apartment and in the world depend on the claims each woman will allow her past to make on her future. Beneatha, "tired of hearing about God all the time," seeks to move beyond her dependence on her family; at the same time, Mama needs to remember that she and Big Walter "went to the trouble" to get their family "to church every Sunday." Beneatha attempts to alleviate the "burden" of her family history, but those memories serve as psychic life-preservers for Mama.

Beneatha, unwilling to yield to Mama, continues to establish a rhetorical space for her worldview within the confines of the cramped apartment:

Mama, you don't understand. It's all a matter of ideas, and God is just one idea I don't accept ... It's just that I get tired of Him getting credit for all the things the human race achieves through its own stubborn effort. There simply is no blasted God – there is only man and it is *he* who makes miracles! (MAMA *absorbs this speech, studies her daughter and rises slowly and crosses to* BENEATHA *and slaps her powerfully across the face. After, there is only silence and the daughter drops her eyes from her mother's face, and* MAMA *is very tall before her*). (51)

Beyond highlighting Mama's physical dominance, the scene calls atten-tion to the conditions that enable Mama to create a house and that establish Beneatha's homelessness. Beneatha becomes subject to Mama's authority and at the same time Mama demonstrates the limits of her agency. Although Beneatha lives in the apartment, her attempt to create space for herself and to move beyond the gender ideals her parents prescribe meets a swift and violent end. Simultaneously, Mama's need to establish discursive order, through her insistence that Beneatha repeat, "in my mother's house there is still God," demonstrates the threat Beneatha poses. At the same time, Mama's insistence on repetition points to the limits of her authority; she must make Beneatha repeat to secure her own sense of social order. This repetition, as with all repetition, rein-scribes Mama's position as it points to what is missing, what is lost. Mama's need for Beneatha to repeat signifies her realization that a generational shift has occurred. The particular words Mama asks Beneatha to repeat demonstrate Mama's subjection. As Judith Butler elucidates, "subjection consists precisely in this fundamental dependency on a discourse we never chose but that paradoxically, initiates and sustains our agency."[36] Mama's physical and verbal response to Beneatha locates her own vulnerability. After achieving her apparent goal by assuming a posture of control, standing "*very tall before*" her daughter, Mama walks "*away from Beneatha, too disturbed for triumphant posture*" (51).

Similarly to Mama's historical counterparts who left the South and headed for Chicago between 1910 and 1920, she cultivated practices, including joining a church, to control the disruption of leaving her home. In general, migrants to the North had to face unsettling realities associated with dislocation. The children of the displaced and unwelcome urban migrants of the Great Migration, whom Richard Wright calls "the first-born of the city tenements," appear in the fiction of Wright, the poetry of Brooks, and the drama of Hansberry.[37] The generational shift – from the 1920s to the 1940s and 1950s – moves the terms of negotiation from the control of the vexed sadness generated by leaving homes in the South, to the control of the memories and economic legacy that threaten to cause the dreams of these first generation northern Negroes to "dry up like a raisin in the sun." The competition for authority between Beneatha and Mama points to their individual desire to achieve social legibility. Both women long for independence, but simultaneously yearn for recognition and validation from the other. Beneatha must assert herself verbally to counter her financial dependence on Mama. Meanwhile, Mama needs Beneatha to perform as her obedient Christian daughter in order for Mama to maintain her position of authority.

The play shows the cracks in the foundation of Mama's position through her interaction with her children and inanimate objects. *A Raisin in the Sun* shows how black Chicago and its encompassing social history participate in constituting the characters. In the play Mama cultivates a small plant; she waters it daily and comments that when she first moved to Chicago she always dreamed of a house with a garden. Given the Youngers' inability to control the space outside their apartment, Mama's plant functions as a willed response to the lack of vegetation urban planning enforces. In African American drama, the clues or symptoms of submerged histories are often contained in the *mise en scène* of the plays. In *A Raisin in the Sun*, the spirited "old plant that ain't never had enough sunshine or nothing" comes to stand in for the deferment of Mama's dream of a home in Chicago (52). The plant serves as a symbolic reservoir that enables her to hold onto the hope she had while controlling the pain of an unsatisfied dream. In preparation for their move to Clybourne Park, Travis presents Mama with a "*very elaborate, wide gardening hat*" (123). The hat functions primarily as comic relief, while it reestablishes Mama's dream of growing a garden. The final scene of the play depicts the Youngers leaving their cramped living quarters on the South Side, embarking on another migration; Mama takes the little plant with her. Her attention to the plant is a choice to remember.

Mama's relationship with her plant adds racial and historical specificity to fort/da; Mama and Big Walter, her husband, have gone to Chicago in search of a home. Freud's depiction of fort/da considers the impact leaving has on the child left behind as a stage in psychic development. My appropriation of Freud's paradigm focuses attention on the individuals who leave. Unlike the dynamics between Freud's mother and child, it seems that Mama and Big Walter were compelled to go. In their new northern environment, the couple create supplements to assuage the rupture their flight causes. Mama's plant allows her to claim some psychic ease in an urban landscape dominated by concrete. Moreover, Mama and Big Walter's migration transforms space from a benign backdrop the subject uses (in Freud's scenario, the child occupies and ultimately manipulates space to consolidate the loss of his mother) to a contentious battleground.

The plant as prop enables Mama to seize some control as it reinforces the limited authority produced by the game that Freud describes. Nevertheless, Mama's gender and age create crucial differences between Freud's fort/da and my appropriation and application of it. In Freud's rendering, the boy cultivates a skill that, according to Lacan, becomes transferred to a more general manipulation of the symbolic field or language that he will continue to use as an adult. Mama, on the other hand, must not only repeat the practices that help to facilitate her approximation of psychic cohesion, but she must also defend those behaviors. To clarify, Mama uses strategies such as caring for her plant and attending church to mediate the loss of home; nevertheless, throughout the play the other characters call into question her ability to provide a home – a psychic space of cohesion and safety. From the beginning of the play, Walter Lee tries to persuade his mother to let him invest the insurance money in a liquor store. In a famous exchange between Mama and Walter Lee, she questions why Walter believes it prudent to invest the money this way. Mama raises a series of objections, some ethical and others practical, as an explanation of her initial decision to not give her son the money. She reasons, "So now it's [money is] life. Money is life. Once upon a time freedom used to be life – now it's money. I guess the world really do change … " To which Walter responds, "No – it was always money, Mama. We just didn't know about it" (74). Mama's practices of tending her plant and attending church with her family keep the pursuit of freedom in view, but her age and gender apparently set her at a critical distance from apprehending the forces that govern her son's world.

Mama accedes to the obsolescence of the strategies she has used to offer some modicum of freedom to her children and gives Walter Lee control of the family finances. I emphasize Mama's gender as the primary barrier that inhibits her from advancing her children's dreams and not chiefly her age since she never considers turning over the family finances to Beneatha as an alternative to empowering Walter Lee. Although Walter is the older sibling, Mama not only gives him control of the money that will be used to start his business, she also asks him to manage the money set aside for Beneatha's education. If one interprets Mama's decision as an attempt to empower her children and grand-child, then one must still question the basis for making Walter Lee the executor of the funds. I assert that the one obvious reason for allowing Walter to manage the portion of the money allocated for Beneatha as well as that set aside for him is not his age but his gender. The play establishes Mama's choice as a mistake in two ways: firstly, by having Walter Lee lose all the money, and secondly, by having Mama alone onstage at the end of the play. Although presented as a poor financial judgment on Mama's part, the transfer of authority becomes a necessary dramatic turn that enables Mama to demonstrate how she never relin-quished her authority completely. Instead of Mama simply making the down payment on the liquor store and establishing a bank account with the remainder of the money for Beneatha's education in order to maintain the cohesion of her family, she allows Walter to assume a level of control that he forfeits, at least in financial terms, by the end of the play.

A Raisin in the Sun stages the apparent lapse in judgment to emphasize the extra steps women must take in order to enhance the functionality of the economy of repeated actions, which through their repetition reconfigure the symbolic order. Through Mama's repeated acts of culti-vating her plant, I argue the play uses a prop to demonstrate how modes of behavior function to secure individuals. In the last scene of the play, after Walter Lee "finally [came] into his manhood" Mama is left alone onstage (151). The stage directions indicate that "*a great heaving thing rises in her and she puts her fist to her mouth to stifle it, takes a final desperate look, pulls her coat about her, pats her hat and goes out. The lights dim down. The door opens and she comes back in, grabs her plant, and goes out for the last time*" (151). Mama must stifle herself and remain in control, unable to access the joy associated with moving, particularly from the South Side of Chicago to a house with a yard. Her mediated affect reorients her understanding of the tools she has cultivated while in Chicago, and even though Mama initially leaves without her plant, the play ends with her returning to the apartment, one last time, to retrieve the symbolic representation of her efforts at homemaking. Although she bypasses these repeated strategies momentarily to enable her son, the play suggests that she must return to them to address the still unfinished business that awaits her in Clybourne Park.

Thus *A Raisin in the Sun* ends with a joyful yet foreboding final scene that suggests the Youngers will continue to struggle even as the play makes available for its audiences and readerships strategies to deploy repetition/reproduction as a mechanism to mitigate perpetual deferment. Chapter 2 continues to investigate the gender specificity of repetition/reproduction as a reparative methodology: Du Bois' *The Star of Ethiopia* demonstrates how historical recuperation might enable the perpetuation of the freedom drive. His pageant creates an opportunity to redefine the relationship between black people and theatricality, which he calls into question in "The Negro and the American Stage." Du Bois asserts:

We all know what the Negro for the most part has meant hitherto on the American stage. He has been a lay figure whose business was usually to be funny and sometimes pathetic. He has never, with very few exceptions, been human or credible. This, of course, cannot last. The most dramatic group of people in the history of the United States is the American Negro.[38]

His ambiguous pronoun "This" troubles the constitution of the Negro through theatricality even as his solution mobilizes the "dramatic" quality of the Negro. Initially, Du Bois' statement may seem contradictory, but if one interprets drama as a medium through which artists and audiences actively constitute humanity then it becomes a mechanism to challenge the enterprise of racism. An understanding of the relationship of blackness to theatricality is essential to the project of dismantling racial hierarchies. Moreover, black drama challenges the status of black people in the US as the referent, the object upon which and through which the drama will be staged. The framing and staging of drama in theatrical production unravels the intertwining of blackness and theatricality through its "alternating play with presence and absence, repression and representation," to borrow a description of theater from Barbara Freedman.[39] Black drama has the potential not only to manipulate where audiences will look but also, as I argue in the next chapter, to reference the psychic forces that drive particular racial formations.

CHAPTER 2

Recuperating black diasporic history

W.E.B. Du Bois' The Star of Ethiopia

At the same time 'human'/'humanity' is not read in the light of 'African-American.'

As an unexplored narrative resource, black personality elaborates human freedom as a single chapter of transition between the beginning and the end.

Hortense Spillers

Thunder sounds, lightning strikes, wild beasts roar, tom toms beat, and one hundred men and women fill the stage in the opening scene of William Edward Burghardt Du Bois' (1868–1963) *The Star of Ethiopia.*[1] The storm that opens Du Bois' pageant, composed of five scenes in twelve episodes, quickly subsides once the Kushites who fill the stage offer a blood sacrifice to Shango, the thunder god. The pageant purposefully intertwines the grandeur of the opening scene – which, in addition, Du Bois scripted to include a lion that crosses the foreground of the stage and a two-hundred-member choir – with mysticism as a method to begin the historical lesson the pageant sought to distill. The force behind the history then, from the beginning of the pageant, is a specific African force that has particular implications for black people in the western world. Originally staged in New York as *The People of Peoples and Their Gifts to Men* (1913), *The Star of Ethiopia* played to thousands in Washington, DC (1915), Philadelphia (1916), and Los Angeles (1925) (Figure 4). As Du Bois explains in "The Drama among Black Folk," twelve hundred African American participants staged the pageant at the American League Ball Park in Washington, DC to a racially mixed, although predominantly African American audience.[2] According to the *Washington Bee*, the cast presented ten thousand years of history in five scenes narrated through music and dance.[3]

Unparalleled in historical scope, *The Star of Ethiopia* revised the American pageant, a form that flourished in the United States from 1905 to 1925. Du Bois' pageant presents an international landscape instead

Figure 4 "The Pageant, 'Star of Ethiopia.' In Philadelphia. Leading characters, and Temple built and decorated by Richard Brown and Lenwood Morris," *The Crisis*, August 1916, 172

of recounting a local history, altering the geographical scope of American pageants at the time. As a result, the play expands the democratic potential of the pageant form and the meaning of American community to include bodies from diverse spaces and geographical locations. Besides stretching the geographical boundaries of the American pageant form, in 1915 Du Bois extended the pageant from a dramatic work that sought to teach a historical lesson to an epistemology of history. Owing to the grand scale of the productions and size of the casts of pageants in general and Du Bois' pageant in particular, its formal qualities made it an ideal medium to further Du Bois' philosophical project – presenting the black world as composed of modern subjects and historical actors. Du Bois imbued the quotidian definition of actor – one who performs an action – with purpose by having ordinary citizens play the part of revolutionary histor-ical actors. In addition, his project entailed demonstrating the relationship between the creation of the black subject and the modern subject. By bridging the cleavage between modern subjectivity and revolutionary subjectivity, Du Bois hoped to quicken African Americans' investment in exercising their democratic privilege to be free acting agents of history. Du Bois first presented the relationship between modern subjectivity and revolutionary subjectivity in his description of double consciousness.

Du Bois' representation of black subjectivity as double consciousness in *The Souls of Black Folk* (1903) remains a hallmark of his scholarship even though black feminist scholars have rightly critiqued his philosophical project, in general, for its gender politics. For example, Hazel Carby argues in *Race Men* that the model of political activism Du Bois presents in *The Souls of Black Folk* is patriarchal. I take seriously Carby's contention that Du Bois presents a limited model of male leadership, which makes his choice to cast the redemptive figure as a woman in the pageant even more striking. *The Star of Ethiopia* provides evidence that Du Bois conceded the importance of freeing the black woman from the restrictive singular role of reproducing the nation long before he articulated that realization in his nonfiction.

His often-quoted 1903 text stands out as the most important book of the Post-Bellum, Pre-Harlem era of the African American literary tradition,[4] so much so that, as Caroline Gebhard and Barbara McCaskill explain, some critics have dubbed the literary period between Reconstruction and World War I the Age of Du Bois. The problem with such a moniker is that it reinforces the singularity of Du Bois and facilitates a model of leadership that feminist critics have decried in Du Bois' body of work; such naming eclipses the significant contribution women writers made during the period. Understanding gender as a critical context within Du Boisian scholarship and considering the impulse to present Du Bois as a singular figure in his generation notwithstanding, I read the pageant as an extension of the groundbreaking work Du Bois begins in *The Souls of Black Folk*, but argue the pageant differs in that it presents the active role women play in transforming the interpretation of race as a visual category that dogs black people throughout the twentieth century. Through Ethiopia's insurgent and mystical, historically past and present performance practices, the pageant presents her physical movements as a counterpoint to the object-ification of the racialized gaze and the gender hierarchies therein.

As with much of Du Bois' creative writing, *The Star of Ethiopia's* gender politics often treads a tenuous line. Nevertheless, Du Bois pur-posefully casts a woman as the figure that re-presents the Negro and the force that generates the movement of history. In the pageant Ethiopia leads the action until slave traders lynch her. She is then resurrected, upon which she resumes her status and conjures the abolitionist movement. Through the creation of Ethiopia, Du Bois addresses the key social issue of the Post-Bellum, Pre-Harlem period and a central theme of this book, the interrelation of the movement from object to subject and the legal movement from enslaved Africans to US citizens. Du Bois makes clear through his use of Ethiopia that the movement from object to subject required responding to specific cultural images that circulated about black women. Even as African American writers participated in the practice of articulating histories of their own, images of the black female as mother dispossessed, as an object with no legal rights to her children, continued to proliferate. In that way, Du Bois' pageant has much in common with black female playwrights' lynching plays, which sought to challenge the status of the black female as mother dispossessed.

In the Post-Bellum, Pre-Harlem period, black writers who were also political activists created strategies to address one of the central concerns of the period – lynching. The theatrical display of mutilated African Americans became the site upon which artists, black and white, advocated for and against black subjectivity. In the aftermath of Reconstruction, lynching became a social event. As Leon Litwack describes, "newspapers ... announced in advance the time and place of a lynching, special 'excursion' trains transported spectators to the scene, employers sometimes released their workers to attend, parents sent notes to school asking teachers to excuse their children for the event and entire families attended ... the action and accompanying festivities."[5] As I discussed in the Overture and will continue to explain later, the union of theatrical display and construction of blackness is deeply related to the philosophical enterprise of slavery. In the Post-Bellum era lynching reflects that union – black theatricality. The close alignment of blackness with theatricality creates a slippage between the two terms that produces mutuality between them.

In Taylor's critique, one of the problems with theatricality is its scripted nature and its predictability. While performance leaves room for improvisation and play, theatricality almost always promises the same outcome.[6] African American playwrights in the twentieth century profit from theatricality's script and the related expectations it imposes on blackness, by drawing from familiar dramatic forms (for Du Bois the pageant) and shocking their audiences into reflection through the insertion of performances that disrupt the expected narrative progress. For example, in the Overture I explain how Suzan-Lori Parks' *The America Play* uses the conventions of blackface minstrelsy to deform race. Du Bois' pageant taps into the democratizing mission at the heart of the pageant form in order to reveal the imperialism at the core of modern US subjectivity that denied the humanity of black people.

At the turn of the century, Thomas Dixon, Jr.'s novel *The Clansman, an Historical Romance of the Ku Klux Klan* (1905) became the text that mobilized a reinvigorated discourse on black inhumanity. Fittingly,

Dixon adapted the novel into a play (1906) that toured throughout the United States and depicted white men violently disciplining white men in blackface for their lascivious advances toward white women. In adaptation, Dixon makes explicit the process of projection, which Orlando Patterson locates at the heart of depictions of black male brutality. Patterson contends, "Like the tick calling the dog a parasite, the stereotype performs an obvious psychological role. Seeing the victim as the aggressor and as the 'white man's burden' is a classic instance of projection: at once a denial of one's own moral perversity and violence and a perfect excuse for them."[7] The adaptation of *The Clansman* for the stage draws the violence and process of projection even more clearly into view. In order for racial dominance to cohere it must be staged, but staging inevitably reveals the drama's mechanics.

In order to justify the policing of black bodies, white minstrels deformed black corporeality through vicious portrayals of black rapists. The desire to fragment the black body in order to re-embody it on prescribed terms points to anxiety concerning the social space of blackness and whiteness and the multiplicity within each category. Although Dixon's work points to a particular type of sexual anxiety, white minstrels also blackened up more generally to abate the pressure of class and ethnic differences.[8] Through their caricatures, the performers simultaneously constituted blackness and whiteness, "holding them in tension with one another and grotesquely exposing the mutual constitution of the former with the latter."[9] As the familiar myth of the black rapist and the avenging lynch mobs evidence, audience members willingly accepted the fractured bodies of white performers as evidence of the ontology of black people, which points to the active process of materialization of the body through the stage.

In 1915, D.W. Griffith commissioned Dixon to write the screenplay for *The Birth of a Nation*. Foregrounding the way sexuality constitutes whiteness in the early twentieth century, Claudia Tate explains the relationship between the film and the political tenor of the time. She argues, "What had been a white male, nineteenth-century contest about capital and nation was, at the turn of the twentieth century, a more mystified struggle about white political privilege now executed as sexual authority."[10] To account for the shift in national identity the Civil War enacts, Dixon's film distills a foundational myth of America – the hypersexual black brute. Stunningly, the film enables the detection of overt and aggressive sexuality simply through the identification of an individual as a Negro, which increases the need to display and maintain surveillance of black people. Ranked as the most profitable and popular American film of its era, *The Birth of a Nation* inspired heated debates marked notably by Du Bois' vehement critique of it in *The Crisis*. Tate explains that Du Bois deployed "chivalric" imagery in *The Crisis* to counter the propaganda which, in the film, engendered a replica of the "displaced persecutory fantasies to police white female sexuality" in mandates for representations of chaste black femininity, a point I continue to explore in Chapter 5.[11] Although present in Du Bois' grounding aesthetic manifesto "The Criteria of Negro Art" (1926) and artistic work, notably *Dark Princess* (1928), *The Star of Ethiopia* marks a more distinct departure from the compulsive policing of black female sexuality as a mechanism to displace the anxiety over the limitations of black male leadership.

Although Du Bois vacillated over time, he recognized and was not alone in recognizing performance as a useful mechanism to reclaim black women's bodily sovereignty, a necessary step in refuting the visual violations. Before the production of Dixon's film black women writers responded to the staging of *The Clansman* in kind, by creating anti-lynching dramas that established women as more than conduits to subjectivity, vessels within which future generations of male leaders could gestate. Angelina Weld Grimké's *Rachel* (1916) is a stunning example of an anti-lynching drama that considers the implications of lynching for black female reproductivity. At the end of the first act, the eponymous protagonist learns that her father and half-brother were lynched. Rachel questions her mother about the current state of black people in the South and declares, "Then, everywhere, everywhere, throughout the South, there are hundreds of dark mothers who live in fear, terrible, suffocating fear, whose rest by nights is broken, and whose joy by day in their babies on their hearts is three parts – pain."[12] Rachel's response to the death of her father and brother becomes commingled with the trauma caused by the racist epithet classmates hurl at her adopted son Jimmy. Taken together, the multiple abuses imposed upon the males in Rachel's life prompt her vow not to have children. A radical stance, *Rachel* is an early play that demonstrates a black female's attempt to take control of the racial trauma and violence endemic to her world through a curtailment of her bodily reproduction. While Grimké's play does not write its protagonist out of what Alys Eve Weinbaum calls the "Race/Reproduction bind" – "a set of presuppositions that naturalize the connection between maternity and the reproduction of racial and national identity"[13] – it does, as Koritha A. Mitchell argues, make the audience aware of the "enduring torture" the families of lynching victims suffer.[14] Through the limitations Rachel places on the constitution of her family, she scripts an alternative trajectory for the production of national identity. Within the intimate theater spaces that housed Grimké's play, Rachel's refusal renders her physical body flexible enough to perform a radical resistance to the materiality implicit in birthing the nation.[15]

Du Bois' pageant loosens the interlacing that the race/reproduction bind signifies as it challenges the ritualized practice of lynching. The black theater in the first decades of the twentieth century, then, can be seen as a form that challenges the restrictions imposed on bodies via race and sex in order to claim modes of affiliation that exceed the nation state. Grimké's *Rachel* and Alice Dunbar-Nelson's *Mine Eyes Have Seen* call into question the social mandates placed on black domesticity as prerequisite to national belonging, while Du Bois' pageant offers global subjectivity as an alternative to national subjection. Appropriating Judith Butler's formulation in *The Psychic Life of Power*, I use the term subjection to describe the construction of subjects; subjection refers to the regulatory, at times violent, mechanisms by which subjects come to be. The pageant presents a female figure who reproduces history and offers an alternative to national belonging by transforming a lynching scene into a revolutionary performance in a global context. The pageant repeats the familiar scene of domestic subjection – lynching – but figures that moment as a repetition with a difference by crafting the scene of Ethiopia's death as the site which births the revolutionary impulse at the heart of black performance through her resurrection. As a result, the pageant positions the black woman as a necessary part of writing the black subject into history.

In order to highlight the impact of the uncanny force of racial representation and the insurgent practices of "African 'survivals'" on the recuperative project of narrating black history, Du Bois' pageant contains a mythical quality that reveals the extra-materiality of history.[16] The mythical quality of the central figure in the pageant gives a shape to the silent, uncanny, ephemeral, and fleeting practices that move in and through history. At the same time, her mystical quality points to the creation of history as occurring between the past and the present, as in-between time. The pageant not only imbues its central character with mysticism; it also creates a mystical quality in its organization. Read allegorically, scene I, episode I, "The Gift of Iron," portrays a Garden-of-Eden-like state, which the imposition of social hierarchies and ethnic conflict threatens in scenes II and III. Marking a fall from grace, scene II, "The Dream of Egypt," and scene III, "The Glory of Ethiopia," depict a once unified black world splitting into factions. Scene III, episode 7, the second episode in scene III (in each scene the numbering of the episodes does not begin again but continues from the number of the last episode), shows Africans' enslavement and violent removal from what remains of their garden-like existence. Scene III also introduces the idea of redemption through the sacrifice of Ethiopia and her resurrection at the end of scene IV. The fourth scene, "The Valley of Humiliation," also depicts the new parameters the black world must negotiate in order to achieve freedom. Accompanied by a slave ship, "'Death' and 'Pain' dance among the prostrate" enslaved Africans in the scene (WB, 1). Finally, scene V, "The Vision Everlasting," displays the struggle to recreate unity after violence and geographical displacement have become woven into the historical narrative. Notwithstanding its biblical allusions to the Fall, *The Star of Ethiopia* does not establish the moral terms of biblical original sin. The allegorical similarities do, however, point to an ethical imperative resulting from the recognition that formerly enslaved Africans cannot go "home" again. The pursuit of freedom requires making use of what appears by way of what has disappeared, what remains after the loss of "continuity" (PA 1).

But even more than that, by making the star of the pageant both Christ-like and a woman, *The Star of Ethiopia* specifies a political agenda necessary to achieve the ideal of freedom.[17] American history and literature both present the dependent relationship between black subject formation and the subjection of black women. In the United States, race has historically been transferred through the mother. The convergence, as Spillers describes in "Mama's Baby, Papa's Maybe," of the legacies that "a child's identity is determined through the line of the Mother,"[18] and Weinbaum's assertion that blackness and national belonging are irreconcilable, establishes the identity of the black woman with reproductive potential as anterior to the issue of citizenship. Recognizing the politically and socially scripted position of black women enables moments of black female subjection to yield a keen insight into the interdependence of racism and sexism. Why does the legacy that black women confirm interrupt incorporation into a certain national body?

Du Bois realized early on that the quest for freedom required that he clearly articulate how members of the black world participated in world history. In so doing, he questioned the relationship between subject formation and historical narrative. He sought to arrest the erroneous formulation that the black world is without history and therefore does not have modern subjects or that black people were premodern and therefore without history. To this end, *The Star of Ethiopia* depicts the social alienation of the black world through the lynching of Ethiopia and thus dramatizes the individual psychic rupture described in *The Souls of Black Folk* as a collective dynamic. Ethiopia's death enacts a communal scene of subjection, which establishes the viewers' (double) consciousness and alienation. The pageant depicts subjection as a necessary stage in the development of world history, and "begins at the 'beginning'" in order to delineate the structure of subjection, "which is really a rupture and a radically different kind of cultural continuation."[19]

Du Bois' representation of subject formation in the pageant precedes Michel Foucault's and Butler's realizations that the discursive positions we are often called to occupy are collective. While Du Bois' pageant implicitly posits such models of identity, it also performs its own revolutionary project. As a pageant, *The Star of Ethiopia* is primarily a visual event that intervenes in the theorization of subject formation by portraying how racial difference acts as a catalyst to a paradigmatic scene of subjection. The death of Ethiopia alienates the black subjects in the pageant and sparks their double consciousness. Her subsequent resurrection creates a symbolic representation of how to reproduce the black revolutionary spirit through resistance to the psychic, social, and physical death instantiated by the trans-Atlantic slave trade and the practices (e.g., lynching) that emerge in its wake.

Hegel's *Phenomenology of the Spirit* and Du Bois' *The Souls of Black Folk* depict similar yet distinctive trajectories of subject formation. The individual participates in a scene of subjection that subsequently causes his alienation. Taking ownership of that alienation and the corresponding benefits it entails, one of which is double vision, allows the subject to appear. Based on these commonalities in the theorists' trajectories of subject formation, the remainder of this introductory section historicizes the visual dynamics that make the black body dangerous and in need of subjection. The second section of this chapter considers the formal attributes of the pageant form and why it serves as a suitable genre to extend the double consciousness theory. The third section examines the implications of Ethiopia's sacrifice and how it qualifies as a scene of subjection. In the fourth section, I situate Du Bois' depiction of double consciousness within the discourse of subject formation and consider how the pageant moves from a scene of subjection to the emergence of alienated subjects. I contend that the narrative progression of *The Star of Ethiopia* follows the philosophical development of revolutionary subject formation. All of the key moments (from subjection, to alienation, to reproduction) that Hegel and Du Bois mark in the formation of subjects occur, with important variations, in Du Bois' pageant. The fifth and final section suggests that *The Star of Ethiopia* presents a gender-inflected model of subject formation that materializes a revolutionary impulse in black culture and its reproduction. In this section, I categorize the revolutionary spirit symbolized in Ethiopia's resurrection as reproductive.

Du Bois wrote *The Star of Ethiopia* during a period when comedic and often degrading images of African Americans crowded American stages and cultural productions. These dehumanizing depictions of black people, typified by *The Birth of a Nation*, circulate alongside the disregard for black life that the practice of lynching epitomizes. Although noted for his exceptional talent, Bert Williams (perhaps the most well-known African American actor of the period) also holds the dubious distinction of appearing in blackface, thereby enacting many of the stereotyped images associated with minstrelsy. Even though Du Bois leveled cautious praise at Bert Williams and his partner George Walker's accomplishments, the designation "Two Real Coons" restricted the parameters for famous American vaudeville performers. In recounting the dramatic legacy of *The Star of Ethiopia* Du Bois writes in "The Drama Among Black Folk," "Cole and Johnson and Williams and Walker lifted minstrelsy by sheer force of genius into the beginning of a new drama" (169). Nevertheless, Williams and Walkers' comedic routines left Du Bois' pageant to confront the predominant images of blackness as either dangerous or buffoonish. As the epigraph to this chapter states, "'human'/ 'humanity' is not read in the light of 'African-American,'" but nevertheless, "as an unexplored narrative resource, black personality elaborates human freedom as a single chapter of transition between the beginning and the end."[20] Spillers articulates a model for reading African American expressive practices as historical projects even as black subjects continue to be denied recognition as historical actors. In response to a visual field crowded with demeaning images, Du Bois created a mystical revolutionary figure to represent the ethos of black performance as a historical epistemology. That epistemology draws from the slippery trickery necessary to repel the force of projection and to mobilize the sustenance of resistance. Yet, as with all models of transformative recuperation, and herein lies the danger, black performance must constantly negotiate the threat of reinscribing the prototypical display inherent in blackness as theatricality.

The sight of Ethiopia bears the weight of blackness as ubiquitously theatrical even as it foregrounds the status of black female representation. In order for Ethiopia to challenge the way that she is seen she must be born again, remade in front of the viewers' eyes. Western thought places a premium on ocular dynamics; appearance facilitated modern slavery. Saidiya V. Hartman's influential *Scenes of Subjection* insists that the gaze, which determines the boundaries between the "valuable" and the "unvaluable," has to be continually monitored and affirmed. She analyzes the visual dynamics of daily indignities that enslaved African Americans suffered at the hands of their captors. For example, Hartman considers the imagery of the auction block, blackface minstrelsy, and melodrama. She categorizes scenes of subjection as visual displays that participate in circumscribing the subjectivity of the black individual on display and affirming the subject position of the white viewer. Realizing the need to garner the individual's coerced agency, scenes of subjection were usually performed within someone's view. Therefore, these scenes, which maintain the boundaries between European subject and African non-subject, also constitute an ethical project that can be done and undone in performance. Through Ethiopia's resurrection she challenges the finality of subjection and offers an afterlife to the disciplining of race.

"THE PAGEANT IS THE THING"

Earlier in his career Du Bois decided that art would play a major role in his work. Arnold Rampersad notes, "Du Bois ventured into the field of belles-lettres. And not by accident but as part of the plan of his life. On his twenty-fifth birth-night (1893) he confided solemnly to his journal that 'these are my plans: to make a name in science, to make a name in art and thus to raise my race.'"[21] The interdisciplinary scholar further confirms his commitment to the arts in his often-quoted essay "Criteria of Negro Art" in which he specifies the relationship he sees between art and political empowerment. He writes, "Thus all Art is propaganda and ever must be, despite the wailing of the purists. I stand in utter shamelessness and say that whatever art I have for writing has been used always for propaganda for gaining the right of black folk to love and enjoy."[22] He imagined a drama with the potential to challenge racism, model the process of history, and cultivate a new way of understanding subject formation.

The pageant's form and theme reflect Du Bois' desire to usher in new possibilities for blackness in theatrical representation. His innovative use of the pageant form included situating it in a long line of dramatic production and positioning it as a response to the paucity of self-empowered representation of African Americans across the color line. Du Bois confirms, "with the growth of a considerable number of colored theatres and moving picture places, a new inner demand for Negro drama has arisen" (DA 169). Although well known for his seminal sociological and historical writing, in 1913 Du Bois responded to the social tenor and expanded his oeuvre to include a pageant. *The Star of Ethiopia* was his first major theatrical project.

What distinguishes *The Star of Ethiopia* is its explicit engagement with the problem of history and the innovative artistic strategies that it offers black dramatists throughout the twentieth century to deal with that problem. Besides creating *The Star of Ethiopia*, Du Bois played several roles in the development of African American theater. He founded the NAACP's Drama Committee, helped found the Krigwa Players, and sponsored the *Crisis* writing contests, which, along with the *Opportunity* magazine writing contests, provided a venue for young writers to publish their work.[23] The writing contests had a similar goal to the pageant in democratizing artistic production. Du Bois notes in "The Drama Among Black Folk" that his interest in theater, and the pageant in particular, stemmed from his recognition that the pageant could serve a pedagogical purpose: to instruct black folk about historiography and establish black people as historical actors.

On October 23, 1913, at the Twelfth Regiment Armory in New York City, Du Bois presented a performance unparalleled in African American dramatic history to an estimated audience of fourteen thousand spectators. The first performance of *The People of Peoples and Their Gifts to Men*, which Du Bois revised into *The Star of Ethiopia* in 1915, was staged at the Armory, only a half block from Broadway, and came at the culmination of the New York Emancipation Exposition consisting of fifteen parts. According to "Three Expositions," an article published in *The Crisis*, leagues presented the parts, including "the industries of Africa," "the work of Negro laborers and artisans," "education," and "church," using maps, charts, models of buildings, and film.[24] According to Du Bois' recollection in "The Drama Among Black Folk," the 1913 staging opened with the cry of "the dark and crimson-turbaned Herald" (169). The pageant was given on Thursday, October 23; Saturday, October 25; Tuesday, October 28; and Thursday, October 30.

Two years after the initial production, in one of the few reviews of the pageant, Du Bois describes the process of mounting it as painstaking, but necessary. He writes in "The Star of Ethiopia," published in December 1915 in *The Crisis*:

I have been through a good many laborious jobs and had to bear on many
occasions accusations difficult to rest under, but without doubt New York
Emancipation Exposition was the worst of all my experiences ... Yet through
it all one thing became clearer – the Pageant must be tried ... We had our ups
and downs with it. It was difficult to get hold of the people; it was more difficult
to keep them. There were curious little wranglings and bickerings and none of us
will forget that dress rehearsal.[25]

In retrospect, the economic and personal hardship resulted in groundbreaking theatrical innovation. Du Bois' pageant is the first American
pageant to attempt to present such an expansive historical narrative. His
pageant also sets the stage for African American dramatists throughout the
twentieth century who attempt projects of historical recuperation. Du
Bois describes the first performances as "singular in their striking beauty,
and above all in the grip they took upon men. Literally, thousands
besieged our doors and the sight of the thing continually made the tears
arise." The mass impact of the production caused him to proclaim in
"The Star of Ethiopia," "the Pageant is the thing. This is what the people
want and long for. This is the gown and paraphernalia in which the
message of education and reasonable race pride can deck itself."[26] Du Bois
uses language that exudes the grandeur of the form ("gown and paraphernalia") and makes palpable the emotion "the *sight*" generates. His 1913
staging proved forceful enough to motivate his consistent effort over the
next decade to stage the pageant, which even in Du Bois' proclamation –
"the Pageant is the thing" – locates his formal choice in relation to but
separate from other modes of theatrical representation. Du Bois' proclamation remixes Hamlet's statement "The play's the thing / Wherein I'll
catch the conscience of the king" in act II, scene 2 of *Hamlet*. While
Hamlet's response to the play he is watching gestures toward action, but
ultimately results in inaction, the structure of Du Bois' pageant incorporates the same community members whom he wishes to inspire toward
action as players in the pageant. Du Bois' rhetorical echo of Shakespeare
locates the theater as a particularly efficacious space to call attention to the
ontology of black performance – repetition/reproduction. Through
the ritualized performances presented in the pageant Du Bois reproduces
the flow of black history.

The Star of Ethiopia is, however, as much a part of an established genre
as a thing in itself. Its formal characteristics reflect the general qualities of
United States pageants, which proliferated throughout the country in the
first and second decades of the twentieth century. In 1905, seventy
participants adopted a form that had been developing in England and

staged *The Gods and the Golden Bowl* "in a pine grove on the Saint-Gaudens estate" in New Hampshire.[27] The pageant honored Augustus Saint-Gaudens, a sculptor, and celebrated the twentieth anniversary of an artists' colony in Cornish, New Hampshire. Building on the enthusiasm surrounding civic celebrations in the United States at the close of the nineteenth century, in 1908 Ellis Paxson Oberholtzer staged a pageant in Philadelphia. His pageant ended a weeklong celebration of the city's founding and cost $60,000. Oberholtzer's successful production in Philadelphia and the staging of a pageant in Springfield (1908) inspired patriotic and hereditary societies, educators, and playground workers to stage pageants. By 1910, David Glassberg informs us, *American Homes and Gardens* declared "America was going 'pageant mad.'"[28] Between 1910 and 1913, the novelty and appeal of the genre led to various kinds of dramatic representation and presentation that used the demarcation pageant as a form of marketing. Responding to the ever-looser application of the term, some of the earliest creators of pageants in the United States gathered in 1913 to devise a strategy to protect the form and its use. The meeting resulted in the formation of the American Pageant Association (APA). During the pageant's emergence in the United States attempts at defining the form, however, were only partly successful. Recently, scholars describe the formal qualities of the pageant as a massive presentation given outside that celebrates a local event or individual. Episodes organize the pageants, which could recall from two hundred to two thousand years of history.

The scale distinguishes the pageant from other modes of dramatic display. Yet at the time of its height in the US, it found much in common with the "varieties of street theatre ... staged in U.S. cities during and immediately following World War I."[29] Masses gathered in New York City for the silent parade of approximately 8,000 black people down Fifth Avenue on July 28, 1917 to protest the East St. Louis massacre and lynchings. In 1920, Marcus Garvey held his first Universal Negro Improvement Association (UNIA) parade for thousands of UNIA members and Harlem residents. Literally transforming the New York City landscape through the visual display of brown bodies, the parades and pageant sought to harness the power of spectacle to redirect the organization of the visual field. The sheer size of the display rips the viewer from the quotidian and requires him or her to attend to the alternative representation being actively cultivated before the eyes. While annual parades need not function in this way, the novelty of these events created a cultural curiosity that served to seize the attention of watchers.[30]

Although maintaining an interest in historical representation, in the second decade of the twentieth century pageants began to take a more explicit political agenda, bringing social practices into question and refusing the genre's characteristic of easy reconciliations. In June 1913, the Industrial Workers of the World staged a pageant in Madison Square Garden for striking silk mill workers in Paterson, New Jersey. Scenes such as "The Workers Dead, the Mills Alive" depicted the exploitation of workers.[31] Naima Prevots notes that *Cave Life to City Life*, a pageant staged in Boston in 1915, was the "first pageant in America to be part of a reform effort."[32] The pageant attempted to change Bostonians' "state of mind" by focusing on industrial progress through education, transportation, innovations in communication, and improved working environments. The industrial revolution and the quest for workers' rights also influence *The Pageants of Sunshine and Shadow*, staged on May 2, 1916 at the City College of New York, which depicts the predicament of child laborers and youth exploitation in general.

The focus of advocating for under-represented groups did not extend to those in the numerical racial minority. With primarily segregated casts, Billy McClain's *The Siege of Vicksburg* (1893) was the first pageant to cast African Americans. Errol G. Hill recounts, "The single entry in the records regarding this show is dated 24 June 1893. It advised that Billy McClain was rehearsing sixty black performers, who would participate in Pain's [Major Ben Payne] spectacular production of *The Siege of Vicksburg*, scheduled to open at Manhattan Beach, Coney Island, on 26 June."[33] The lack of diversity in the casting of pageants highlights how African Americans were often absent from European American depictions of history. Inserting themselves into US communities or stage representations of their own, African Americans also staged pageants that incorporated the formal revisions *The Star of Ethiopia* made to the pageant form. African American pageants focused on the ideals of democracy and education, while also emphasizing uplift. Moreover, they often represented African American history (such as Amiri Baraka's *Slave Ship* discussed in Chapter 6), instead of the regional history European American pageants presented.[34]

Americans staged pageants as an expression of democracy. The scale of the pageants necessitated that communities of people work together to produce them. Consequently, the leaders of the pageants envisioned that diverse groups of people would interact and grow to understand themselves as part of one community. Many pageant leaders believed that educating and involving community members in the development and staging of pageants enacted enlightened democracy. The three principal

groups involved in producing American pageantry (professional dramatists, educators and playground workers, and patriotic and hereditary
societies) disagreed on its overall purpose and utility; nevertheless
throughout the twentieth century, many African American dramatists
shared a belief in art's transformative power.

Although the pageant form has a long history in western culture
that dates back to medieval drama, in "The Drama Among Black Folk"
Du Bois specifies a relationship between black religious activity and the
dramatic forms that he draws on in his pageant. In the essay he creates a
correlation between African pageantry and, for example, the "'Shout' of
the church revival." The sound of the familiar shout coincides with the
spiritual attributes of Du Bois' pageant and draws attention to how
the politics of black theatricality and the assumed fixity of blackness
may serve as a point of departure for the all-encompassing and diverse
history *The Star of Ethiopia* presents. While I seek to locate Du Bois'
pageant in black theater history, Susan Gilman notes that the pageant
places Du Bois in "the much less well-known context . . . of black popular
history." Gilman recalls the familiar images of Marcus Garvey parading
through New York City as one example of "his mission . . . to dramatize
Africa in history" – a mission Du Bois shared.[35] The focus on popular
versus academic edification reveals the pageant's multiple pedagogical
valences while it places certain pressures on the formal characteristics of
black drama as an inherently popular form, pressures that Langston
Hughes feels even more intensely leading up to and during the New York
production of *Tambourines to Glory* and that James Baldwin registers
during the New York production of *Blues for Mister Charlie*.

Much to Bertolt Brecht's hypothetical dismay, the pageant's ability to
entertain coincided with its ability to garner an emotional and spiritual
reaction, similar to the affect that produces the shout of the church
revival. In the predominantly segregated world of the first decades of
the twentieth century, the fervent expression of a historicized affect in
public (note Du Bois offers an acoustic genealogy of sorts in his situating
the pageant form in line with the shout) offered an alternative to the
demureness central to the "politics of respectability," which encouraged
black women to counter the representations of blackness as implicitly
theatrical through pious and reserved public displays.[36] The evocation of
a familiar sound of the church revival locates the quotidian in black
revolutionary performance as depicted in the pageant. *The Star of Ethiopia*
emerged in light of these common performance models. At the same time,
the mysticism of *The Star of Ethiopia* has much in common with medieval

pageants. An editorial for *The Crisis*, "A Pageant," presumably written by Du Bois, states that "A pageant is not a tableau or playlet or float. It is a great historical folk festival, staged and conducted by experts with all the devices of modern theatrical presentation and with the added touch of reality given by numbers, space and fidelity to historical truth."[37] Du Bois rooted the pageant form in African history, folk culture, and modern dramatic and technological innovation. In that sense, *The Star of Ethiopia* modernizes the pageant form, transforming its focus from the local to the global, drawing from a patchwork of influences, using modern lighting and effects while emphasizing the importance of folk culture and ritual practice.

Through an incorporation of the old and the new, the sacred and the socially profane, *The Star of Ethiopia* extends and revises the United States pageant form by incorporating elements of African American drama, including the use of African and African American music and ritual. Similar to *The Souls of Black Folk*, Du Bois' 1915 pageant draws from African American and western music, consisting of spirituals, original compositions inspired by African music, and "two selections from Verdi's *Aïda* that accompanied the Egyptian episodes."[38] Two articles published in the *Washington Bee*, "The Music of the Pageant" and "The Great Pageant," described *The Star of Ethiopia*'s music, which Mr. J. (John) Rosamond Johnson, one of the composers of the Black National Anthem, directed.[39] J. Rosamond Johnson collaborated with his brother James Weldon Johnson in the composition of the anthem "Lift Every Voice and Sing" and the brothers worked with Robert "Bob" Cole to form a song-writing trio that produced two operettas, *The Shoo-Fly Regiment* (1906) and *The Red Moon* (1908). The operettas were staged on Broadway with all-black casts. The trio also contributed music to *Sleeping Beauty and the Beast* (1901), *In Newport* (1904), and *Humpty Dumpty* (1904).[40]

The all-star quality of the 1915 production team did not end with Rosamond Johnson. It also drew on some of black America's most distinguished soldiers, historians, and civil rights activists. United States Army Colonel Charles Young, who was one of the Buffalo soldiers, the third African American to graduate from West Point, and the first appointed to the rank of Colonel, contributed original compositions to the pageant, including his opening tom-tom piece called "Prelude Primitive," and the songs "Chant of the Savages," "Song of the Faithful," "When Darkness Descends," the "African Chant," and the "Welding Song." In addition, African British composer Samuel Coleridge-Taylor contributed two pieces, the "Imaginary Ballet" and "Motherless Child."

The pageant also featured African American folk music such as "Walk Together Children." To further bolster the commercial appeal, Du Bois inserted prominent black scholars and artists into his productions. Figures for the 1915 production included the highly respected historian Charles H. Wesley and civil rights activist Marcy Church Terrell.[41] And if the star appeal did not engage viewers, the familiarity of the narrative would. Du Bois' pageant would have attracted an audience familiar with the form and ready to see a historical lesson. For the 1915 production, the *Washington Bee* published the script four days before opening night, giving audience members access to the story before they watched it. Using advertisements in the *Washington Bee*, Du Bois solicited contributions to finance the pageant and recruited cast members from the Washington, DC metropolitan area; they were asked to assist in making their own costumes.

Through the narrative arc, which works its way from ancient Africa to modern America, and by creating a community through the process of staging, the pageant communicates a central and consistent strand of Du Bois' race theory – the common history of dark people in the world. The history beckoned Du Bois' telling. Two years after the original production of the pageant, he describes in an article entitled "The Star of Ethiopia" how he questioned whether he would be "tempting fate to try it again. And then, after all, there was no money. There was war and there was trouble."[42] Yet even in light of the mounting obstacles, Du Bois refused to abandon the idea of the pageant; he refused to let it rest as a part of his rich intellectual and artistic past. He decided to try once again to stage the pageant, but in Washington, DC under the stars and sky. Similar to the first production in New York, Du Bois recalls the organizational and financial difficulties he encountered while preparing for the 1915 production. In light of the foreboding obstacles, he writes, "Six thousand human faces looked down from the shifting blaze of lights and on the field the shimmering streams of colors came and went, silently, miraculously save for the great cloud of music that hovered over them and enveloped them. It was no mere picture: it was reality."[43] In total 13,000 spectators came to witness Du Bois' pageant in the District of Columbia. Although Du Bois' depiction of his pageant in visual terms remains consistent, several characteristics distinguish the 1915 production, most notably a significant change in plot.

The circumstances of the first production of the pageant (to celebrate the fiftieth anniversary of emancipation) differed significantly from the circumstances of the 1915 one. The impact of World War I weighed heavily on Du Bois and emerged in his revisions. The 1913 production focused on the gifts black men and women gave to the world. Divided into six scenes, the original version presented a veiled woman who directs the action. In the first scene the veiled woman enters "commanding in stature and splendid in garment, her dark face faintly visible" (ox 306). She enters carrying fire and iron. As she moves across the stage drummers begin to play tom-toms and "anvils ring at the four corners. The arts flourish, huts arise, beasts are brought in and there is joy, feasting and dancing" (ox 306). The combinations of sounds that accompany the shrouded woman in the 1913 version draw attention to her presence onstage. The familiar imagery of the veiled woman in the 1913 version recalls Du Bois' description in *The Souls of Black Folk* of the material separation between white and black worlds in which he was "shut out from their world by a vast veil" (8). The 1913 version of the pageant shifts the position of the veil from a spatio-temporal one to a material object. Du Bois continues his play with the veil as symbol and object in the multi-genre compilation entitled *Darkwater: Voices from within the Veil* (1920) and in the 1915 version of the pageant. In *Darkwater* he also reproduces the imagery of Ethiopia present in the 1915 version of the pageant, drawing together the reproductive power of Ethiopia and the power of the stage-curtain-like veil to reveal or conceal the action.[44] Through the manipulation of the veil, *Darkwater* emphasizes the feminist undercurrents that I locate in the 1915 version of the pageant.

The 1915 version transforms the pageant from an informative celebration of black people's gifts to the world to an elaborate presentation that emphasizes the revolutionary impact of black performance on world history. The reasons for this shift were not only Du Bois' theoretical and philosophical transformations but also social ones. The mounting number of lynching victims and the proliferating negative images of black people in the midst of World War I had a significant impact on the revisions to the pageant. Brent Hayes Edwards describes the impact of World War I on the Harlem Renaissance:

As he [Du Bois] put it later, a "world view" of the color line was all the more indispensable in the wake of a series of earthshaking events in the second decade of the century, most of all "that great event of these great years, the World War." What Nathan Huggins terms the "post-war effort to thrust Negro social thought into an international arena" is a constant thread in the work of black intellectuals of the period no matter what their ideological outlook.[45]

In focusing on the implications of his work on international politics, Du Bois was no exception. His commentary in *The Crisis* and the shift of his focus in the pageant suggest that not only in the "wake of a series of earthshaking events," but also in the midst of these events, Du Bois felt compelled to respond. As Du Bois clarifies in "World War and the Color Line" (1914), "Many colored persons, and persons interested in them, may easily make the mistake of supposing that the present war is far removed from the color problem of America ... This attitude is a mistake."[46] Du Bois saw the war as a global manifestation of race prejudice and a result of a history of imperialism. He argued, "The Negro problem in America is but a local phase of a world problem."[47]

The name Ethiopia marks this shift in Du Bois' focus from national to international dynamics; the "mysterious woman" (1913) becomes Ethiopia in the 1915 version (Figure 4). The accompanying change to the name of the pageant invokes the discursive history of the words "Ethiopia," "Ethiop," and "Ethiopian." In *The Negro* Du Bois discusses Ethiopia as a geographical region and a pseudonym for the continent of Africa. He explains, "Africa is at once the most romantic and the most tragic of continents. Its very names reveal its mystery and wide-reaching influence. It is the 'Ethiopia' of the Greek, the 'Kush' and 'Punt' of the Egyptian, and the Arabian 'Land of the Blacks.'"[48] The *Oxford English Dictionary* confirms Du Bois' association of the term with ancient Greece. The term "Ethiop" or "Ethiopian" occurs in Milton's *Paradise Lost*, and Shakespeare's *As You Like it* and *Romeo and Juliet*. In these Renaissance texts, the term Ethiopian is used to mean a swarthy or black person. Milton and Shakespeare use the term in association with the continent of Africa in general and not a specific country. Du Bois draws from this vague, mythical, and mystic sense of Africa, as he invents his own mythologized history. His blatant act of reproduction in the naming of the pageant recalls the prophetic biblical verse: "Princes shall come out of Egypt, and Ethiopia shall soon stretch forth her hands unto God" (Psalms 68:31), which infuses Ethiopia with a revolutionary impulse.

Moreover, this act of naming signifies a change in Du Bois' priorities and a corresponding alteration of the visual dynamics of the pageant. As Edwards clarifies, however, before Du Bois made his famed proclamation in *The Souls of Black Folk* – "the problem of the twentieth century is the problem of the color line" – he had already given a speech in London entitled "To the Nations of the World" (1900) in which he first uttered his signature declaration.[49] While Du Bois' international interest emerged well before the calamities of World War I, it is noteworthy that the 1915 version of *The Star of Ethiopia* contains a shift in geographical emphasis, from national to global, and a change in characterization that echoes

Figure 5 "From the Pageant: 'The Star of Ethiopia,'" *The Crisis*, December 1915, 90

Du Bois' rhetoric in "World War and the Color Line." The 1915 version of the pageant transforms a dark veiled woman bearing the gifts of black people into Ethiopia, a revolutionary Christ-like figure who calls attention to herself by directing the action of the play. As the director of the action, Ethiopia calls for audiences to recognize her as the central character and therefore focus their gaze on her (Figure 5).

Du Bois' commentary on the 1916 performances in Philadelphia and the 1925 performances in Los Angeles suggest that after he transformed *The Star of Ethiopia* for the 1915 performances he continued to stage a similar version of the pageant. In fact in "The Drama among Black Folk" Du Bois describes the 1916 staging as "technically the best" and "possibly the end of the series" (169). Although there is no evidence that these performances ever occurred, an announcement for the Washington, DC production says the pageant "will be repeated in Boston, Baltimore, and other cities South and West" (Figure 6). For over a decade, incurring financial loss and one impediment after another, Du Bois continued to pursue the pageant, which he argued was a necessary and productive mechanism "to reveal the Negro to the white world as a human, feeling thing" (DA 171). The affective and communal qualities of the pageant served to draw the audience into the action and, correspondingly, implicate them in the scene of subjection.

Figure 6 "The Star of Ethiopia," *The Crisis*, April 1915, n.p.

A PARADIGMATIC SCENE OF SUBJECTION

The structure of *The Star of Ethiopia* does not call for the audience to identify with Ethiopia but instead to pay attention to her and identify with the collectivity she leads. In scene III, episode 7 a fatigued Ethiopia enters the divided land of the blacks. Although she attempts to mediate the fighting, by the middle of the scene "there ensues the real battle of Islam and Fetish." Prior to the *real* battle, minor skirmishes had been quelled among the groups, spanning hundreds of years of African history, accompanying Candace (a title used by the female rulers of Ethiopia, one of whom defended the country against Greek and Roman invasion in 30 BC),[50] Sheba (the ruler of an ancient empire located in modern day Yemen, who lived in the tenth century BC), the Mononotapa (a kingdom, also spelled Monomotapa, in southern Africa from 1450–1629, located in modern day Zimbabwe and Mozambique), Mansa Musa (a fourteenth-century king of the Mali empire located in West Africa), and Mohammed Askia (a late fifteenth-century king of the Songhay empire located in West Africa), who had all gathered at the temple for a feast and a performance (WB, 1). Note that the pageant draws figures from throughout the contin-ent of Africa and one from Asia to compose this royal court. The temporal incongruity of the scene, once again, points to the way Du Bois chose to blend African history and mythology to situate black people as historical subjects, a technique contemporary writer Pauline Hopkins (1859–1930) uses in her novel *Of One Blood*. In the pageant the collapse of time suggests a relationship among the different empires and the modern black subject who comes to be, historically, through the incursion of the trans-Atlantic slave traders at the end of the scene. The conflation of time and space may rightly raise the ire of late twentieth-century black diasporic critics. In doing so Du Bois risked calling into being a static model of community that undermined the fluid possibilities made available through his act of historical recuperation. He dangerously elevated a singular history over multiplicity – a gesture that mirrors the trauma enacted when any singular figure stands in for the multiplicity of the whole. His tactic, however, does have its redemptive aspects. Through his blending, he enabled the multiplicity that surely categorized his audience to find a singular reflection in history and therefore recognize themselves as a community. Scene III depicts the breakdown of community, but through the ritual reenactment of that history the participants and audience had access to communion that Du Bois hoped would engender a reinvigorated investment in community (the gospel play form creates a similar dynamic, which I consider in Chapter 4).

The visual dynamics shift in episode 7 as additional groups of people take the stage. Characterized in the pageant as Mohammedans and fetish worshipers in battle, the groups fight as Christian priests appear.[51] In the Du Bois papers the priests are directed to walk to the front center of the stage, directions that specifically call attention to the Christian priests. Whether or not the priests actually took centerstage, the fighting serves as a distraction that allows the Spanish, Portuguese, Dutch, and English slave traders lurking behind the priests at some distance to enter and wait undetected while the battle for "The Star of Freedom" plays out (WB, 1). Foreshadowing the outcome of the battle, angels hide the star as Ethiopia appears at the Temple. Once there, she secures the star as the greedy slave traders approach the victorious Mohammedans to purchase other Africans from the victors. After the traders have manacled the enslaved, they notice Ethiopia looking on. Members of the audience, already having witnessed Ethiopia's power to direct the masses of people onstage, might have noticed her watching from above on a rock. If not, once the slave traders direct all of their attention to her the audience would have begun to notice that Ethiopia has been watching. Such a perspective – watching Ethiopia watching – highlights the way power makes individuals subject to a gaze. In the beginning of episode 7, Ethiopia retains her power and thus makes the slave traders subject to her gaze.

The pageant relies on the primacy of the visual to establish the social positions of figures onstage in order to show how the visual may also reposition the generative possibilities of the body, particularly the black female body. It is important to note that Ethiopia's name distinctively weds her to the material; in as much as she is mythical and transcendent she is also material and consistently becomes woman before the eyes of the audience. Her materiality reinforces the importance of visual perspective in the pageant. As Oyèrónké Oyěwùmi makes clear, "The reason that the body has so much presence in the West is that the world is primarily perceived by sight. The differentiation of human bodies in terms of sex, skin color, and cranium size is a testament to the powers attributed to 'seeing.'"[52] In *The Star of Ethiopia*, Du Bois attempts to challenge the visual regimes that participate in structuring subjects by asking the audience to participate in a scene of subjection that does not render the subject an object of the gaze.

The end of scene III marks a rupture introduced by the caustic violence that will, from now on, inform the representation of black subjects, black performance, and the historical epistemology that black performance demonstrates. In Scene III, episode 7 the audience has seen the slave drivers capture and enslave Africans. Then the slave drivers "discover her and set fire to the Rock as she flees. She burns, lifting the Star of God, and the Rock becomes her tomb. There is darkness" (WB, 1). The enslaved Africans watch as the fire consumes Ethiopia and the star of freedom transcends; the audience now watches a community of actors watching. A transformative event although extremely destructive, the burning has restorative power. The charred rock, smelted under the heat and pressure of the fire, gives birth to performance practices, which draw from memories of the past but refine them under the new urgent pressure of the present.

The burning fire exemplifies the productive power of waste, staging an intervention in the break between objection and subjection. The exertion of violence toward Ethiopia represents "the performance of waste," which according to Joseph Roach consists of "the elimination of a monstrous double, but one fashioned by artifice as a stand-in, an 'unproductive expenditure' that both sustains the community with the comforting fiction that real borders exist and troubles it with the spectacle of their immolation."[53] As with many of the performances considered herein, the display of violence produces non-value – waste, which black drama, through repetition/reproduction, endows with value by offering alternative modes of interpreting cultural production. For Ethiopia, her non-value transforms into value through her return in scene IV, where she is resurrected with a sword in hand that she uses to command the revolutionary activity of the black world.

As Ethiopia dies, the pageant calls for the audience's gaze to shift from her to the hundreds of actors onstage. Engulfed in flames, Ethiopia's physical body is removed from view, which begs the audience to redirect its attention to what is present, what remains onstage. In any scene of subjection the witnesses construct the moment as much as the participants. Public violence disseminates terror through the consumption and memory of the audience. While the narrative and spatial position of Ethiopia onstage would have drawn attention to her, once the flames consume her the mass of stage onlookers directs the audience's attention. The burning of Ethiopia, the star, and the rock demonstrates the terrorism endemic to the experience of slavery while it also establishes public acts of violence as defining this newly formed black community and the modern world. Scene V harnesses the potential of this new subjectivity, remembering Ethiopia as the material sacrifice that ruptures the historical narrative and provides practices of freedom.

Ethiopia's sacrifice engenders an opacity that aligns her subsequent insurgent performance with other mystically opaque black women in the fiction of Hopkins' *Of One Blood* and the dancing of Ada (Aida) Overton Walker. Ethiopia's performance circulates in the performative space Daphne Brooks' "veiled ladies" create.[54] As Brooks explains:

"dubbed the 'veiled ladies' of mystical exhibitions because of their putative ability to 'cross over' the 'veil' separating life and death, mediums were no doubt icons of exploitation and abjection."[55] Nevertheless, in an African diasporic context, these women resist "'the segregation of the dead' by summoning up ancestral spirits from an idealized re-membered homeland."[56] The veiled ladies in *Of One Blood* and Walker's *Salome* create a critical context for Ethiopia's performance, marked by mysticism, political insurgency, and historical recuperation, that replaces the physical veil in the 1913 production of *The Star of Ethiopia* with a performance of opacity in the 1915 one.

Of One Blood features three generations of prophetic women, Hannah, Mira, and Dianthe Lusk. Mira, a slave woman, does not raise her three children (Dianthe, Reuel Briggs, and Aubrey Livingston), who through happenstance reunite in the novel to form a love triangle. The novel focuses on the deceptions and Herculean efforts best friends Reuel and Aubrey make to win Dianthe. Reuel and Aubrey first see Dianthe performing in a concert as a member of the Fisk Jubilee Singers. She is a virtuoso soprano and the melodic tone of her voice attracts Reuel and Aubrey's attention. She strikes a particular chord with Reuel, since earlier on the day of the concert he had a vision of a figure with Dianthe's face. An apparitional Dianthe visits Reuel again before he finally meets her. Reuel, a Harvard medical student, is called to the hospital to treat a comatose patient, Dianthe. All the other medical personnel have given up on the train crash victim. But when Reuel sees her lovely face he does everything in his power to revive her and successfully brings her out of her stillness with a potion; however, her memory is gone. Dianthe's memory loss, an apparent boon for Reuel, enables him to rename her Felice Adams, integrate her into their white circle of friends, and wed her. Just as things are falling into place, Reuel's fortunes turn when he is unable to find a job to support his wife. The only job he can secure is as a medic on an expedition to Africa. Intent on saving his marriage and therefore supporting his wife, he leaves her in the care of Aubrey (his best friend and brother) while he journeys to Africa. Aubrey secretly desires Dianthe and agrees to help as he plans to have Reuel killed while in Africa.

Aubrey almost has his way until the phantomatic return of their mother Mira disrupts the central characters' best-laid plans. Aubrey convinces Dianthe to be his wife by blackmailing her and severing communication between her and Reuel. Countering Aubrey's coercive rhetoric, Mira appears to Dianthe. "She neither looked at Dianthe nor did she speak; but walked to the table and opened a book lying upon it and wrote; then coming back, stood for a moment fixed; then sank, just as she rose, and disappeared."[57] Dianthe, untroubled by this woman from within the veil, looks to see what she wrote and finds Luke 12 underscored: "'For there is nothing covered that shall not be revealed.' On the margin, at the end of this passage was written ... Mira."[58] Mira prompts Dianthe to begin to question her belief that Reuel has not written to her since departing for Africa. "As a phantom, Mira's materializations in the novel are all connected to the issue of legibility – more specifically, to making coded and 'hidden' signs visible and comprehensible to the protagonists," according to Dana Luciano.[59] I would agree and argue that, as Mira reveals Aubrey's duplicity to Dianthe and Reuel, she intensifies her opacity.

Aubrey describes Mira as the servant his father hypnotized to entertain party guests. In one such instance, Mira foretold of the coming of the Civil War and emancipation and as punishment the elder Mr. Livingston sold Mira. Her bodily freedom violated in her sale, she also bears the mark of Mr. Livingston's incursion in the persons of her three children. Mira's reproductive role is not an uncommon one for an enslaved black woman in the US, and while the novel does suggest that through her a royal legacy is born in the person of Reuel who goes on in the novel to become the ruler of an imaginary kingdom called Telassar in Ethiopia, I focus on the way Mira, from within the veil, disrupts the unfolding of the narrative and alters the perception of the three central figures. Through her opaque veiled performance she reconfigures the historical trajectory of the novel and demands that the characters reevaluate themselves. In that way, Mira acts as a force of history.

When Mira appears before Reuel in Africa she enables him to see a letter Aubrey wrote to a treacherous servant, Jim Titus, accompanying Reuel on the trip to Africa; Aubrey charged the servant to kill Reuel. While abroad Reuel is falsely informed that his wife has died in a boating accident. But through the second sight Mira provides, Reuel realizes that Dianthe lives and that Aubrey has betrayed him. Reuel confronts Jim and with his dying breath Jim reveals that Dianthe, Aubrey, and Reuel are siblings. The incestuous love triangle reinforces Mira as a tragic mulatta but not one whose mixed race pins her body in an intractable quicksand-like grip. Rather, Mira serves as a conduit to Reuel's realization in order to produce the haunting force of history. As a historical actor who ruptures the veil between the worlds of the living and the dead, she performs resurrection. Resurrection inserts chaos where order once stood. It is in the rupture caused by death that the freedom drive, "an interminable struggle," may flourish.[60] Resurrection disrupts the purportedly natural progression of materiality toward death. Through an unlawful return, resurrection creates a fissure between what came before and what comes after (for example, BC and AD); a break in time that must be accounted for in and through the return. What I am calling an act of resurrection, which features a return of the dead, enacts a significant shift in time that is not completely discontinuous with what came before, but nevertheless changes the way in which we understand historical time. In Mira's act of return, she changes the course of events and reveals her reproductive power as more than exclusively bodily.

Moving between past and present, Mira veils her body, which draws attention to her performance as a force of history. She transitions from an object of sexual exploitation and physical labor to a prophetic voice through the exploitative practices of the elder Mr. Livingston. His indiscretion leads to Mira's perpetual insurrection. Ada Walker's performance as Salome also demonstrates an ability to draw attention away from her body and focus attention on her performance. She purposefully identifies herself with the biblical figure Salome and inserts herself in the early twentieth-century *Salome* craze in Europe and the US to draw attention to her ability to adopt different identifications as a black professional dancer. Her ability to change roles and change the role of Salome functions as another example of veiling that both obscures the black female body and reveals the performative work it does.

The original biblical narrative of Salome told in the Gospels of Mark and Matthew features an allegory of dangerous female sexuality that each adaptation of the tale reinscribes. To participate in the *Salome* craze one had to negotiate the erotic pull central to the original narrative. In the Bible, King Herod jails John the Baptist for performing miracles and condemning Herod's decision to marry his brother's wife. Subsequently, King Herod hosts a celebration with Queen Herodias and her daughter who entertains the other guests by dancing the dance of the seven veils. Her dance seduces Herod into granting her any request and she asks for the head of John the Baptist on a plate. Herod grants her request, crystallizing the sequence as an allegory of the danger of women's sexuality.

Transforming the narrative of Salome from an age-old cautionary tale to a modern narrative exploring female desire, Oscar Wilde's *Salome* shifted "the energy of the narrative away from prurient heterosexual male desire and toward a roving, open-ended sexual expressiveness rooted in the female performer's potential agency."[61] His ability to claim some space for female desire did not account for the complex negotiations Walker had to make as a black middle-class woman trying to guard against the "dominant, already scripted notions of 'deviant' black female sexuality necessitated" by assuming a posture of modesty. While seemingly odd that Walker should pick a dance laced with eroticism as a woman who sought to establish herself as a choreographer of the middle class, she also sought recognition as a modern choreographer. Salome then served as her opportunity to insert herself into a tradition synonymous with modern dance. As dance critic Jayna Brown observes, Walker's "dances were also about a politics of black self-representation. Her efforts presage the efforts of later black dancers, such as Katherine Dunham and Pearl Primus, at cultural recovery. These efforts are always mediated and shot through with contradictions."[62]

As Brown and Brooks note, Walker inserts herself into modern dance and claims a middle-class respectability for herself and black dance. Walker performed *Salome* at the end of Bert Williams' and her husband George Walker's *Bandanna Land.* In *Bandanna Land* Overton Walker had to contend with Williams' parody of her dance in which he dressed in drag and performed a grotesque burlesque interpretation of her movements. Nevertheless, she introduced modern dance into the space of the black Broadway musical. Critics have noted the major impact of her innovation in a space primarily closed off to women's innovation. Adding to Brooks', Brown's, and David Krasner's important work, I argue Overton Walker participates in the making of black global citizens central to the formal innovations of Hopkins and Du Bois.[63] The performances of all three artists' veiled ladies take place in forms that make history and position the performers as agents of history.

Hopkins, Du Bois, and Walker believed that art could further the political goal of positioning African Americans as full national citizens even as artistic forms exposed the limitations of national belonging for black subjects. All three challenged the conventions of their chosen artistic forms and included women who transcend physical barriers to draw attention to the constitution of race as a physical barrier. Luciano notes how *Of One Blood* deploys melancholic imagery to demonstrate national belonging. For Luciano, melancholia in Hopkins' novel is "a historical condition – the very condition, indeed, of being historical."[64] She insists that the pervasive haunting in the novel points to a national lack that *Of One Blood* addresses through the return of the dearly departed. She claims that "foregrounding the revivification of the (living) dead as a means of addressing the psychological, psychic, and cultural wounding that marked African and Anglo-American subjectivity at the turn of the century," the novel's "bicontinental, transhistorical narrative performs an act of critical memory that both reframes the notion of melancholia and resituates possibilities for African American community."[65] *Of One Blood* mobilizes the national melancholia in order to give a second life to the figures that haunt the national consciousness. Walker's *Salome* and Du Bois' *The Star of Ethiopia* also feature women from within the veil who not only return from the dead but also challenge the physical death black women suffer through the objectification of their bodies.

Hopkins' investment in mobilizing the past as a method of democratizing the black populace motivated her to use the adventure plot. She developed "stories devoted to uncovering 'hidden' pasts, histories, and civilizations. Her 'unrealistic' tales ... exemplify what Houston Baker has called the critical function of the black public sphere."[66] Walker hoped to show that black people could experience as performers the participatory democratic privilege that Hopkins cultivated through a readership. "In this era of disenfranchisement and thwarted socio-economic opportunities, Walker recognized the value in aesthetic self-making and representational autonomy."[67] She charged, "unless we learn the lesson of self appreciation and practice it, we shall spend our lives imitating other people and depreciating ourselves."[68] Walker, conscious of the politics of mimicry (a category I consider in greater detail in the next chapter), shifted the framing of her body through her insertion of a modern dance into an all-black musical form. She sought to elevate the dance and black musical theater, offering her audience cues, which many did not take, for how to interpret her performance.[69]

The Star of Ethiopia similarly recouped familiar forms in an attempt to reposition black people in general and black women in particular as national and global subjects. Du Bois drew from the spectacular displays that dominated the modern landscape, from lynching to massive parades, and coupled the two forms to mold an aesthetic that demanded the black populace participate in the staging. The sheer size of the pageant required a communal participation unlike theater in general. The democratic work of the pageant takes place throughout the rehearsals and meetings because in those gatherings community members had the opportunity to practice the collaboration key to Du Bois' vision of social uplift. The actual production offered a culmination to the alternative visual field Du Bois' pageant desired to produce, shifting the black subject from a death-bound figure to a transcendent one with the option of participating in the national body but with recourse to an international space of belonging.

This chapter considers the particular implications of the ritualized death and rebirth of Ethiopia as a representation of historical narrative and the pursuit of national belonging (in Chapter 6 I examine in detail the implications of blood rites for Afro-Christian ritual and African American drama). Shelby Steele's description of ritualized history in the Black Arts Movement period remains applicable to *The Star of Ethiopia*. Quoting Amiri Baraka, he explains that ritual creates a reciprocal relationship between the performers and the audience. Ritualized history creates an emotional connection that, as Steele argues in "Notes on Ritual in the New Black Theater," is empowering for the audience.[70] The sense of empowerment supports David Krasner's assertion in "'The Pageant is the Thing': Black Nationalism and *The Star of Ethiopia*" that the pageant foreshadows an emerging Black Nationalism more fully articulated during the Black Arts Movement. I emphasize that instead of repressing the material female sacrifice, which haunts many Black Nationalist dramas of the Black Arts Movement period, through Ethiopia's resurrection the pageant demonstrates the rupture caused by her death and the alternative perspective born out of it.

DISAPPEARANCE AND REAPPEARANCE: PERFORMING THE RUPTURING OF THE GAZE

If the loss of Ethiopia can be thought of as a visual representation of alienation through her consumption, the transcendence of the star, and the introduction of physiognomy as the primary demarcation of social hierarchy and power, then scene III, episode 7 has much in common with the way Du Bois represents subjection in *The Souls of Black Folk*. The pageant performs the challenge *The Souls of Black Folk* poses to Enlightenment formulations of subjects, by demonstrating the precariousness of looking, especially at individuals, groups, and histories. In *The Souls of Black Folk* Du Bois' double consciousness particularizes psychic rupture as emanating from the construct of race. In addition, Du Boisian double consciousness establishes an affective relationship created by seeing oneself through the eyes of a contemptuous other. Du Bois focuses the relationship between subject formation and the split gaze, described by Hegel in *Phenomenology of the Spirit*, by connecting the rupture of the gaze to racial recognition. The psychic and social revision that *The Souls of Black Folk* demands of the formulation of double consciousness commands a particular form of appearance in the pageant. In the pageant, unlike *The Souls of Black Folk*, the subject at the center of the scene of subjection is a woman. Similar to Hegel's depiction of subjectivity formation in the "Lordship and Bondage" scenario, the slave drivers' act of terrorism has a dual effect: firstly, it results in the objectification of the enslaved Africans, and secondly, it solidifies the white Europeans' collective authority. The pageant adds another stunning twist, however, by way of a "dispossessive force objects exert," which the resurrection of Ethiopia and subsequent insurrection of the black world demonstrates.[71] In this way, building on the critique of Hegel that Paul Gilroy locates in Frederick Douglass' autobiographies, Ethiopia's "inclination towards death and away from bondage is fundamental."[72]

The simultaneous need to affirm the history of the black world and to keep the black subject from being "torn asunder" by the two warring selves compelled Du Bois to move beyond Hegel's formulation of consciousness. Hegel uses the famous allegory of lordship and bondage to describe the development of consciousness. In his paradigm the lord's self-consciousness depends on making the bondsman subject to the lord:

> The lord relates himself immediately to the bondsman through a being [a thing] that is independent, for it is just this which holds the bondsman in bondage; it is his chain from which he could not break free in the struggle, thus proving himself to be dependent, to possess his independence in thinghood. But the lord is the power over this thing, for he proved in the struggle that it is something merely negative; since he is the power over the other [the bondsman], it follows that he holds the other in subjection.[73]

The lord and bondsman have a preexisting triangulated relationship; the lord depends "immediately" on the bondsman by way of "[a thing] that is independent." The power that defines one man as lord, a negotiator of capital, and the other as bondsman, a laborer, also designates the lord as implicated in the subjectivity formation of the bondsman. The lord has power over the bondsman via his power over capital. The lord is not inherently privileged, but placed in a position of power by leveraging his relationship with the bondsman over an independent entity.

The bondsman does not depend on the lord for his "independent consciousness," but, based on the established power dynamics, the lord determines the bondsman's servitude. The bondsman guarantees the lord's knowledge of himself. The lord appears – comes into being – by way of his status, and represents the spectrum of power that subjects the bondsman. At the same time, the lord depends on the bondsman's labor for his certainty. Similarly to Du Bois' depiction of double consciousness, the bondsman knows the role that he plays in solidifying the lord's consciousness. The circumstances of the encounter inscribe the lord's and bondsman's identifications, the lord's knowledge of himself by way of the bondsman and the bondsman's knowledge of himself by way of the lord. As Sandra Adell explains, "the 'lordship and bondage' relationship ... exists as self-consciousness only insofar as it is acknowledged as such by another self-consciousness which it must supersede ... This process of suppression ... according to Hegel, 'has been represented as the action of *one* self-consciousness.'"[74] Hegel's model represents consciousness as doubled, dependent on seeing oneself through and in relationship to another, dependent on and necessarily imagined as independent of the other. Anthony Bogues' reading of "Lordship and Bondage" is useful here. He posits "that the slave turns away from the object of work but does not turn toward the master. Instead the slave turns to a series of practices of freedom."[75] The staging of this familiar philosophical showdown allows Du Bois to demonstrate embodied practices of freedom that not only mimic historical events but also create alternative social practices, practices of freedom.

Several decades after his Hegelian intervention in the first chapter of *The Souls of Black Folk*, Du Bois revises the movement from consciousness to double consciousness, revealing the specific implications double consciousness has for the black subject. It is important to note, nonetheless, that as Paul Gilroy points out, Hegel's famous passage "can be used to offer a firm rebuke to the mesmeric idea of history as progress ... because it provides an opportunity to re-periodise and reaccentuate accounts of the dialectic of Enlightenment."[76] In that way, the pageant recoups some of the latent potential of "Lordship and Bondage" left only partly articulated in *The Souls of Black Folk*. I am not the first to highlight the broader implications for Du Bois' theorization of subjectivity. Many scholars note the way Du Bois' double consciousness influences political, social or philosophical movements,[77] or they examine how the theories of Du Bois' western predecessors influence his construct.[78] My goal in revisiting the most often-cited moment in Du Bois' oeuvre is to demonstrate the way racial identity creates a particular form of alienation for the modern subject and how that alienation informs the shape of history and formation of community in *The Star of Ethiopia*. The practices of freedom cultivated in the pageant depend on the slave's understanding of herself as clearly distinguishable from her oppressor through the choice to seek freedom.

Du Boisian double consciousness entails a judgment, imbued with social history. In *The Souls of Black Folk* Du Bois writes, "It is a peculiar sensation, this double consciousness, this sense of always looking at one's self through the eyes of others, of measuring one's soul by the tape of a world that looks on in amused contempt and pity."[79] By qualifying double consciousness as a "peculiar sensation," Du Bois immediately focuses attention on the subject's constitution "through the eyes of others ... [looking] in amused contempt and pity." Echoing Du Bois' sardonic question "how does it feel to be a problem?", the inherent judgment implied by the act of "measuring one's soul" by the tape of an antagonistic and foreign world theorizes subjectivity based on an embittered struggle. The idea of struggle and communion haunted Du Bois throughout his life. Ultimately, he knew that the quest for freedom required more than the liberation of an individual subject. In scene IV, episode 10 of the pageant, Du Bois communicates liberation as a collective endeavor:

The great march of Ethiopia. She waves her sword; the roll of tom-toms is heard and the Furries [*sic*] of Insurrection rush in led by Nat Turner. She waves her sword again, and to the march "Walk Together, Children," Toussaint and the Haytians [*sic*] march in, Ethiopia waves her sword the third time, and to the time of "Marching through Georgia," the soldiers an [of] the Civil War march in. (WB, 1)

Du Bois' depiction of historical collectivity situates a revolutionary impulse at the heart of black liberation that neither physiognomy, time, nor space can bind. It also explains how the pageant functions as an ideal form of historical recuperation in the early twentieth century in its ability not only to stage collectivity but also to demonstrate the possibility of extra-state political formations. While Du Bois depicts enfranchisement in the nation state as central to his social project throughout most of his life, he also understood black liberation would require practices of freedom that exceeded the framework.

Though not bound by physiognomy, physical racial distinctions inform the visual quality of Du Bois' depiction of subjection. The way that Du Bois describes perhaps his first scene of subjection – in "Of Our Spiritual Strivings," the first chapter of *The Souls of Black Folk* – shows how the visual takes hold of the subject:

In a wee wooden schoolhouse, something put it into boys' and girls' heads to buy gorgeous visiting-cards – ten cents a package – and exchange. The exchange was merry, till one girl, a tall newcomer, refused my card, – refused it peremptorily, with a glance. Then it dawned upon me with a certain suddenness that I was different from the others; or like, mayhap, in heart and life and longing, but shut out from their world by a vast veil.[80]

In the moment when the little girl refuses Du Bois' greeting card, "with a glance," she makes him feel "different from the others." In that instant he becomes an outsider. Even though he longs for inclusion he is "shut out ... by a vast veil." The veil subjects black people to the gaze of the white world, as it clarifies the view of the black subject. It creates a psychic separation that mimics the physical ones. The little white girl's privileged status in the classroom causes Du Bois to hold her "in common contempt" with his other classmates who reside on the other side of the veil. And similar to this rejection, he notes in *The Souls of Black Folk* that when "they approach me in a half-hesitant sort of way, eye me curiously or compassionately, and then, instead of saying directly, How does it feel to be a problem? they say, I know an excellent colored man in town," these outrages actively inform his theory of black subject formation.[81] Thereby, double consciousness extends beyond the scene of subjection to theorize the interpellation and continual maintenance of the black subject. While Du Bois depicts the scene of subjection as a visual event, the subsequent process of naming that reorientation, of taking hold and living behind the veil, resonates with what Foucault describes as normalizing discourses.

The Star of Ethiopia participates in Du Bois' philosophical project by staging a visual event that includes an active response to being shut out by a veil. As with Brooks' veiled ladies, Du Bois' Ethiopia perforates the veil. In the wee wooden schoolhouse the other classmates' presence and implicit support underpins the power of the tall girl's refusal. It is, in part, through her affiliation that she alienates Du Bois. *The Star of Ethiopia* presents a different dynamic. Ethiopia's death inscribes the collective alienation of the enslaved Africans, giving them the power to determine the direction of their historical narrative. In the pageant, Ethiopia not only represents the potential for redemption, she also symbolizes the power of history. Her death signals the enslaved Africans' difference. The pageant, as a visual event performed for an audience, also stages the implicit dynamic between Du Bois and his other classmates. As I have said, however, the structure of the pageant encourages audience members to empathize with the alienated subjects instead of further solidifying their otherness. The audience's assumed resistance to the discursive promise of otherness implied in the scene of subjection enables the revolutionary history the pageant depicts following the scene of subjection.

The Souls of Black Folk implies that in order to combat the social structures that create double consciousness, black people must be established as historical actors who participate in the crafting of history. As a result, Du Bois' famous 1903 collection questions the representation of history as a progressive narrative. He redirects the trajectory of history that Hegel's famous genealogy sets in motion, arguing, "After the Egyptian and Indian, the Greek and Roman, the Teuton and Mongolian, the Negro is a sort of seventh son, born with a veil and gifted with second-sight."[82] In calling the Negro "a sort of seventh son," Du Bois adds the Negro to Hegel's model of historical progress. In "Repetition as a Figure of Black Culture," James Snead comments, "Hegel (like most of Europe) was confused by the African: where did blacks fit into 'the course of *world history?*'" Snead continues by quoting Hegel, who says:

In this main portion of Africa there can really be no history. There is a succession of *accidents and surprises.* There is *no goal*, no state there that one can follow, no subjectivity, but only series of subjects who destroy each other. There has as yet been little comment upon *how strange a form of self-consciousness* this represents . . . What we actually understand by "Africa" is that which is without history and resolution, which is *still* fully caught up in the natural spirit, and which here must be mentioned as being on the threshold of world history.[83]

Following Hegel's logic, the subject emerges from an ordered existence within a state. Correspondingly, social structures emerge through the efforts of self-conscious individuals building from their history and working toward a goal. The mythical structure of the pageant challenges Hegel's claim that Africa is on the threshold of modernity by presenting the centrality of Africa to progression of world history and all modern social structures. The pageant suggests that the modern world depicted in the final episode depends on Ethiopia's life and death in Africa and resurrection in the US. Ethiopia stretches forth her wings and diasporic freedom movements ensue.

THE BLACK FEMALE SUBJECT REPRODUCING HISTORY

The process of situating the black subject outside of history resulted not only from imagining Africa as premodern but also from what Weinbaum calls "the race/reproduction bind." She clarifies, "The word 'bind' expresses the inextricability of the connection between race and reproduction – the fact that these phenomena ought not to be thought of as distinct, though they have all too often been analytically separated."[84] Her work considers how the intertwining of race and reproduction pervades modern conceptions of nation states and becomes folded into intellectual, political, and social theories. The idea of female biological reproduction as the mechanism by which racially "pure" nations sustain themselves contributes to the rhetoric depicting black female reproduction as dangerous. Within the twisted logic of national and racial purity, white female reproductivity must be guarded and assured to facilitate the making of the modern nation, and the black female's legacy as disavowed property must be reiterated and solidified. In the United States, securing the nation against the threat of miscegenation and gifting of capital resources entailed reaffirming black women's limited maternal or bodily agency. The brutalization of the black female body has a long history in American literature and culture that precedes *The Star of Ethiopia*, notably depicted in *Incidents in the Life of a Slave Girl.*

The Star of Ethiopia is a stunning representation of the gender politics implicit in imagining history as a production that is independent of the economy of reproduction. Just as the black female body serves as the object by which national resources, but not the United States itself, are imagined to be cultivated, representations of the black male body also affirm the United States, but often through ritualized scenes of subjection. The imagery of lynching in the US is predominantly black and male. Scholars have given much thought to the function of representations of lynching. In fact, in Chapter 4, I theorize the "sound of lynching." For my purposes here, I will focus on how representations of lynching have a ritualistic purpose that *The Star of Ethiopia* draws from and subverts. Du Bois' depiction of his rebuff in the schoolhouse demonstrates the way the black male serves as the prototypical other in narratives of historical belonging and subject formation. By depicting a black female in a horrific scene of subjection and scripting her resistance to that social alienation, the pageant calls attention to the material histories of black women as historical actors; histories denied by the discursive legacies that codify national belonging.

The familiar images of crowds of people surrounding a victim of lynching, some gathering to watch a lynching take place, others posing for the camera, suggest the way the act itself, and its mimetic reiteration through photography and postcards, acts to make the spectator feel integrated into something bigger than himself or herself. While in religious ritual this something is metaphysical, in lynching it is the nation, state or community. Referencing Mary Douglas, Orlando Patterson concurs in *Rituals of Blood: Consequences of Slavery in Two American Centuries* that "sacrifice enacts and symbolically recreates a disrupted or threatened social world, and it resolves, through the shedding of blood, a specific crisis of transition. It is a brutal rite of passage enacted not primarily for the individual but for the community."[85] For example, the ritualized burning of Zachariah Walker atop a bonfire, as depicted in Toni Morrison's *The Black Book*, reflects a social insecurity on the part of the Coatesville, PA mob, not only considering the blatant and excessive force used to carry out his execution but also

Figure 7 "Christmas in Georgia A.D. 1916," *The Crisis*, December 1916, 78

the positions of the spectators. The focus of many of the members of the crowd is not on the burning body but the camera. Moreover, many of the audience members' postures – posing and smiling – suggest an investment in capturing the event as a part of an archive and not, necessarily, participating in the event itself. Such postures place a greater emphasis on remembering the event than on the singular death of Walker. The spectators anticipate the continual negotiations of power authorized by archiving the image of Walker's corpse, which although it is at the forefront of the picture seems to serve as a backdrop to the interest of those in the photograph. Clearly the execution of Walker, who was accused of killing a police officer, served to reestablish a set of power dynamics threatened from within.

Compare the crowd of spectators surrounding Walker's body with an image from *The Crisis* of a lynching victim as a Christ-like figure (Figure 7). The image of the lynching victim as Christ-like figure intercedes in the representation of the black male body and its relationship to national identity, creating a typological signification at the site of ritualized sacrifice. The image of the lynched figure transformed into a crucifixion shifts the body from object through which power is exchanged to subject, the very broker of the exchange. The sacrifice of the Christ-like figure could be thought to pay for the redemption of the US as nation. Werner Sollors' *Beyond Ethnicity* and Eddie S. Glaude's *Exodus!* each describes the sense of community that Anglo-Americans and African Americans garner through their use of biblical typology. Drawing from the story of Exodus, marked by the movement from enslavement in Egypt to liberation and nation-hood in a land promised by God, Anglo-Americans imagined the US as their promised land, while African Americans thought of the United States as like Egyptian bondage. The images of the black Christ-like figure in *The Crisis* and *The Star of Ethiopia* complicate African Americans' typological imaginings by emphasizing the sacrifice of the black body as woven throughout the intricate networks supporting the project of modernity in addition to the constitution of a particular nation state.

   The Star of Ethiopia intertwines Ethiopia's death with African American biblical typography, and in so doing transforms the gender politics of the black body in pain. Simultaneously, the pageant reorders the visual repre-sentation of black savior or emancipatory figure as male. The pageant distinctively models the possibility of redemption at the end of black female sacrifice and therefore pushes at the very boundaries of the notion of modern subjectivity. It challenges the illogic of slavery at the heart of modernity, and its subtending formulations of the modern subject, through the image of a female salvific figure. Similarly, "The Damnation of Women," an essay in Du Bois' collection entitled *Darkwater*, "stage[s] world history through and as a maternal genealogy [that] fundamentally revises the monumental history of 'The Star of Ethiopia,'" according to Gilman.[86] While I find Gilman's attention to what she calls the citation of *The Star of Ethiopia* in "The Damnation of Women" a singular and important contribution to the study of Du Bois' work, she focuses, as do other critics, on the 1913 version of the pageant and does not conceptualize it as an ongoing production with significant differences. Whereas Gilman rightly notes that Du Bois reproduces the imagery present in *The Star of Ethiopia* in "The Damnation of Women," I do not find a progression in Du Bois' feminism from *The Star of Ethiopia* to *Darkwater*. Rather, I see each of the iterations as a part of a long cycle marked by crosscurrents.

   Du Bois' pageant reproduces the history of modernity with a difference by including the narrative of slavery and the logic it demands of all modern subjects. Literary theorists have explored the gender politics of "scenes of subjection" and their relationship to emancipatory narratives. At the same time, African American studies theorists have considered the vexed politics of black female biological reproduction. My situating the reproductive activity in *The Star of Ethiopia* as fundamental to the freedom drive at the core of the African American literary tradition extends the work of Saidiya Hartman and Fred Moten while it creates a point of intersection among African American studies, performance studies, and literary studies. In the opening chapter of *In the Break*, Moten makes use of Hartman's theorization of scenes of subjection to establish the acoustic history of the black radical tradition. Beginning with the same scene that Hartman depicts in the introduction to her book, Moten describes the now infamous beating of Aunt Hester in *The Narrative of the Life of Frederick Douglass*. While Hartman recalls or, more precisely, attempts not to recall the scene, Moten depicts Aunt Hester's beating to show how Douglass' emancipatory narrative depends on the objection and repression of Aunt Hester's screams. Of this well-known scene of torture, a young Douglass writes:

I have often been awakened at the dawn of day by the most heart-rending shrieks of an own aunt of mine, whom he [Captain Anthony, Douglass's first master] used to tie up to a joist, and whip upon her naked back till she was literally covered with blood ... The louder she screamed, the harder he whipped; and where the blood ran fastest, there he whipped longest.[87]

The *Narrative* juxtaposes Aunt Hester's screams to the often-cited scene of the enslaved Africans going to the Great House Farm "for the monthly allowance for themselves and their fellow-slaves." Douglass describes them as "peculiarly enthusiastic," singing spirituals and dancing.[88] The juxtaposition of the two sounds could be read as a call and response that reveal what Du Bois and Zora Neale Hurston have both described as the resistance embedded in singing spirituals.

Moten's rereading of the beating of Aunt Hester foregrounds the gender dynamics at stake in her brutalization and provides a point of departure for me to recuperate black female reproduction as a revolutionary site of black performance. He asserts that the juxtaposition in the *Narrative* models for the reader how to move from slavery to freedom. He warns that focusing on the scene of the singing enslaved going to the Great House Farm requires de-emphasizing Aunt Hester's scream. Douglass narrates Aunt Hester's beating and then describes the enslaved singing spirituals and dancing. For Douglass, that movement, from slavery to freedom, is predicated on a turning away from female suffering; he stops listening to Aunt Hester's scream and starts listening to his fellow slaves singing spirituals. Moten provocatively explains, "enslavement – and the resistance to enslavement that is the performance essence of blackness (or, perhaps less controversially, the essence of black performance) is a *being maternal* that is indistinguishable from a *being material*."[89] In his incisive claim, he pinpoints the act of double listening as a liberatory practice. Seeing double becomes listening double and once again reframes looking through active resistant participation in the scene of subjection. Moten argues that in order for Douglass' narrative to achieve its prescribed end of emancipation – for him to move from object to subject, from slavery to freedom – he must distance himself from Aunt Hester's scream because the discourse of slavery requires the consistent reiteration of the black female's materiality. Nevertheless, the acoustic materiality of her protest becomes incorporated and reproduced through the sorrow songs. Therefore, the quelling of the sound of Aunt Hester's voice from one scene to the next does not permanently silence the sound.

What is at stake when Aunt Hester disappears from the *Narrative*, and how does her disappearance help explicate Ethiopia's death in scene IV of the pageant? As Moten notes, "Douglass and Hartman confront us with the fact that the *conjunction* of reproduction and disappearance is performance's condition of possibility, its ontology and its mode of production."[90] To disappear from view is not synonymous with dissolving. Rather, black performance functions through opacity and on what Ralph Ellison calls "the lower frequencies" as a means to rework and recoup the material, which is indistinguishable from the maternal. The intersection of disappearance and reproduction specifies black performance as a historical project that resists elision. At the same time, the acoustic reproduction Douglass' narrative establishes also bears the trace of physical reproduction and its tie to the black female body as property. Moten claims Aunt Hester's scream as part of the performance legacy of black subject formation and emblematic of the ontology of black performance. In an effort to establish another site of female recuperation, I focus on Du Bois' deployment of a black female salvific figure. Instead of focusing on acoustic materiality and the interruptive rupture it inaugurates, I reclaim black female reproduction as black performance that engenders historical, sexual, and political practices; practices that must repeat in order to offer strategies for the emergence of the black subject's pursuit of freedom.

Creating a multifaceted meaning of reproduction in relation to Ethiopia, Du Bois points to spaces of agency for black women in black performance at the intersection of reproduction and disappearance. Reproduction is not the making of the same thing. Instead, it is a process that demonstrates the successful completion of crafting something new. I am not using the term reproduction to signify that the performances depicted in Du Bois' imaginative work are mechanically reproduced. A mystified look that meets Ethiopia's resurrection in scene IV follows the horrified look Ethiopia's public death produces in scene III. Ethiopia's second coming symbolizes the potential for new vision created by alienation from the scene of subjection. Nevertheless, the assumption of that power is not automatic, as Butler explains: "Where conditions of subordination make possible the assumption of power, the power assumed remains tied to those conditions, but in an ambivalent way; in fact, the power assumed may at once retain and resist that subordination."[91] The fifth scene clarifies how the frightened enslaved Africans make use of the power made available by Ethiopia's death and rebirth. This scene depicts the abolitionist movement. As the abolitionists battle with the slave drivers, Shango emerges, sings, makes a gesture, and resurrects Ethiopia. In this liberatory moment, Ethiopia transforms from sacrifice into salvific figure. She also establishes the line of the father through the daughter. Ethiopia returns in scene IV holding the star in one hand and a sword in the other. The image of Ethiopia standing at the right hand of Shango resists the impulse to turn away from material remains in the pursuit of freedom. Her position creates an occasion for the black world to learn "who the female is within itself," to quote Hortense Spillers.[92] Ethiopia waves her sword, and the community onstage performs a revolutionary history. Characterized by "The men of Palmares" and "The Haitians led by Toussaint," the black world revolts. Ethiopia brings together the psychic and physical remains, which results in self-generative forces. Her reappearance in scene IV with sword in hand ushers in the revolutionary activity. Notably the nature of revolution the pageant depicts highlights Du Bois' investment in a humanism that presupposes the master's tools can dismantle the master's house.

The Star of Ethiopia presents blackness as the pursuit of freedom through historical (re)enactment. Giving Ethiopia a material and metaphysical presence in the narrative, the pageant resists freezing her as a material point of contact and departure. In the pageant, instead of producing children, Ethiopia expands the reproductive possibilities for the black female in the scene of subjection. She directs the reproduction of black performance and the gaze of the spectator. Imagining a black woman as a guiding force in subject formation and black performance is a way to subject the unavoidable model of subjection to radical breakdown.

The next two chapters also consider the potentially transgressive movements of black heroines. Zora Neale Hurston's *Color Stuck* and Langston Hughes' *Tambourines to Glory* present the possibilities and limitations of performance practices as mechanisms to address structural inequality. Satirical mimesis characterizes the cakewalking in Hurston's play and the religious performances depicted in Hughes' drama. The playwrights deploy familiar modes of black performance in order to question the black collectivity in which *The Star of Ethiopia* culminates. Hurston's and Hughes' plays call attention to the limits of black performance and the uses of repetition.

CHAPTER 3

Reenacting the Harlem Renaissance

Zora Neale Hurston's Color Struck

Bodies erect, prancing smoothly, the dancers draw the whole stage, well, almost the whole stage, and the entire audience into frenzy. For seven minutes the characters in Zora Neale Hurston's *Color Struck* (1926) cakewalk across the stage. There is no evidence that *Color Struck* was ever performed. My reading of the play, however, reflects the staging implicit in most dramatic work. The climactic cakewalk in the middle of the play eclipses the struggle that leads up to it, emphasizing what has been achieved. The beautiful carefree dancing, read outside of its historical context, seems to have no political import. In "On Freedom and the Will to Adorn: Debating Aesthetics and/as Ideology in African American Literature," Cheryl Wall explains that in Richard Wright's 1937 review of Hurston's *Their Eyes Were Watching God* Wright linked "Hurston to a politics he deemed reactionary and to a quest for the beautiful which, to him, served no 'serious' purpose."[1] Wright established a binary opposition between Hurston's choice of subject matter – focusing on the abundance of beauty in African American culture – and what he deemed serious political art. In this chapter, I question the oppositional relationship between the quest for the beautiful and political empowerment through black performance. Foreshadowing the conceptual frame Hurston estab-lishes in "Characteristics of Negro Expression" (1934), the cakewalking in *Color Struck* presents a performance practice that embodies the conflicts of the community imagined in the play and reflects the larger struggle the New Negro community faces over its racial and national identities.[2]

Color Struck's plot is deceptively simple. The play depicts a classic love triangle that develops within a group of young people from Jacksonville, Florida on their way to a cakewalking contest in St. Augustine, Florida. *Color Struck* is set at the turn of the century, the height of cakewalking in America and Europe. Spearheaded by George Walker, his vaudevillian partner Bert Williams, Stella Wiley, and Ada (Aida) Overton Walker, the duos transformed the cakewalk from a dance enslaved Africans performed for themselves and at the behest of slave masters into an international craze; as Walker describes it, they "were able to put a premium on Cake-walking, and at one time, in 1902 and 1903 ... had all New York and London doing the Cake-walk."[3] Most theorists, including Elin Diamond and Jacqui Malone, describe the cakewalk as a strut. Additionally Malone specifies the improvisational quality implicit in the dance and in all forms of black vernacular dance. While the erect torso and extended leg charac-terize the dance, descriptions and modern interpretations of it allow for much variation. Leading up to the contest depicted in *Color Struck*, the female protagonist, Emmaline (called Emma) consistently fights for her boyfriend John's attention. While John consoles and chides dark-skinned Emma for what he characterizes as her unfounded jealousy, he also encourages the affection of light-skinned Effie. Along with the play's commentary on the politics of colorism, *Color Struck* adds a twist to this classic love triangle by interrupting the progress of the plot with dancing scenes. In fact, the emotional climax of the play occurs in scene III, which presents the cakewalking contest, a purposeful reordering of early twentieth-century revue sketches that concluded with a "jubilant" cakewalk.[4] If the action that leads up to the contest seems to depict Emma as a jealous melodramatic girlfriend, the third and fourth scenes of the play arrest that judgment. From the climactic third scene to the structural critique Emma makes at the end of the play, *Color Struck* focuses on the costs of modern "progress."

One such ideal is the figure of the mulatto. The mulatto, "a taboo and a synthesis," serves as a model for the New Negro who exhibited a way of

Although not well known, *Color Struck* in many ways is an archetypal text of the Harlem Renaissance. The play won second prize in the *Opportunity* magazine writing contest announced in June 1925 and the periodical *Fire* published it in 1926. Similar to Nella Larsen's *Quicksand* (1928) and *Passing* (1929), Wallace Thurman's *The Blacker the Berry* (1929), Jessie Redmon Fauset's *Plum Bun* (1929) and *Comedy American Style* (1933), and Langston Hughes' "Cross" (1925), "Mulatto" (1927), "Father and Son" (1934), and *Mulatto* (1935), Hurston's play depicts a deep affective cost embedded in identifying as a New Negro. Her play along with the aforementioned texts investigates the way the New Negro, as cultural imago, produces what Hortense Spillers calls "neither/nor" identities.[5] Associated with the way individuals view and access others, holding them to an imaged ideal, I use the term imago to position the New Negro as a construct that has psychic significance for those unable to assume the ideals it glorifies.

One such ideal is the figure of the mulatto. The mulatto, "a taboo and a synthesis," serves as a model for the New Negro who exhibited a way of being in the world that easily incorporated black people into US modernity.[6] During the Harlem Renaissance color became one of the primary bodily features upon which writers imaged ideals, a shibboleth for inclusion. Sherrard-Johnson's study, *Portraits of the New Negro Woman: Visual and Literary Culture in the Harlem Renaissance* is one of several studies that figure the mulatto/a as constitutive of the Harlem Renaissance. She contends that "obsession with color reflects both white and black anxieties about identity in the midst of modernization."[7] Although always present, the mulatta further emphasized the gender and class dynamics infused at the site of sexuality. "As a passing figure and a representative of the trope of the New Negro movement, the mulatta underlines how gender oppression and anxieties concerning sexuality and sexual difference constituted the New Negro movement's racial discourse."[8] Further explicating the relationship between the New Negro and the mulatto/a, Sherrard-Johnson and Hazel Carby focus on the mulatto/a as a figure between white and black America who serves as a site of projection of racial difference and accommodation. As an ideal and site of projection, the mulatto/a figure serves as a limit point to national inclusion and a boundary to racial equality. She becomes both hero and villain, freeing the desiring subjects from confronting their own investments in colorism. *Color Struck* intercedes in this process of projection and disavowal by focusing on the way the mulatta as New Negro imago creates a neither/nor identity for dark-skinned black women. Anticipating the critique of colorism in Thurman's *The Blacker the Berry* and Fauset's *Comedy American Style*, Hurston's play presents the tragedy of hierarchies of color, by suggesting that colorism implicitly asserts that certain bodies deserve discrimination more than others. In the play performance exacerbates and exhumes the laden psychic configurations that enable colorism.

While *Color Struck* should be read alongside the novels, novellas, poems and plays of the Harlem Renaissance that consider colorism, Hurston's play singularly mimics the dynamic of exclusion that colorism creates, through the staging and deployment of the cakewalk. The third scene calls for the audience to participate in the cakewalking and therefore to encourage the light-brown-skinned John and mulatta Effie and exclude dark-skinned Emmaline. Despite Emma being the main character, critics justify her alienation in the climactic third scene by arguing she has an unrealistic emotional attachment to John. As a result, many dismiss *Color Struck* as melodramatic, even considering Emma's insightful enunciations at the end of the play.[9] Alternatively, I read Emma and John's relationship as a metaphor for the dynamic identifications the reemergence of the New

Negro identity after World War I necessitates. Additionally, Emma and John's relationship must be viewed through the dramatic sequencing of the play. The negotiations between Emma and John signify a political struggle over what qualified as useful identifications with regard to class, gender, geographical location, and performance for African Americans during the Harlem Renaissance. Emma's inability to participate in the cakewalking in scene III should be read within the historical context of the dance – a dance that presented gestures featured in black minstrel performances and central to primitivism. At the same time, mulatta Effie participates in the cakewalking scene and through her dynamic performance hijacks space between the social figures of the respectable race woman and the erotic primitive Jezebel, reinforcing the fugitive status of the neither/nor identity.

IDENTIFYING: MAMMY/MULATTA, EITHER/NEITHER

The slapstick comedy deployed in the opening scene of *Color Struck* situates the play in the theatrical history of black minstrelsy as it establishes a connection between Post-Bellum and Harlem Renaissance performances. It also establishes Hurston's theatrical tradition, which she draws from in her now infamous collaboration with Langston Hughes on their play *Mule Bone: A Comedy of Negro Life*. Imagine the sound of a train, boisterous laughter, and several people talking at once. As you adjust your hearing to the layers of sound, a curtain opens to a group of Negroes, men wearing *"'plug' silk hats," "sunflowers in their button holes,"* and women with colorful highly adorned dresses who scramble to find seats on a train. Organized in pairs, one couple, *"miss[es] a seat three times, much to the enjoyment of the crowd."*[10] As the passengers settle down the dialogue of the play begins. The playfulness central to the opening scene of *Color Struck* recalls the mirthful opening of Williams and Walker's hit musical *In Dahomey* (1902), which featured "two real coons." For those familiar with the confidence game that opens *In Dahomey*, *Color Struck's* mimicry of black minstrel tropes immediately registers as a red herring. While the humorous play draws the audience, it should also place the careful viewer on guard.

The opening of the play purposefully displaces its critique of Harlem Renaissance propriety by setting the scene at the turn of the century. During the Harlem Renaissance, social practices and performances served as mechanisms to legitimize and differentiate identities. The opening scene of *Color Struck* presents working-class black people living in the

South at the turn of the century, seemingly unaffected by the images of respectability circulating in Negro periodicals. Wall argues that unlike Hurston's contemporaries, "no tragic mulattoes people [Hurston's] fiction"; Hurston depicts folk culture instead.[11] Wall's comment suggests the figurative tension mapped onto actual bodies that Hurston seeks to arrest by using an embodied medium that calls attention to the legacy of black theatricality and the limits scripted blackness places on black people. *Color Struck* moves from playful to serious and comedic to tragic to implicate the viewer in taking pleasure in modes of representation that lock the black subject in place. Similarly to modern US melodrama, Hurston cultivated an audience through familiar images like those of the opening scene. The sheer force of Hurston's comedic voice suggests the desire that her audience revel in the display. Nevertheless, Hurston also asks her audience to consider the cost of such pleasures. The multiplicity of voices expressed in *Color Struck* differentiates it from melodrama in that it does not come to a neat resolution by the end of the play but instead asks the audience to make sense of the ethical dilemma located at the site of taking pleasure in pain.

Hurston makes a similar move in "Characteristics of Negro Expression." A manifesto on black performance, Hurston's at once playful and serious essay inspires joy and laughter similar to what many twenty-first-century black audiences express when they go to see a gospel play or a Tyler Perry production that features familiar if derogatory and stereotypical images of black life. Unlike the often buffoonish comedy of the Chitlin Circuit, Hurston's essay masterfully describes the Negro's ingenious and yet ridiculous linguistic, stylistic, and aesthetic inventions, coining phrases such as "more great and more better" and "funeralize" to register the joy of recognition and inspire critical consideration of the costs of the joy.[12] Hurston creates the tension between uninhibited pleasure and careful consideration by drawing parallels between black and white cultures. She explains, "Now the people with highly developed languages have words for detached ideas. That is legal tender. 'That-which-we-squat-on' has become 'chair.' 'Groan-causer' has evolved into 'spear,' and so on. Some individuals even conceive of the equivalent of check words, like 'ideation' and 'pleonastic.' Perhaps we might say that *Paradise Lost* and *Sartor Resartus* are written in check words."[13] Hurston's sarcasm is palpable. She marks the value of certain modes of cultural expression amounting to "legal tender" and then derides them by suggesting their abstractness equals that of black cultural expressions. Hurston ridicules the culturally motivated assignment of value as she pokes fun at the people with "highly developed languages" and the Negro's vernacular expression. Her essay stages scripted black performances with predictable outcomes, but she, and herein lies the critical edge of her essaying performance, defies the expected outcomes, undermining them at every turn and refusing our expectations in order to compel the reader to examine his or her desire. In one passage she describes "a robust young Negro chap" flirting with a Negro girl and concludes ironically "these little plays by strolling players are acted out daily in a dozen streets in a thousand cities, and no one ever mistakes the meaning." Her affirmation of the observer's indisputable interpretive mastery undermines its validity as it draws the reader in as a player in the drama. The push and pull of her prose creates the rhythm of the elusive offbeat characteristics of Negro expression.

Reversal marks every aspect of Hurston's signature essay. Therefore one must read for the contrary when Hurston defines the drama implicit in Negro life, which is the source material for her folk art. She writes, "Everything is acted out. Unconsciously for the most part of course. There is an impromptu ceremony always ready for every hour of life. No little moment passes unadorned."[14] The will to adorn is not static; as a principle that supports many modes of expression it is used to negotiate relationships both internal and external to the black communities imagined in Hurston's oeuvre. It points to the excess attributed to black culture as it highlights the excessive weight of projection black culture must bear. Expressed through the references to black minstrelsy, in *Color Struck* the will to adorn portrays both the joy and the struggle embedded in the "freedom already achieved" while it offers a strategy to achieve "freedom yet denied."[15]

At the same time, signaling a shift in the social and racial dynamics of the country, the mimicking of minstrelsy in *Color Struck* celebrates the freedom momentarily to forget struggles over national and racial identity. Unwilling to credit this assumed freedom as an unmediated privilege, the play illuminates the disparity between an individual community member's ability to fully enjoy his or her national identity and his or her ability to forget racial limitations and to benefit from the performances. Throughout the play Emma (the darkest character in the play, and as a result, the character least able to experience national belonging) demands that John (the light-brown-skinned male protagonist) try to satisfy her insatiable desire to be loved. Emma's consistent requests appear to represent her *personal* lack. They demonstrate shortcomings in the objects of black cultural identification, however, if read in relationship to the structural apparatus of the play – the stage directions, scene progression, and settings. *Color Struck* portrays the New Negro projecting his physical slippage, his physical inability to approximate whiteness, onto his darker and even more forcibly radical sister. The first three scenes of *Color Struck* comment on and extend the theorization of the New Negro by situating its emergence through bodies in motion.

The representation of colorism, which was widespread during the Harlem Renaissance, "as pervasive as Jim Crow," reflects one aspect of the problem some Harlem Renaissance artists had with the ideal of the New Negro.[16] Henry Louis Gates explains, "The 'New Negro,' of course was only a metaphor. The paradox of this claim is inherent in the trope itself, combining as it does a concern with time, antecedents, and heritage, on the one hand, with a concern for a cleared space, the public face of the race, on the other."[17] Gates traces the trope of the New Negro from its use in the late nineteenth century to its belated deployment in the Harlem Renaissance. The cultural demands of the Harlem Renaissance, or what Gates calls "a paradox ... of self-willed beginning," called for repudiating histories of revolutionary and black-minstrel-like perform-ance, which for the cakewalk were one and the same. Alongside the cakewalk's deployment as a key part of many turn-of-the-century black performances, the dance also served as enslaved Africans' mode of mocking ridicule. The cakewalk, therefore, in its early twentieth-century enactments represents the history of the Old Negro and the possibilities of the new one.

The artistic transformation associated with Alain Locke's codification of the New Negro movement in his anthology *The New Negro* necessi-tated creating distance from the Old Negro. Locke designated the politics of the New Negro by saying:

Of course, the thinking Negro has shifted a little toward the left with the world-trend, and there is an increasing group who affiliate with radical and liberal movements. But fundamental for the present the Negro is radical on race matters, conservative on others, in other words, a "forced radical," a social protestant rather than a genuine radical.[18]

Locke's attempt to highlight the way American society produces a "forced radical" is both supported and undercut by calling the New Negro a conservative. As Gates notes, "Locke's New Negro was a poet, and it would be in the sublimity of the fine arts, and *not* in the political sphere of action or protest poetry, that white America (they thought) would at last embrace the Negro of 1925."[19] The tactic of creating an image worthy of incorporation unavoidably denies the material reality of black people.

Although ideals always serve to exclude the actors, *Color Struck* questions the investment in approximating the New Negro as an ideal.

In particular, *The New Negro* had specifications that served to divide African Americans into privileged and subordinate categories. In the introduction to Locke's collection, he claims that "for generations in the mind of America, the Negro has been more of a formula than a human being – a something to be argued about."[20] Foregrounding the constructedness of the Negro in the American imagination, Locke does not indicate how his project participates in creating an unattainable, but nevertheless socially powerful, cultural ideal of its own. He strategically codifies a division through this new politicized body named the New Negro, which would manifest itself in differences among black folk. Locke's formulation attempted to negotiate the radical politics of some New Negroes and the legacy of enslaved Africans' distant performances. At the same time, his categorization, by omission, created a frame for the women of the Harlem Renaissance. Although Locke does not directly engage gender, through his use of imagery, metaphor, and citation, as Wall notes, he establishes a masculine tone that informs the remainder of the volume. For the women of the Harlem Renaissance, the artistic revolution Locke's categorization of the New Negro calls for requires confronting the protocols of respectability established by the New Negro women at the turn of the century.

The New Negro woman represented an idealized identity formed to negotiate the political struggles urban African Americans experienced following Reconstruction. Foreshadowing a legacy that would haunt the Harlem Renaissance, she presented a refined, dignified public face, which embraced certain aspects of the collective character and repudiated others. Foregrounding the respectability of black women in opposition to charges of their moral inferiority, Nannie H. Burroughs asserts in "Not Color, but Character," published in *Voice of the Negro*, an Atlanta-based periodical that circulated from 1904 to 1907, "it is the duty of the Negro women to rise in the pride of their womanhood and vindicate themselves of the charge by teaching all men that black womanhood is as sacred as white womanhood."[21] Burroughs insists that educating men about black women does not differ with regard to race. The New Negro woman's ability to reach across racial lines informed her activism.[22] At the same time, her comment reflects an impulse on the part of the New Negro woman to counter the legacy emerging from what Mrs. Addie Hunton describes as the Negro woman being made subject to "compulsory immorality."[23] The New Negro woman sought to defend against the discursive history resulting from the sexual abuse enslaved black women suffered. The need to defend Negro womanhood reflects the social history of disavowal that black women faced at the turn of the twentieth century and that was central to W.E.B. Du Bois' recuperation of Ethiopia as discussed in the previous chapter.

In order to more easily assimilate these New Negroes into the northern urban culture, Locke defined certain aspects of their collective character as markers of identity. He attempted to codify a cosmopolitan class of Negroes. During the Harlem Renaissance vernacular forms (spirituals, blues, ragtime, and cakewalking, for example) signified the history of slavery and the geographical and socioeconomic conditions that underpinned it. Vernacular culture became equated with poor, rural, uneducated African Americans and challenged what Evelyn Brooks Higginbotham calls the politics of respectability. She contends the politics of respectability emerged out of the discourse of self-help and required Negroes to create a public image that demanded the respect of the world. This new public self acted as "proof of the race's uplift from the degradation of slavery and from the disparaging images of Sambo and the blackface minstrelsy."[24] The politics of respectability responded to the philosophical belief that race created an ontological difference – race was thought to be in the blood. Therefore, as a justification for slavery, black people were said to be biologically incapable of participating in a free society. The same belief system, of an inherent inferiority on the part of black people, underpinned Jim Crow laws and segregation. Black and white people could not and therefore should not live together, eat together, or go to school together. The politics of respectability worked through the loss of dignity African Americans suffered by focusing on the aspiration toward a new ideal. The politics of respectability emerged as a performative response to the depiction of the Negro as "the sick man of American Democracy."[25] The tragedy of the politics of respectability mirrored that of the mulatto: as long as Homer Plessy or any of his kin had any black blood they were doomed to fall short of complete assimilation into American culture. The desire for the nearest approximation motivated the fierce policing of black propriety.

Harlem Renaissance literature explores the implications of aligning phenotypes with modes of performance. The mulatta adheres to the politics of respectability that Irene Redfield in Larsen's *Passing* exemplifies, and negotiates primitivism as depicted by characters such as Clare Kendry in *Passing* and Helga Crane in *Quicksand*. The images of respectability look back to the Victorian era while the figure of the seductive animalistic tragic heroine points to a modernist impulse that entangles class, color, and standards of behavior. Class privilege distinguishes the central characters in *Passing* and *Quicksand* from the protagonist Emma Lou of Thurman's *The Blacker the Berry* whose name, no doubt, aligns her with Hurston's main character. Thurman served as one of the editors of *Fire*, the periodical in which Hurston first published *Color Struck*. In Thurman's novel, one of few depictions of the plight of a dark-skinned woman from the period, the protagonist is the only member of her family not part of the blue vein circle, "so named because all of its members were fair-skinned enough for their blood to be seen pulsing purple through the veins of their wrists."[26] Emma Lou, the product of her mother's first marriage, learns from her family that "the tragedy of her life was that she was too black,"[27] a tragedy her sex and class compound. Even though Emma's family has enough money to send her to the University of Southern California, when she arrives she is unable to pledge the Greek letter sorority, because unlike Verne, another dark-skinned female student, Emma Lou is not a bishop's daughter and she does not drive a big Buick. Emma Lou has enough money to access but not to participate in the organizations defined, in part, by their opposition to her color. Emma Lou's struggle, which the novel repeatedly suggests would not be so great if she were a boy, has as much to do with her desire for white skin as the repeated rebuffs she suffers throughout the novel.

In addition to establishing the specific stakes of color for a woman during the Harlem Renaissance, *The Blacker the Berry* introduces performance into the negotiation of race. In a scene that imagines a conversation among key figures of the Harlem Renaissance, a character named Truman relates colorism to the theater. He explains, "Then, too, since black is the favorite color of vaudeville comedians and jokesters, and conversely, as intimately associated with tragedy, it is no wonder that even the blackest individual will seek out someone more black than himself to laugh at."[28] Essentializing the creation of hierarchies, Truman acknowledges the history of blackness and theatrical display. As I discuss in the Overture, the visual systems of codification necessary to maintain slavery aligned the production of blackness with theater. Truman's comment extends that idea to the Harlem Renaissance by specifying the way darkness in particular, and not all shades of black people, becomes associated with vaudeville. In the conversation, *The Blacker the Berry* alludes to the opening scene of William Wells Brown's *Clotel; or, the President's Daughter* (1853), which features the auction of the main character "with a complexion as white as most of those who were waiting ... her features as finely defined as any of her sex of pure Anglo-Saxon."[29]

Whereas Clotel's status on the auction block, and not her physical appearance, confers her blackness, by the publication of *The Blacker the Berry* the color black becomes aligned with the stage.

While *The Blacker the Berry* makes explicit the relationship between blackness and theatricality, Langston Hughes' *Mulatto* (1935) leverages colorism to draw attention to the constitution of the mulatto figure in actions rather than in the blood. Hughes' play questions the naturalness of the familial structure by depicting an explosion of rage. Oedipal conflict marks Colonel Tom Norwood and Robert's relationship. Bert's conflict with his father, however, does not center on their triangulated relationship with Bert's mother and Colonel Tom's lover Cora. Although the two men often negotiate their relationship through Cora, she is not the central object of desire as in the Freudian rendering of oedipalization. In *Mulatto*, what Bert lacks, what he is willing to kill for, is his father's recognition. As taboo as incest, Colonel Tom granting recognition to his son would implode the social order of modern, southern gentility and legitimate the intimate intermingling of white and black people in Hughes' drama. Colonel Tom, therefore, must refuse Bert in order to define a coherent home, a southern white home; in this familial drama, Bert may only occupy the positions of laborer and servant, *not son*.

In response to Colonel Tom's rejection, Bert, who is the spitting image of his father, performs appropriated white privilege. He tells his brother William, "He's half white, and he's gonna act like it" and mocks, with his use of a heavy accent, his neighbors who warn, "You can't argue wid whut folks, man. You better stay out o' this Junction. You must ain't got no sense, nigger."[30] His most explicit appropriation of whiteness establishes how performance bolsters the value of light skin. Bert demands, "Look at me. I'm a'fay boy. (*Pretends to shake his hair back*) See these grey eyes? I got the right to everything everybody else has. (*Punching his brother in the belly*) Don't talk to me, old slavery-time Uncle Tom."[31] Although Bert confirms the relationship between physical appearance and behavior that he seeks to undermine in order to allow his incorporation within a restricted genealogy, his behavior points to the ratifying gestures and postures that stabilize colorism. While Bert tenaciously claims white privilege, he must disparage William to displace his inadequacies onto his sibling, calling him an Uncle Tom. William reminds Bert of their shared racial difference from Colonel Tom, therefore William signifies what Bert so deeply wishes to reject when the protagonist calls himself a Norwood. Hughes' play establishes the fluidity of racial categories and the unreliability of the visual as a marker of inclusion or exclusion. In order to shore up the permeable visual field, individuals were socially mandated to perform certain social and cultural roles.

Realizing the denigration of certain cultural forms during the period, Hurston resisted the artistic restrictions the public persona of the New Negro demanded and, instead, drew from vernacular culture in her art. Critics have objected to her use of the vernacular, specifically her representation of the folk – rural, southern, black Americans. From claims that the folk Hurston presents exist outside of modern time to claims that her representations lack any political import, Hurston's resistance to predominant images has inspired and troubled critics.[32] Her use of folk culture foregrounds a more general concern about whether representation, particularly via performance, serves to reify at best and reinscribe at worst the very modes it seeks to critique. Even if Hurston's play challenges the investment in the mulatta as culture icon, how may we interpret the pleasure the humorous, minstrel-like images generate? Diamond argues the play deploys those images in order to destroy them, yet the pleasure, arguably, still remains.

The appropriation and commodification of black culture, as Hurston presents it in *Color Struck*, highlights the social and cultural stresses that inform the process of communal identification and the theater. Through the process of identification, Hurston produces satirical humor to create a self-reflexive view. The fact that the laughter remains provides the risk of further dehumanization and the opportunity for future reflection. At the same time, Hurston's use of vernacular culture creates an alternative historical epistemology. For example, the introduction of a Jim Crow car in the beginning of *Color Struck* and the conversation about migration at the end both point to specific historical and political issues that the play negotiates. For Hurston, the burden of representing an authentic black culture coupled issues of class with critiques of gender politics. Moments in Hurston's work in which she challenges the psychic structures that encourage African Americans to conform to the "inferior values of the dominant culture" speak as much to the gender politics of the twenty-first century as they did to the Harlem Renaissance.[33]

The history of colorism and the pressures to strive toward realizing the ideal of the New Negro woman explain why from the beginning of the play Emma epitomizes melodrama – race melodrama, that is. The opening scene of the play shows an argument among Jacksonville's best team of cakewalkers, Emma and John. Emma playfully chides John, "John! John, don't you want me to love you, honey?" and he responds, "(*turns and kisses her slowly*) Yes, I want you to love me, you know I do.

But I don't like to be accused o'ever light colored girl in the world. It hurts my feeling. I don't want to be jealous like you are" (9). John's affectionate rebuttal forces Emma into a defensive position, making her "jealousy" seem unfounded, whereas in fact he actively encourages Effie's attention. John's ability to marshal credibility at will and render Emma's response excessive stems from the racial and gender privilege the audience grants him. Emma appears melodramatic – "invariably a term of opprobrium, even when used simply descriptively" – when the audience categorizes John as the hero and invests in his success even in the face of trying circumstances.[34] Melodrama is a "'mode of excess' ... that cuts across periods, cultures, and art forms, as an 'imagination' dominated by a Manichaean worldview."[35] As Susan Gilman astutely suggests, race is melodrama in the US, or in Hurston's play darkness is melodrama, rendering any and all of Emma's emotional displays excessive, unruly, out-of-line, overboard, and extreme.[36] But to dismiss Emma's affect as melodramatic does not account for the social regulatory forces that establish the norm as in opposition to her femininity, darkness, and poverty.

Moreover, the eroticism of John's language and performance – he "*turns and kisses her slowly*" – establishes Emma as an emotional outsider who simply cannot appreciate the love of a good black man. As Sandra L. Richards explains, if one were to imagine a staging of *Color Struck*,

The body (Emma's body) onstage, through its carriage gestures, and spatial relationships to other bodies, resonates with social history ... Spectators see a woman described as "black" in the company of a boyfriend said to be "light brown-skinned," competing against a single female who is described as "a mulatto girl."[37]

The visual signifiers within the play serve as cues to the way the play structures the process of identification as much as the dialogue does, if not more so. In the opening scene, John appears as a loving, affectionate, handsome, likable character. He attempts to comfort Emma as he blames her for their argument. His affection further demonizes Emma, the jealous dark woman.

Although John pretends that Emma's nagging insecurity over her complexion is totally manufactured, his actions, especially read within the larger context of the play, provide contrary evidence. In the moments before John and Emma board the train, Dinky, a secondary character, escorts Effie to her seat and denies his girlfriend Ada for a chance to gain Effie's affection. When Effie rebukes him and another man on the train announces "(*with head out of window*) Just look at de darkies coming!

(*With head inside coach*) Hey, Dinky! Heah come Ada ... " Dinky runs out of the train to meet her (7). The juxtaposition of Dinky's proposition and the playful, although disparaging, comment of the other man on the train provides a context to understand the subtle advances John makes toward Effie. "Darkies," a common racial slur, might be read as the co-optation of the western discourse on darkness if Emma did not physically represent it. In *Playing in the Dark: Whiteness and the Literary Imagination*, Toni Morrison describes darkness as "this haunting ... from which our early literature seemed unable to extricate itself."[38] Therefore, as John demonizes Emma's actions their physical juxtaposition would perform the inextricable haunting that the play's staging and dialogue necessitate. Emma's presence alongside the other central characters creates a theatrical specter that haunts the New Negro ideal. John explains, "Emmaline nearly made us get left. She says I wuz smiling at Effie on the street car and she had to get off and wait for another one." Later Emma responds, "Jes the same every time you sees a yaller face, you *takes* a chance" (8). The "*takes*" thus dramatizes the conscious sacrifice implicit in attempts to obtain whiteness. The emphasized word draws the focus of the reader or watcher to what is being sacrificed when John chances his relationship with Emma for the possibility of a relationship with "a yaller face."

The two arguments between John and Emma that frame the opening sequence of *Color Struck* do not prevent the couple from expressing some happiness by practicing their cakewalk in the aisle of the train. Hurston writes, "*Wesley begins to play 'Goo Goo Eyes' on his accordion, the other instruments come in one by one and John and Emma step into the aisle and 'parade' up and down the aisle ... They two-step back to their seat amid much applause*" (8). The performance easily makes John's hurtful reminder to Emma that her body signifies a racialized psychic battle that he would rather not take up seem like a distant memory. The initial cakewalking in the play serves to relieve some of the tension created through Emma and John's confrontation.

Riffing on the formal qualities of many African American dramatic performances of the late nineteenth and early twentieth century which almost always featured a cakewalk, *Color Struck* centralizes the cakewalking, and therefore implicitly begs for the audience's attention, only to question it in scene IV. Adding to the rich history of doubling at the heart of the cakewalk, the play mimics the dance and implies a critique. Hurston defines mimicry in "Characteristics of Negro Expression" as "not so much a thing in itself as an evidence of something that permeates his [the Negro's] entire self and that thing is drama."[39] Hurston's "mimicry" insists that identity is cultivated through performance; for the Negro the performance is of dissemblance. The cakewalking in the first scene of the play enacts doubling which relates to the historical and cultural circumstances that created the "New Negro." In many ways, the history of the cakewalk is the history of the New Negro. The cakewalking in *Color Struck* depicts mimicry as central to the process of identifying as a New Negro.

As a poor dark-skinned woman living in the South, Emma has the most difficulty approximating the identity of the New Negro. *Color Struck* demonstrates how identifications demand the privileging of certain desires. The identity of the New Negro facilitates divisions within the black community imagined in the play. So certain members of the community – those light, appropriate, mobile, and male enough – can claim a closer approximation to whiteness. Through the ubiquitous incompleteness Locke's definition of the New Negro imposes, *Color Struck* highlights the social mechanisms that repeatedly support a community ideal predicated on the denial of lack. The irresolution of the process of assimilation informs the Harlem Renaissance, and underpins the critique I argue *Color Struck* makes of the New Negro as imago. Hurston's play reveals that although cultural practices like the cakewalk open up spaces of resistance for the African American community in the play, if privileged members of that community are constantly striving toward the unattainable goal of assimilation, the whole community will suffer the casualties and not just the Emmas in it. The play clarifies that despite the constant pressure of self-hate, which repeatedly pushes Emma away from John, the melodrama that characterizes her is a communal expression of desire to end the perpetual internal struggle the racially split subject characteristically experiences. In *The Souls of Black Folk* Du Bois claims that it is the Negro's "dogged strength alone (that) keeps it (his two souls, two thoughts, two unreconciled strivings) from being torn asunder."[40] In moments where the characters in the play exhibit the will to adorn through dance they are able to momentarily mask this psychic battle.

TOWARD A VERNACULAR HISTORY: THE STORY OF THE CAKEWALK

The historical legacy of the cakewalk informs its use in *Color Struck*; as a result, the cakewalking at the center of the play communicates the transformation of power dynamics. The cakewalk mutated from a dance enslaved Africans used to mock white slave owners into a dance white and black Americans use to entertain, for the most part, white patrons. Consequently, the cakewalking in *Color Struck* has what Spillers calls "a signifying property *plus*."[41] Within a psychic geography, the cakewalk acts as a trace of the legacy of and response to slavery. Yet each subsequent reiteration of the performance demonstrates the community's continued negotiation of slavery and its aftermath. As the physical expression of a psychic paradigm, the dance communicates the constant ambivalence and struggle that results from being a partial citizen – almost American but not quite, "almost the same but not white."[42]

Highlighting the cakewalk's history as a form that communicates the process of identity formation, in *To Wake the Nations: Race and the Making of American Literature*, Eric J. Sundquist explains the origins and performances of the cakewalk leading up to its appearance in *Color Struck*. He traces the emergence of the cakewalk from African tribal celebrations, specifically the African circle dance, to the slaves' ring-shout. He contends that the cakewalk incorporated ritual into the plantation labor structure, embedding in the meaning of the dance celebration and satire. Sundquist goes on to note, as does David Krasner, that enslaved Africans used the cakewalk to imitate white people strutting. The enslaved Africans mimicked the enslaver to demonstrate the contradictory identity of the elegant, southern gentlemen who facilitated slavery. The dancer magnified his difference by mimicking the slave owner and revealed the hypocrisy embedded in American democracy. Consequently, in each historical reiteration of the cakewalk, the dancer negotiates the distance race creates between himself or herself and citizenship. By focusing on the deployment of the cakewalk in that cultural moment, Sundquist and Krasner call attention to an ideal deployment of mimicking, resulting in authority turned upside down.

The story of the cakewalk does not end on the plantation. As with many subversive black cultural forms, the cakewalk would be appropriated by both white and black performers to entertain white and black audiences. During the post-Civil War era and even earlier, Sundquist explains, the cakewalk "concluded many minstrel shows, a grand promenade in which couples dancing in a circle competed with fancy improvised steps and struts."[43] Ironically, the blackface imitations by white people of "black" gestures were based on enslaved Africans' imitations of their white slave-masters; "fundamentally at issue is the question of who is 'imitating' whom in this legendary two-step romp."[44] The white performers used blackface to solidify their status as white people and therefore citizens, and to distance themselves from African Americans. Yet in each performance the blackface minstrels were actually mimicking the white group whose position, at least in part, they desired to occupy.

By 1896 the cakewalk had become the most popular aspect of the minstrel show, and was becoming a mechanism to authenticate both white and black actors. The cakewalk's appearance in Sam T. Jack's *The Creole Show* in the 1890s and Will Marion Cook and Paul Laurence Dunbar's 1898 production of *Clorindy, or the Origins of the Cakewalk* transformed it into a national phenomenon.[45] The production of *Clorindy* also served to further complicate the dance. In the musical, the dancers performed the cakewalk to music steeped in the black minstrel tradition. Dunbar would later lament the lyrics he wrote for *Clorindy*, vowing "never to write such lyrics again (a vow he didn't keep)." Critics, however, commended Cook's score; specifically, "James Weldon Johnson praised Cook's music for its 'musicianly treatment of ragtime.'"[46] The oppositional histories of the lyrics and the music signify the tension the black theater community feels over drawing from mocking impersonations of black people in popular cultural forms. Through black minstrelsy the cakewalk became wedded to blackness through performance. Interestingly enough, though, in as much as black and white minstrelsy confers a racial consolidation (for black performers it may also confer rupture), the insurgent playfulness at the heart of the cakewalk remained and enabled Hurston to change the joke and slip the yoke, to borrow a phrase from Ralph Ellison, of the theatrical mandates on blackness.

At the turn of the twentieth century, the desire to gain access to American institutions continued to trouble African American artists and performers, which compelled some artists to modify their performances in response to the demands of white audiences. It did not take long for black performers to learn that audiences, whether on Broadway or in Harlem, were most interested in musicals. George Walker, a premier black performer of the early twentieth century, describes the circumstances that led to the success of the production *In Dahomey*. He explains, "all that was expected of a colored performer was singing and dancing and a little story telling, but as for acting, no one credited a black person with the ability to act."[47] While Europeans and white Americans enjoyed the latest primitivist rage, black performers and artists recognized the cakewalk as both a triumph and a "sometimes compromising and painful enigma."[48] By using the dance in a satirical musical that calls into question the logic of racial hierarchies, the cakewalk in *In Dahomey* resists, albeit subtly, mimesis.

Ada (Aida) Overton Walker (1880–1914), one of the chief practitioners of the cakewalk and the wife of George Walker, also used the dance to trouble the history of pejorative stereotypes associated with slavery. Nevertheless, as with the reception of *In Dahomey*, Walker's clients refused to call into question the familiar visual representation of the cakewalk and deliberately read the dance outside of the strategic contexts she chose to present. By the beginning of the twentieth century, white and black people alike cakewalked to navigate in and among social circles. As David Krasner describes, Walker instructed affluent white clients in New York City how to do the cakewalk, but "it was reconfigured with some ingenuity to accommodate race, gender, and class identities in an era in which all three were in flux." Walker's clientele desired to engage with the "authentic blackness" they associated with "the cakewalk, along with ragtime, blues, and black theatre."[49] Walker's classes foreshadowed an impulse, fully expressed through the identity of the Harlem Renaissance New Negro, to reference but in some ways differentiate blackness through performance. Therefore Walker's choreography became a hybrid, merging her interpretation of cakewalking with the preconceptions of a white culture that became captivated with the form. "Cakewalking transformed the ever-present 'push and pull' of the Negro into a perambulatory spectacle which weaved in and out of a seemingly endless vortex of cultural 'imitation' to deploy a dynamically fluid representation of African American identity. It was, according to Walker herself, 'more of a walk [and] less of a dance.' In other words, cakewalking served as a performance of travel that literally walked the color line of identity politics."[50]

Yet she could not upset completely the materialization of her body. Such reconfiguration would require a complicit relationship between her and her clients. Similarly to the imagery used to describe the body of Nella Larsen's protagonist, Helga Crane, in *Quicksand*, Walker's dark body served to authenticate the dance and highlight the deep fissure between the white and black communities Walker wanted to bring together. Her strategies suggest the limitation of shifts in comportment outside of critique, and yet stage explicit resistance to visual representation as completely coherent and obvious.

The idea of "authentic blackness" became a tenacious force constantly demanding the attention of the Harlem Renaissance artists. Hurston offers a performative response to the desire to locate the "real" black culture. In "Characteristics of Negro Expression," she explains:

It is obvious that to get back to original sources is much too difficult for any group to claim very much as a certainty. What we really mean by originality is the modification of ideas. The most ardent admirer of the great Shakespeare cannot claim first source even for him. It is his treatment of the borrowed material.[51]

Hurston's definition unmakes "originality," figuring all cultural production as a repetition that unravels and reconstitutes what has come before. At the same time, Krasner's analysis of Walker's dance classes reveals the thirst for authentic blackness that motivated her clients.[52] He notes that "Walker represented the acceptable alter-ego whites wanted in order to confirm their superiority; for whites, she represented the exotic as well as the sophisticated Other."[53] Walker's audience found ways of negotiating the stereotypical and troubling images that the New Negro wanted to avoid because her clients never felt at risk of embodying the exotic, authentic blackness that fascinated them, even though they brushed ever so close as they attempted to discipline their bodies to match Walker's form. Instead of seeing Walker as a model of the race, she became a stunning and palatable anomaly. As *Color Struck* makes stunningly clear, even as an anomaly Walker's performance could not interrupt her identification as the representation of authentic blackness; it did, however, place her clients in a spectrum of embodiments of blackness visible to the critic as an archival audience member.

CAKEWALKING IN 'COLOR STRUCK'

A generation later, Hurston attempted to recoup the cakewalk and all the twists and turns of its cultural legacy. Instead of attempting to work around social constraints, she incorporates the tension they create into the dramaturgy of the play and in turn modifies those boundaries through the dancing. The dance movements in *Color Struck* summon the cakewalk's celebratory historical legacy that its subversive use during slavery and deployment in variety shows exemplifies to foreground the concurrent vexed relationship to black middle-class respectability and black performance history. The cakewalking in Hurston's play intertwines the threads of a larger national history into a local narrative. The space Walker opened up as the acceptable other, but alter ego nonetheless, made room for Hurston's critique. Walker's attempts to reposition the dance outside of its most recent stereotyped lineage by refining the movements and only performing it in certain settings forced her to manage the competing desire for respectable representations of blackness against the longing of her white clientele for a primitive and authentic blackness. At the same time, Walker existed within a generation of dancers that used "the cakewalk as a lampoon of black middle-class social present-ations. It critiqued black bourgeois retention of the prim, well-behaved, Victorian models for civilized deportment and the black bourgeoisie's sensitivity to white approval," doubling Walker's mode of self-presentation as neither primitive nor assimilationist.[54]

The struggle enacted in Walker's performance establishes the dynamic of neither/nor central to the mulatta in the Harlem Renaissance and key to an understanding of how *Color Struck* situates that dynamic as intraracial. The constant ambiguity Emma expresses allows the characters in *Color Struck* to represent the will to adorn through the dancing scenes in the play, while the destructive desire for whiteness, or the closest approxima-tion to whiteness, light-skinned Effie, still threatens what has been achieved. The struggle for a freedom yet denied limits the productivity of the dancing in the opening scene (the actors are dancing in a Jim Crow car). Although Emma's constant pleading with John emphasizes his desire for Effie and her light skin, Emma also desires John, at least in part, for his physical proximity to whiteness.

The momentum of the play and subversion of visual dynamics hinge on the audience's enjoyment of and investments in the cakewalking. Therefore, the performance in scenes ii and iii must intensify at the same rate as Emma's unbearable sense of anxiety, which corresponds to John's increasing investment in fulfilling his personal desire. In an attempt to calm Emma's suspicions, John explains, "Ah don't make you! You makes yo' self mad, den blame it on me. Ah keep on tellin' you Ah don't love nobody but you. Ah knows heaps uh half-white girls Ah could git ef Ah wanted to. But (*he squeezes her hard again*) Ah jus' wants *you*! You know what they say! De darker de berry de sweeter de taste!" (10). Unfortu-nately, Emma is only momentarily reassured. When Effie offers John a piece of pie and he accepts, Emma interprets his action as another betrayal and complains that John is "jus' hog-wile ovah her cause she's half-white" (10). Emma does not seem to want to be white. Conversely, she wants the self-love that she privileges as only attainable through approximating whiteness. Emma desires that she appear to John the same way that Effie looks. For Emma John is the desired love object. *Color Struck* politicizes Emma's loss by predicating her inability to satisfy her desire on her complexion.

To foreshadow the separation of performance from bodies and of theatrical representation from the production of blackness, *Color Struck* disallows the darker and more phenotypically black Emma's participation in the cakewalk contest. When the master of ceremonies finally calls

Emma and John to the stage to dance, Emma refuses. She is finally given the chance to assert herself onstage, to celebrate freely and in public with her peers, but she cannot continue to participate in this process of authentification. Emma, consumed with fear and unable to recall that she is part of the larger social group, pleads:

EMMA Naw, John, Ah'm skeered. I love you – I – (*He tries to break away from her. She is holding on fiercely*).
JOHN I got to go! I been practicing almost a year – I – we done come all the way down here. I can walk the cake, Emma – we got to – I got to go in! (*He looks into her face and sees her tremendous fear*) What you skeered about?
EMMA (*hopefully*) You won't go it – You'll come on go home with me all by ourselves. Come on John. I can't, I just can't go in there and see all them girls – Effie hanging after you – .
JOHN I got to go in – (*he removes her hand from his coat*) – whether you come with me or not. (11)

John does not realize that when Emma asks him to go "home" she is not only talking about a physical structure but also an atmosphere of relative psychic cohesion. His response does indicate his awareness that what he wants challenges what she needs. The transition from the first person singular to plural and then back again reflects John's desire to negotiate his wants at the expense of Emma's needs. Ultimately, John's decision to dance with Effie, Emma's mulatta rival, instead of heeding Emma's request that they "come on go home" secures his personal investment in her as an object of desire, an investment suggested throughout the play, and establishes Emma's request as a call that echoes the militant history John chooses to forget.

The interaction leading up to the cakewalking in *Color Struck* emphasizes the way the sacrifice of the personal to collective interest is accomplished both from within the community and by the larger group. The play expresses the difficulties the racialized subject faces in trying to assimilate into the national fabric. It also depicts the emergence of the New Negro through access to limited mobility (for example on the Jim Crow car) and the freedom of expression but only within certain spaces and under certain eyes. The emergence of the New Negro renders invisible those African Americans unable to attain this ideal. Like many texts of the Harlem Renaissance, *Color Struck* depicts the painful erasures necessary for the constitution of the larger community. Associating Emma with dark skin, and eventually the South and poverty, the play communicates the danger of disavowing vernacular culture and, by association, of performance that disavows its own traditions.

Through cakewalking *Color Struck* calls attention to the social and political implications of willful forgetting. John's inability to hear Emma, rendering her psychically mute, transforms into the physical invisibility that plagues Emma when she "*springs to her feet and flings the curtain wide open*" (11). Emma, unable to be so free and so inhibited at the same time, does not perform the cakewalk, and thus is left alone, bemoaning her inability to forget her racial struggles. With rage she says:

He went and left me. If we is spatting we done had our last one. (*She stands and clenches her fists*) Ah, mah God! He's in there with her – Oh, them half whites, they gets everything, they gets everything everybody else wants! The men, the jobs – everything! The whole world is got a sign on it. Wanted: Light colored. Us blacks was made for cobblestones. (11)

Emma qualifies her position as human sacrifice by aligning blacks with cobblestones. She also articulates that her pain stems from "them half whites," usurping her ability to get everything she wants; that is, to satisfy her desire, even as she herself longs for the affection of a light-skinned man. Emma never critiques what is desired. And she never expresses anger toward the white community, African American males in particular, or herself. She turns all of her resentment toward light-skinned black people. Emma loses the will to struggle for the freedom she has been denied because she allows her envy of other black people's physical approximation to whiteness to consume her. The juxtaposition of the climactic cakewalking scene and Emma's complete alienation from the community reestablishes the dangerously subversive nature of the dance. In the same way that cakewalking challenged the tyranny of the plantation by claiming a site for expression, cakewalking in *Color Struck* celebrates the legacy of black communal spaces seemingly free of domination. Emma's position, off to the side, serves as a reminder of the larger context in which the dancing takes place.

Up until this moment the desire for inclusion pushed Emma into action. The concurrence of the psychic need for the fulfillment of desire and willful creativity exemplified through the music and dance that permeates the first three scenes of the play models the potential healing that an introjection of past gains *and* losses enacts, and also points to the potential dangers caused by the incompletion of the process. As a practice refined over time, the cakewalking in the third scene both characterizes the present expression of freedom and projects possibilities for future liberation. Cakewalking allowed enslaved African Americans to clear a space for expression and still go unnoticed by the gaze of the slaveholder, modeling a form of productive opacity complicated by the hypervisibility of the dance in the first decades of the twentieth century.[55] In Hurston's play, however, the repetition of the cakewalk forecloses Emma's ability to appear before the eyes of others. By scripting Emma's disappearance the play supplements the visual field through a reference to psychic structures.

Color Struck evokes the cultural history of the cakewalk, setting the play in the first decade of the twentieth century and dressing the characters in *"gaudy, tawdry best of 1900"* (7), and then uses the dance to disrupt the narrative progress of the play and thereby emphasize the stakes of affiliation. Symbolically the choices the play asks its audience members to make, for example where to focus their gaze and whom to sympathize with, demonstrate the way that losing something one loves, whether it is a desired object such as a mate, a child or a dear friend, or a desired ideal such as democracy, freedom, culture or home, coupled with the possibility of gaining something one desires in return, such as elevated class and social status, constitutes the individual and his or her community. Leveraging potential losses for gains constitutes the individual. In *The Psychic Life of Power*, Judith Butler explains that the ego is constituted through losses and that the internalization of loss creates the boundary between the psychic and the social world.

Color Struck does not present the consistent negotiation of wagering losses for possible future gains as easy, simple, or unmediated. Instead, the play presents the consequences of not using the affect that results from a continuous and contentious negotiation with the past. Hurston's play demands an engagement with the affect resulting from the partial success and partial failures necessary for the emergence of the New Negro. Understanding the coercive forces that encourage certain cultural performances and their repetition not only raises a critical consciousness about identity formation but also offers insight into the psychic and social matrices that serve as the structural foundation for racism, sexism, and classism.

Mirroring the psychic process of racial melancholia – the transformation of the ego through the management of communal losses – every performance of the cakewalk in *Color Struck* focuses the audience's attention on the dancers and away from whatever else occurs in the scene. The backdrop to the dancing is lost in the visual focus on the cakewalk. Racial melancholia diverges from melancholia, in part, by considering group identifications and processes of mourning. While Sigmund Freud defines melancholia as an individual mourning without end, the process of mourning Freud describes, if recontextualized, creates a productive space to understand "psychic and material processes of assimilation."[56] David Eng and Shinhee Han depict racial melancholia as a "structure of feeling,"[57] while Dana Luciano describes it as "a historical condition."[58] *Color Struck* elaborates racial melancholia by demonstrating how choices about the configuration of personal and communal narratives – what will be included and what will be left out – create mandates for the future. As the play elucidates through the disjunction between its narrative and structure, the choice to acquire implicitly necessitates a choice to reject. By looking at the dancing in the third scene of *Color Struck* the audience must look away from something else, Emma. Unlike the looking away that fuses the audience into a revolutionary subjectivity in *The Star of Ethiopia*, the looking away in *Color Struck* begs the audience to consider how communal formation registers as a loss. While Ethiopia's death functions as a sacrifice in Du Bois' pageant, Emma's sacrifice is not in the service of collective empowerment but a consequence of fragmented advancement. Hurston's play directs visual movement, shuttling back and forth between acquisition and loss or between acceptance and rejection, which indicts the New Negro as a dangerous social fantasy.[59] At the same time in *Color Struck*, "the work of mourning" emerges as a constant resignification of prior performances.[60]

Racial melancholia causes the individual to question how he or she is both part of and alienated from the larger group, as it pressures each individual's ability to form group affiliations. The discourse on racial melancholia considers the meeting ground of identity formation and racial construction as a locus for addressing both individual and group identifications. Although Freud categorizes melancholia as pathology, Eng and Han make clear that racial melancholia is a process, not pathology. Borrowing from Freud's distinction between mourning (the process of slowly retracting libido from a lost object and subsequently displacing that libido onto a new object) and melancholia (the process of mourning without end over the lost object because the subject is unable to fully displace his or her libido onto the new object or ideal), the theorists use the term racial melancholia to describe common everyday "processes of immigration, assimilation and racialization."[61] By focusing the analysis of "the work of mourning" on groups instead of individuals, racial melancholia calls attention to the way loss creates group identities and group ideals. Freud claims, "in mourning it is the world which has become poor and empty, in melancholia it is the ego itself." [62] Also, "melancholia ... is a loss of a more ideal kind."[63] Melancholia describes how the process of acquisition and loss forms the individual. Racial melancholia turns the psychic structure of melancholia toward groups and collective ideals.

The inability of people of color to fully access their rights as citizens, to fully introject their histories into national narratives places the ideal of democratic citizen within the framework of racial melancholia. As a black subject in America, the repeated and consistent processes of racialization, reminding the individual that he or she is subject to but not completely recognized by the state, make it difficult, if not impossible, to "get over" slavery, to move beyond the lost object. Therefore, even though Hurston rejected "the 'inner psychology of characterization' just as she resisted the one-statement folk play form decreed by her admired teachers and friends," the structure of racial melancholia foregrounds a communal structure of feeling resulting from a racialized sense of alienation and is therefore an appropriate formulation to understand the affective and political stakes of *Color Struck*.[64] The identification of the New Negro exemplifies the outcome of the psychic struggle of racial melancholia. And as *Color Struck* illuminates, the process of naming comes at a price.

Dark-skinned Emma signifies the stratification that complexion causes within the black community and also the psychic matrix that perpetuates interracial divisions. By the end of the play, *Color Struck* reveals that the reason for Emma's continuous feelings of loneliness and physical isolation is her status as a battle site for a freedom not yet achieved. In each of the three locations of the play – in the Jim Crow car on the way to the cakewalk contest, at the contest, and in her home – Emma asks John to confess his love. His response is doomed to produce a non sequitur of sorts, because even if John were to acquiesce, which he does not, his constant reassurance alone cannot dam her rushing fear that no one could love a dark-skinned woman, not even her. The seeming paranoia Emma expresses over losing John throughout the first three scenes of the play comes to fruition, by her own doing, when she finally leaves him. Her decision to leave makes sense within the psychic economy of the racially melancholic subject. The potential loss of John per se does not threaten Emma. Instead, she constantly struggles with the idea that as a dark-skinned woman she does not warrant love. Emma's pursuit of John reflects her attempts to come to terms with an unattainable idealized concept of beauty. She thinks that John's love would enable her finally to end the confusion caused by her inability to incorporate the losses she experiences as an ostracized member of her community.[65] The racial melancholia that Emma comes to symbolize (she must constantly face racialization in the play and the limits it imposes on her) has devastating personal ramifications, but also, more significantly, it holds accountable members of the black community imagined in the play for the intraracial conflict that enables their social freedom. Emma comes to stand in for the unresolved and irresolvable process of assimilation but she does not function as the source of the desire to assimilate.

Color Struck represents the dynamics of racial melancholia not only through its dialogue and visual dynamics but also in its structure. The stage directions transform the theatrical space to create a melancholic setting; Hurston's script specifies that the *"Fervor of spectators grows until all are taking part in some way – either hand-clapping or singing the words. At curtain they have reached frenzy"* (12). The engagement of the crowd both on and off the stage should result in expressive catharsis and emotional explosion. The play calls for everyone in the theater to participate actively in the performance. By demanding the complicity of the whole theater, Hurston's play creates a community of viewers alongside the imagined community onstage. *Everyone*, including the audience, performs an approximated fullness (we are still at a contest in the Jim Crow South), which the play juxtaposes to Emma's inconsolable lack. The community both on the stage and in the audience performs a united celebration that remains wholly inaccessible to Emma. Left completely alone – abandoned by John, the staged community, and the audience – Emma, who first acts defiantly (flinging the curtain wide open) toward the spectacle of John and Effie performing an award-winning cakewalk, eventually *"creeps over to a seat along the wall and shrinks into the Spanish Moss, motionless"* (11). *Color Struck* positions Emma's motionless body off to the side yet still as a part of the scene to create a visual representation of melancholia. She represents the past that cannot be fully introjected, a past that sets the ideal of identification as a New Negro at a critical distance.

John and Effie's award-winning cakewalk signifies their shared social privilege. As a whole, the cakewalk contest poorly mimics latent performances of identification practiced on the plantation, resulting instead in the performance of identity – an attempt to approximate John and Effie's social status as New Negroes who have moved beyond the oppressive legacy of slavery. During the Harlem Renaissance, African Americans negotiated lost identifications with African culture and the partial success and partial failure of identifying as New Negroes. In *Color Struck*, the cakewalk serves as a performative practice that exemplifies the struggle over identification resulting in this new identity. The complex status of the cakewalk as a social practice exhibiting a signifying property *plus* includes one layer of signifying in the cakewalk's initial goal of satirizing the process of coercive identification the white slave owner enacts on the enslaved African. Nevertheless, the cakewalk also represents a double-layered identification both desiring the power of naming that the slave owner once possessed (we call ourselves New Negroes now) *plus* mourning the lost identity the current matrix of power makes disappear. Emma's invisibility calls attention to the partial failures of the strategic cakewalk that the dancers perform across a tightrope of identifications.

At the same time, the dance's hypervisibility and Emma's invisibility in the scene qualify the performance as an idealized American fantasy, which relies on her physical presence and social illegibility. In a reading of Ellison's *Invisible Man*, Anne Cheng explains the relationship between cultural exclusion and racialization: "If the ideology of 'American cultures' sustains itself via the repeated exclusion and staged reincorporation of excluded others, then one may begin to read 'racialized America' ... as a fantasy built on absences."[66] A generation before Ellison introduced his invisible protagonist, Hurston used a dance so layered in meaning that its performance erupts in frenzy to highlight the ways American identity hinges on a battle between presence and absence. Emma's invisibility represents the human losses that enable divisions within the African American communities. The cakewalking scene requires Emma's body onstage, but it also requires that the activity on the stage render her invisible. The psychic weight that Emma bears literally causes her to disappear, transforming her into a ghostly figure who, by the end of the play, will attempt to reappear through maternity. Hurston scripts our blindness, relying on the persuasive power of the cakewalk to prohibit seeing Emma. At the same time, the scene challenges the viewer to participate in subversive looking, to look at the cakewalking and see Emma at the same time. Such a mode of looking challenges the optic regime central to the hegemonic legacy of the dance and asserts the subversive power of opacity.

Although the performance of the cakewalk has the potential to render Emma invisible in the third scene, it makes her mute throughout. While the play challenges the viewer to adjust his or her focus away from the pleasure of the cakewalking in scene III, *Color Struck* demands, through-out, an alternative acoustic register to hear Emma's cries to go home, which can be translated as her desire to be both, as Morrison describes it in her essay "Home," "free and situated."[67] John cannot hear Emma. When Emma begs John to "come on go home" she challenges the lure of the contest. That challenge does not vanish when Emma sinks into the

Spanish Moss. Instead it is relocated to an alternative register of hearing. Emma's pleas may be understood as providing a soundtrack to the visual opacity produced in scene III that aligns with the opacity in Du Bois' pageant and Overton Walker's performance of Salome as discussed in Chapter 2.[68] Her sounding seeks to cultivate "subversive expression" that "reposition[s] readers, [viewers, and listeners] by leading them away from the attitudes and assumptions of the master class."[69] Emma's tragic invisibility at the end of scene III underlines the traumatic costs of opacity to women of color and asserts the ethical imperative the audience must bear in order to transform that opacity into a political strategy.

TRANSFORMING THE IMAGE OF THE TRAGIC MULATTA

In order to reorient the acoustic and visual dynamics established in the first three scenes of the play, the final scene does not take place in public. Showing the communal disavowal that has been created, scene IV takes place in Emma's dark home. Certainly the structure of racial melancholia *Color Struck* creates does not exempt Emma from the complicit role she plays. Nonetheless, in the same way that Eng and Han describe racial melancholia as a collective state that results from societal pressures, *Color Struck* depicts Emma's inability to completely repudiate her destructive desire as inexorably linked to the will of her community. John cannot fill up the fissures of doubt that appear as Emma's constant jealousy throughout the play because his complexion gives him the privilege of categorizing her feelings as overreactions.

To accommodate the shift in the focus of the play from the communal to the individual as a part of the community, the play not only shifts locations, which creates a different tone, but also time – twenty years has elapsed since the cakewalking contest. While Hurston's play recalls the variety shows performed in the first decade of the twentieth century, which usually ended with a cakewalk, it has a different structure, ending with a belated scene that follows the cakewalk. The shifts in time, space, and structure create a new rubric with which to hear and see Emma. In the final scene of the play, Emma contends that John's gender and complexion give him access to mobility and opportunities that she is denied. In scene IV, John returns to Emma after traveling to Philadelphia and achieving financial prosperity. Emma explains that although John married a dark-skinned woman, he took advantage of his status as a light-brown-skinned man and by extension his ability to integrate himself more fully into US mainstream culture. She reminds him that his success is dependent on her failure: "Ah aint got a whole lot lak you. Nobody don't git rich in no white-folks' kitchen, nor in de washtub. You know Ah aint no school teacher an' nothin' lak dat" (13). Emma initially responds to John's return with suspicion and anger. She continues to assert that her pain stems from the betrayal of the black community, arguing an internal communal violence has been exacted.

The communal loss that Emma epitomizes has not solely resulted in sadness. Unfortunately, it has also transformed into hate. Emma's state serves as a cautionary tale, a warning of the possibility of forgetting the subversive history embedded in cultural practices like the cakewalk in an effort to make those practices more assimilable to American culture. *Color Struck* demands negotiation with the past and the resulting affect stemming from that memory. John's return in the final scene of the play is filled with inequality, which Emma pinpoints when she calls attention to his mobility. The couple's ability to share the goal of collective liberation from the color-caste legacy of slavery does not depend on John's remaining in the South. Rather, it requires that he acknowledge that her disavowal underpins his privilege. Emma asks John to share the grief that she must confront and that he chose not to see or hear.

John is unable to empathize with Emma. Nevertheless, I maintain *Color Struck* shows how the conditions that render the mulatta tragic also alienate Emma as a dark-skinned woman living in the South. Emma, as a result of these very conditions, does not register for critics as a sympathetic character. The play questions why the mulatta figure evokes sympathy while Emma induces irritation. In the introduction to *Iola Leroy, or, Shadows Uplifted*, part of the Black Women Writers Series, Hazel Carby discusses the frequent turn to the mulatto figure in African American fiction. She argues that the mulatto figure "enabled an exploration of social relations between the races . . . and it enabled an expression of the sexual relations between the races, since the mulatto was a product not only of proscribed consensual relations but of white sexual domination."[70] If, as Carby claims, the mulatto figure primarily served to provide a framework to examine the space between the races, *Color Struck* reveals some less often theorized desires that motivate such explorations. The play disrupts the easy separation of the drive to explore cross-communal social relations and the drive to acquire white privilege. More pointedly, *Color Struck* begins and ends at the sites Carby argues the mulatto figure opens up, in a Jim Crow car in the South and in a conversation about Emma's mulatta child respectively. In a bold, strategic turn at a time when African Americans were rapidly leaving the South, and when Locke was proclaiming "Liberal minds to-day cannot be asked to peer with sympathetic curiosity into the darkened Ghetto of a segregated race life," Hurston illuminated the darkened ghetto of segregated race life to comment on the construction of sites of interracial contact.[71]

Color Struck engages the idea of cross-cultural relations through the invocation of the Jim Crow train car in the opening scene of the play. Dark-skinned Emma insists that light-skinned Effie poses a threat. Emma's accusations reveal the infrastructural meeting ground between the races even in the absence of any white characters. The desire for Effie that many of the characters in the play exhibit exposes an overarching structure of power predicated on the physiognomy of the subject. Hurston challenges the New Negro and the nation to carefully consider how the trace of yesterday enables the attractive American scene Locke describes.

Traditionally, the train car has been a site of symbolic importance, especially during the Harlem Renaissance, because it symbolizes mobility and northern migration. The Jim Crow car in *Color Struck* does not take us north; it travels south from Jacksonville to St. Augustine, Florida. The migration depicted in *Color Struck*, alternatively, functions as a critique of the gender politics of travel. Images of movement occur throughout the play: the Jim Crow car departs in the first scene, Emma begs John to go home with her in the third scene, and John returns from his northern migration to Philadelphia in the fourth scene. While Emma struggles to move in the play, at times begging for assistance, *Color Struck* presents John's darker, "irrational," female companion hindering his movement. John freely participates in the cakewalking that occurs in the Jim Crow car in the opening scene. He cakewalks expertly in the climactic third scene, and he moves to Philadelphia once he has ended his relationship with Emma. She, conversely, feels apprehension about moving and longs to go home. The dancing in the play liberates John while it only provides temporary relief to Emma because it does not address the larger inequalities that stifle her. Although all the characters travel in a Jim Crow car, Emma cannot integrate herself into the performance of social freedom; she continues to produce a slippage.

Emma has been constituted through perpetual racialization; she cannot access collectiveness since she is not seen as part of a collective. Moreover, Emma, implicated by her own desire symbolized by her mulatta child, is still unable to articulate what she really wants. John returns to Emma to reclaim her, to make her his wife. Since his departure, Emma has had a mulatta child whom she keeps hidden. When John returns, Lou Lillian (Emma's daughter) is physically sick and intermittently cries out for help. Emma ignores her daughter as she asks John, "you love me – you really want me sho' nuff?" (13). Her question coupled with her denial of Lou Lillian is emblematic of her inability to articulate what she really needs. Even as John offers himself to Emma he remains unattainable, a perpetually lost love object. The unarticulated question will go unanswered.

Lou Lillian represents both Emma's shame and her desire to achieve cohesion. Her presence calls attention to Emma's constant attempt to be what she feels she can never be: loved by black people and accepted by white people. When Emma finally leaves her home to summon a doctor, John notices that Lou Lillian groans, "water, so hot." He responds by offering the girl a drink. When Emma reenters the home she sees John attending to Lou Lillian and misconstrues his actions as another betrayal. She accuses, "I knowed it! (*She strikes him*) A half white skin" (14). John is able to subdue Emma and finally leaves, this time for good. Emma's shame, which the darkness that shrouds her home symbolizes, and her insistence that her daughter's long, straight hair remain hidden even after John sees it, come from her recognition of the complicit role she plays in the structure of racism, and by extension in the colorism that entombs her. Emma's inability to express herself costs her John and her daughter. Her trip to the doctor comes too late, and her daughter dies. Emma's enunciation of her final line in the play – "Couldn't see" – testifies to the fact that she did not know what she so desperately needed.

Emma's final line of the play damns her and indicts the audience members who could not see her in scene III, reinforcing the connection between the dynamics of visual representation in theatrical production and psychic frameworks. At the same time, *Color Struck* communicates that, although dangerous, walking the tightrope of identifications shows individuals and groups how to access and use subversive histories. Drawing on the history of cakewalking, the play presents the sacrifices made in the name of "progress." The cakewalking in *Color Struck*, however, reproduces and therefore reorients the social and cultural history of the dance by insisting that the introjection of losses gives the viewer a keener eye, enabling him or her to see both the dancing and Emma at once.

Hurston draws from the performance tradition of vernacular forms to critique the processes that install bourgeois black culture when they come at the expense of the folk. Her contemporary, Langston Hughes, also draws inspiration from vernacular forms. But instead of anticipating how intraracial dynamics would inform the composition of his audience, he assumes that a common investment in familiar modes of representation will produce the joy and pleasure of recognition. Although his trickster protagonists inaugurate the gospel play form, *Tambourines to Glory* demonstrates the high stakes of black vernacular performance, especially during the politically and racially charged era of the Civil Rights Movement.

CHAPTER 4

Resisting shame and offering praise and worship

Langston Hughes' Tambourines to Glory

Essie Belle Johnson, one of the female protagonists of Langston Hughes' *Tambourines to Glory*, sings "Upon this rock I build my church. The gates of hell shall not prevail" and convenes the first meeting of Tambourine Temple.[1] The meeting takes place on a curb in Harlem "*above* the gutter." Essie and Laura, called the Reed sisters "even if [they] ain't no relation," do not actually occupy a building; Essie's song attracts an audience and thus inaugurates their church (192). Her melodic and soulful singing inspires the crowd as it introduces the tension between secular and spiritual necessity central to the play and fundamental to the African American sermonic tradition. Poverty motivates Essie and Laura to start their church, but as the gospel song Essie and Laura sing suggests, *Tambourines to Glory* is also interested in mobilizing the double-voiced quality intrinsic to gospel music, which aims toward triumph over material defeat *and* spiritual death. Therefore, even though the rock is Jesus, the location of the singers establishes the intersecting need for a spiritual and a material foundation.

Situated in Harlem after World War II in the burgeoning years of the modern Civil Rights Movement, *Tambourines to Glory* deploys the African American sermon, using it as an effacement of race- and class-based shame. In many texts of the period, African American writers communicate the shame associated with poverty. Ubiquitously repeated in *Native Son* (1940), the definitive quality of Bigger Thomas's existence is shame. Instead of turning anger and pain inward, *Tambourines to Glory* demonstrates how to deflect intrusive and judgmental gazes. The play provides a sly defense against the visual dismissal Du Bois posits as the source of his double consciousness in the opening pages of *The Souls of Black Folk*. The ability, however, to anticipate such visual slights comes at a cost. The sermons, often sung in the play, highlight the powerful possibilities and simultaneous costs of sly and deflective African American performance traditions. This chapter analyzes the religious activity *Tambourines to Glory* depicts as a part of African American worship practices, the cultural customs in Harlem in the wake of World War II and in the midst of the Cold War, and the politics of the flourishing Civil Rights Movement. This modern morality play suggests that the ethos of black Christianity requires a progressive social performance structured by a tradition of reading between the lines.

STAGING THE AFRICAN AMERICAN SERMON

Tambourines to Glory is "a dramatization of a very old problem – that of good versus evil" localized by the black community imagined in the play (184). The plot of the first gospel play follows the material development and spiritual decline of Tambourine Temple. As the church develops, the women's personal lives also take significant turns. Owing to Essie's new source of income, she can finally send for her daughter Marietta. Laura's newfound wealth enables her to buy clothes, cars, and liquor. And thanks to financial prosperity, Laura can now woo her young boyfriend. By the end of the play, Laura kills her lover, Big-Eyed Buddy Lomax, for cheating on her with a younger woman. The drama, however, does not focus primarily on Essie's and Laura's personal lives. Instead it considers the implications of their spiritual lives for the communal organization – Tambourine Temple. The personal profit the women enjoy comes at the expense of the church, and the play indicts the women for that transgression more than any other.

While the moral theme of the play traverses the color line, *Tambourines to Glory* depicts the manifestation of this very old problem through culturally specific humor and music. The play continues Hughes' lifelong goal to create art about black people that reveals the ingenuity and the inherent beauty of blackness. In the play Hughes celebrates the black church even as he parodies it. Through exaggeration and stereotype, the play interprets the black storefront church and the religious practices performed there "from within rather than from without."[2] Mikhail Bakhtin, considering how parody functions in language, writes that "As in stylization, the author employs the speech of another, but, in contradistinction to stylization, he introduces into that other speech an intention which is directly opposed to the original one."[3] As Henry Louis Gates, Jr. clarifies, "The mode of parody . . . depends on the utilization of another text's words" in order to deal, according to Glenda Carpio, "with the stress and pain of a bad situation."[4] Bakhtin and Gates note the citational quality of parody, which is also central to the black sermonic form. I add, following Carpio, an examination of parody in terms of bodily citations that disrupt the mimetic performance of black preaching in the play.

In the opening scene as Laura tries to convince Essie to start her church, Laura insists, "Listen to my spiel. I can whoop and holler real good" (192). Her consolidation of black preaching into sound calls attention to the key signifiers of the performance. The whooping and hollering serves as a key to the validity of the performance and the understanding of it as preaching. She continues as the stage directions indicate that "*She mounts a pile of furniture imagining herself as a preacher*" (192). Fascinating in their specificity and yet openness, the stage directions allow the actress and director to create the comportment of a preacher in Laura's mind's eye. As she mounts the pile of furniture, her carriage has to be convincing enough for the audience and Essie to momentarily forget the setting and accept Laura's preacherly persona as legitimate. Laura explains:

I'll tell them Lenox Avenue sinners: You all better come to Jesus! The atom bomb's about to destroy this world and you ain't ready. Get ready! Get ready!
Lord above, I am lost
I have strayed from the cross
And I cry, Yes, I cry, save me now! (192)

Laura references the contemporary threat of the cold war and infuses it with familiar fire and brimstone rhetoric but then makes a shift in rhythm and tone. After the urging repetition of "Get ready" she shifts from the accusatory to the introspective and cries for help. Her repetition of "Get ready" serves as both a call and a response, which models for her audience the interaction that she would like them to produce. She urges them to "Get ready" as she offers them a rhetorical phrase to grab on to, remember, and repeat. She then renders herself vulnerable to reinforce her dual position. Laura acknowledges her shortcomings and failures as a Christian and takes hold of the promise of redemption.

In her confession and plea for guidance she embodies parody. On the one hand, Laura stands on a pile of furniture imagining herself as a preacher. On the other hand, she presents herself in voice and action, presumably, as a downtrodden sinner. While she voices the words of the lost she still assumes the raised position of the preacher and as she calls for personal healing – "save me" – she actually desires the transformation of her fellow Harlemites not into pious believers but generous congregants. The play does not specify Laura's gestures, but the rhyme scheme, change in tempo, and shifts in tone of her short speech suggest an ebb and flow of intensity (from the insistent cry of "Get ready" to the softer admission "I am lost" to the repentant plea "save me now") that imply variations in bodily position. While the eyes may look accusingly straight ahead at the audience as she charges "Get ready," she may look down in shame with the admission of being lost, and then upwards with her plea to be saved. The more exaggerated the gesture, the more humorous the scene. In this scene, however, humor would undermine the play's narrative goal of establishing Laura's trickery.

In drawing from a medium that depends on the intersection of verbal and bodily citations, the play demonstrates the way that gesture and movement constitute the body. As I have argued throughout this book, the fact that identity is constituted through performances and mediated by regulatory structures – now a familiar notion – creates a stranglehold on black bodies. The ideological matrix of race in the US demands that only certain performances may constitute particular bodies. *Tambourines to Glory* makes use of one of the most highly authorized performances of blackness – preaching – to demonstrate how actions constitute the individual, using a break between actor and character (between Laura and the preacher figure) to arrest temporarily the tragicomic racial pageant that is US culture. In 1963, black audience members where unwilling to separate the actors from the characters and, therefore, the play did not realize its potential to produce civil unrest. Yet the related performances of Tyler Perry as Madea in the late twentieth century and early twenty-first century have garnered the willing participation of audiences.

As described above, *Tambourines to Glory* presents embodied parody, using characteristic gestures (for example, arm and foot movements) and intonation. The delivery of a good sermon depends as much on what is said as how it is said. In order to analyze the performance of an African American sermon, one must consider it as an experience complete with visual (movement), acoustic (moans, shouts, and grunts), and rhetorical cues ("can I get an amen"), a set structure, and audience interaction and expectations. In *I Got the Word in Me and I Can Sing It, You Know*, Gerald L. Davis explains that the African American sermon has a performative history, regardless of denomination, invoked in each repetition. Often the success of the performance depends on reinforcement of or divergence from this tradition. He specifies, "The sermon structure identified ... as African American describes sermons preached from hundreds of Black pulpits across America, without regard to denominational affiliation. That sermon structure is cultural."[5] *Tambourines to Glory* makes a gender- and class-based cultural intervention by parodying the mid-twentieth-century black storefront church and evoking the style of the African American sermon while debasing the subject. Although the black church remained a space that gender mandates restricted in the first half of the twentieth century, Chicago made room, as Wallace Best explains, for an "eclectic assortment of women to exercise ecclesiastical power" in the 1930s and 1940s that "did not always represent or lead to changing attitudes with regard to women in ministry, but it did grow from the opportunities to work in the public realm that urban culture afforded."[6] Parodying the style of the African American sermon, the play ridicules social mandates for respectability that were particularly restrictive for women and counters the shame associated with poverty.

Hughes' play extends the performative power of the African American sermon style by incorporating it into the form of the gospel play. The backdrop of the play creates a mechanism to understand the socialization of the form and its use in everyday interaction. More specifically, through humor the play signifies on the double-voiced quality of the African American sermon. That quality allows the sermon to speak to both spiritual and material needs at the same time. Ideally, the spiritual tenet directs the corresponding appropriation of biblical example for the parishioners' lives. In *Tambourines to Glory*, Laura and Essie borrow and subsequently revise biblical language to further Tambourine Temple and by extension themselves; thus, they bend and redirect the sermonic form. The play highlights the dangers and corresponding costs of the repetition/reproduction of African American performative traditions, using the sermon as its example par excellence.

Hughes developed the performative practices honed in *Tambourines to Glory*, distinguished as the first gospel play, for over a decade. In each performance of the sermonic form, Hughes' drama reproduced the ontology of black performance and enabled an enactment of the pursuit of freedom. The movement of black preaching in Hughes' work situates his drama as a part of a longer and ongoing action. Just as *The Star of Ethiopia* might be read as a part of the circuit between, within, and through *The Souls of Black Folk* and *Darkwater*, so too might we understand *Tambourines to Glory* within his larger body of work. Hughes experimented with the use of music, religious themes, and humor in his plays. Before writing *Tambourines to Glory*, he wrote two plays that explored the use of music and religious themes: *Don't You Want to Be Free?* (1937), a religious drama written for the Harlem Suitcase Theater, and *The Sun Do Move* (1942), a play that explores the existential and social meanings of the spirituals. *The Sun Do Move* traces the passage of the protagonist, Rock, from enslavement to freedom. The play notably expresses Rock's movement through both dialogue and music. Similarly incorporating music and humor, *Tambourines to Glory* also presses the limits of the comedic voice Hughes develops in his urban comedies (e.g., the familiar tales of Simple), by embedding that performance of survival within a gospel play. Exploring Hughes' early use of humor, Leslie Catherine Sanders contends, "The genesis of *Tambourines to Glory* lies in Hughes' urban comedies of the 1930s, *Little Ham* and *Joy to My Soul*, as much as it does in personal history or in his exploration of the dramatic possibilities of black religion."[7] The light-hearted local comedy of *Little Ham* and *Joy to My Soul* becomes intensified in *Tambourines to Glory*, which enters into the national debate concerning civil rights.

Hughes' play secularizes African American sermonic ideals by presenting an economic revelation through comedy, gospel, and the sound of preaching. In *Black Preaching*, Henry Mitchell claims one of the chief mandates of "hermeneutics is to convey the revelation in its contemporary context."[8] He further specifies that the African American preacher's task has always been to deliver the message in the common language and style of the parishioners using readily recognizable examples. The play reorients the message of redemption, looking to save "the souls of black folk" that James Brown, the godfather of soul, invokes.

Even as Hughes' play builds on black performance traditions in an attempt to establish a precedent for the gospel play as an aesthetic, criticism of *Tambourines to Glory* uniformly critiques its formal qualities. In *The Development of Black Theater in America: From Shadows to Selves* (1988), Sanders argues that the play fails because "Hughes tried to include in *Tambourines to Glory* almost every successful aspect of his literary and dramatic career; he succeeded in realizing none of them." Further, she argues that the play's single major flaw is Hughes' mixture of forms. "The implicit acceptance and faith that folk forms demand as responses, and the act of celebration they embody, rarely can exist simultaneously with manipulation of the dramatic perspective and a plot that concerns misrepresentation of the image portrayed."[9] Joseph McLaren recounts the history and reception of Hughes' gospel plays in "From Protest to Soul Fest: Langston Hughes' Gospel Plays" (1997); he does not take a position about the blending of forms in the play. Instead, he offers both negative and lukewarm reviews as evidence of the play's reception. In a subsequent less critical treatment of the play, "I've Wrestled With Them All My Life," Sanders argues that the major shortcoming of the 1963 staging was its venue. She contends the play would have attracted a wider audience if it had been performed in a location that drew black spectators. She elaborates on the problems of the theater's location in "'Also Own the Theatre': Representation in the Comedies of Langston Hughes" (1992), asserting the poor reception of the play clearly indicates that Hughes needed a theater of his own.[10]

The problem of the venue distinguishes *Tambourines to Glory* from some of Hughes' earlier plays and introduces the dynamic quality of audience interaction central to the gospel play form. What Sanders and others describe as a problem or limitation of form remedied through a shift in venue points to the larger cultural critique of space made in African American drama, which the varied locations of Tambourine Temple specify. In 1963, the US could not provide a space to hold the black nomadic movement of the preacherly form that passes through *Tambourines to Glory*. On its way through, black preaching brushes up against a class and gender critique similar to that offered in *Color Struck*. Attempting to harness the power of black preaching on the move, the play deploys folk forms to address universal ethical issues, just as the African American sermon conveys biblical content in vernacular form. As Susan Bennett argues, "A crucial aspect of audience involvement, then, is the degree to which a performance is accessible through the codes audiences are accustomed to utilizing, the conventions they are used to recognizing, at a theatrical event. Intelligibility and/or success of a particular performance will undoubtedly be determined on this basis."[11] Therefore, *Tambourines to Glory* might have experienced at least some commercial success if its audience had been familiar enough with black preaching but not threatened by the deconstruction of it that is key to a parody. The interpretive histories audience members bring to the dramatic event were, in this particular instance, also informed by the politics of representation central to performances of civil unrest during the Civil Rights Movement.

Conversely, in the last decade African American gospel plays have achieved enormous financial success, which accompanies a greater divide along class lines in the representation of black people and the secularization of the black freedom movement. Gates discusses the phenomenon of the gospel play and the competing implications the form has in terms of class affiliation and vernacular culture in the late twentieth century. In "The Chitlin Circuit," through a close reading of Adrian Williamson's *My Grandmother Prayed for Me*, he explains:

All the very worst stereotypes of the race are on display, larger than life. Here, in this racially sequestered space, a black audience laughs uninhibitedly, whereas the presence of white folks would have engendered a familiar anxiety: *Will they think that's what we're really like?* If this drama were shown on television – in an integrated forum – Jesse Jackson would probably denounce it, the NAACP would demand a boycott, and every soul here would swap his or her finery for sandwich boards in order to picket. You do not want white people to see this kind of spectacle; you want them to see the noble dramas of August Wilson ... By contrast, the Chitlin Circuit plays carry an invisible racial warning sticker: for domestic consumption only – export strictly prohibited.[12]

Similarly to the dynamic in many churches in America, the Chitlin Circuit remains a predominantly segregated setting. The protest that Gates predicted, however, did not take place when *Diary of a Mad Black Woman* (2005), written and directed by the reigning king of the Chitlin Circuit, Tyler Perry, premiered with the highest box office revenues for the week, grossing $50.6 million. Notably, *Diary of a Mad Black Woman* does not deploy some of the familiar clownish figures from some of Perry's other dramas or the literal coming to Jesus moment depicted in his *I Can Do Bad All By Myself* (2009). Nevertheless, Perry still appears in drag as the central figure, Madea. Perry's performance as the headstrong, chainsaw-wielding matriarch raises the question of who is in fact the mad black woman of the title: the main character Helen (Kimberly Elise) or Madea? A central question if one considers Hughes' play, the first gospel play, as a critique of gender politics that exclude women from liberation struggles.

Although purposefully exaggerating the stereotypical image of the Mammy as asexual, Perry as Madea creates an opportunity for the audience to delight in recognizable and humorous images while achieving some distance from them. On the one hand, Perry's stature (he stands over six feet tall), the clownish gray wig he wears as Madea, and the excessive violence he often performs call attention to the performative nature of his role and draw a critical question about the materialization of the Mammy figure. At the same time, the humor reflects a concretization of sex that interrupts any gender critique the Madea films might offer. Part of the joke is that we *know* a man plays Madea. Perry's performance may be read within a history of black male comic acting that the virtuoso legacy of Richard Pryor epitomizes. A master of parody, Pryor's audience members "laugh not only at the ease with which they can recognize the stereotypes that Pryor imitates but also at the irony of both his accurate portrayal of distortion and the fact that he gives those distortions real referents," as Carpio argues regarding Pryor's performances.[13] Perry's slapstick buffoonery does not match Pryor's genius. Moreover, Carpio notes that Pryor's impersonations require no use of costume, while Perry dons an elaborate one. Yet Perry taps into a cultural imaginary – the Mammy – that his audience desires and at the same time can repudiate a performance. His ability, like Pryor's, to portray a distortion and give "those distortions real referents" secures the viewer and gives her liberty to laugh. Laughter is further licensed by Perry's use of costume, which suggests the malleability of the body in general as it fixes the black female body as material in service of the audience. Whereas the stereotypical portrayal of the angry black woman alongside the characteristic redemption scene appealed to Perry's audience, Hughes' representation of the seductress, redeemed by the end of the play, and her foil the old church lady, did not attract patrons. The composition of African American theater audiences has changed since Hughes premiered *Tambourines to Glory*, but the performance of black preaching, with its implications for gender, still retains many of its signature properties and possibilities.

By the time *Tambourines to Glory* made its New York premier in 1963, Malcolm X and Dr. Martin Luther King, Jr. had already gained national prominence. Although Hughes attempted to make adjustments to the development of the plot to account for the seven-year lapse from its inception to its New York debut, the humorous tone of the play did not match the volatile and often angry tenor of the time. *Tambourines to Glory* critiques the black church, an institution fundamental to the Civil Rights Movement. At the same time, the play highlights the danger in undermining vernacular cultural forms, specifically the African American sermon, which served as a model for political protest during the Civil Rights Movement. The negative reception of the 1963 staging of *Tambourines to Glory* evidences the disruption Hughes' use of vernacular expression caused during a historical moment focused on integration. In 1963, it seems, the patrons and the critics found difficulty in separating the form from the institution – in separating black religious practice from the church – because in that moment they were intimately intertwined and interdependent. Moreover, audiences were in no mood for parody; theatergoers craved "revolutionary theater" – note the violence central to James Baldwin's *Blues for Mister Charlie* (1964), Amiri Baraka's *Dutchman* (1964), and Adrienne Kennedy's *Funnyhouse of a Negro* (1964).

BEING "PUT OUTDOORS": DISPOSSESSION, EVICTION, YOU'VE BEEN KICKED OUT

Seemingly of another time, the opening scene of *Tambourines to Glory* signifies on depictions in *Invisible Man* (1952) and Hughes' own play *Angelo Herndon Jones* (1935), even as it resonates with a scene from Toni Morrison's *The Bluest Eye* (1970). The eviction scene, probably most famously depicted in Ellison's *Invisible Man,* had a cultural currency before his hyper-realistic portrayal. As Morrison recounts in *The Bluest Eye,* a novel set during World War II, the stock market crash of 1929 and the ensuing Great Depression that persisted until 1941 still lingered in Americans' minds even after the start of the war and improvements in the economy. Morrison's young female narrator, Claudia, describes being "put outdoors" as the signification of this lingering threat:

Outdoors, we knew, was the real terror of life. The threat of being outdoors surfaced frequently in those days. Every possibility of excess was curtailed with it. If somebody ate too much, he could end up outdoors. If somebody used too much coal, he could end up outdoors. People could gamble themselves outdoors, drink themselves outdoors. Sometimes mothers put their sons outdoors, and when that happened, regardless of what the son had done, all sympathy was with him. He was outdoors, and his own flesh had done it. To be put outdoors by a landlord was one thing – unfortunate, but an aspect of life over which one had no control, since you could not control your income. But to be slack enough to put yourself outdoors, or heartless enough to put one's own kin outdoors – that was criminal.[14]

Claudia indicates that behavior cannot control whether or not someone is "put outdoors," which qualifies it as "the real terror of life." In contradiction, the rhetoric of the 1920s New Negro specified codes of conduct that could solidify African Americans' social position. The threat of being "put outdoors" draws attention to the material limits of performance as a strategy of social inclusion. Claudia also qualifies, however, that "every possibility of excess was curtailed." Acknowledging the lack of complete control, the people in Claudia's community policed the aspects of their lives they could influence. Even as she depicts a passive relationship to socioeconomic structures, Claudia states that "To be put outdoors by a landlord was . . . unfortunate, but an aspect of life over which one had no control." The characters in Hughes' and Ellison's texts take a different position. These authors stage highly choreographed responses to being "put outdoors." The writers challenge the amorphous power of landlords that Claudia categorizes as a part of life "over which one had no control."

Langston Hughes' *Angelo Herndon Jones* depicts the potential for revolutionary change through political organizing in response to amorphous social networks of power. Written the same year as Clifford Odets' *Waiting for Lefty,* it is a propaganda play about the African American communist organizer Angelo Herndon Jones. Set during the Great Depression, the play stages the eviction of a mother and daughter, Ma Jenkins and Viola. The community in the play responds to Ma Jenkins and Viola being "put outdoors" with revolutionary social action, the force of which grows in response to Jones' voice. The play takes place over the span of three days. On the second day, the Landlord, accompanied by deputies, evicts Ma Jenkins while Viola is out trying to find work. Viola returns and finds her mother in despair and with all their furniture sitting on the street. In the next scene, the play interweaves the action of Viola going to an Angelo Herndon Jones meeting with Ma Jenkins praying, which anticipates the critique of religious practice alienated from social action that *Tambourines to Glory* stages. *Invisible Man* raises a similar question, but with irony.

As modeled in *Angelo Herndon Jones*, in *Invisible Man* and in *Tambourines to Glory*, eviction inspires oration. *Angelo Herndon Jones* shifts from the image of Ma Jenkins praying in the street to the sound of a speech: "(*The lights go out, but in the darkness, growing louder and louder, there is the sound of applause, and Herndon's voice is heard speaking*)."[15] In classic agitprop style, Herndon's voice, presumably coming from offstage, directs the attention of the crowd:

VOICE ... I tell you let them imprison me. Let them send me to the chain gang, but a thousand Angelo Herndons will arise to take my place. A million Angelo Herndons. All over the country in every city and town! I am the working class. (*applause*) Black and white unite to fight. (*The strains of the INTERNATIONALE are heard. Then VIOLA's voice speaking to BUDDY*)
VIOLA And all our things are out in the street, Buddy. On the sidewalk in the night, in the cold.
BUDDY You hear that, comrades, what Viola says? She and her mother's been thrown out of their room by the landlord.[16]

The voice coming from offstage drives the action onstage; the sound of the male voice encourages formation of community and also functions as a trope of disembodied power that Amiri Baraka upsets in *Slave Ship*. The lack of specificity of the voice enables its universal quality. The play ends as Buddy rallies the other spectators, who now see themselves as comrades, to action. In a utopian resolution, the group constituted of both black and white workers departs, resists the restraints of the police, and carries the furniture back into the apartment.

The utopian vision presented in *Angelo Herndon Jones* requires the elision of difference and therefore had been eclipsed by the Cold War by the time Ellison published *Invisible Man* and Hughes staged *Tambourines to Glory*. *Invisible Man* suggests that the remedy to economic struggle must be found within the frame of the capitalist economy. The evolution of events in *Invisible Man* is strikingly similar to the eviction scene scripted in *Angelo Herndon Jones*. As Ellison's unnamed protagonist walks down the street he notices "the sullen-faced crowd" and describes the eviction as startling. In the same moment he begins to process the scene and once he notices a crying woman sitting next to the furniture on the street his surprise turns to "foreboding" and "a quick sense of uncleanliness."[17] The feeling of "uncleanliness" drives his reactions to the eviction even as he becomes a primary advocate for the evicted couple. Before he is compelled to action, *Invisible Man* explains the reason the protagonist felt "unclean." Seeing the sobbing old woman, he realizes "that what I'd taken for junk was actually worn household furnishings" (268). Recognizing the forlorn elderly woman forces the protagonist to reevaluate his initial assumption that "junk" had been placed where it belonged, on the street. At first the protagonist failed to realize that the "junk" was in fact prized possessions because he refused to *see* the sobbing woman; his subsequent realization reflects biological and cognitive processes. The protagonist's vision focuses attention on the emotional and social factors at play in all of the eviction scenes.

The feeling of uncleanliness in response to the eviction in *Invisible Man* points to a divergence between Ellison and Hughes in social philosophy. Ellison's depiction imbues the unnamed protagonist with shame as an affect, a feeling of inadequacy. Beginning in the 1970s, a group of scholars including Silvan Tomkins, Helen Block Lewis, Donald L. Nathanson, Andrew Morrison, and Léon Wurmser revised many of the popular psychoanalytic beliefs about shame. These scholars agree that shame emanates from a biological source manifested through, but not solely located in, visual interaction. Disrupting the gender bias embedded in Freud's depiction of shame as a response to "genital deficiency," Donald Nathanson points out that shame is an innate characteristic that life experiences complicate and refine.[18]

Following J. Brooks Bouson, I am interested in thinking of shame as a collective manifestation of a socially motivated affect. Bouson describes the way that shame as "some sort of failure of the self," usually associated with "weakness, defectiveness, and dirtiness," gets folded into blackness.[19] Recounting one of the most recognizable articulations of racial shame, Bouson explains:

The black Antillean psychiatrist Frantz Fanon provides a vivid account of the shame sufferer's doubleness of experience in his remarks on the black feeling of inferiority that "comes into being through the other" and in his description of the experience of being seen as the object of contempt – as a "Dirty nigger!" in the eyes of whites. Viewed through the shaming gaze of whites, "Negroes are savages, brutes, illiterates." Fanon describes his feelings of being "dissected under white eyes, the only real eyes," and having his body "given back" to him "sprawled out, distorted." The fact that he wants to hide from the gaze of whites – "I slip into corners, I remain silent, I strive for anonymity, for invisibility" – reveals his reactive desire to defend against feelings of shameful exposure.[20]

Bouson also refers to the phenomenon which, discussing Du Bois in Chapter 2, I categorize as his incorporation of affect into his conceptualization of the black psyche, noting his depiction of double consciousness as "this sense of always looking at oneself through the eyes of others, of measuring one's soul by the tape of a world that looks on in amused contempt and pity." Similarly, Judith Halberstam writes that the racial shame associated with blackness, as articulated by Fanon and Du Bois, "records in a dramatic fashion (a blush, vertigo, overwhelming panic) a failure to be powerful, legitimate, proper – it records the exposure, in psychoanalytic terms, of the subject's castration, be it racial, gendered, class-based, or sexual."[21] Bouson and Halberstam recall these classic moments to point to how racism functions to constitute blackness.

Bouson's analysis, however, mainly focuses on shame as a result of and not as a cause of action. In other words, if shame is an innate affect then the subject needs it. Therefore, one could imagine instances in which shame protects the subject. Shame can account for both passive displays (the subject drawing into himself and averting another's eyes) as well as aggressive action (the subject attracting the attention of another in anticipation of the judgmental gaze). In the latter, it is just as plausible to conceptualize performances of black pride as a collective response to shame, rather than as a result of it. Moving from individualized scenes of shame to the collective inscription of shame through racial metaphors reveals how race pride, as an anti-shaming gesture, managed the competing affect produced by what Toni Morrison calls the "funkiness" of blackness.[22] At the same time the theatricality of the shamed subject and of the racially marked subject makes both postures ripe for sly refusal: knowing the familiar scripts makes them vulnerable to parodistic flips that invert and explode the organizing principles of the scene. *Tambourines to Glory* demonstrates the longstanding social importance of black religious practice as a mode of psychic fortification, a resistance to racialized shame.[23] The play reveals the affective dynamic that exists in anti-shame identifications (e.g., "black is beautiful") built on race pride and their history in vernacular forms of expression. Bouson claims, "Until the black revolution of the 1960s, 'To be called "black" in America meant to live in a state of shame...'"[24]

The eviction scene in *Invisible Man* makes the distinction that some characters cannot call on historical memories as psychic fortification. The unnamed protagonist does not look away from the eviction scene because *he* has been exposed; the scene depicts a collective exposure affected by a common history. As he absorbs the scene before him, he notices

a self-consciousness about them, as though they, we were ashamed to witness the eviction, as though we were all unwilling intruders upon some shameful event; and thus we were careful not to touch or stare too hard at the effects that lined the curb; for we were witnesses of what we did not wish to see, though curious, fascinated, despite our shame, and through it all the old female, mind-plunging crying. (270)

The protagonist does not feel ashamed that the eviction is taking place; he feels ashamed of what the eviction says about him. Witnessing implicates him in the event, but their race intensifies the tie he feels. The novel notes that the marshals performing the eviction are white. Moreover, many of the belongings of the evicted couple have racial implications: "'knocking bones,' used to accompany music at country dances, used in black-face minstrels ... a straightening comb ... scattered across the top of the chiffonier were nuggets of High John the Conqueror, the lucky stone" (271). Later on the crowd knocks over a drawer and out spills "a yellowing newspaper portrait of a huge black man with the caption: MARCUS GARVEY DEPORTED" along with "a fragile paper, coming apart with age, written in black ink grown yellow. It read: FREE PAPERS" (272). The material history brought to daylight for everyone on the street to see immediately recalls an ongoing, palpable, brutal social dynamic embodied in the white men who have been given the authority to come into a black community and throw two elderly black people out onto the street. In witnessing, the protagonist recognizes his lack of agency and feels ashamed.

In contemplating the affective confusion the scene inspires, he realizes suddenly that "it was as though I myself was being dispossessed of some painful yet precious thing which I could not bear to lose" (273). The forced loss of the "painful yet precious" material history embodied in the objects strewn about the street motivates the protagonist to take action. Attempting to mediate the loss of what he cannot bear to lose, he begins to speak. Initially his speech calls on the rhetoric of scientific Marxism. He tells the now enraged crowd, "'Black men! Brothers! Black Brothers! That's not the way. We're law-abiding. We're a law-abiding people and a slow-to-anger people," and before he finishes his second phrase "they stopped, listening" (275). But he, nevertheless, continues to try to persuade the crowd by tapping into the emotion that he sees in their faces.

Altering his approach, the protagonist's speech uses techniques from the African American sermonic tradition, which Spillers calls "the African-American's prototypical public speaking."[25] He continues: "'What are we to do?' I yelled, suddenly thrilled by the response. 'Look at him,' I cried. 'Yes, just look at him!' an old fellow in a derby called out as though answering a preacher in church. 'And look at that old couple . . .' 'Yeah, what about Sister and Brother Provo?' he said. 'It's an ungodly shame!'" (277–78). The protagonist attempts to liberate the dispossessed couple by calling for the action of the community. By asking a series of questions he intimates that some action, some "law-abiding" action, should be taken: yet he does not elucidate what that action should be. He employs repetition, a classic characteristic of the African American sermonic form, to reproduce an insurgent history, but ironically forestalls the power of his message by repeating the phrase "the law-abiding thing." Speaking out of both sides of his mouth, Ellison's protagonist reiterates law-abiding to point to the inadequacy of "playing by the rules." The repetition of the phrase highlights that law-abiding people end up on the street. The protagonist uses repetition to communicate a message of liberation for him and the crowd from the history – the racialized, funky junk – that turns the law-abiding into the dispossessed. Even in advocating for the couple the protagonist feels ashamed. He does not condemn the judgment of non-value made by putting the couple out on the street. Rather, he condemns the exposure of the objects that trigger painful memory. In his speech, he indirectly admonishes the elderly couple for cluttering up the street with their junk in part because their junk implicates him.

Foregrounding the importance of audience participation and collectivity, the unnamed protagonist's speech gains momentum from the spontaneous responses members of the crowd offer. Replying to a man who cries, "Hell, they been dispossessed, you crazy sonofabitch, get out of the way!" (278), the protagonist answers, "'We're dispossessed,' I said at the top of my voice, 'dispossessed and we want to pray. Let's go in and pray. Let's have a big prayer meeting . . . Take it all, hide that junk! Put it back where it came from . . . Hide it, hide their shame! Hide *our* shame!'" (279). Rhetorically creating a distance between himself and the elderly couple, the protagonist preserves the "painful yet precious thing that he cannot bear to lose" while keeping it at bay. He demonstrates shame of the private practices now made public, even as his public performance draws on the social history of blackness that he scorns.

Although the protagonist's speech rhetorically draws from the structure and content of the African American sermon, his message significantly deviates from that tradition. In the African American sermonic tradition, the interaction between the preacher and the audience is supposed to be transformative. The protagonist advocates that the crowd help him "Hide *our* shame!" The participatory nature of the eviction scene in *Invisible Man* mirrors the dynamic created in the cakewalking scene in *Color Struck.* In both, the audience participates in shaming a member of the community by conceding to the categorization of their behavior as inappropriate and worthy of scorn. In psychoanalytic terms shame often "follows a moment of exposure," which explains the protagonist's insistence that the crowd must hide the couple's belongings.[26] Contrary to the overriding conclusion of the African American sermon, "the ultimate triumph over defeat and death," the gesture toward concealment acquiesces to the judgment from the outside that induces shame.[27] The African American sermon works to liberate the subject and, as mentioned, locates that liberation in the community. It responds with strategies to manage and confront, instead of simply yield to, shame.

A confluence of social demands and limitations occurs in the eviction staged in *Tambourines to Glory*, but affective motivations for the response by the two female protagonists are markedly different from those of Ellison's protagonist. Once Laura (whom Hughes notes "should be performed by a compelling personality, one not merely pretty, but capable of projecting sunlight, laughter, easy-going summer and careless love") convinces Essie (whom Hughes describes as "the good old earth, solid, *always* there come sun or rain, laughter or tears, the eternal mother image") that they should start a church, Essie "*Suddenly rises, looking upward*" and declares, "With faith! And I mean that! Right now, tonight! Laura, I just got a vision. A voice tells me to take you up on this – and try to save *you*, too" (193). When Laura finds Essie on the street she is not ashamed. In fact, finding Essie makes Laura hopeful.

The context of Essie's prophetic vision, including the conversations that precede it, reflects a set of psychic dynamics that establishes a tone for the sermonic song that follows. Before Laura finds Essie on the street, Essie has two conversations both marked by humor:

YOUTH Lady, what happened to you?
ESSIE Evicted, that's all.
YOUTH Damn! Ain't that enough?
ESSIE No need to use profanity, son.
YOUTH Excuse me, ma'am. (*As he exits he turns*) But I still say damn!

WOMAN (*Stops and speaks kindly*) Poor soul! Even though it is May, it's not warm
    yet. I hope you don't have to sit out here all night.
ESSIE I reckon God'll provide for me. My credit's run out.
WOMAN Don't you have any relatives?
ESSIE Not a soul in New York.
WOMAN Not even a husband?
ESSIE When I had one he warn't much good.
WOMAN You can say that again! Neither was mine. (190)

The young man and woman do not feel implicated in what has happened
to Essie; they do not demonstrate shame. Instead they sympathize with
her, the woman more so than the young man. The change in tenor reflects
racial and historical dynamics that differ between *Tambourines to Glory*
and *Invisible Man*. Unlike the scene in *Invisible Man*, *Tambourines to
Glory* takes place in a black community and under the gaze of members of
that community, in line with the distinction Gates makes between modes
of representation for insiders and outsiders. Moreover, while *Invisible
Man* shows how the tension of the eviction scene inscribes a painful
history onto the crowd, the eviction scene staged in *Tambourines to Glory*
presents the everyday.

RESETTING SCENE ONE

The opening scene of *Tambourines to Glory* sets the tone for the play and
therefore underwent significant thematic and structural revisions in the
seven years from the play's inception to its New York premier. The
revisions to the opening scene mark an impulse in Hughes' work toward
repetition/reproduction. A similar case could be made for the multiple
ways Hughes explores the figure of the mulatto in short story, poetry,
and drama. He repeats and revises the story, giving new social life to it in
subsequent iterations. As stated earlier, the production history of a play
serves as an exemplar of the dynamic interactive quality of literary
history. The earliest version of act 1, scene 1, written in 1956, takes place
in Laura's government-subsidized apartment. The women decide to better
their lives by using some of the money they collect from relief to start a
church. The physical dynamics of Laura's apartment mirror the Youngers'
apartment in *A Raisin in the Sun*. Although Hughes never staged Laura's
apartment as a part of the opening scene of the play, domestic life
in Harlem was one of his ongoing concerns. In 1944 he contemplated
the living conditions in Harlem in an essay entitled "Down Under
in Harlem." He recalls:

under the hill on Eight Avenue, on Lenox, and on Fifth there are places like this –
dark, unpleasant houses with steep stairs and narrow halls, where the rooms are
too small, the ceilings too low and the rents too high. There are apartments with
a dozen names over each bell. The house is full of roomers. Papa and mama sleep
in the living room, the kids in the dining room, lodgers in every alcove, and
everything but the kitchen is rented out for sleeping.[28]

Hughes opens the essay by explaining the social and economic diversity
among African Americans. He focuses, though, on Negroes not "smart
enough and lucky enough to be among Dr. Du Bois's 'talented tenth'
and be a race leader and to go to the symphony concerts and live on that
attractive rise of bluff and parkway along upper Edgecombe Avenue."[29]
The essay attempts to explain the riots that broke out in Harlem in
1943. Notably, Baldwin discusses the same riots as he mourns the
passing of his father in "Notes on a Native Son." Not only does Hughes
make light of Dr. Du Bois' talented tenth, he also confronts the
hierarchy that makes the inhabitants of Sugar Hill better than those
"under the hill."

The transformation of the opening scene points to Hughes' concern to
tightly fuse the economic, emotional, and spiritual concerns of the play.
He began writing the first version of *Tambourines to Glory* on July 14, 1956
and finished on July 24. Once complete, Hughes turned the play into a
novel published in 1958. In August 1959, the Theater Guild accepted
Tambourines to Glory and rehearsals of the play began on August 15,
1960. On Labor Day, September 5, 1960, when the show was staged at
the Westport Country Playhouse in Connecticut, it received positive
reviews. Arnold Rampersad explains, "In a poll, 314 out of 386 patrons
like the show 'very much,' and many were sure *Tambourines to Glory* was
ready for Manhattan." Yet "On religious, moral, and political grounds,
several observers found the play in appalling taste." The critical perception
of the "taste" of the play communicates a division along class lines between
Hughes' imagined audience and the one that attended the Westport
production. Often distinctions coded as taste break down along lines of
expressivity – the more expressive and emotive the display, the less tasteful
it is deemed. The Westport audience's responses reflect an audience
demographic that revisions to *Tambourines to Glory* could not satisfy.
Nevertheless, Hughes "composed a new prologue, new songs, a new
opening scene, and a closing sermon to improve the tone."[30]

He changed the opening scene of the play because he understood his
critics as barometers of the changing times. He maintained nonetheless
that "'People forget . . . that comedy, as well as tragedy, can be used as a

weapon of social criticism."³¹ The 1956 version presents Laura and Essie in the opening scene sitting in a tenement room. In this version "*Essie sits in her coat cleaning her fingernails*" and complains, "Oooo-ooo-o! Sure is cold in this place. Old Landlord ought to keep the heat up even if the calendar does say spring" (ov). After complaining about the living condi-tions, Laura suggests that they start a church. In the opening scene of the August 1959 version, Laura enters with a blanket around her shoulders carrying a bottle of wine. The women discuss the scarcity of food along with the unseasonably cool temperatures before Laura suggests that Essie "Get holy" and "sanctify" herself. The July 16, 1960 version contains distinct changes from the previous scripts. The first scene of the play dramatizes an agent repossessing a chair from Essie's tenement (IV). The repossession acts as the catalyst for Essie and Laura to found Tambourine Temple. Hughes does not add the eviction scene to the play until the October 1, 1960 version marked "(after Westport) version as sent to Anne Meyerson." Following the new prologue, the October 1960 version includes the eviction scene that remains the opening sequence of the first act of the play. The 1960 version also contains the first rendition of "Upon this Rock."

The circumstances articulated in the framing of the play limit the threat of judgment and, as Laura reminds Essie, inspire strategies for managing economic poverty: "You know Bishop Longjohn right over there on Lenox Avenue? That saint had three whores on the block ten years ago. He's got a better racket now – the gospel!" (191). Responding to the ethical issues Essie raises, Laura is insistent:

LAURA ... Let's start a church. Huh?
ESSIE Where?
LAURA On the street where the Bishop started his – outdoors – rent free – on the corner.
ESSIE You mean down here in the gutter where I am.
LAURA On the curb – *above* the gutter. We'll save them lower down than us. (192)

Instead of responding to Essie's eviction with shame, Laura responds with humor. The two women do not share the same beliefs: Laura is on relief, while Essie refuses to claim relief (in the 1963 version); Laura wants to purchase their Bible on credit, while Essie says they should found the church with faith. Nonetheless, Laura and Essie share a common eco-nomic status and therefore an investment in transforming their state. "*As Laura stares in amazement, Essie, her face flooded with radiance, mounts her pile of furniture and sings*":

ESSIE Upon this rock I build my church.
The gates of hell shall not prevail.
Upon this rock I build my church.
With strength from God I shall not fail.
(*Essie snatches Laura's wine bottle and throws it away. Laura, falling into the spirit of the thing, cries out dramatically*)
LAURA The call has come and I have heard!
BOTH The gates of hell shall not prevail!
ESSIE I shall not doubt His holy word.
BOTH With strength from God I shall not fail.
(*Gradually as they sing, windows open and heads pop out. Two or three passers-by stop to watch and listen. Then a few more gather on the street ... The passers-by cry approval and join in their song. The street is filled with music*). (194)

The playfulness of the women's song, which results in the same kind of call and response motivated by the speech of Ellison's protagonist, reflects cunning. By depicting the capitalist system as something to be manipulated instead of as a threat, *Tambourines to Glory* calls for Essie and Laura's empowered response to the eviction. This impromptu song is sermon-like because it delivers a liberatory message of material and spiritual transcendence, activates call and response, is structured by repetition, draws on the inherent musicality of the African American sermon, and "catalyzes and embodies movement."[32] Also, this song demonstrates how parody is embedded in many lines of the play.

The familiar melody and rhythm of "Upon this Rock" uplifts and entertains passers-by, and inspires them to join in. Anyone passing in the street could assume that Essie has chosen to deny her lack of material solvency any authority over her spirituality. The lyrics of the song come from a conversation between Jesus and Simon Peter in the Gospel of Matthew, in which Jesus responds to Peter's proclamation that Jesus is "the Christ, the Son of the living God" (16:16) by replying, "And I say also unto thee, That thou art Peter, and upon this rock I will build my church; and the gates of hell shall not prevail against it" (16:18). The rock is faith in Jesus, both in the Bible and in the song. Jesus responds to Peter's act of faith when he says, "upon this rock I build my church." Essie appropriates that line, trading the spiritual message for secular empowerment. Shifting the significance of the line, the "gates of hell" that shall not prevail are the material limitations of poverty. Essie's faith in the corruption of Harlem encourages her investment in Tambourine Temple.

Laura and Essie's song is not insurgent but self-serving. The crowd that forms as Essie and Laura sing shares their economic insolvency and therefore feels connected to the multilayered message. In the classic sense, "the church goer hears double, or in excess, because it is between the lines of Scripture that the narratives of insurgence are delivered."[33] The sermons given in *Tambourines to Glory* bind the community to a conwoman's mentality, fixed on the transfer of money, not on the transcendence of position. Similarly to the trickery depicted in Suzan-Lori Parks' Pulitzer Prize-winning play *Topdog/Underdog*, which I discuss in Chapter 7, *Tambourines to Glory* presents the sly activity of the confidence woman as central to the constitution of community. The audience must knowingly participate in the con in order for it to work. The willingness of the audience reflects the working of capitalistic ideology that the play facilely manipulates. Hearing Essie and Laura's song demands a form of listening in which the lines of the sermon are tripled.

Not just any speech given in front of an audience qualifies as a sermon. Audiences anticipate the African American sermon will reference its social history as a response to displacement and rhetorical history as a form containing strategies of uplift that rely upon listening between the lines. And just as the audience of Ellison's protagonist "stopped listening" when his speech did not produce the insights it expected, the audience of any sermon may stop listening if its expectations regarding form and content are not met. The listener's participation in the African American sermon is essential to the form and therefore a good sermon inspires listening.

Sermons in the African American tradition explore the concept of freedom as existential and social. By modeling strategies of identity – class affiliations, as demonstrated in Angelo Herndon Jones's speech, racial affiliations, as demonstrated in Ellison's protagonist's speech, or social affiliations, as demonstrated in the sermon Essie and Laura sing – the speaker creates an opportunity for interpretation and self-reflection. Therefore, as Spillers elucidates, "we perceive it [the sermon] fundamentally as a symbolic form that not only lends shape to the contours and outcome of African-Americans' verbal fortunes under American skies, but also plays a key role in the psychic configuring of their community."[34] The sermon provides a model for reading that then creates the possibility of forming a community just as a theater event presents an opportunity for active learning.

Similar to the audience dynamics Du Bois, Hopkins, and Overton Walker actively cultivated in the early twentieth century, the call and response of the sermonic form create protocols for reading that cultivate an "expansive literacy."[35] As crucially as Frederick Douglass' pursuit, the gospel play borrows from the sermonic form, including the audience in the production of the event and therefore training audience members to play their part as interpreters and producers of words, songs, sounds, and gestures. Just as literacy provided Douglass with a set of tools that led to empowerment, improvisation, and freedom, the structure of the gospel play enables audiences to learn liberatory practices through active participation in the event. The setting of the gospel play and the inclusion of the audience in the theatrical production allows a sense of communion that enables community. While Douglass' literacy enabled his individual freedom from physical bondage, the gospel play form creates a structure of empowered interaction and participation that has the potential to result in collective forms of expansive literacy.

The play attempts to transform the transformer, or in other words, reaffirm black religious practice, one of the very processes that enables the reformation of black people in the Americas; the play, however, suggests Harlem has mutated and abandoned its cultural history. Black Christianity emerged as enslaved Africans in America tried to make sense of their lives under the brutal conditions of slavery and "in the light of biblical texts, Protestant hymns, and Christian testimonies."[36] The history of black Christianity, as exemplified in the spirituals, always advocated an insurgent existential *and* social deliverance from oppression. In Hughes' play, Laura perceives her condition as primarily economic. Creating Laura and Essie as foils, *Tambourines to Glory* references the prophetic strand of black Christian thought. Cornel West describes this strand, saying it is "guided by a profound conception of human nature and human history, a persuasive picture of what one is as a person, what one should hope for, and how one ought to act."[37] Structured through sermons and driven by humor, the play calls for a progressive religious practice that relates human behavior and the individual's ability to act to a history of economic struggle. Therefore, understanding "how one ought to act" is always in tension with the range of possibilities open to the characters in the play. Laura and Essie manipulate cultural practices that bridge existential and social freedom movements. The play questions the efficacy of the forms when emptied of their existential meaning.

The familiarity of the sermonic form almost renders it retrograde; a direction of movement Hughes smartly taps into. Through reversals of the meaning of scripture, for example the manipulation of the metaphor of the rock, Hughes taps into the "incongruity" that humor produces. "We laugh when our expectations are somehow disturbed ... At its best, the humor of incongruity allows us to see the world inverted."[38] To clarify, I am not suggesting that the narrative development of Hughes'

play offers surprises. As a matter of fact, it follows classic formal characteristics of melodrama – a "'mode of excess' … that cuts across periods,
cultures, and art forms, as an 'imagination' dominated by a Manichaean
worldview," as Gilman remarks – characteristics whose relevance to *Color
Struck* we have already seen in Chapter 3.[39] Hughes purposefully draws
from the scriptedness of theatricality in crafting the formal conventions of
the gospel play, only to strategically deploy comedy and the con to
unravel the set expectations and present the possibility of creating civil
unrest in the form of cultural critique.

GIVE THE PEOPLE WHAT THEY WANT: HUGHES' CHANGING FORM

Before Hughes began experimenting with the potential of black Christian
performance traditions, he contemplated the social power of black Christianity in general. More than two decades before Hughes wrote *Tambourines
to Glory*, he wrote a poem entitled "Good-bye, Christ" (1931) that would
torment him for years. Ten years after writing the poem, in response to
attacks critics and former supporters made, Hughes wrote a press release
called "Concerning Good-bye, Christ." In the release he explains:

Almost ten years ago now, I wrote a poem in the form of a dramatic monologue
entitled GOODBYE, CHRIST with the intention in mind of shocking into
being in religious people a consciousness of the admitted shortcomings of the
church in regard to the condition of the poor and oppressed of the world,
particularly the Negro people.[40]

Even though Hughes addresses both white and black Americans in
"Good-bye, Christ," he strategically argues that his poem meant to shock
"particularly the Negro people." Throughout his career Hughes primarily
wrote about African Americans. His intended audience does not, however, circumscribe the readers he summons in the poem, by that time an
international readership. Hughes' poem emphasizes forms of oppression
shared by the working class and people of color. In the aftermath of
World War II and the Red Scare, Hughes seems to have shifted his
political goal from shocking his audience to cajoling it.

"Good-bye, Christ" identifies the church's proselytizing as problematic if it is done in the absence of social and political mobilization for civil
rights. Hughes clarifies his concern in recounting a trip to the South in
1931. He describes regions of the nation in which African Americans were
denied the opportunity to exercise voting rights. The Scottsboro trial

intensified his dismay over the systematic denial of the opportunity to vote – the most fundamental practice of democracy. Upon returning from his tour of the South, Hughes visited the Soviet Union. The juxtaposition of human suffering in "our American Southland" with governmentally supported civil rights in the Soviet Union ("There were no pogroms, no lynchings, no Jim Crow cars") forced Hughes to question the function of Christianity in the United States. He asserts, "To me these things appeared unbelievable in a Christian country. Had not Christ said, 'Such as ye do unto the least of these, ye do it unto Me'? But almost nobody seemed to care ... It was then that I wrote GOOD-BYE, CHRIST."[41] The impulse "to shock into being a consciousness," particularly for black people, had not left Hughes by 1956, but he chose to adopt a different tone. Instead of infusing his verse with rage, he utilized the same irony associated with the blues and present in his blues poetry. But he turned that irony into parody in *Tambourines to Glory*. The danger of all parody, as with irony, is that the viewer will not realize that the art is self-reflexive. Even though the tone of Hughes' work changed throughout his life, from his Marxist-proletariat writing in the 1930s to his use of comedy and return to music as a formal device in the 1940s, 1950s, and 1960s, his investment in creating art that displayed the richness and political power of black culture as a social force remained consistent.

The boldness Hughes shows in an often-cited essay, "The Negro Artist and the Racial Mountain," abates, slightly, by the time he writes *Tambourines to Glory* (1962). In the essay he states:

We younger Negro artists who create now intend to express our individual dark-skinned selves without fear or shame. If white people are pleased we are glad. If they are not, it doesn't matter. We know we are beautiful. And ugly too. The tom-tom cries and the tom-tom laughs. If colored people are pleased we are glad. If they are not, their displeasure doesn't matter either.[42]

Hughes defines his aesthetic through a repudiation of shame. He refuses to allow protocols of behavior to restrict him as an artist, knowing that if he acquiesced in shame he would implicitly support restricting the expression of "individual dark-skinned selves." In "The Negro Artist and the Racial Mountain" Hughes implies that shame helps to police certain prescriptions for blackness. His concern about the reception of *Tambourines to Glory* suggests that it did matter to him "if colored people are pleased" with his work. The changes he made to the script evidence that he allowed audience response to influence the story he would tell.

Although his unabashed nature might have tempered as he aged, Hughes' choice to write a gospel play communicates his consistent investment in vernacular forms as the inspiration for his work. He deployed traditional forms of African American expression, without fear or shame of the "painful yet precious" history the tradition recalls. Therefore, even though "As a rule, Hughes stayed away from religious topics and themes," as Arnold Rampersad explains, "he loved and respected the distinctive manifestations of black religious practice ... Hughes' most extended use of religious material occurs in his plays, where his impulse to record the drama of black music and black religion found appropriate form."[43]

Tambourines to Glory takes the highly crafted forms of the African American sermon and gospel music and imbues them with comedy, then uses them to critique the black church. Gerald L. Davis summarizes the characteristics of the performed African American sermon: "it usually has three or more units structured formulaically, is organized serially in performance, and is given cohesion through the use of thematic and formulaic phrases."[44] Hughes further elucidates the guiding artistic models for *Tambourines to Glory* in the author's note that precedes the play. He explains, "*Tambourines to Glory* is a fable, folk ballad in stage form, told in broad and very simple terms – if you will, a comic strip, a cartoon – about problems which can only convincingly be reduced to a comic strip if presented very cleanly, clearly, sharply, precisely, and with humor" (184). The Harlemite's description of the play as a comic strip confirms my categorization of the play as a parody. For over twenty years, Hughes explored the profound aesthetic insight that can be gained by drawing from vernacular culture. He states that "*Tambourines to Glory* is, on the surface, a simple play about very simple people" (184). Anticipating the problems with the staging, Hughes insists that all of the play's "performers should be sensitive enough to appreciate the complexities of simplicity" (184).

In the same way that Hughes manipulated poetic forms such as the folk ballad to offer structural models for *Tambourines to Glory*, the blues poetry that he is most well known for informs the play's gospel song lyrics. Hughes notes:

Much of the meaning of *Tambourines to Glory* lies in its songs, so both Laura and Essie should be actresses who can sing. As if it were a rhythmic ballad, the overall conception of *Tambourines* must have rhythm – as "John Henry," "Casey Jones," "Stackolee," "Lord Randall," and "Mack the Knife" have rhythm. This the staging must achieve. When the curtain falls, the final effect must be that of having heard a song – a melodic, likable, dramatic song." (184)

He indicates in an interview for *The New York Times* entitled "Poems to Play: Langston Hughes describes the genesis of his 'Tambourines to Glory'" that gospel music inspired him to write the play. He heard a connection in the music between the secular and the spiritual. More than anything else, Hughes wanted the music to transform the theater and create an environment in which "participation might be encouraged – singing, foot-patting, hand-clapping, and in the program the lyrics of some of the songs might be printed with an invitation to sing the refrains along with the chorus of Tambourine Temple" (184). The interactive nature of the gospel play once again required an audience familiar with the vernacular traditions Hughes drew from.

INSPIRING INFLUENCES

Similarly to the cohesion created by the hushed organ music floating behind the sermon in many African American churches, the melody of "Upon This Rock" continues from scene 1 to scene 2, creating a seamless transition and inducing the song-like quality that Hughes desired. Still on the curb above the gutter, the second sermon more clearly illustrates the implications of Tambourine Temple being founded in the street. Having planned the second service, Essie and Laura's meeting has a familiar structure. Essie begins with an invocation: "Grant us your grace, Jesus! Fill us with Thy word, Lord, and bless this corner on which we, Your humble servants, stand tonight. Hear us, Lord, I pray Thee! Amen!" (195). In this modern morality play, Essie's prayer positions her as a believer. She asks that the words of the sermon enter the hearer and fill him or her. Seeking release from want or need, her words aspire to liberate. We find Laura, fittingly, concerned with more pragmatic matters; she complains, "We got to get an audience, Essie. Ain't nobody paying you no attention. (*She shakes her tambourine violently*)" (195). If the audience had been participating in the singing and hand-clapping, once Essie began the invocation they would have stopped. Therefore Laura's complaint could address the play's congregation and the audience simultaneously. In response to the lack of interaction, Laura begins to solicit engagement, and as she speaks a crowd gathers.

The humor, absent from Essie's prayer, returns as Laura begins to minister through the spoken word. The play does not make light of the African American sermon, as a thing in itself. *Tambourines to Glory* calls attention to how the object becomes mutated and changed through performance. It parodies the black church by keeping the African

American sermonic structure constant and invoking comedy through the content and location of the message. Laura speaks:

Yes, you sinners, I say, *Stop*! Stop in your tracks now and listen to my words. (*As she speaks gradually a crowd gathers*) Lemme tell you how I got the call. It was one night last spring with Sister Essie here, right on the street, I saw a flash, I heard a roll of thunder, I felt a breeze and I seen a light and a voice exploding out of heaven cried, "Laura Wright Reed," Take up the Cross and Follow Me!" Oh yes, that voice said, told me to come out on this corner tonight and save you! You young man laughing and about to pass on by. Stop! (195–96)

Besides the young man laughing, nothing in the beginning of Laura's sermon indicates the insincerity of her words, although based on the actress' intonation and gesture the scene could shift from the familiar lilt, exaggerated pauses, and musical meter of the African American preacher into a comedic exaggeration of those sounds. Laura references Matthew 16:24 when she says "Take up the Cross and Follow Me." In the Gospel, Jesus prophesies his death and resurrection to the disciples, and "Then Peter took him, and began to rebuke him, saying, Be it far from thee, Lord; this shall not be unto thee. But he turned and said unto Peter, Get thee behind me, Satan. Thou art an offense unto me; for thou savorest not the things that are of God, but those that are of men" (Matthew 16.22–23). Jesus admonishes Peter for his lack of faith. In order for Jesus to save Peter, the other disciples, and the world, he must suffer and die. Peter, acting in response to the love and fear he has for Jesus' physical safety, begins to rebuke him. The Messiah proceeds to say, "If any man will come after me, let him deny himself, and take up his cross, and follow me. For whosoever will save his life shall lose it; and whosoever will lose his life for my sake shall find it" (16.24–25). Outlining the danger and the sacrifice intrinsic in being saved, Jesus emphasizes that in order to "take up his cross, and follow me," man must "deny himself." The process of being saved requires the cultivation of an imaginative and transgressive will to power.

Laura dissipates the transformative power of the Gospel by appropriating the prophetic encounter and applying its tenets to her religious scheme. Her transformation, as she describes, moves her from "sin's gutter" to the "curbstone of life." Evoking her conversation with Essie from the previous scene, Laura's comment would amuse the audience who would remember her saying, "We'll save them lower down than us ... The ones that do what you can't do – drink without getting sick. Gamble away their rent. Cheat the Welfare Department – more'n I do.

Lay with each other without getting disgusted ... Them's the ones we'll set out to convert" (192). The comedic quality of Laura's speech depends on drama's ability to manipulate time, and on the security of realist drama that places the audience in a privileged position of knowledge and therefore immune to the con (Suzan-Lori Parks' *Topdog/Underdog* suspends this sense of safety). In the temporal configuration of the play, scene 2 takes place days after scene 1, yet in the stage directions the band is told to continue playing "Upon this Rock" to create cohesion between the two scenes. The sequence of days, eclipsed in a few minutes of the play, allows the congregation to invest in Laura's sermon. The real time between the scenes allows the audience to laugh at Laura's joke and hear the perversion at the core of her sermon.

In the play, Laura is an offense to the Gospel but a likable and humorous character nonetheless. As a modern morality play, *Tambourines to Glory* illustrates that cultural forms create communities and therefore have ethical imperatives. As the audience laughs and enjoys Laura's display they participate in her iniquities. Her mocking humor grows as the sermon builds. Having alluded to the costs of salvation by evoking Matthew 16:24, she persists:

LAURA Yes, because time is a candle – and everybody's burning time. Don't let your candle burn down before your soul gets right. Time is your electric light bill. Everybody is burning lights. Pay your bill before your lights is turned off and your soul is left in darkness.
ESSIE Pay your bill! Pay your bill!
LAURA Sinner, don't let your lights go out before your soul gets right. I'm gonna pay my bill tomorrow, yes! And you pay yours – take care of Con Edison. But let your soul get right tonight. (196)

Following a musical interlude, Laura finishes by saying, "Everybody! Sing with us as you put your contributions in our tambourine. Better than in some juke box for the devil to get ... Brother you can't get saved for nothing" (196–97). For the purpose of her payoff, Laura masterfully conflates spiritual deliverance with her personal, economic prosperity. The price of the mock sermon points to the theater audience's own position in the capitalist circuit the players manipulate. Traditionally, the African American sermon appropriates survival strategies from the Gospel to use in the daily lives of the parishioners. Laura's competence "in the interpretation and manipulation of systems of signs," however, has grown to the point that she has moved beyond survival strategies and on to profit.[45] Laura tells the audience that it can atone for its sins by giving her, as representative of the church, money.

Instead of lauding Laura's cunning, the play condemns her actions by aligning her with the devil figure, Big-Eyed Buddy Lomax. Following the collection of the offering, a police officer summons Laura and extorts money from her, but before he finishes a young man named Buddy appears and convinces the officer to leave. In the 1963 version Buddy opens the play with a soliloquy and introduces himself, saying:

I'm the Devil ... In this play, according to the program, you might think I'm Big-Eyed Buddy Lomax – if I didn't tell you in front, no, I'm not. Big-Eyed Buddy is just *one* of my million and one names. I've got plenty of names, had plenty – some pretty big ones – Hitler, for example. *Yes, Hitler was me ...* Katherine the Great – I put on drag sometimes. Iago. Brutus – *et tu, Brute* – right on back to Cain ... The Devil comes in various guises – and disguises. I'm disguised now. I am not the *me* you see here – tall, handsome, brownskin. I am not always dark – sometimes I'm white ... I speak all tongues ... In Harlem I'm cool, in Spain I'm hot. In Katanga I'm Tshombe. Sure, I have my troubles, get shot up once in a while, ambushed, assassinated. But, quiet as it's kept, I love being the Devil because I raise so much hell! Watch me this evening. I'll find work for idle hands – stagehands – to do. Unemployed actors, too. The Theater Guild put me up to this. (188)

Medieval morality plays have characters who represent vices and virtues. In this modern morality play, the characters are types with particular characteristic vices. In his soliloquy, Buddy qualifies himself as a particular incarnation of the devil – "tall, handsome, brownskin" – yet he still possesses the characteristic ability to tempt. Laura as the sultry street-smart vixen does not, however, require much temptation. Her relationship with Buddy undermines the gender critique the play offers by presenting Laura as a conwoman and therefore a sly manipulator of ideological structures.

The African American sermon, a form that Laura demonstrates she can deliver and deform, is the primary commodity Tambourine Temple trades in. Laura's performance contributes not only to the development of her character but also to the development of her congregation. Framed in the moral terms of good versus evil, the play questions the political, psychic, and social responsibility of the black church. Moreover, *Tambourines to Glory* investigates the ethical responsibility the performer has to the form.

GOING TO THE CHURCH

The play's next sermon takes place, fittingly, in a converted theater. But before Laura and Essie occupy that space, they move from the curb to a storefront church. Hughes explains in an interview with Lewis Nicholas, "Tambourines is based on the store-front churches that dot Harlem, churches that anyone can start by declaring himself a minister and opening for business ... Most of them are run by men of good will, pious, trying to help the community and area, but there is an occasional bad seed that mars the record."[46] Farah Jasmine Griffin aligns the emergence of storefront churches with the Great Migration. Even though Hughes writes *Tambourines to Glory* well after the height of the northern migration, Essie indicates in the first lines that she is a transplanted southerner and has no family to call on in New York. Griffin elucidates: "The rise of the storefront church and the ascendancy of gospel music within the established churches is an indication of the intraracial conflict that was intensified when the large numbers of poor blacks migrated to Northern cities."[47] The play codifies class distinctions by depicting a start-up church which ministers to people in the gutter, calling attention to the need for an institution such as Tambourine Temple.

The relocation of the church, from curb to storefront to theater, symbolizes the progressive transformation of the performance of the sermons. Laura and Essie do not deliver a sermon in the storefront church, described as showcasing *"behind the rostrum, a large mural of the Garden of Eden in which a brownskin Adam strongly resembles Joe Louis and Eve looks just like a chocolate Sarah Vaughn. Only the Devil is white"* (205). Act I, scene 5 begins directly after a church service. Instead of showcasing the sermon, the scene depicts the result of the performance. Laura and Essie commence with a meeting of the Trustee Board, but before they can begin, Brother Bud, a member of the church, interrupts:

BUD I kind of stuck around to see if you can help me. My wife is sick, I'm out of work, and my grandchild is hungry. (*Essie immediately puts her hand in her tote-bag*)
LAURA Essie! ... Brother Bud, Jesus will help you.
BUD He don't come to earth very often.
ESSIE Meanwhile, here brother, here!
(*Essie hands him some money. Laura shrugs*)
BUD Thank you, Sister Essie! Thank God! And bless you both! (206)

All communities coalesce through a commonality, whether a shared belief, history, experience, or interest. Tambourine Temple forms a community based on a common belief in the tenets of Christianity, a common history that the participants' investment in the church activities illustrates, and a common interest that the parishioners' donations fund. Therefore, when

Brother Bud asks the two leaders of the church for financial assistance, he does so having already invested in the community. Laura's unwillingness to assist Brother Bud juxtaposed with Essie's immediate response highlights the irony of the backdrop behind the two women.

The racialized Garden of Eden focuses attention on temptation external to the black community; Laura's response to Brother Bud, however, clarifies the troubles within the church. The mural attempts to turn the associations of blackness with evil and whiteness with purity on their heads by blaming whiteness, as a racial category, for introducing sin into the Garden of Eden. At the same time, Laura, sitting in a storefront church that she helped to found, consistently acts as the instrument that introduces sin. By the end of the trustee meeting Laura tells Essie that she is going to start selling holy water from the sink "as soon as the bottles come" (208). Although Laura sets up the church schemes, the moral barometer of the play does not find Essie guiltless. The outcome of the play represents the culmination of an ongoing battle between good and evil.

Similarly to the climax of Zora Neale Hurston's *Color Struck* and Du Bois' *The Star of Ethiopia*, the height of the action in *Tambourines to Glory* involves a spectacular display. Borrowing from African American religious practice, scene 7's entertainment value hinges on its theatrical display. The scene opens with a church service set in "*a newly converted theatre. It is a bright and joyous church. Besides an electric organ, there is a trio of piano, guitar, and drums – Birdie Lee is the drummer – with a colorfully robed Choir on tiers in the background, some Singers holding tambourines*" (219–20). Music remains essential to the church service and the structure of the play. The musicians, at this point familiar to the audience, all play distinct roles in the play. Birdie Lee joins Tambourine Temple after the first formal service on the curb. Early on she demonstrates her ability to offer a powerful testimony. Her passion for the Lord annoys Laura; Birdie tends to steal the show. The musicians prepare the congregation and the audience for the service. Accompanying Deaconess Hobbs and two tall Deacons, Deacon Crow-For-Day and Deacon Bud, the music coming from behind the closed curtain creates the tempo for the devotions. Deaconess Hobbs begins singing, "I cannot find my way alone. / The sins I beat I must atone / And so I pray the light be shone / To guide me as I go through this world" (220). Echoing John 14:6 in which Jesus tells the apostles, "I am the way, the truth, and the life: no man cometh unto the Father but by me," her song asks for intervention and guidance as it utilizes the easy-to-follow and inviting rhyme scheme of many gospel songs.

Similarly to the mural that hung in the storefront church, Deacon Crow takes centerstage and begins to testify, creating a backdrop for Laura's sermon. He testifies, "In my sinful days, before I found this church, I were a dyed-in-the-wool sinner, yes, dyed-in-the-wool, sniffing after women, tailing after sin, gambling on green tables" (222). The enunciation of the words and imagery could, once again, create a comic effect (imagine an actor reenacting "sniffing after women," taking deep breaths in and out through his nose and leering as he struts across the stage) or he could enact a pious affect that would induce sympathy. Based on his name and the formal attributes of the gospel play, I consider the former rather than the latter performance more fitting. His fervent recollection continues:

CROW I shot dices. Now I've stopped. I lived off women. Uh-huh! No more! I make my own living now. I carried a pistol, called *Dog* – because when it shot, it barked just like a dog … I drank likker.
BIRDIE Me, too! Me, too!
CROW It made me fool-headed. Thank God I stopped.
BIRDIE Stopped, stopped, stopped!
CROW I witnessed the chain gang, the jail, the bread line, the charity house – but look at me now!
BIRDIE Look, look, look!
CROW I lived to see the chicken crow for the day, the sun of grace to rise, the rivers of life to flow, thanks be to God! Lemme tell you, I've come to the fold! I've come – (*He sings and the whole church bears him up*)
Back to the fold –
How safe, how warm I feel
Yes, back to the fold!
His love alone is real. (222–23)

Based on the general practice of testifying, as Deacon Crow continues his testimony his tempo would quicken and the variation in his intonation would intensify, increasing the energy and force of his performance and calling for the participation of the congregation. He amens himself, saying "I lived off women. *Uh-huh*" – a model for the parishioners of an appropriate response. By agreeing with himself and changing his tempo as he agrees, he mimics the classic structure of the African American sermon. Therefore, even in the absence of Birdie's response, the testimony demonstrates the process of transformation; one embedded in the structure of the telling. His increasing tempo and final change to melody, moving from speaking to singing by the end of his testimony, elicits the participation of the entire congregation on the stage ("*the* whole *church bears him up*").

The setting of act 1, scene 7, as described in the play, stages viewership in a way that mirrors the dynamic between the audience in the theater and the performance of Hughes' play on the stage. Tambourine Temple's latest location, a converted theater, reflects the visual dynamic the play creates between the audience and the actors onstage: just as the play takes place in a theater, so does the church service. The congregation could see the physical remains of the old theater in their new church. Similarly, Deacon Crow's testimony shifts the dynamics of the space. A testimony acts as a mechanism of praise and as a model for liberation. His testimony contains his echo, which Birdie triples. The congregation, hearing Deacon Crow and Birdie, are encouraged to join in and repeat the song he begins. The congregation's participation could have invited a fourth, although simultaneous, echo from the audience. The singing and testifying usher Laura into the pulpit. As she enters, Birdie sings, "I'm gonna testify! / I'm gonna testify! / I'm gonna testify! / Till the day I die. / I'm gonna tell the truth. / For the truth don't lie. / Yes, I'm gonna testify!" And Laura begins her sermon by echoing Birdie, chanting "No, the truth don't lie!" (224). United by the singing, Laura integrates into the service seamlessly and quickly takes advantage of her position.

She continues the service by giving the scriptures for the week, what she calls "Lucky Texts." For each text she instructs the congregation to drop a quarter in the Tambourine. This is a scheme Buddy suggests to encourage members of the congregation to play the numbers; Laura's lucky texts are rumored to represent numbers that will win. Her lucky scripture warns against the Lord's judgment of the wicked. Beginning at Psalms 9:19, the Bible says, "Arise, O Lord; let not man prevail; let the nations be judged in thy sight. Put them in fear, O Lord: *that* the nations may know themselves to *be but* men. Selah." Laura's preaching parodies the performance of the African American sermon by exploiting the structure created through the testimonies to further defraud the congregation. She begins the service by referencing the scripture, but she never reads or explains it. Following Deacon Crow's testimony, which focused on the dangers of gambling, Laura, inadvertently, reads a scripture that warns against man's hubris. As in Laura's sermon on the curb, her sermon in the theater predicates transformation on a wager instead of sacrifice. By corrupting the subject of the sermon, she undermines the form as "the primary instrument of moral and political change within the community."[48] She enters into the preestablished tempo presumably to move the service forward but stalls it instead. Laura forestalls the only conclusion a "sermon" can come to, "the ultimate triumph over defeat and death" and therefore denies the congregation access to change.⁴⁹ While the congregation might find Laura's performance entertaining or amusing, the audience would also notice that the play foreshadows the repercussions of her actions.

In act II, scene 3, to the sound of a "*shimmer of tambourines,*" a "*drum roll,*" a "*crash of cymbals,*" and a choir led by Essie, Laura mounts the rostrum of Tambourine Temple and begins her last sermon, as it transpires, as pastor of Tambourine Temple by selling holy water "directly from the Jordan River" (254). In another scheme devised by Buddy, Laura began selling tap water in little bottles to the parishioners so she could buy a mink coat, a Cadillac, and "a hi-fi set – for Buddy" (208). As is her custom, Laura never gets around to actually delivering a sermon. Instead she calls for testimonies, singing "Who will be a witness for my Lord? / Who will be a witness for my Lord / On the day of jubilee?" (245). Birdie responds to Laura's call, and while Birdie testifies, Essie and her daughter Marietta find Buddy's dead body lying in the Robing Room covered in blood. Before entering the pulpit, Laura had an altercation with Buddy concerning another woman and she killed him.

Once again, *Tambourines to Glory* provides the audience with a privileged perspective. Having witnessed the fight between Buddy and Laura, Laura's call for a witness mutates the double-voiced quality of the sermon, imbuing it with a foreboding quality where humor had previously dominated. Before Laura assumes her place on the rostrum, she accuses Buddy of cheating on her. He admits to the cheating and tells her that she does not have the authority to chastise him. He goes on to degrade her and slap her "*full in the face*" (242). Feeling completely humiliated and lost, Laura, having anticipated an altercation with Buddy, waits for him to pull her close to him, pulls out a knife she "borrowed" from Essie's purse, and stabs Buddy as he tries to kiss her.

Upon finding Buddy, Essie immediately tries to save him, and in the process gets covered in blood. The transference of blood from Buddy to Essie symbolizes Essie's essential role in all of Laura's hustles and serves as a visual cue that she is implicated in Buddy's death. The police arrest Essie for Buddy's murder, but eventually release her when Laura admits to the crime. Upon release, for the first time since the impromptu sermon on the street corner Essie preaches to the congregation, instead of selfishly appropriating the idiom for personal gain. The play signals the renewed quality of this sermon by having Essie participate in the making of it. As the choir sings, Laura joins Essie on the rostrum. Essie presents Laura as evidence of the power of transformation. But she makes clear that Laura will not be held guiltless of her crimes.

Tambourines to Glory depicts the powerful possibilities for enhancing the community through the African American sermon, even in the midst of corruption. As Laura enters, her remorse and sadness replace her usual light-heartedness and fervor. She admits, "I have come to confess to God, before this church and before the world tonight, that I have sinned, I have sinned, sinned, sinned" (255). Laura performs the first two steps toward forgiveness – admission and repentance – but the rest of her sermon points to the change most central to the play. The repetition of "sinned" leads to a song, which reintroduces the spiritual component to the performance of the sermonic form as depicted in the play. In the middle of the song "*She speaks against the music*" (255). Laura invites the congregation to participate in the sermon through the song. By speaking against the music she calls attention to her individuality. The movement of drawing the audience in and then alienating herself demonstrates a model of leadership that does not undermine the church body. Her performative strategy in the song provides survival techniques for her parishioners even in her absence.

The absent presence Laura establishes resembles mainstream theater audiences' diminished desire for certain vernacular performances. In the seven-year span between inception and premier, Hughes witnessed significant political and social changes. As both Leslie Catherine Sanders and Joseph McLaren argue, *Tambourines to Glory* did not enjoy a successful run in New York (it only ran for three weeks in its initial staging) because it did not attract an audience who could appreciate it. Arnold Rampersad elucidates, quoting Loften Mitchell:

the failure of the show had little to do with Langston's competence. "The attack on the black storefront church was not only justifiable, it badly needed to be made. But I'm not sure that whites were interested in such a matter, so the theater patrons stayed away. But there wasn't anything superficial about the play. Religion meant a lot to Langston."[50]

Mitchell's quote in conjunction with Sanders' and McLaren's critiques raises the question: What audience could have appreciated *Tambourines to Glory* in 1963? More than the negative reviews of the play, the protests that the play inspired point to a political challenge embedded in this particular black performance. Even though the African American community demanded art that openly addressed interracial conflicts and the fight for civil rights, Hughes maintained that the intraracial drama *Tambourines to Glory* explores provided political strategies, strategies that could aid the Civil Rights Movement. He hoped to engender feelings of race pride that would defer the consuming desire for integration – not to offset investments in integration completely, but to highlight the characteristics of Negro expression that served as bedrock for centuries of resistance. These repeated actions, whether the rhetoric and distinctive gestures of an exemplary preacher or the virtuoso steps of a cakewalker, reproduce a revolutionary identity. Although vexed and often co-opted as exemplified in *Tambourines to Glory*, Hughes saw the ability to revel in and learn from virtuoso black performance as a key component to obtaining social justice. His critics disagreed. Theater audiences stayed away.

Evidenced as early as 1959 in Lorraine Hansberry's *A Raisin in the Sun*, integration was on everyone's mind, including theatergoers'. Even though Hughes wrote the play in 1956, by the time it was staged in 1963 white theatergoers had lost interest in drama that overtly drew its idiom from vernacular culture without challenge, and black theatergoers were critical of the political implications of a play that critiqued the black church in a moment when the church served as a bedrock of political action. Nevertheless, two months after the historic March on Washington, in the midst of political unease, *Tambourines to Glory* opened at the six-hundred-seat Little Theater on Forty-Fourth Street near Broadway. And, as expected, the audience immediately interrogated the play's political position.

The controversy that swirled around the play reveals that Hughes' audience shifted its perspective and that he did not keep pace with its current politics. At one point, "A rumor spread that a picket line would oppose the show. According to Jobe Huntley," the composer of the play, "Langston was determined to counter-picket, and even prepared a sign that read 'YOUR MAMA LIKES GOSPEL SONGS.'"[51] Hughes never had the chance to picket; the show closed before any protests were staged. Nevertheless, Hughes' response demarcates his expected audience as black people and reinforces his choice to draw on black culture, both comedy and tragedy, as the guiding idiom for his art. The comedy embedded in the play and its troubled initial staging demonstrate the political terrain that shifted under Hughes' feet. The dynamic power of the African American sermon informed much of the rhetoric of the Civil Rights Movement and influenced James Baldwin's drama, which I take up in the next chapter. The philosophical imperative of freedom and uplift through racial pride drove Langston Hughes' aesthetic from the very beginning. Unfortunately, his use of the idiom fell victim to social "progress" because *Tambourines to Glory* questioned the relationship of the idiom to the institution in which it flourished.

CHAPTER 5

Resisting death: the blues bravado of a ghost

James Baldwin's Blues for Mister Charlie

The way we find Richard Henry in the opening scene of *Blues for Mister Charlie*, "face down in the weeds," recalls perhaps the only lynching victim Americans know by name and sight.[1] Emmett Till's body haunts James Baldwin's play of 1964 much like Toni Morrison's "ghost in the machine."[2] In 1955 the fourteen-year-old black boy was brutally murdered in Money, Mississippi, for allegedly whistling at a white woman. Although the protagonist of *Blues for Mister Charlie*, Richard Henry, does not represent Emmett Till, Till's tragic death and the staging of his funeral nonetheless echo throughout the play. As Till's surrogate, to borrow a term from Joseph Roach, Richard's role in the social drama may exceed and differ significantly from the one that Till played even as Richard fills with soundings the vacancy Till left. *Blues for Mister Charlie* uses a legacy of acoustic resistance modeled in African American cultural productions to present the competing historical narratives that culminated in Till's death, the 1963 death of Medgar Evers (a civil rights activist), and the deaths of thousands of other lynching victims. This chapter provides a critical lens to interpret why certain histories remain ghostly and others emerge as part of the "official" story. Baldwin's play demonstrates, through the articulate, haunting speech of Richard Henry, how the acoustic legacies left by the victims of lynching inform the shape of historical narratives. Through the play, Baldwin situates the death of Till as a sequence of events that may not be consolidated by one moment in time.[3] The dismembered remains of the victims of lynching have a visual legacy in historical and artistic texts. Intervening in the visual history of lynching, the play, however, does not translate onto the page Till's alleged whistle, Evers' cries for desegregation, or the moans of lynching victims that preceded them. Instead, it theorizes the processes that mute certain sounds and amplify others.

As others have argued, including Marvin Carlson, Joseph Roach, Elin Diamond, Herbert Blau, Richard Schechner, Bert O. States, Harry

J. Elam, Jr., and Alice Rayner, the theater is essentially a ghosted space filled with the possibility of arresting judgment and forcing "recognition or reknowing or unforgetting" in Rayner's terms.[4] The disruptive force of the theater inheres in its ability to render a familiar sight unfamiliar. For example, as I have argued in previous chapters, *The Star of Ethiopia* and *Color Struck* rendered the black female body unfamiliar through opacity and elision. African American theater has the ability to make the "familiar world suddenly [seem] strange and new or impossible" through the repeated display of black bodies and the simultaneous reproduction of (un)familiar performances.[5] The disjunction or connection between certain bodies and certain acts has the potential to recalibrate looking and recall the ghostly histories that supplement viewing practices and therefore are left purposefully unsaid. As Carlson notes, "theatre is in an important sense haunted by a preexisting text."[6] Throughout this book I have shown how race as a discursive category and political force establishes viewing practices that haunt the African American theater and enable the critical work of many of the plays I discuss even as they limit the commercial viability of several of them. *Blues for Mister Charlie* bridges a gap between theater as a ghosted medium and other forms of cultural production by demonstrating the way other modes register ghosting through the acoustic.

Frederick Douglass and W.E.B. Du Bois strategically represent the sound of spirituals to structure the narrative progress of their most often-cited works, *The Narrative of the Life of Frederick Douglass* and *The Souls of Black Folk* respectively. As I discuss in Chapter 2, in the former the juxtaposition of Douglass hearing his Aunt Hester screaming and hearing his fellow enslaved Africans singing spirituals creates the conditions that necessitate the development of his concept of self. The sounds that Douglass hears remain an absent presence, but the narrative demonstrates how those sounds inform who Douglass becomes. Similarly, in *The Souls of Black Folk* Du Bois frames each chapter with epigraphs of musical notation. The musical notation or "the sonic signs," as Alexander G. Weheliye explains, "cannot form a mimetic merger with spirituals."[7] Therefore, the epigraphs serve a double purpose, representing but not replicating a cultural sounding, and structuring the narrative histories presented in *The Souls of Black Folk*. Douglass and Du Bois offer strategies to liberate repressed histories signified in acoustic legacies. The structures of their texts point to the ghostly sound of loss in all narrative, by organizing their narratives through sounds that are an absent presence. The sound of loss always supplements the representation of a fullness that does not exist.

The Life of Frederick Douglass and *The Souls of Black Folk* model strategies of narration and demand interactive modes of reading. Baldwin, like Langston Hughes in *Tambourines to Glory*, activates the interactive modes of engagement represented in Douglass' and Du Bois' texts in order to attune the listener's ear to the potentially reparative sound of the ghostly – to what Ralph Ellison calls "the lower frequencies."[8] Baldwin first conceptualizes the theater as a space in which such reparations may take place in his first play entitled *Amen Corner* (1955), which like Hughes' gospel drama takes place in a storefront church. In the notes for *Amen Corner* Baldwin explains how his theater relates to a method of healing: "I knew that out of the ritual of the church, historically speaking, comes the act of the theatre, the *communion* which is the theatre. And I knew that what I wanted to do in the theatre was to recreate moments I remembered as a boy preacher, to involve people, even against their will, to shake them up, and, hopefully, to change them."[9] Some Christians believe that during the service of communion transubstantiation occurs, the wafer and the wine becoming literally the body and the blood of Christ. Baldwin's use of the word "*communion*" indicates the transformative life-giving power he associated with the theater in its ability to give human form to what had previously only been understood as objects – black people in the US. The transubstantiation that *Blues for Mister Charlie* enacts also signals the theater's ability to conjure and, as importantly, name the dead. Baldwin's play suggests the persistent presence of the lynching victim as a part of the national fabric. In the context of the play the lynching victim becomes Richard Henry, a young, brash, vulnerable musician. The communion Baldwin describes, unlike some forms of the Christian one, does not attempt to reclaim the body; it strives to resurrect Richard's voice, to name it, to incorporate it, and to hear its troubled cries.

This chapter interprets how the narrative structure of *Blues for Mister Charlie*, following the legacy of sounding that Douglass, Du Bois, and Hughes exemplify, elucidates the political and historical importance of representation of the sounds of lynching. In *Passed On: African American Mourning Stories*, Karla F.C. Holloway explicates a relationship between artistic representations of historical events and the affect the actual events generate. Using the sorrow songs as an example, she argues, "African American cultural practices – music, literature, and visual arts – all used the facts of black death and dying as their subject. There was an overlap of fiction and fact, artistic subject and streetscape, lyric and conversation. The spirituals, those 'sorrow songs,' also of course, captured black melancholy."[10] Building on Holloway's astute analysis, my formulation of the sounds of lynching references many soundings in historical and artistic representations. Historically the sound of lynching, to borrow from Fred Moten, could be best categorized as a mo'nin', a sound that registers and communicates mourning. In music, Billie Holiday's weathered and complicated voice – a voice that sounds like the singer has "been through something," heard in her rendition of Lewis Allen's lyrics "Strange Fruit" – is the sound most readily associated with lynching.[11] Neither of those sounds fully encapsulates the sounds of lynching, but they point to legacies that inform the sounds. In this chapter, I trace a history of the sounds of lynching in order to propose that *Blues for Mister Charlie* intervenes in and extends that tradition in response to a turning point in the Civil Rights Movement. To move from the historical repetition of lynching and its acoustic legacy to artistic reproductions of those sounds is to move from ghostly memory to the introjection of history, from the incorporation of loss to the "work of mourning."[12] *Blues for Mister Charlie* does not replicate the sounds of lynching that echo as its backdrop. The play represents some of the social, psychic, and historical legacies that could produce such ghastly sights and did produce such ghostly sounds, and comments on the relationship between those sounds and the process of historical narration.

THE VISUAL DYNAMICS OF LYNCHING

Lynching is a social mechanism par excellence for disciplining communities. In *Discipline and Punish: The Birth of the Prison*, Michel Foucault theorizes the interdependence of public violence and community consolidation. He asserts, "The public execution did not re-establish justice; it reactivated power."[13] Foucault contends that public displays of violence served a reciprocal purpose: they established the status of the discipliner and subordinated the disciplined. Maime Till Bradley attempted to shift the power dynamics implicit in the visual dominance of lynching by presenting her son's mutilated corpse open for public view in a casket instead of hanging from a tree or shrouded to bar display. Bradley's radical choice to display her son's corpse created a space to examine the peculiar American calculus that equates quotidian expressions of masculinity – whistling at a woman – combined with blackness as a deadly threat. Bradley demanded that the nation see what was done to her son and in so doing reoriented the visual legacy of lynching. Historically, lynching victims' bodies were photographed, included on postcards, and presented as evidence of the violence that could and would be enacted on black Americans. Elizabeth Alexander reports the circumstances of Till's funeral.

She describes, "hundreds of thousands of mourners 'in an unending procession, later viewed the body' at the funeral home. A photograph of Till in the casket . . . ran in *Jet*, and largely through that medium, both the picture and Till's story became legendary."[14] The image of Emmett Till's mutilated body, displayed at the funeral home and on the cover of *Jet* magazine, directed the nation to look with horror. Till Bradley's choice to display her son's corpse asserted that he died not because he "whistled" at a white woman, but because his whistle, whether real or fictional, registered as an imminent threat.

For decades the lynching scene has informed America, Americans' consciousness, and Americans' artistic production. Artists, including Jacob Lawrence, have depicted lynching as a historical phenomenon with vast significance that continues to inform cultural production after the death of the victim. What Jacqueline Goldsby calls the "cultural logic" created by lynching dramatically reemerged in response to the viciousness of Till's murder, which occurred just months after the Supreme Court's decision in *Brown* v. *Board of Education* (1954).[15] The surprising reemergence of a haunted national legacy established Till as a symbolic representative of the lynching victim among thousands. As Moten explains, "The fact that whatever force Till's death exerted was not originary does not mean, however, that the force wasn't real. For even if his death marks panic and even if panic had already led to the deaths of so many so that that death was already haunted . . . something happened."[16] The vicious nature of Till's murder recalled the disfigured physical remains of many others. Bradley's decision to augment the visual legacy of lynching by displaying her son's corpse called for an analysis of the "force" exerted in every lynching. At the same time her decision to present his corpse alongside photographs of Till "created for the audience" what Elam calls "a 'reality check,' a moment that traumatically ruptures the balance between the real and the representational. It is a moment that, in the dissonance, generates demands that the relationship between the real and the representational be renegotiated."[17] Foregrounding the elusive presence of the real in theatrical display, the funeral stages a young man's corpse to organize the perpetual horror, fear, trauma, and grief of lynching. Instead of satisfying the mimetic desire of its audience, *Blues for Mister Charlie* takes a cue from Bradley's stage directions and creates a reality check by obscuring the lynched body from view while calling attention to Richard's embodied performance. The play responds to Till's death, but also recalls the deaths of the many thousands that had already gone by giving an acoustic materiality to the victims of lynching.

Till's disfigured corpse marks only part of the visual legacy that *Blues for Mister Charlie* dynamically transforms. In the wake of Till's death and funeral, images of Till's mother, the court proceeding, and the rallies mounted to protest Till's murder permeated national newspapers. Till's death coincided with the explosion of the technology of photography. "With more than half of the American public plugged into television networks and just as many pursuing photography on their own or in magazines devoted to that art, Bradley and the black press understood that, in 1955, they and the rest of the nation were living in what Heidegger called 'the age of the world picture.'"[18] Following the images of Till's death and funeral and the trial, photographs of protests filled periodicals during the Civil Rights Movement. Sit-ins at lunch counters and protest rallies still emblematize the era. In addition, in the year leading up to the production of *Blues for Mister Charlie* on June 12, 1963, Medgar Evers, a NAACP field secretary, was assassinated after suffering threats for his investigation into the murder of Till. A few months later on September 15, 1963, the Ku Klux Klan bombed the Sixteenth Street Baptist Church in Birmingham, Alabama, which resulted in the death of four girls: Addie Collins, Cynthia Wesley, Denise McNair, and Carole Robertson. As Baldwin outlines in "Notes for Blues," the preface to *Blues for Mister Charlie*, the play is in some distant way based on the death of Till but "when [Evers] died, something entered into me which I cannot describe, but it was then that I resolved that nothing under heaven would prevent me from getting this play done" (xv). In the playbill Baldwin dedicates the work "to the memory of Medgar Evers, and his widow and his children, and to the memory of the dead children of Birmingham."[19] The confluence of events in 1963 necessitated that Baldwin reconsider Till's death in relation to a long legacy of death and destruction. Serving as a turning point in the African American theater history explored herein, *Blues for Mister Charlie* questions the limitations of strategies of resistance predicated primarily on reorienting visual display, especially considering the popular medium of photography. Noting the limitations of photography as a medium for telling Till's story, Goldsby contends that "The images that do exist forestall the hard fact that a missing one points toward, which is that photography's capacities to document the real are not indisputable, and that the medium is more fully capable of *depicting* (not documenting) 'what must be imagined, what can[not] be actually seen – what can[not], in any verifiable way, be known.'"[20] While *The Star of Ethiopia* and *Color Struck* call attention to what the audience fails to see, the plays do not go so far as to suggest that visual media cannot communicate black revolutionary force; that it is unseeable. Instead they use the apparatus of the theater to reorient vision and obscure certain sights. By turning to the acoustic, the play highlights another mode of civil disobedience and questions the ability to capture black revolutionary practices.

By altering the setting of the "scene of subjection," to borrow a phrase from Saidiya Hartman, Bradley usurped some of the power of the lynch mob.[21] Till's mother, however, was not the first family member of a lynching victim to challenge the authority of the mob. Therefore, her actions must be read within the historical context that precedes them. In "Exquisite Corpse," Ashraf Rushdy describes some of the responses of Bradley's precursors:

In 1889, after a mob broke into a Barnwell, South Carolina, jail and lynched eight African American men, the local black community displayed its solidarity at the funeral. More than five hundred people lined the street, and several women implored the Lord to "burn Barnwell to the ground." The community refused to bury six of the men, claiming that the whites who killed them should bear that responsibility. In Virginia, Joseph McCoy's aunt refused to bury the body of her nephew, who was lynched in 1897. "As the people killed him, they will have to bury him," she explained. The body, whether buried or left to the elements, had become a symbol of the injustice and barbarism of the white community, the failure of the nation's founding principles: Let the dead bury their dead.[22]

Family members and community members decided to respond to the brutality of lynching by transferring the symbolic weight of the death from the victims to the "whites who killed them."

Instead of utilizing the dense visual history formed by the historical responses to lynching, *Blues for Mister Charlie* takes up a different tactic; it obscures lynching from view and does not emphasize its physical results. The play calls attention to the aural history that has been overlooked by focusing on the visual evidence. The reorientation in *Blues for Mister Charlie* from the visual to the acoustic marks a consideration of what Toni Morrison posits as the "racial 'unconsciousness' or awareness of race."[23] In *Playing in the Dark* Morrison considers how racial unconsciousness informs the narrative choices of American writers. She goes on to question how the racial unconsciousness of the writer contributes to the formation of "literary whiteness" and "literary blackness." Using the logic implicit in Morrison's inquiries, Baldwin's act of narration comments not only on the creation of American literature but also on the shape of all American literature and its reception. The acoustic history the play echoes explains how racial unconsciousness interrupts, informs, and reroutes historical narration.

Although the unconscious is usually understood as an individual's possession, Morrison's formulation of racial unconsciousness serves as a metaphor for the function of ghostly narratives. In "The Unconscious" Freud explains that "We have learnt from psycho-analysis that the essence of the process of repression lies, not in putting an end to, in annihilating, the idea which represents an instinct, but in preventing it from becoming conscious. When this happens we say of the idea that it is in a state of being 'unconscious.'"[24] He further elucidates, "we can produce good evidence to show that even when it is unconscious it can produce effects, even including some which finally reach consciousness."[25] As J. Laplanche and J.-B. Pontalis explain in *The Language of Psychoanalysis*, Freud indicates that the unconscious "in its 'topographical' sense ... comprises the repressed contents which have been denied access to the preconscious-conscious system by the operation of repression."[26] Freud's primal scene consists of the impression produced by the child witnessing the parents having sex, which, according to David Eng, sets the stage for images to be "(re)constituted, (re)presented, and (re)produced at a later time through deferred action."[27] Freud's primal scene draws into being the unconscious and its function. The primal scene leaves a trace that the subject can only identify after the fact. The trace, the image, nevertheless exists and informs the formation of the subject. Morrison's figuration seeks to decipher the formation of narratives and identities, including racial ones, that prevent certain voices from being heard. Therefore, the idea of racial unconsciousness draws from Freud's formulation and reorients it as a metaphor and, as a result, suggests the way the visual dynamics of race create a trauma that informs unspeakable narratives marked by ghosting.

RACIALIZING THE ACOUSTIC MIRROR

To further extend Morrison's metaphor, the rupture Freud's primal scene provokes could be reoriented by the trans-Atlantic slave trade as the sequence of events that sets in motion American writers' racial unconscious. Similarly, *Blues for Mister Charlie* reconfigures another of Freud's fundamental formulations, also described as a cut. The play establishes a stunning addendum to Freud's representation of sexual difference – a visual difference – as *the* primary difference. Freud depicts the castration crisis as the moment when the male child first learns to manage the difference of the female child and not, strikingly, his own difference from her. As Freud portrays it, the male, racially non-marked and hence implicitly white child initially experiences the castration crisis when he sees that the female child does not have a penis:

> when a little boy first catches sight of a girl's genital region, he begins by showing irresolution and lack of interest; he sees nothing or disavows what he has seen, he softens it down or looks about for expedients for bringing it into line with his expectations. It is not until later, when some threat of castration has obtained a hold upon him, that the observation becomes important to him: if he then recollects or repeats it, it arouses a terrible storm of emotion in him and forces him to believe in the reality of the threat which he has hitherto laughed at.[28]

The little girl poses an uncanny psychic threat to the male child because her body establishes the possibility of physical castration. To quote Freud, "the uncanny is that class of the frightening which leads back to what is known of old and long familiar."[29] The female body serves as the site that orients a previous or future psychic cut, which continues to haunt the male throughout his life. Notice, Freud depicts an uninterested little boy who manages the difference he notices in the little girl through disavowal; he refuses to acknowledge what he has seen. And only later does the boy, confronted by what he perceives as the implications of what he saw at the site of the girl's body, remember the female body as dangerous and threatening.

In *The Acoustic Mirror: The Female Voice in Psychoanalysis and Cinema*, Kaja Silverman revolutionizes Freud's paradigm, by arguing that difference is first registered through hearing, not through sight. Theorizing what she calls an "acoustic mirror," Silverman contends that before the child sees himself as different from others he notices the difference between his voice and the voice of his mother. By situating the loss of the mother's voice as primary, Silverman upsets the gender hierarchy implicit in Freud's model. Her challenge to Freud also enables analysis of the racial dynamics implicit in his depiction of the castration crisis. Reorienting Freud and anticipating the implications of Silverman's analysis, *Blues for Mister Charlie* establishes the anatomic difference associated with race as a necessary part of the force that perpetuates psychic division, the force that recalls a prior loss. Silverman contends that the little boy's visual recognition of physical difference is a by-product of a preexisting psychic process: he associates the threat of losing the penis with another loss, the loss of the mother's voice. Baldwin's play explains the visual threat the black male body poses, by recouping another, overlooked acoustic history of loss – the sounds of lynching. In the same way that the little boy represses the loss of his mother's voice, *Blues for Mister*

Charlie suggests American narrative has repressed the suffering of African Americans and the sound of their mo'nin'.

Blues for Mister Charlie narrates a dangerous struggle for self-definition waged primarily among men. Richard, a disillusioned recovering drug addict, returns to his hometown after migrating to the North to escape the social restrictions of the South and to pursue a musical career. Once he returns, he begins to challenge his town's most sensitive social conventions. For example, he carries around pictures of white women in his wallet, he brags to his friends about the relationships he had with these women, and he has a public verbal altercation with Lyle Britten, a white store owner. Richard's actions qualify him as dangerous because his anatomical difference has already registered him as a threat. Therefore, all of Richard's actions have an uncanny quality. The way the white community in the play reads Richard's body relates to "what is known of old and long familiar." Interpretations of his actions, therefore, must contend with the preexisting history of racial strife in the South. When Richard returns, he upsets his friends and family because he undermines all of the social mechanisms arranged to keep black men "in their place" and to alleviate the threat black men pose to the psychic economy of the townspeople. Since Richard threatens what Lyle knows and finds familiar, he feels no remorse when he kills Richard.

American racial politics encourages black men to act with servility. Richard, however, views the performance of humility as an acceptance of the association of blackness with danger. Early in the play, Richard criticizes his father, Meridian Henry, a minister and a symbol of nonviolence, for acquiescing in the racial politics of their town. In a conversation with his grandmother Richard recalls, "I didn't want to come back here like a whipped dog. One whipped dog running to another whipped dog. No, I didn't want that. I wanted to make my Daddy proud of me – because, the day I left here, I sure as hell wasn't proud of *him*." Remembering the death of his mother and Meridian's lack of response to her death, Richard charges, "I just wish, that the day that Mama died, he'd took a pistol and gone through that damn white man's hotel and shot every son of a bitch in the place." Even though Richard knows his father lacked the power to confront the hotel owner or management without inciting further violence, he nevertheless organizes his ideal of masculinity in opposition to the image of his father, "whipped, whipped, whipped" (20). In order to diffuse the threat Richard's father's racial difference triggers, Meridian had to appear totally without power. The separation between psychic and social freedom is inexplicable for Richard, which is why he refuses to perform in ways that might aid his social mobility if the cost is his subjective state. When Richard rejects the coupling of blackness with danger, he calls attention to the structures in his town that demand a certain performance. The play questions the relationship between performance and anatomical difference by focusing on how the sound of Richard's voice continues to inform the narrative progress of the play after Richard is murdered.

Blues for Mister Charlie derives its narrative coherence from Richard Henry's voice, a voice that echoes historical and artistic representations of the sounds of lynching, including the mo'nin' of mourning, the whistle of Emmett Till, and the "Ghost of a yell" reverberating from the lynching mob.[30] Richard's voice moves the focus of lynching from the event – what happened – to the causes of the event – why did this happen? The stage directions say, "*For the murder scene, the aisle functions as a gulf. The stage should be built out, so that the audience reacts to the enormity of this gulf, and so that Richard, when he falls, falls out of sight of the audience, like a stone, into the pit.*" Consequently, as the play opens, "*In darkness we hear a shot. Lights up slowly on Lyle, staring down at the ground. He looks around him, bends slowly and picks up Richard's body as though it were a sack. He carries it upstage and drops him*" (2). At the end when the death scene is reenacted, Richard again falls out of sight. While his falling body represents the loss experienced in each lynching, his haunting return throughout the play models how to transform the affect associated with loss into insurgence.

Blues for Mister Charlie exists within the genealogy of the lynching narrative. Like its predecessors, it calls attention to the impact of lynching on American identity and history. Depictions of lynching scenes pervade early twentieth-century American literature. During the late nineteenth and early twentieth centuries, the reiteration of lynching across the southern landscape reflected and normalized it as a mode of discipline. Consequently, even though lynching was an uncommon practice in 1955, and certainly in 1964, the "meanings made an excess in time; over time, assigned by a particular historical order," to borrow a phrase from Hortense Spillers, they continued to inform the national landscape.[31] Even though black communities created strategies to resist the morbid display of mutilated black bodies, the repetition of those images over time informs our historical understanding of lynching. As Rushdy suggests in his analysis of the brutal lynching of James Byrd in 1998, "African American men have long been portrayed as comic buffoons or dangerous criminals, and a large segment of this nation remains incapable of imagining black suffering."[32] Once again the body, covered by the history of racial construction, serves as a shibboleth of black performance, authorizing certain stereotypes (the black man acting as violent criminal) and making certain realities undecipherable (the black male experiencing pain).

LITERARY REPRESENTATIONS OF THE SOUND OF LYNCHING

The lynching narrative not only qualifies as a significant national narrative, but it also occupies a specific space in American drama. In the introduction to *Black Female Playwrights: An Anthology of Plays before 1950*, Kathy Perkins explains the proliferation of lynching in America up until the 1930s. She states, "an estimated 3,589 blacks, including 76 women, were lynched between 1882 and 1927." Citing John Hope Franklin, she continues, "'In the very first year of the new century more than 100 Negroes were lynched, and before the outbreak of World War I the number for the century had soared to more than 1,100.'"[33] Perkins takes note of Georgia Douglas Johnson's *A Sunday Morning in the South* (1925), *Safe* (1929) and *Blue-Eyed Black Boy* (1930) as well as Regina Andrews' *Climbing Jacob's Ladder* (1931) as distinguished plays by black women about lynching. The black female playwrights of the 1920s locate the domestic sphere as the primary site of loss in their lynching drama. Instead of focusing on the death, they consider the cultural logic that requires black death.[34] Meanwhile, black male playwrights were also interested in this peculiar form of American discipline. W.E.B. Du Bois' *The Star of Ethiopia* and Langston Hughes' *Mulatto* (1935) also qualify as lynching narratives. In both of these texts the lynching scene establishes the power of the white community while it simultaneously instantiates the human sacrifice of black people as central to the development of communities.

What distinguishes Baldwin's play from Du Bois' pageant, which also features an afterlife for its main character, or Hughes' *Mulatto*, which features a complicated outspoken male protagonist, is the way the formal attributes of the play introduce a "multidirectional flow of time" that allows "free will and historical fatalism to coexist."[35] Similarly to the critiques hurled at Hughes' innovative use of form in *Tambourines to Glory*, Baldwin's unconventional play received vehement critiques from Robert Brustein in *The New Republic* (more recently known for his public debate with August Wilson over multiculturalism) and Philip Roth in the *New York Review of Books*. Brustein charged, "*Blues for Mr. Charlie*, certainly, is the embodiment of everything [Baldwin] once professed to deplore, being 'notoriously bloodthirsty' propaganda of the crudest sort, with little existence either as truth, literature, or life ... No doubt,

Baldwin's material is partly to blame. Any work inspired by the Emmett Till case is almost automatically destined to be melodrama."[36] Disparagingly labeling the play melodramatic by aligning it with the death of Till, Brustein fails to account for the very history that he names. In historicizing the sequence of events that led to him writing the play, Baldwin reproduced the melodrama that is race in the US in the midst of complicated and contradictory characters. He arranged his stage in halves and situated Richard's grave and the final site of communion in the center, in the break. The historical materialism Baldwin cultivates in the play feeds off the stereotypical melodrama Brustein abhors, while it disrupts the pleasure of melodrama by offering contested communion instead of easy reconciliation at the end of the play. As unpleasurable as the reality check enacted in Till's funeral, Baldwin's play disrupts the formal conventions of melodrama, assigning neither guilt nor blame to any single figure or group; he asks his audience to discover "the material reality of what is not," the embodied consolidation of race.[37] Brustein misnames his frustration with Baldwin and his dissatisfaction with Baldwin's noncommercial theater.

While Baldwin had gained national prominence for his novels and essays, his dramatic form raised the ire of critics. In his transition to Broadway, he attempted to claim the theater as a space of redress that could not be found in the courtroom or in the church. By 1964 the crushing blows of the death of Evers and the Sixteenth Street church bombing, just weeks after the March on Washington, required a change in tactic. *Blues for Mister Charlie* registers that shift with the imagery of a gun in the pulpit. And even though Baldwin felt the segregation of the church served as a fundamental flaw that limited its social power, he did not lose faith in the power of communion. His abiding faith in the power of collectivity motivated him to integrate Broadway by lowering ticket prices to a maximum of $4.80: the "top price is the lowest on Broadway for a show." In addition, he used "his West End avenue apartment as headquarters" recruiting friends to call people and encourage them to see the show.[38]

Blues for Mister Charlie challenges audience members to cross the aisle by intervening in a highly visual tradition. The visual dynamics of the tradition work to systematically silence the victim of the lynch mob, which the play counters by giving voice to Richard, the victim of a lynching, after his death. The play further transforms the lynching narrative by drawing from the blues as an idiom that distinguishes the function of Richard's voice. Ralph Ellison's defining description of the blues elucidates why it serves as a fitting medium for Baldwin to bring to light the structures, shrouded in darkness, that enable lynching. Ellison writes:

The blues is an impulse to keep the painful details and episodes of a brutal experience alive in one's aching consciousness, to finger its jagged grain, and to transcend it, not by the consolation of philosophy but by squeezing from it a near-tragic, near-comic lyricism. As a form, the blues is an autobiographical chronicle of personal catastrophe expressed lyrically.[39]

Baldwin's play emphasizes the interplay between the personal and the political, as it jerks the repressed sound of black suffering into consciousness. Through its structure, the play references the repeated sounds of lynching and reproduces the cadence of the blues tradition in a manner that reveals the sounds in all their mutations as acoustic regimes constituting and constituted by America. In this, Baldwin situates lynching victims as national sons that refuse the quiet the lynch mob imposes. The play begs its audience to finger the jagged grain – the painful, seeping tear – inflicted during the struggle for civil rights.

Contextualizing the psychic import of acoustic resistance embedded in African American literature, *Blues for Mister Charlie* demonstrates the insurgent possibilities of acoustic materiality. Prior to Baldwin's depiction of Richard's haunting voice, Jean Toomer described a different kind of acoustic excess enacted at the site of a lynching. "Blood-Burning Moon," one of the short stories in the first section of *Cane*, depicts a black man, Tom Burwell, who is lynched for fighting and killing a white man, Bob Stone, in a fight over a black woman, Louisa. As in *Blues for Mister Charlie*, in this story societal constraints challenge the black characters' ability to act. Thus, as expressed through changes in the form of the story, from prose to poetry, the characters must invent modes of expression, practices that exceed the limitations of the social narrative.

Throughout *Cane*, as Farah J. Griffin explains, the paradoxical relationship between black people and the state manifests itself in the imagery of nature's physical properties: "The title 'Blood-Burning Moon' is taken from the African-American religious tradition of sermons and spirituals where the image of the blood-colored moon serves as an omen for the crucifixion of Christ."[40] Griffin emphasizes the spiritual implications African Americans have attributed to their experiences in the US. Indeed, "Blood-Burning Moon" imagines African American history as messianic time. Griffin further clarifies, "Whereas here, in the first Southern section of the text, the moon is linked with the crucifixion of a black man, in the final Southern section it will signal the possible redemption of black people."⁴¹ "Blood-Burning Moon" also depicts the thematic relationship between the protagonists' physical properties and the racial politics of the South. The story describes Louisa as "the color of oak leaves on young trees in the fall."⁴² Aligning Louisa with the leaves of the tree, a characteristic image of the lynching scene, questions the agency she has in the drama that will unfold around her, while the description also places her as both central and at a critical distance from the root of the issue. Similarly, Tom's blood will be the sacrifice paid for his "impudent" challenge to Bob's authority and it will be fittingly offered at the site of a larger threat, in an abandoned factory, a symbolic representation of the economic costs of emancipation to the South. Instead of adding his blood to the red Georgia clay, Tom's blood participates in a different kind of nation-building. His blood is fittingly offered at the site of a factory, a symbol of the industrial revolution.

Following a psychic progression played out forty-one years later in *Blues for Mister Charlie*, "Blood-Burning Moon" highlights the dangerous need for totalizing perception that facilitates racial construction. The story begins with a depiction of Louisa's ambivalence over which one of her suitors she will respond to, white or black, Bob or Tom. Louisa's choice, however, is quickly revealed as the fiction that it is when Bob begins to ruminate over black women's newly established physical agency, especially since "his family still owned the niggers, practically."⁴³ The narration of the character's thoughts explains the implicit challenge that Louisa and Tom present. Louisa's newly found independence threatens Bob because it signals a larger social change taking place in the South. Her agency also evokes African Americans' ever-present spiritual and psychic self-possession, even during slavery. Moments later, after Bob has seemingly conquered the psychic threat that Louisa's agency posed to him and his concept of the nation by imagining the satisfaction he would get from raping her, he still wonders, "was there something about niggers that you couldn't know."⁴⁴ Bob's desire to know helps explain the drive to create racial fictions as a supplement for the inaccessible knowledge of another. Even though the singing that Bob hears and finds confusing prevents him from "knowing" the black people in the factory town, it does not prevent their physical domination.

Through the spilling of Tom's blood and the representation of the sound of lynching, the story instantiates the physical contribution black people have made to the US's history and landscape. After fighting with Bob and eventually cutting his throat, Tom is apprehended, bound, and dragged to the factory. "The big man shoved him [Tom] through the door. The mob pressed in from the sides. Taunt humming. No words.

A stake was sunk into the ground. Rotting floor boards piled around it. Kerosene poured on the rotting floor boards. Tom bound to the stake." Tom is depicted as quiet: "his eyes were set and stony. Except for irregular breathing, one would have thought him already dead."[45] In African American literature the lynching victim is often depicted as quiet if not silent in the face of demise. Writers portray black people performing with dignity in death to counter the dehumanizing stereotypes ascribed to African Americans and used to justify lynching. In "Blood-Burning Moon," after "a great flare muffled in black smoke shot upward," the only sound heard is the mob yelling. "Its yell echoed against the skeleton stone walls and sounded like a hundred yells. Like a hundred mobs yelling. Its yell thudded against the thick front wall and fell back. Ghost of a yell slipped through the flames and out the great door of the factory."[46] Although the "Ghost of a yell" comes from the lynch mob, it reveals part of the acoustic legacy echoed in Richard's haunting voice, which is also filled with Till's "infamous" whistle. The "Ghost of a yell" draws attention to the lack of any other sound. "Blood-Burning Moon" emits an acoustic silence that mirrors the narrative silences made present through representations of lynching victims.

Moten extends theorization of the thick acoustic history of lynching, saying "you need to be interested in the complex, dissonant, polyphonic affectivity of the ghost, the agency of the fixed but multiply apparent shade, an improvisation of spectrality, another development of the negative."[47] Moten implies that ghosts always have a sound that must be attended to, a sound that can be read back alongside the visual to enrich and explain it. The sound, however, is complex and dissonant because it calls on historical narratives some US citizens would rather forget. As a result, those sounds manifest themselves as the "polyphonic affectivity of the ghost"; sounds that signal the return of the repressed, the history of mo'nin'. Recalling the famous photo of Emmett Till's corpse displayed on the cover of *Jet* magazine, Moten argues that the photo had an acoustic materiality: "to publish the photograph" was "to restage death and rehearse mo(ur)nin(g)."[48] Moten's language, calling the photography a *re*-staging of death, indicates viewers had seen this kind of death produced under different circumstances. Furthermore, his contention that the photography "rehearse[d] mo(ur)nin(g)" implies its inability to fully actualize the process of grieving, and instead it functions as a mechanism to prepare for that actuality. The temporality Moten's choice of words implies places the mo(ur)nin(g) of Till in a melancholic frame. Assuming that a rehearsal proceeds a staging and that funerals function as the site in which the mourning process begins, Moten's description of the photograph, which appeared on the cover of *Jet* after Till's funeral, implies a yet unfulfilled anxious anticipation of the relief felt by letting go of the lost object. As explained in Chapter 3, melancholia or mourning without end aptly describes the process of black suffering. Yet the haunting "polyphonic affectivity" of the photograph creates a strategy for working through Till's loss and the national legacy it implies. Moten goes on to explain, "Something is remembered and repeated in such complications. Transferred. To move or work through that something, to improvise, requires thinking about morning and how mourning sounds, how moaning sounds. What's made and destroyed."[49] The moaning evoked by mourning Till transforms the polyphony that the lynch mob activity produces. Yet the two do not function in isolation. A more productive formulation would emerge by considering how the sound of the lynch mob, the transgressive whistle, mourning sounds, and moaning sounds collectively inform the sounds of lynching. Such a formulation would attend to the intertwining of grief and pleasure heard in and through mo(ur)nin(g). The painful erotic pleasure central to the process is a clue to deciphering a similar force at work in the practice of lynching.

Blues for Mister Charlie, also structured through the acoustic interruption, the interruption of Richard's voice, extends the representation of the sounds of lynching by calling on another acoustic history. And as may be inferred from the title of the play, the blues idiom inflects Richard's voice, which allows it to recall the horror of lynching while critiquing the social structures which encourage the practice. The title of the play participates in the dual signification process characteristic of the blues, ironic in its mocking of the loss of Mr. Charlie, the mythical overseer and boss character, and foreboding in its promise to explain the process of that loss. *Blues for Mister Charlie* uses three distinct aspects that I identify as part of the blues idiom. Recognizing the blues as (1) an inherently US form, (2) a form that is marked by its investment in personal expression, and (3) a form that makes political interventions through its commentary on sexuality and love, *Blues for Mister Charlie* makes a literary intervention through the blues idiom.

The blues provides an acoustic history that informs what Richard's voice reveals to the characters in the play about themselves and about the United States. The blues, originating at the crossroads of African and American music, incorporates the inherent dichotomy between African Americans and the concept of nation. In "African Slaves/American Slaves: Their Music" Amiri Baraka writes that blues is "the product of the black man in this country; or to put it more exactly the way I have come to think about it, blues could not exist if the African captives had not become American captives."[50] Baraka limits his analysis to a specific gendered identity. Nevertheless, he distinguishes the initiating societal pressures that ushered in the blues by noting that the trans-Atlantic slave trade resulted in the genre. He also makes clear the consistent restrictions black Americans as both African and American captives experience. The blues, as songs of the American captives, demand a certain performance of Richard's voice.

By invoking the blues, the play also demonstrates how the personal informs the social. Lynching signifies terror and panic. In order to move beyond the terror, Baldwin's play attempts to disarm the public display. The blues, as Cheryl Wall argues in *Worrying the Line: Black Women Writers, Lineage, and Literary Tradition,* "offer a way of contextualizing the 'private story.'" She goes on, quoting Baraka:

In the musical tradition, the persona of the individual performer dominates the song, which centers on the singer's own feelings, experiences, fears, dreams, acquaintances, and idiosyncrasies. As Amiri Baraka (then LeRoi Jones) argued in *Blues People,* "[E]ven though its birth and growth seems connected finally to the general movement of the mass of black Americans into the central culture of the country [during and after Reconstruction], blues still went back for its impetus and emotional meaning to the individual, to his completely personal life and death."[51]

Richard haunts deeply personal scenes in the play, and, as Baraka indicates, the scenes derive their "emotional meaning" from the individual. The scenes focus on how Richard's haunting informs the individual's self-perception. The acoustic is not inherently more private than the visual, but the specific idiom – the blues idiom – that the play deploys lends itself to the personal. *Blues for Mister Charlie* does not turn to *the* acoustic, but echoes *an* acoustic legacy, the cry of many thousands gone, the "Ghost of a yell" emanating from the mob, and the whistle of Emmett Till, through a personal (African) American form.

REMEMBERING RICHARD

The blues song, in *Blues for Mister Charlie,* mourns the inability of Parnell James, a white lawyer whose class privilege allows him to serve as the mediator between the white and black communities, to acknowledge his social privilege. In the trial of Lyle Britten for the murder of Richard

Henry, Parnell is called to testify for the prosecution. Parnell has information that could confirm Lyle's guilt. But he decides to withhold that information from the court. As a result, Richard's story never becomes part of the public record. Nonetheless, through a flashback that interrupts his testimony, Parnell realizes how Richard's death secures his performance of white American masculinity. Even though Lyle denies killing Richard, he offers a justification for Richard's death; while on the stand, Lyle claims that Richard assaulted his wife. When the state questions Parnell about the same encounter, he recalls, "I – I knew of a fight. It was understood that the boy had gone to Mr. Britten's store looking for a fight. I – I cannot explain *that*, either" (113). When the prosecution challenges Parnell to offer more specific details concerning the fight, he justifies himself: "We were all very much upset. Perhaps he was not as coherent as he might have been – perhaps I failed to listen closely. It was my assumption that Mrs. Britten had misconstrued the boy's actions – he had been in the North a long time, his manner was very free and bold" (113). Parnell presents the discrepancy between his testimony and Lyle's as a lapse in memory.

Immediately before Parnell takes the stand, the play flashes back to him in his bedroom, contemplating his sexual desires for black women. In order for Parnell to negotiate his anxiety over Richard's death, he has to regress to a personal, sexualized space. He thinks:

Richard would say that you've got – black fever! Yeah, and he'd be wrong – that long, loud, black mother. I wonder if she's asleep yet – or just lying there, looking at the walls. Poor girl! All your life you've been made sick, stunned, dizzy, oh Lord! driven half mad by blackness. Blackness in front of your eyes. Boys and girls, men and women – you've bowed down in front of them all! And then you hated yourself. Hated yourself for debasing yourself? Out with it Parnell! The nigger-lover! . . . Jesus! I've always been afraid. Afraid of what I saw in their eyes? They don't love me, certainly. You don't love them, either! Sick with a disease only white men catch. Blackness. What is it like to be black? To look out on the world from *that* place? I give nothing! How dare she say that! My girl, if you knew what I've given! Ah. Come off it, Parnell. To *whom* have you given? What name did I call? What name did I call? (106)

Parnell's disjointed flashback, marked by the incursion of echoes of Richard's voice, exposes the motivations for his testimony. He does not commit perjury to protect Lyle. Instead, Parnell lies to protect himself, to halt the revelation Richard's probing voice produces. Parnell fears what admitting Richard's innocence reveals about him. If Richard were innocent then Parnell would have to confront his limitations and insufficiencies.

Parnell's anger with Richard, "that long, loud, black mother," is a manifestation of the challenge Richard poses to the way Parnell sees himself.

The choices made in staging the Broadway premier of *Blues for Mister Charlie* heightened the impact of Parnell's confessional soliloquy. The April 1964 ANTA Theater production of the play used no scenery.[52] The production depended on the effects of lighting to communicate the shifts in time and space. Both white and black characters occupy the stage at the same time; however, when the black characters present their stories they move downstage while white characters move upstage, and similarly the white characters move to the front during their scenes.[53] Placing individuals from one community in the shadows, with those of the other illuminated but occupying the stage at the same time, the production of the play, like *Color Struck*, creates a spatial dynamic that complements the psychic history it presents. The representation of the segregated society through the splitting of the stage creates a seeming dichotomy that the mutually constitutive nature of blacktown and whitetown troubles. In different parts of the stage there is an incursion of sound from one community to the other. Furthermore, by not having scenery the ANTA production emphasizes the temporal incongruity of the play, its taking place in and out of time, and facilitates the structuring of the play through flashbacks.

The flashbacks staged in *Blues for Mister Charlie* elaborate on the cutting that Freud describes. Freud depicts the male subject deploying strategies he developed to counter the threat of castration in moments when he feels threatened. In *Blues for Mister Charlie*, characters register a threat in the moments before the flashbacks. As a part of the play's structural apparatus, the flashbacks expose why the character feels threatened and what the character thinks he or she might be losing. While the victims of lynching were often castrated, the idea of castration serves as a symbolic threat to both men and women. To highlight the common threat of cutting, across gender lines, is not to undermine the physical brutality experienced by lynching victims, but instead to point to a concurrent history of violence. The flashbacks as interruptions or cuts draw attention to the cultural histories that exemplify the process of castration.

Silverman qualifies the acoustic realm as a suitable space to historicize the anatomical loss Freud describes as the castration crisis. She depicts the auditory as one of the spheres, if not the most important one, in which the child, either male or female, learns to distinguish between self and other – between his or her own vocal self and the mother's voice. In the moment of distinction the mother's voice becomes excess. The child's realization that the voice is not a part of the self, the realization that the child cannot contain the voice, is both traumatic and necessary. Nevertheless, the child creates strategies to manage the loss of the mother's voice. Freud attempts to present the castration crisis as an initial splitting, as the male child's first introduction to the potential of loss. Silverman counters Freud, arguing "there is a castration which precedes the recognition of anatomical difference – a castration to which all cultural subjects must submit, since it coincides with separation from the world of objects, and the entry into language."[54] Silverman locates the threat of castration, the threat of losing part of the self, as not gender specific but a common bill that all individuals must pay to enter into language. Silverman explains, "According to the terms of Freud's own argument, if the spectacle of female castration strikes the male viewer as 'uncanny,' he himself must already have experienced castration ... he too inhabits the frame of the unpleasurable image."[55] When the male child realizes his anatomical difference, he is already in pursuit of the phallus, which is "a signifier for symbolic knowledge, power and privilege."[56] Parnell and Lyle's power depends not only on their sex but also their gender, within the social and political landscape of the United States. Therefore, every mechanism the male formulates to defend against the threat of castration, directed toward the object, the white female, will always fall short, since "what seems to confront him from without, in the guise of the 'mutilated' female body, actually threatens him from within, in the form of his own history."[57]

By feigning amnesia on the witness stand and, consequently, denying Richard's innocence and Lyle's guilt, Parnell masks his inadequacies, which he fetishizes as blackness. In "Fetishism," Freud says, "the fetish is a substitute for the woman's (the mother's) penis that the little boy believed in and – for reasons familiar to us – does not want to give up."[58] The little boy Freud describes creates a fetish, or a penis, at the site of the mother's body to protect against the threat of castration. *Blues for Mister Charlie* complicates Freud's formulation by presenting how creating a fetish always also inscribes race. Eng contends, "racial fantasies facilitate our investment in sexual fantasies and vice versa. As such, they must be understood as mutually constitutive, as drawing their discursive legibility and social power in relation to one another."[59] *Blues for Mister Charlie* demonstrates how, in the same way that the boy acts to secure his ego against the threat of the mother's "lack," fetishism can function racially to secure "a grown man" who experiences "a similar panic when the cry goes up that Throne and Altar are in danger, and similar illogical consequences will ensue."[60] Nevertheless, for lynching, as Harvey Young clarifies, the fetish's "power is both contained within and emerges from materiality."[61] The play serves to undermine the brutal pull and seeming stasis of the lynching victim's remains and the fetish object they have historically become by rendering Richard's material body ghostly.

To defend against the difference that the male subject sees at the site of the female's body, he creates a fetish. The fetish also serves to interrupt the fear that he will become her. In *Racial Castration* Eng further delineates the racial dimension of the castration crisis. In a reading of David Henry Hwang's *M. Butterfly*, Eng analyzes the "logic" of fetishism for the Asian American male body: "Hwang's drama resists, reverses, and ultimately revises Freud's traditional paradigm by opening it upon a social terrain marked not by singular difference but by multiple differences."[62] Highlighting the intersecting identifications implicit in all human existence, Eng clarifies how Freud's paradigms create hierarchies within subject positions. He continues: "rather than seeing at the site of the female body a penis that is not there to see, Gallimard refuses to see at the site of the Asian male body a penis that *is* there to see ... The white diplomat's 'racial castration' of Song thus suggests that the trauma being negotiated in this particular scenario is not just sexual but racial difference."[63] The history of racial mythology surrounding Asian and African American male bodies differs significantly. Eng's analysis of Hwang's drama, however, establishes a protocol for reading the function of the fetish in *Blues for Mister Charlie*. In Baldwin's play, similar to Hwang's, the threat is not the site of a penis not there to see, but instead a penis that *is* there to see: blackness is the fetish created to manage the black male's imagined anatomical "excess." In the history of lynching, blackness comes to signify a physical threat. The visual display associated with lynching, therefore, demonstrates the management of that threat. Parnell imagines Richard to be hypersexual in order to negotiate the lack he associates with himself. Richard's hypervirility threatens Parnell as it secures him and justifies Lyle's actions. In a dream world, Parnell can admit he is "Sick with a disease only white men catch" (106). Making such an admission in court would tear at the very fabric of his being. Therefore, in the courtroom he must project onto Richard insufficiencies that counterbalance the fear Richard's manner produces, a manner that "was very free and bold," a manner that justified his death.

Blues for Mister Charlie perpetually intertwines Richard's sexuality with his identification as a black man. Richard's hypervirility mirrors the excess attributed to blackness and the excessive materiality of the voice, the other that the child cannot incorporate, and therefore, in defense, eventually repudiates. Silverman contends that "the male subject later hears the maternal voice through himself – that it comes to resonate for him with all that he transcends through language … the male subject subsequently 'refines' his 'own' voice by projecting onto the mother's voice all that is unassimilable to the paternal position."[64] The play depicts the loss of Richard as incomplete by flashing back to him throughout. Parnell attempts to refine his own voice by projecting onto Richard all that is unassimilable to his position. Yet Richard's voice and the words he speaks remain a haunting trace that interrupts the narrative structure of the play. The process of haunting is connected to what Moten calls the "resurrection of reconstruction."[65] Moten contends that the Civil Rights Movement attempted to redress some of the failures of Reconstruction and, as a result, resurrected the haunting legacy of slavery. Richard's return creates an uncanny fear in the residents, both black and white, of his hometown and occurs as his peers mount Civil Rights demonstrations. Seeing Richard's death within the expanded historical frame created by Moten's assertion calls attention to the scope of unfinished historical business made material in one death and filling a tradition of sounds.

One of the final scenes of the play establishes the haunting quality of Richard's voice and presents the social and cultural paradigms that his bold performance of black masculinity challenges. The play explains not only why Richard must die, but also why his death "marks panic" – not the emergence of panic, especially since "panic had already led to the death of so many," but a genuine sense of frantic urgency nonetheless.[66] This scene, remembered after Richard's death, continues to haunt Lyle. Even after Lyle has murdered Richard, he must continually relive the death scene to secure his ego. Richard questions his murderer:

Why have you spent so much time trying to kill me? Why are you always trying to cut off *my* cock? You worried about it? Why? (*Lyle shoots again.*) Okay. Okay. Okay. Keep your old lady home, you hear? Don't let her near no nigger. She might get to like it. You might get to like it, too. Wow! (*Richard falls.*) (120)

Richard's final spoken lines, in the play and in the chronology of his life, illuminate the investments Lyle has made to secure his ego. While Richard can only physically die once, he asks the question, "Why have you spent so much time trying to kill me?" The temporal incongruity Richard expresses signals the perpetual threat he represents as black masculinity embodied. He continues, "Why are you always trying to cut off *my* cock?" His second question points to the threat of castration: it highlights the way psychic and physical forms of castration collapse at the intersection of a particular black male body to guard against the intrepid performance of black masculinity that Richard enacts and the subversive histories he echoes. Even though a distinction exists between the bodily penis and the symbolic phallus, "access to the phallus is still predicated upon possession of the penis."[67] Therefore when Richard says, "Okay. Okay. Okay. Keep your old lady home, you hear? Don't let her near no nigger. She might get to like it. You might get to like it, too," he reveals to the audience the process of fetishization and the secret desire on the part of Lyle to possess blackness. When Lyle kills Richard (Figure 8) he does so to secure his position in the social order of the town. Richard, however, continues to haunt Lyle through his final spoken words, which draw attention to Lyle's inability to kill what really troubles him. Richard's haunting voice also serves as a metaphor for the relationship between foreclosed and national narratives.

Baldwin revisited the relationships among communal belonging, ritual-ized violence, and whiteness in his short story "Going to Meet the Man" (1965). The narrative depicts a white police officer named Jesse who struggles with temporary impotence. As Jesse lies in bed with his wife, he remembers two incidents of ritualized violence: the first from earlier that day when he brutally attacked and nearly beat to death a Civil Rights leader; and the second from his childhood when he witnessed the lynching of a black man named Roger Whitlow. Similarly to *Blues for Mister Charlie*, flashbacks structure "Going to Meet the Man" and serve as explanation for the inadequacies of the white male protagonist. While the lynching scene in Baldwin's play seems to recall a past now gone, "Going to Meet the Man" situates the history of lynching as a personal racial and sexual primal scene that enables the protagonist to brutally beat another man. His memory validates his action and causes anxiety that constricts his ability to have sex with his wife since his desire is tied to sadistic rituals of racial hate "by means of which he and other participants [in the lynching] released themselves in a communal orgasm."[68] By remember-ing an event in which racial violence served to feed communal desire and fostered collectivity, Jesse reconciles his conscience to his brutal act against a defenseless black man in police custody and copulates with his wife as he tells her "Come on, sugar, I'm going to do you like a nigger, just like a nigger, come on, sugar, and love me just like you'd love a nigger."[69]

Jesse's act of violence allows him to express uninhibited desire after he psychically and linguistically projects deviance onto an imagined black figure whose role he assumes, directing his wife to play along, and the real life body of the prisoner he brutally beats. The transfer of desire occurs

Figure 8 Actors Al Freeman and Rip Torn in *Blues for Mister Charlie* at the ANTA Theater, January 1, 1964, directed by Burgess Meredith

through the structure of Jesse's memory, which the story characterizes as sounds. Jesse entered the police station after the arrest of a number of Civil Rights activists. When he got to the jail, he recalls, "They were still singing and I was supposed to make them stop."[70] His strategy: to beat the ringleader into submission and then order him to order the rest of the singers to stop. But even if they had halted their verse, which they did not, no one could quiet the mo'nin' that echoes through his head. From the sound of "I stepped in the river at Jordan" that he heard driving home from Whitlow's lynching, to the sound of the scream he uttered when Whitlow looked him in the eye, to the "terrible sound, something between a high laugh and a howl" that he expresses before he copulates with his wife, a soundtrack of suffering "out of the darkness of the room, out of nowhere" finds him and comes "flying up at him, with the melody and the beat."[71] The soundings described in the story intertwine black suffering with a national suffering rendered invisible but still audible to those who refuse to see – a ghostly sound that breaks in on Jesse and forces him to contend with the long-lasting effects of his inauguration in a culture of brutality that gains power – sexual and social – through the suffering of black folk.

While Jesse's directive to his wife in the final scene of "Going to Meet the Man" links blackness to hypersexuality to satisfy the correlation he makes between racial brutality and sexual release, in the play Lyle attempts, by connecting black masculinity to hypermasculinity, to elicit a performance of humility, passivity, and compliance from Richard. Richard's taunting suggestion that "She might get to like it" acknowledges both Lyle's and Richard's investment in ascribing an elevated virility to Richard. Considering Richard's own failures as a musician, and his inability to cope with the demands of living in the North, his statement also implies his own need for Lyle to perceive him as a threat. Lyle and Richard's co-investment in imagining Richard as a virile sexual threat explains the homoerotic quality of Richard's final statement, "You might get to like it, too." The idea that Lyle and his old lady "might get to like it" explains why Lyle must symbolically always try to cut off Richard's penis. Lyle kills Richard to temporarily evade exploring the implications of the desire and pleasure he derives from not only disciplining Richard, but also from seeing Richard as a threat who needs discipline.

On the rare occasion that ideological means of discipline do not elicit the desired performance, physical action must ensue. Before Richard charges that Lyle has spent so much time trying to kill him, he asserts "You can't dance because you've got nobody to dance with – don't you know I've watched you all my life? *All my life!* And *I* know your women, don't think I don't – better than you!" (119). In this scene Richard tries to trump Lyle. He argues that he is not hypermasculine; he is just more of a "man" than Lyle. Their mutual practice of objectifying women supplements both Lyle's and Richard's masculinity. In the narrative Richard would die no matter how he responded to Lyle. As the narrative relates to the psychic relationship that *Blues for Mister Charlie* illuminates, however, Richard dies because there are no other terms for him to use in response to Lyle. And, chillingly, there are no other terms that Richard or Lyle would want Richard to use.

Unable to permanently quiet Richard's intrusive voice, Lyle recalls his final interaction with Richard after he has got away with murder. Richard's voice interrupts Lyle as he is leaving the courtroom. After a jury of his peers acquits him of murder, Lyle still cannot escape his personal inadequacy, which he categorizes as Richard's hypermasculinity. Lyle recalls this scene, musing, "Do you know what that nigger said to me?" (118). Richard's willingness to taunt Lyle even in the face of death disrupts Lyle's sense of power and inscribes an indelible mark on his psyche. Instead of securing his ego by killing Richard, Lyle liberates Richard's voice, causing its further incorporation, its permanent remembrance.

MEMORY AND HISTORY: IMAGINATIVE INNOVATIONS

Blues for Mister Charlie uses the imaginative process of rememory to satisfy the impulse to make use of histories, even traumatic and shameful histories. Toni Morrison coined the term "rememory" to describe the communal nature of recuperation: "First of all, I must trust my own recollections. I must also depend on the recollections of others. Thus memory weighs heavily in what I write, in how I begin and in what I find to be significant."[72] Situating herself within a literary tradition, Morrison quotes Zora Neale Hurston, who said, "Like the dead-seeming cold rocks, I have memories within that came out of the material that went to make me."[73] Explicating Hurston's statement, Morrison continues, "These 'memories within' are the subsoil of my work. But memories and recollections won't give me total access to the unwritten interior life of these people. Only the act of imagination can help me."[74] Both Morrison and Hurston refer to the organic quality of memory. They suggest that memory is palpable, that it exists in the material world, and that the past has a tangible existence in the present. While Hurston claims memory as constitutive – coming "out of the material that went to make" her – Morrison describes it as a necessary, fertile base. Establishing themselves as part of a tradition, the writers recognize how memory functions, and categorize their work as moving from that "site of memory" to the imaginative process of creating a narrative.

Morrison's or even Hurston's depictions of recuperation, of digging up the past, reflect an epistemic practice historical legacy necessitates. Douglass' *Narrative* and Harriet Jacobs' *Incidents in the Life of a Slave Girl* are two paradigmatic texts of the African American literary tradition that foreground the need to document and recoup individual and communal histories. The aesthetic and political goals of Hurston's, Baldwin's, and Morrison's work differ distinctly, however, from the writing of formerly enslaved African Americans, who were forbidden to read and write by law. While Hurston, Baldwin, and Morrison all see themselves as intervening in the historical narrative, they emphasize their work as necessary because it is imaginative.

Musing on his writings' relationship to history in a 1979 interview with Kalamu ya Salaam in which Baldwin looked back on the Civil Rights Movement, his position as a writer, and his role in American culture, he said, "The role of the writer *is* to write, but this is a cryptic statement. What I meant is that a writer doesn't dance. His function is very particular and so is his responsibility. After all, to write, if taken seriously, is to be subversive. To disturb the peace."[75] Baldwin's choice of language infers the historical disruption he hoped to cause. The very act of writing, when done correctly, creates detours from the planned trajectory. When Salaam questioned him about his responsibility as a writer in the United States, he specified, "it involves my concept of my responsibility to people coming after me and to people who came before me ... *To, in a sense, tell their story, so that others can understand from whence they came* ... Yes. I consider myself to be a witness."[76] The twofold enterprise of being a US writer seems paradoxical in that it entails causing historical and political breaks even as it necessitates building bridges between past and future generations. Nevertheless, as Baldwin seems to suggest, the disturbances may, in fact, guarantee a new way to respond to the people coming after and to the people who came before. As a writer Baldwin assumes ethical imperatives that reflect a sense of communal responsibility. Indeed, Baldwin transposes his identification as a witness onto the American public in his turn to drama. The act of witnessing informs Baldwin's generic choice and the formal qualities of *Blues for Mister Charlie*. Anticipating the premier of the play, Baldwin emphasized in an article for the *New York Times* that "I knew this had to be a play. I knew I had to tell this story in this form."[77] The act of witnessing implicates the viewer in the action of the scene. Therefore, the stage directions of the play, which create a gulf onstage, solicit the viewers to recognize how that gulf mimics the political experience they perpetuate in America. The stage directions coupled with Richard's haunting presence dramatize a feeling of vulnerability. In writing and staging *Blues for Mister Charlie*, Baldwin sought to bear witness to more than the tragic death of this individual young man; he sought "to bear witness to the reality and the power of light" (xv). That is to say, he hoped to inspire introspection by clarifying the dynamics that culminated in Richard's death through theatrical non-display, which he marshaled to secularize the power of the church in an effort to save those who had already been lost and those who might yet perish.

For Baldwin the act of remembering delineates possibilities in the present. He depicts the present as a working out of the past, as a return of the repressed. Baldwin wrote in "Many Thousand Gone" that "We cannot escape our origins, however hard we try, those origins which contain the key – could we but find it – to all that we later become."[78] Similarly, in *A Rap on Race* he explains, "If history were the past, history wouldn't matter. History is the present, the present. You and I are history."[79] The way Baldwin conceptualizes history allows him to reorient and transcend death, seeing it as not only loss, but also possibility. Correspondingly, the way Baldwin describes history informs his choice to organize *Blues for Mister Charlie* through the voice of a ghost. The play obstructs looking at Richard's dead body, but does not suggest that he loses his intelligibility. Throughout, Richard haunts Whitetown and Blacktown as a historical force made present. The play gives a material structure to the imaginative process through the flashbacks that call Richard to the stage. Often summoned by music, Richard haunts *Blues for Mister Charlie* to satisfy the psychic needs of the living characters. Whitetown and Blacktown need Richard, and if he were not there they would have to invent him.

For African Americans, the mode writers use to engage the past holds particular importance. Barbara Christian clarifies the specific function of remembering for African Americans: "that concept could not be at the center of a narrative's revisioning of history until the obvious fact that African-Americans did have a history and culture was firmly established in American society."[80] Christian pinpoints the relationship between value and historical tradition within literary studies by acknowledging how the legibility of a text depends on the reader's prior knowledge. She confronts the same model of subjectivity that compelled Du Bois to write black folk into history, as she points to the construction of all history as a judgment and a choice. Recognizing the constant presence of the past creates an opportunity to imagine possibilities for the spaces between the gaps of history, "which contain the key – could we but find it – to all that we later become."[81] In Baldwin's effort to imagine a landscape that had yielded the tragic death of Till and that would resist and eventually stall the efforts of the Civil Rights Movement, he bears witness to the submerged, the forgotten, and the repressed.

Blues for Mister Charlie does not suggest that Richard's death is anomalous but ties it to the uncanny quality of American narrative. As Richard's haunting voice reveals the personal motivations of many of the characters, his living body represents a necessary American fantasy. His particular version of masculinity corresponds to what Baldwin categorizes as the "American ideal." He contends, "The American *ideal*, then, of sexuality appears to be rooted in the American ideal of masculinity. This ideal has created cowboys and Indians, good guys and bad guys ... butch and faggot, black and white. It is an ideal so paralytically infantile that it is virtually forbidden – as an unpatriotic act – that the American boy evolves into the complexity of manhood."[82] Born from genocide and slavery, the "American ideal" disrupts bridging the chasm between Whitetown and Blacktown. Baldwin poses the "complexity of manhood" as a challenge to the binary oppositions listed as the result of the "American ideal." In order to evolve into the complexity of manhood, each American boy would have to negotiate his identity as a meeting ground of "punks and studs," for example, and not a repudiation of one or the other. Deemed unpatriotic, such an investigation would undermine the alleged distance between the two identities. Therefore, rejecting one identity – the Indian, the bad guys, the punks, the stud, the softies, the faggots, the white men – protects the other identity and the nation from erosion.

As the play unfolds, the implications of the tension between the established binary, white and black masculinity, grows. Throughout, Richard remains the character who continually draws attention to the tenuous yet powerful relationship among blackness, the phallus, and national identity. Nevertheless, Richard fails to ever completely realize how he facilitates that relationship. In a conversation with his friends Pete (Lincoln Kilpatrick) and Juanita (Diana Sands, who invented the role of Beneatha in the Broadway production of *A Raisin in the Sun*), Richard explains his romantic experiences in the North. He brags, "I got a whole *gang* of white chicks in New York. That's *right*. And they can't get enough of what little Richard's got – and I give it to them, too, baby, believe me" (25). As Richard boasts, he leverages his status as an object of desire to manipulate and punish white women. Enacting a purportedly subversive dynamic, he strikes back at the white world in the only way that he knows. Baldwin's play does not suggest that black men do not participate in displacing their insufficiencies onto women. Unfortunately, Richard learns too late how to live in the world instead of just respond to it. Through his verbal performance, Richard facilitates the structure – the duality embedded in the "American ideal" – that produces blackness as threatening.

Still, Richard acknowledges the psychic approximation to fullness he establishes through these unsatisfying relationships. In the same conversation, he remembers the loneliness and frustration he attempted to satisfy through sexual escapades. He recalls how, late at night after performing at a club for ungrateful patrons and demanding managers, "you'd make the scene and somehow you'd wake up in the morning and the chick would be beside you, alive and well … you'd manage not to strangle her … And you get out of there and you carry this pain around inside all day and all night long. No way to beat it – no *way*" (29). Although Richard never fully realizes how he participates in the social relationships he despises, his life becomes the currency to pay for the debt he incurs through this (mis)appropriation of power. Just as Parnell projects what is inassimilable to his position onto Richard, "that long, loud, black mother," Richard displaces his rage at the managers and the patrons in the clubs, who personify white privilege in general, onto "some pasty white-faced bitch" (29). Projection involves separating off a part of the self that the subject disdains and casting it out into the world. The thing Richard hates and sees in others fully materializes as a part of him in this verbal exchange. Ironically, while Richard knows he risks punishment for sleeping with white women, his life and death suggest that his performances of black masculinity, marked by bravado, have worked to partially attenuate the full impact of the cut.

Richard's strategy is not wholly unsuccessful because it recognizes the physical implications of the American ideal. In Lyle's trial, Richard's father Meridian Henry succinctly delineates a correlation between black masculinity and its representation as threat to the nation. He responds to the questions of Lyle Britten's lawyer, saying:

I tried to help my son become a man. But manhood is a dangerous pursuit, here. And that pursuit undid him because of *your* guns, *your* hoses, *your* dogs, *your* judges, *your* law-makers, *your* folly, *your* pride, *your* cruelty, *your* cowardice, *your* money, *your* chain gangs and *your* churches! Did you think it would endure forever? that we would pay for *your* ease forever? (103)

Meridian's speech characterizes Richard's search for expression – his verbal and physical performances – as a dangerous pursuit necessary to "pay for" the ease of Whitetown. As Meridian clarifies, in order to pay the price for the expensive acquisition of the American ideal Richard had to be undone. But the dangerous pursuit of manhood undoes both White-town and Blacktown. At times, the American ideal necessitates obscene displays of violence and, in certain instances, death.

Baldwin situates love as an affect necessary to reorient the lynching narrative and forestall the continuous sacrifice of black male bodies at the altar of the American ideal. But he circumscribes the utopian quality of love by highlighting the difficulty in loving anyone, especially across the racial divide. In the closing lines of "The Fire Next Time," Baldwin uses the metaphor of lovers to describe the type of commitment that would enable Americans to "end the racial nightmare, and achieve our country, and change the history of the world."[83] Baldwin demands that the coming together of white and black Americans across the racial gulf that divides the country be like that of lovers. Using the sexually charged language of romantic love, Baldwin points to the urgent need for intimacy among racial groups. Harkening back to Du Bois' signature formulation, Baldwin's insistence that "the relatively conscious whites and the relatively conscious blacks" must "end the racial nightmare" gestures toward a psychoanalytic theory of love. In *An Outline of Psycho-Analysis*, Freud explains that love requires the lover to sacrifice part of his or her ego, part of his or her self, in service of the beloved: "It is only when a person is completely in love that the main quota of libido is transferred onto the object and the object to some extent takes the place of the ego."[84] Ideally the exchange between lovers would be mutual. By describing the relationship that could predicate change in "our country" as "like lovers," Baldwin emphasizes the necessary sacrifice and risk needed to achieve "our country." Romantic love, love between lovers, is unlike any other form of love (the love between a mother and son, or sister and brother) because it demands an extraordinary amount of trust.

In a similar fashion, Baldwin ends act II of the play with a reconcili-atory gesture that demonstrates the type of trust and sacrifice necessary to create community. The flashback staged at the end of act II creates a break, a technical device developed in the blues. In a conversation between Parnell and Juanita, Richard's girlfriend (Parnell, Meridian,

Figure 9 Actress Diana Sands in *Blues for Mister Charlie* at the ANTA Theater, January 1, 1964, directed by Burgess Meredith

and Pete all express sexual interest in Juanita which the defense presents as Juanita's sexual excess in the trial scene; see Figure 9) responds to Parnell's questions about her relationship with Richard. She recalls:

No. That train has gone. One day, I'll recover. I'm sure that I'll recover. And I'll see the world again – the marvelous world. And I'll have learned from Richard – how to love. I must. I can't let him die for nothing. (*Jukebox music, loud. The lights change, spot on Parnell's face. Juanita steps across the aisle. Richard appears. They dance. Parnell watches.*) (78–80)

The flashback to Juanita dancing with Richard recalls an event that taught Juanita how to love. She explains that she must "recover" before she can see the world again. By juxtaposing the flashback with Juanita's explanation the play creates a pedagogical moment, emphasizing that modes of seeing are learned. In an effort to contextualize the backward-looking glance required to see the scene move forward, the play offers the structure of the break. A break – categorized in the blues as "a very special kind of ad-lib bridge passage or cadenzalike interlude between two musical phrases that are separated by an interruption or interval in the established cadence" – occurs so that Richard and Juanita can perform for Parnell.[85] The play's flashback appropriates the structure of the blues break. Richard and Juanita demonstrate the level of intimate contact that is necessary if Parnell is to intercede successfully between Whitetown and Blacktown.

The performance, ushered in by loud jukebox music, participates in what Angela Davis describes as another characteristic of the blues, which "linked it [love] inextricably with possibilities of social freedom."[86] Disruption (a dramatic cut) occurs to show Parnell how Juanita will be able to "see the world again." Music interrupts Juanita and Parnell's interaction, which inspires Juanita to step across the aisle – a structural form similar to the gulf we see in the opening scene of the play and the oceanic Middle Passage explored in the next chapter. The ending of *Blues for Mister Charlie* becomes a fait accompli if read outside of this exchange between Juanita and Parnell. The play does not allow Parnell and Juanita to have the intimate communion symbolized in the dance scene; nonetheless, it does allow room for understanding within more circumscribed boundaries. Baldwin's play ends by highlighting the difficulty of unity. The only way to forestall the vicious division in the courtroom in act III is by attending to the intimate dancing bodies at the end of act II.

Blues for Mister Charlie insists that the cure to the plague that sickens American culture is not to be found in the courtroom. The cure is to be found in an engagement of the abject, in attention paid to the notes off the scale. The play calls for intimate contact with ghostly pasts as an indispensable step to realizing our country. African American theater's engagement with the ghostly through a turn to the cut, modified by the blues break, is a theme I continue to examine in the next chapter. Similarly to Baldwin, Baraka and Wilson find that self-consciousness and American identity lend themselves to an imaginative exploration through, to quote Avery Gordon, "haunting rather than 'history' (or historicism)" because haunting "best captures the constellation of connections that charges any 'time of the now' with the debts of the past and the expense of the present." The nature of haunting requires "not a return to the past but a reckoning with its repression in the present, a reckoning with that which we have lost, but never had."[87] The haunting in *Blues for Mister Charlie* models one such mode to explicate what prevents the nation from dealing with its racial nightmare and to unlock the latent possibilities for what the nation could become.

CHAPTER 6

Rituals of repair

Amiri Baraka's Slave Ship
and August Wilson's Joe Turner's Come and Gone

> Some things you forget. Other things you never do ... Places, places
> are still there. If a house burns down, it's gone, but the place – the
> picture of it – stays, and not just in my rememory, but out there in
> the world.
>
> Toni Morrison, Beloved

August Wilson's *Joe Turner's Come and Gone* depicts Herald Loomis' search
for his song – his purpose in life. His quest, posited as a search for his
estranged wife Martha Pentecost, carries him to distant places and necessitates unexpected encounters. In act 1, Loomis describes the circumstances
that separated him from his wife, recalling how Joe Turner, "brother of
the Governor of the great sovereign state of Tennessee, swooped down,"
kidnapped him, and kept him for seven years.[1] Similarly to many tales of
existential crisis, Loomis' narrative features a traumatic event that creates a
detour from what he perceives as his predetermined path. Once released,
Loomis tries to locate his family but only finds his daughter, being cared
for by his mother-in-law. He resumes his position as caregiver and
continues to look for his wife, a search that draws him to Seth Holly's
boarding house in Pittsburgh, 1911. Through the constant turnover
endemic to a boarding house, the setting of the play incorporates mutability in the seemingly stable materiality of the stage set. The individuals
who reside in the house contribute to its material properties – the things
that make it a boarding house. Therefore, when the boarders change so
too do the material conditions of the setting of the play. The malleable
nature of the setting foregrounds the way the play as a whole will draw
into question some of the basic tenets of setting in realist drama.[2]

The setting also enables unlikely collaborations. As a resident in the
boarding house, Loomis meets the other central character of the play,
Bynum Walker, a man in his sixties who performs rituals and is known
throughout the community to be a conjurer. Loomis, whose tragic
upheaval by Joe Turner renders him agnostic, must collaborate with

Bynum and Martha in order to find his voice. Marked by Loomis' resistance throughout, their ritualistic collaborations create as much dissonance as harmony and may equally qualify as confrontations. Nevertheless, in this chapter I deploy the language of collaboration to distinguish reparative work as arduous. The ostensibly antithetical phrase "collaborative confrontations" further specifies the nature of repair staged in *Joe Turner's Come and Gone*. The play features conflicts whose resolutions require uneasy alliances. Bynum plays an important role in the first two collaborative confrontations that structure the play, while Martha incites the third. Collectively, the altercations allow Loomis to find what he categorizes as his "starting place in the world" (72).

As reflected in Loomis' figurative language, the play addresses psychic fortification through geographies. The site of each confrontation, either real or envisioned, figures prominently in Loomis' repair and serves to refocus the African American reparations movement, which too often is primarily associated with monetary compensation for the losses suffered due to trans-Atlantic slavery. As stated in the Overture, reparations or atonement can take many different forms, including the exchange of money or property, reinstatement of sovereignty or political authority, public acknowledgement of wrongdoing, and group entitlements. In order to establish the case for reparations for the descendants of Africans enslaved in the United States, many legal scholars point to the victories other injured groups in the United States and abroad have won and note the compensation small groups of African Americans have obtained. The US government has sponsored reparations through Indian settlements and the 1988 Civil Liberties Act. In the article "Moving toward Reparation," Ronald Roach recounts that, in the aftermath of World War II, Israel and the descendants of the Holocaust were granted compensation from West Germany and Swiss banks. Following the precedent of redress for other injured groups by the US federal government and governments and private businesses abroad, the Florida and Oklahoma state legislatures have also compensated small groups of African Americans for acts of violence. According to Ronald Roach, in 1994 the Florida legislature passed a bill granting payment to the victims and descendants of Rosewood, a black town destroyed by mob violence in 1923. The state of Oklahoma made amends to the descendants of the victims of the 1921 Tulsa race riots, "where about 300 Black people were killed and striving Black businesses were destroyed."[3] All of these cases establish a legal precedent for African American reparations. Randall Robison, Roach, and David Hall emphasize that the monetary compensation they advocate primarily serves as a mechanism that would enable educational and psychological benefits.

Focusing, once again, on a legal remedy that would demand the subject seeking repair receive redress from the injuring party, the most recent manifestation of African Americans' pursuit of reparations for slavery, according to Vincene Verdun's often-cited essay, "If the Shoe Fits, Wear It: An Analysis of Reparations to African Americans," began in 1989 following the passage of the Civil Liberties Act (1988), which granted $20,000 and an apology to the descendants of those who suffered in the Japanese American internment during World War II. That legal victory reinvigorated a movement that began during the Reconstruction era and, according to Verdun, has had four significant surges since the attempts to grant relief to emancipated slaves following the Civil War. Although for Verdun the emergence of the latest battle for African American reparations came in 1989, in an interview with Ronald Roach for *Black Issues in Higher Education*, Randall Robison, the author of *The Debt: What America Owes to Blacks*, concedes the backlash against affirmative action in the 1990s also contributed to the latest movement for African American reparations.

All of the legal remedies seeking reparations reinforce the static notion of nation states and implicitly facilitate the very nationalism that fostered slavery. The burdens of nationalism – i.e., patriarchal structures, purport-edly bounded geographies, and racial hierarchies – limit legal modes of redress. Nevertheless, in "Black Liberation/Socialist Revolution" (1984), Amiri Baraka, a prominent figure in the Black Arts Movement[4] and an artist whom Wilson has claimed as a key influence,[5] argues that the development of a black sovereign nation would serve as a method of reparation.[6] Although Baraka ties self-determination firmly to the materiality of nationalism and the geographic specificity of the black belt in "Black Liberation/Socialist Revolution," nationalism functions as one approach in a spectrum of methodologies leading to self-determination. Baraka consistently uses the term self-determination to communicate an active resistance to alienation – seeing the world through "somebody else's and not our own" eyes in a Du Boisian sense of double consciousness[7] – and an investment in the continuous pursuit of democracy.[8] Baraka has offered several different models of how self-determination may be accomplished in political, economic, and aesthetic realms, including through the development of a nation in the black belt region of the US. While the practices that lead to self-determination change, the condition remains the same. The fluid, and I would argue therefore redemptive, nature of self-determination renders it useful as a theoretical concept even as it suffers under the weight of prior associations, particularly nationalism.

Baraka has acknowledged the way his investment in Black Nationalism limits his larger philosophical claims; limitations one could also identify in *Joe Turner's Come and Gone*. In the revised introduction to *Black Fire*, one of the most important anthologies of the Black Arts Movement, Baraka recalls the collapse of the Black Arts Repertory Theater (BART), a model of political and aesthetic activism because it demonstrated how to cultivate a black cultural-nationalist institution. BART served as another Black Nationalist model of how to cultivate self-determination. "The Black Arts Repertory Theater School self- (and FBI) destructed because 'Black' is not an ideology and so the unity gained under that finally nationalist but reductionist label, though it was an attempt to locate & raise the National Consciousness, could not hold."⁹ Baraka notes the limitations of the term "black" as a rubric for coalition-building; such limitations do not prevent Wilson from entitling his well-known Theatre Communications Group speech "The Ground on Which I Stand" (1996). "Wilson's discussion of land, the ground on which he stands, is both material and figurative. The land he wants to claim for black theatrical production is a geographic as well as a symbolic space within the American theater system," according to Harry J. Elam, Jr.¹⁰ In his speech Wilson offers a model of cultural nationalism which situates race as "the product of a shared gene pool that allows for group identification, and it is an organizing principle around which cultures are formed. When I say culture I am speaking about the behavior patterns, the arts, beliefs, institutions and all other products of human work and thought as expressed by a particular community of people."¹¹ Wilson's assertion that race serves as the "organizing principle around which cultures are formed" places him in a slippery position that at least four decades of black feminist thought has sought to address. Black feminists have pointed out, for example, that while a first-generation working-class Jamaican American living in New York City and a sixth-generation affluent African American living in South Carolina might both identify as black, the Jamaican American may have more in common in terms of behavior patterns, arts, beliefs, and institutions with a first-generation working-class Anglo-Latina living in New York City than the aforementioned African American. Wilson makes a murky assertion, prioritizing race as the primary cultural signifier in the late twentieth century. Moreover, Wilson's choice to evidence his claim by citing race as the "most identifiable ... part of our personality" and "category of identification" emphasizes a visual dynamic that, according to him, supersedes other modes of identification. My goal is not to retread this well-beaten path; instead it is to identify self-determination as a redeemable concept that emerges in *Joe Turner's Come and Gone* and Baraka's pageant, *Slave Ship* (1969), even though the concept cannot be disentangled from its relationship to Black Nationalism.

Baraka (then LeRoi Jones) characterizes self-determination using Malcolm X as a model. Baraka figures Malcolm X as the archetype of self-determination, focusing attention on how the assassination of President John F. Kennedy, Jr. (1963) helped to bolster the political force of Malcolm X's rhetoric. Baraka argues that Kennedy's assassination "is the context for the confirmation of Malcolm's call for Black political Self Determination [and] corresponds to Black perception that Kennedy's murder removes the 'helping hand' of White liberalism for Black people, forcing them to go it alone!"[12] In Baraka's depiction of the months leading up to Malcolm X's assassination, Malcolm X emerges as a leader in a collective anti-imperialist movement. Yet *The Autobiography of Malcolm X* depicts enlightenment notions of self-transformation that centralize the ability of the individual to marshal his will and transcend the limitations that encumber him, according to María Josephina Saldaña-Portillo.[13] Moreover, although Baraka notes that Malcolm X develops a democratic – including "Muslims, Christians, Nationalists and Socialists" – vision of self-determination at the end of his life, by focusing on Malcolm X as a figure leading a movement Baraka reifies patriarchal power structures that require an assumption of male leadership and individual transcendence.[14]

Unlike Black Nationalism, which one cannot separate from the bounded, geographically specific, patriarchally inflected, nation state model of political organization, Wilson's play and Baraka's pageant locate mutable sites as central to self-determination and ultimately to the reparative process. Wilson's play and Baraka's pageant recall negotiations of space central to this book. The playwrights herein, as demonstrated in *The America Play* and *A Raisin in the Sun*, locate the promise of space in its constitution through repetition/reproduction and not in the opposition of place and movement. For example, in the 1969 Chelsea Theater production of *Slave Ship*, the director Robert Moses and set designer Eugene Lee transformed the theatrical space into a slave ship that travels through the Middle Passage. The Middle Passage in Baraka's and Wilson's theater resists the belated dichotomy of oppression and resistance. The introduction to *Black Imagination and the Middle Passage* clarifies how a philosophy of history emerges in relation to political configurations situated outside the oppression/resistance dichotomy. According to Maria Diedrich, Henry Louis Gates, Jr., and Carl Pedersen, their volume is "defined by what Homi Bhabha calls the space in-between, rejecting the stringent opposition between above and below, between civilized and savage, that informs discourses of slavery's defenders and its opponents."[15] Most simply, the Middle Passage is the name given to the second leg of the triangulated route ships took exchanging goods for enslaved Africans. Ships departed from Europe with goods to be traded for captives in Africa who would then be traded for goods in the Americas. Although the Middle Passage corresponds to a specific route, it also reflects the commodification of African captives into slaves and the acts of resistance enslaved Africans carried out to defend themselves against becoming goods. The editors of *Black Imagination and the Middle Passage* launch their critique from a physical location – the space in-between – that enables multiplicity. I adopt the philosophy that underpins their language for an additional reason. I also categorize it as one that emerges in the aftermath of utopian formulations of community built on consensus, and understand the space in-between as an oscillating position constantly in motion.

The Black Arts Movement artists faced haunting yet enabling recollections of the collaborative failures of the Civil Rights Movement. For example, elsewhere I examine the events that led to Baraka and others learning of Martin Luther King, Jr.'s death, as depicted in Ed Bullins' introduction to the 1968 black drama issue of *TDR/The Drama Review*. King's death functions as an event in a series of events that marked the transition from Civil Rights to Black Arts Movement modes of artistic production.

The piece ends with a foreboding remark, which underscores the consuming chaos that produces the matter-of-fact tone: 'Someone I knew stopped me and said that there were riots started in Harlem. I thanked him, silently hoping that our new theatre building had been missed by fire this time, and began walking fast toward 14th. The warm rain began falling, and I hailed a cab.' Bullins' comment recalls James Baldwin's essay *The Fire Next Time* (1963), which warns that if Americans do not take action, the country's racial nightmare will end in apocalypse. The fires this time, erupting across the country following King's death, had been burning since 1964. Bullins' allusion establishes the precarious balancing act that these artists attempted to hold, situating revolutionary change between bourgeois individualism and despair. Bullins' ambiguity provides a complicated answer to the question of why the black aestheticians would forge ahead in light of their limitations. They continued on in the hope that the fire had missed them *this time*.[16]

The pre-sentimental ambivalence that informs Bullins' comment resounds in a conversation Toni Morrison depicts in *Beloved* (1988) between Denver and her deceased grandmother, Baby Suggs. Denver recalls her grandmother warning "there was no defense" against white folks. She questions "then what do I do?" And Baby Suggs responds, "Know it, and go on out the yard. Go on." In *Beloved*, the space within the yard purportedly offers more safety from the often violent incursion of whiteness than the space beyond it. Nevertheless, in order to survive she must go on out the yard and save herself.

The artists of the Black Arts Movement, fully aware of their inability to defend themselves completely against the alienating affects of racism and to form sturdy coalitions based on the limiting term "blackness," practiced self-repair. The forms of repair they devised address the immediate social and physical deaths that correspond to the failures and losses of the Civil Rights Movement and to the more belated history of loss associated with trans-Atlantic slavery. While all theater sets require audiences to imagine an absent geographical presence, a place that may only appear before their eyes for the limited time of the theatrical event, black drama leverages this convention to comment on materiality. The movement of a ship and the geographical ambiguity associated with trans-Atlantic slavery (enslaved Africans could be transported to a number of geographical locations in the Americas) introduces perpetual movement as a mechanism to address the loss of the nation state that enslaved Africans suffered. The pageant *Slave Ship* takes audience members for a harrowing ride that features a set configured as half of a split-level ship mounted on springs so that it actually rocks back and forth.[17] By dramatizing the movement through the Middle Passage, the pageant locates the ever-changing theater space as a site of repair. Similarly in Wilson's play the central character must move in order to find his "starting place in the world" (72). I purposefully return to Wilson's geographically inflected language to point to the poetics of the play as an exemplar of how to reconceptualize place as a fluid category. By the end of the play, Loomis has found his "starting place in the world," yet he is as nomadic as he was at the beginning. Loomis' ability to find his voice requires that he travel to Seth's boarding house; there he has a vivid vision of the Middle Passage. By activating two sites characterized by their lack of material history and their transmutability, the pageant and play comment on the role of theatrical production in cultivating psychic geographies that might attend to the paucity of material history available to the progeny of the trans-Atlantic slave trade. Instead of seeking to compensate for material losses – the loss of nation states – by claiming new homelands, these dramatic works offer a methodology that calls into question the desire for stable locations. In so doing, they demonstrate the process of materialization through performance, which functions as the ontology of black performance – repetition/reproduction. In performance, *Slave Ship* transforms the Chelsea Theater into a slave ship and reveals the process of materialization. The slave ship shifts from a historical artifact to a site imbued with the personal affective responses of each audience member.

By refiguring the geography associated with the reparations movement from an actual physical nation to mutable spaces, these dramatic works also shift the emphasis of reparations. More often than not the term "reparation" refers to one individual or group compensating another. The physical rituals that Loomis enacts in the play are never singular but, much like the theater as a form, require collaboration. Similar to *Slave Ship*, which stages the Middle Passage by drawing the audience into the action, Wilson's play requires collectivity among the characters onstage. This chapter, unlike the others in this study, focuses on two dramatic texts, asserting that repair often requires collaboration. Baraka's pageant and Wilson's play feature journeys depicted in geographical terms but manifested in temporal shifts. Similarly, my analysis of *Joe Turner's Come and Gone* and *Slave Ship* as well as the other literary texts discussed here advocates an appreciation of temporal shift in literary and dramatic studies, recognizing that literature is in a perpetual state of reproduction and therefore not limited to the date of publication.

Loomis' journey enacts a temporal shift that also critiques the materialism central to many calls for reparation, which assume material compensation will atone for the losses suffered due to slavery. At the end of the first act, Loomis has a vision in which he sees the bones of formerly enslaved black people emerge from their watery graves and walk on water. His vision defies the temporal finality of death and the laws of physics. Through his vision, he transitions from being "outside of time" to inhabiting messianic time (22). Being outside of time in *Joe Turner's Come and Gone* means living in a way that does not fulfill one's purpose. Alternatively, messianic time requires, as Walter Benjamin has specified, a historical materialism that not only "brush[es] history against the grain" but also challenges the very foundation of materialism.[18] Benjamin's model of messianic time eschews teleology and "enable[s] a revision not only of the historical but of temporality as such, forming hiccups in the machine of 'universal history,' hiccups that do not suspend or dispense with this chrono/logical mode as much as they provide pathways to the clefts and folds within its very configurations," to borrow Alexander Weheliye's useful explanation.[19] For Loomis, inhabiting messianic time leads to a remedy for his being outside of time. In order to occupy messianic time, he must learn how to interpret his prophetic vision, which ends the first act of the play. Through the act of interpretation, Loomis learns that his vision serves to augment the material world around him, from the boarding house as the setting of the action of the play to his physical body. His vision exists along a continuum of "clefts and folds" that include the sounds in *Slave Ship* and the dancing of the juba in Wilson's play, which I discuss later. These performances enable generation (those coming after and the act of creation) genealogies, which accounts for the descents of black performance as ones in which "the end is in the beginning and lies far ahead."[20]

Generation genealogies serve as models of literary history that disrupt the ostensibly linear understanding of Baraka and Wilson's relationship as a passing down from the elder artist to the younger one and the models of nation-building that inheritance supports. In the Overture, I discuss how Suzan-Lori Parks locates the Middle Passage as generative primal scene. If you consider the staging of the Middle Passage in *Slave Ship* and *Joe Turner's Come and Gone* as reproductions of a generative primal scene, then these dramatic works foreground a productive reciprocity between the two artists. Past and future productions of them generate a past that serves as a legacy of black theater. In such a model a director could make use of the dancing and sounding found in the production histories of both works in future productions of either. Such a configuration of black theatrical history displaces the singularity of the autobiographical mode that features Wilson describing his artistic precursors. Wilson is often represented as claiming inspiration from the four Bs – the blues, Baraka, artist Romare Bearden, and writer Jorge Luis Borges.[21] Even though Wilson acknowledges that "my own youth is fired in the kiln of black cultural nationalism as exemplified by Amiri Baraka in the sixties," he has also made comments that assert his autonomy as an artist.[22] In 1987 when David Savran asks Wilson what playwrights influence him, Wilson retorts "None, really." But then he revises, "Baraka wrote a book called *Four Revolutionary Plays* which I liked."[23] In an interview with Sandra Shannon in which she questions him about the four Bs, Wilson clarifies this seeming contradiction concerning Baraka's influence. He explains, "So Bearden has become more of an influence from art. Baraka less so. Mainly the ideas that Baraka espoused in the sixties as a black nationalist – ideas that I found value in then and still find value in. Baraka's influence is not so much upon the way that he writes or his writing style other than the ideas of the sixties that I came through and improved a lot using that influence."[24] Wilson's response to Shannon freezes Baraka in his Black Nationalist phase. It also renders Baraka's work static in ways that drama in particular resists.

Despite Wilson's response, I question the idea of influence as a one-way street and would instead like to conceptualize it as a feedback loop that infuses dramatic works with fragments that disrupt a linear formulation of influence.[25] Feedback, according to the *Oxford English Dictionary*, is "the return of a fraction of the output signal from one stage of a circuit, amplifier, etc., to the input of the same or a preceding stage," thus creating a loop. The *OED* 2004 draft addition defines feedback as "the effect whereby sound from a loudspeaker reaches a microphone feeding the speaker, thereby distorting the sound, and typically generating a screeching or humming noise; this distorted sound, esp. (in *Music*) created as a deliberate effect, usually through the amplifier of an electric guitar."[26] Noting the purposefulness of creating "noise," the new millennial usage of the word also defines feedback as a possible constitutive element of the originating sound. Applying the concept of the feedback loop to literary history would allow the generative noise produced when the stage directions in *Joe Turner's Come and Gone* call for Loomis "*to speak in tongues*" to "distort" (52) the sound of the screams produced in Baraka's *Slave Ship*. Instead of foregrounding the life of the author, such a methodology considers the artistic work as in relation to a number of influences, including what came before and after its initial production or publication.

THE ARCHITECTURE OF SLAVERY

The mounting of dramatic work renders the genre an exemplar of the way literature in general is perpetually in process. As a sketch of events that will occur onstage, the pageant, more than other dramatic forms, depends on the collaborative process, the eventfulness of each production. Although the characters in the pageant speak, the stage directions describe the majority of *Slave Ship*'s action in ways much like the structure of *The Star of Ethiopia*. The published version functions as an outline for the action. Organized through vignettes, the published version of Baraka's pageant moves from the hull of a slave ship to a plantation to an auction block to a church to a party. Baraka decides to wade in the murky waters of the Middle Passage to locate sounds that reside in, emanate from, and traverse the watery gravesite of millions of Africans. Baraka's historical pageant thereby, as a printed document and historical event, transforms the theater literally into a slave ship. Structurally as a pageant, *Slave Ship* demands improvisation from the writer, director, musicians, and set designer. My examination considers the published version of it and the 1969 production as a collaboration that exceeds the singularity of either one.

The published version offers directions with regard to the mood, sounds, and progression of the pageant that have specified the experiences of audiences. The published text calls for a cacophony of sounds – groaning, squeaking, screaming, and rocking – to assault the audience as the smell of incense gives way to fecal material. "These smells and cries, the slash and tear of the lash, in a total atmos-feeling" characterize the pageant.[27] In response to the 1969 Chelsea Theater production, critics have noted the ingenuity of the director Robert Moses and set designer Eugene Lee in creating the feeling of being on a slave ship. The entire theater, from the wood paneling on the walls to the incorporation of the audience in the performance, became a performance space. In the auction block scene, audience members were encouraged to participate in the bidding, and in the final scene, black audience members were urged to join the revelry and dancing.[28] Audience members were purposefully packed together and seated on hard wooden benches to create a feeling of discomfort that mirrored the cramped conditions of enslaved Africans on the ships, contributing to Baraka's notion of an atmos-feeling. Elam elucidates, "Moses eliminated any distance the audience had from one another or from the performers. Walter Kerr remarked, 'Black bodies seem to come straight through the floor of the slave ship.' The production disrupted the spectators' normal expectations of theatrical proxemics and aesthetic distance." [29] "The lower level of the set, the dark hold that came just about as high as one's nose when one was seated on any of its four sides, forced the audience to hunch over in order to see what was happening during the first part of this play," according to Dan Isaac.[30]

The uncomfortable nature of the atmos-feeling of *Slave Ship* taps into a racialized affective dynamic central to the creation of the enslaved. In the twentieth century, Du Bois describes this dynamic as feeling like a problem, the feeling of double consciousness, in which "one ever feels his two-ness."[31] Double consciousness theorizes the internalization of objectification that renders the black subject aware of her simultaneous coincident status as object and subject. While *Slave Ship* references some of the sequence of events that transformed black people into chattels – confinement in the cramped hull of the ship and objectification atop the auction block – in an equally important move it calls forth the fear, shame, alienation, pain, and sadness, to name some of the emotions, that come to represent the affective dynamic of the Middle Passage. As Baraka explains, self-determination seeks to combat feeling like a problem.

Through its set design and formal characteristics, *Slave Ship* calls attention to the affective dynamics of racialization, shifting emphasis from the physical ones. If physical difference was the primary organizing principle of the trans-Atlantic slave trade, and I do not think that it was, the choice to begin the pageant in darkness with occasional sounds that give way to putrid smells and "cries, the slash and tear of the lash" shifts the focus away from the dubious ocular dynamics of the body to the feeling of being in those bodies. In other words, the scripting of the opening scene demonstrates "how race and ethnicity can be understood as 'affective difference,' by which I mean the ways in which various historically coherent groups 'feel' differently and navigate the material world on a different emotional register," to quote José Muñoz.[32] Although the discussion of double consciousness in *The Souls of Black Folk* situates physical difference as a cause that results in feeling like a problem, the pageant's scripted opening sequence has the potential to create a theatrical atmosphere that may leave the entire audience feeling brown. By producing a theatrical event that has the potential to activate the affective dynamics associated with racialized difference, the pageant provides the opportunity to de-link the material body from feeling like a problem and to resituate the problem as one of historicity.[33]

Production choices serve as interpretive models of the affective dynamic *Slave Ship* creates and has the potential to evoke. Although the published version begins in darkness in the hull of a ship, the 1969 Chelsea Theater production began with an African tribal vignette. As Kimberly Benston explains, "the African sensibility is depicted as quintessentially religious. We witness a complex fertility rite involving the dances of warriors, farmers, and priests; chants and praises to harvest and protective gods; the whirling dance of the masked fertility goddess; and the culminating expression of social order through a hierarchical procession leading from the youngest child to head priest."[34] By beginning the pageant with African-inspired rituals, the 1969 production established a social order that white slave traders rupture by the end of the first vignette. The rupturing of the preexisting social order becomes the psychic sexual tear the pageant seeks to repair; note that the ritual features a fertility goddess.

Framing the pageant through reproductive social order introduces nationalism if we interpret the progress of the opening scene as sequential – the dance of the fertility goddess leading to social order.

What Alys Eve Weinbaum calls the "Race/Reproduction bind" – "a set of presuppositions that naturalize the connection between maternity and the reproduction of racial and national identity" discussed in Chapter 2 – reemerges in the 1969 production of the pageant and limits the reparative possibilities.[35] Reflecting on the Black Arts Movement and its relation to Black Nationalism, Baraka comments, "it is still my contention that we were revolutionaries, albeit saddled with the weight of nationalism, which does not even serve the people. In fact, in the US, since White nationalism is the dominant social ideology, reactionary Black nationalism merely reinforces the segregation and discrimination of the oppressors."[36] Following Baraka, I hold onto the assertion of *Slave Ship*'s revolutionary improvisational potential, even in light of the 1969 production, one in a series of enactments of the pageant. The difference between the published version (a written archive that the reviews augment) and the production (a repertoire of performance) exemplifies *Slave Ship*'s improvisational quality. The multiplicity within the material history calls attention to the flexibility of the pageant and enables interpretation of not only what occurred but also what possibilities the event enables in the present. In other words, the choice to open the pageant with an African-inspired ritual reflects a limited point of view with regard to freedom dreams. Nevertheless, by staging an alternative opening scene, the 1969 production calls attention to the collaborative process inherent in all theatrical production.

Although Baraka wrote the pageant, Moses and Lee participated in forming its theatrical quality. The definitive quality of the pageant is what Moten calls the "tragic–elegiac."[37] Moten's coinage uses the dash to draw multiplicity into singularity while retaining a compound structure. The compound word enables an epistemological restructuring that animates loss through mourning. Instead of adhering to what Moten describes as the "oscillation between happiness and despair, resurrection and mourning," he provides a term that enacts "ensemble and the improvisation that allows us to experience and describe it."[38] An ensemble-like quality also applies to Wilson's relationship with Lloyd Richards, who directed Broadway productions of Lorraine Hansberry's *A Raisin in the Sun* and Wilson's *Ma Rainey's Black Bottom, Fences, Joe Turner's Come and Gone, The Piano Lesson, Two Trains Running,* and *Seven Guitars.* While working with Richards, Wilson won two Pulitzer Prizes for drama among numerous other awards. In a 1991 interview Sandra Shannon asked Wilson about his collaboration with Richards, and Wilson responded by describing his first time working with the director. He recalled attending a rehearsal assuming that he would answer all the questions. At one point, an actor asked a question about a character, Toledo, and Richards responded. Wilson reflected, "Not only was it correct, but it gave me insight. I said, 'I didn't know that about Toledo.' This went on, but from that moment I visibly relaxed. I said, 'Everything's going to be all right. Pop knows what's he's doing.'"[39] Richards' insights helped develop *Ma Rainey's Black Bottom* and Wilson's next five plays.

The collaboration between the white director Bartlett Sher and the cast of the 2009 revival of *Joe Turner's Come and Gone* sparked controversy because of Wilson's desire that a black person direct his plays. After his death in 2005, his wife Constanza Romero approved Sher as director of the revival of the play. The *New York Times* described the collaboration as an "unusual" and "by all accounts a happy one, between a white director and an almost entirely black cast on Broadway, a rarity itself. At times the actors were directing the director, as they discussed the ways that black Americans relate to one another and to their white neighbors and nemeses. 'I've learned more from this cast than any group that I've ever worked with,' said Mr. Sher, who won a Tony for 'South Pacific.'"[40] A good collaboration requires balance. Although Sher lacked the cultural acumen that enabled Richards to know things about Wilson's characters that the playwright did not know, his social capital as an award-winning white director promised payoffs at the box office that would ostensibly compensate for the uneven relationship between the director and actors.

The collaborative process central to the production history of *Joe Turner's Come and Gone* and *Slave Ship* enables an ongoing investigation of the Middle Passage as a mobile site, geographically mutable and affectively particular in its rehearsal in African American literature. It is a site that through its cultivation of affective dynamics disrupts the Middle Passage as an unmarked grave – the site of irreparable loss – or as the space that marks the "spatio-temporal discontinuity that impedes our direction (home) or the narcotic belief in some spectral reemergence from its depths."[41] What would it mean to understand the Middle Passage as the site of a communal rupture – meaning break and breakthrough – and to think repair in those terms? This is not a matter of each individual finding a way home, but to consider repair as cultural practices that depend on collaboration, which might enable a collectivity to emerge from the muck. Baraka's theater exemplifies not only how the Middle

Passage served to create a common affect but also how that feeling might translate into reparative practices through ritualized reproductions onstage. In the 1969 production of *Slave Ship*, the Middle Passage becomes "a generative break" (as Moten would say), "one wherein action becomes possible, one in which it is our duty to linger in the name of ensemble and its performance."[42] Through the performance of *Slave Ship*, the audience (those who bore witness and those who continue to bear witness to its reproduction through the archive) had the opportunity to experience a common affect and hear the acoustic materiality that still echoes as a reminder.[43]

LOSS AND/AS REVELATION

Baraka's pageant thrusts theatergoers into an acoustically modulated theatrical communion. The published version of *Slave Ship* calls for several different types of sound, including "hideous screams" represented onomatopoeically by "AAAAAIIIIIIIEEEEEEEE" (251) and humming "like old black women humming for three centuries in the slow misery of slavery hummmmmmmmmmmmmmmmmmm" (253). Both directives for sound include a graphic representation that may translate into the elusive acoustics the pageant attempts to render. To further specify the sound, *Slave Ship* uses simile – like old black women humming for three centuries in the slow misery of slavery. Simile creates an analogous relationship that provides a reference point. Additionally, the simile conjures a ghostly sound. The reference requires a deconstructive approach to acoustic history.

The creation of sound in the absence of having heard it, whether the lynching victim's voice or the scream of an enslaved black woman, does not mean that it did not happen or that it does not continue to echo. In fact, the African American acoustic tradition offers several models of the scream that might inform an interpretation of Baraka's reference. The screaming of the enslaved women in the pageant could draw from the sound of Abbey Lincoln's scream in the song "Triptych" (1960), the heart-wrenching scream associated with Ornette Coleman's saxophone, and free jazz more broadly. Baraka notes, "Ornette Coleman's screams and rants are only musical once one understands the music his emotional attitude seeks to create. This attitude is real, and perhaps the most singularly important aspect of his music."[44] In order to hear the echo of Lincoln's and Coleman's screams in the voice of Baraka's enslaved woman, however, we must listen differently. The pageant requires the

audience's willingness to adopt the "emotional attitude" alienation produces and to listen for absences because an echo is always part of the
whole but never a complete sounding. *Slave Ship* creates the dynamic for
such listening by having the sound of the scream emerge from darkness.
The limited visibility draws attention to the sound of the actresses' voices,
the close proximity of the bodies to the right and left of you, the hard
wooden bench underneath you, and the acrid smells that envelop you. In
order to hear the metaphorical sound of "old black women humming for
three centuries," the theater must become a site of origins that disrupts the
linearity and irretrievability of beginning even as it reinforces the sexual
cut inscribed at the site of a primal scene.

Slave Ship's theatricality is dissonant – it jars the audience out of its
complacency and attunes it to the process of listening. Dissonance
reinforces Morrison's claim in *Beloved* that "in the beginning there were
no words. In the beginning was the sound" (259). Dissonance sounds the
way alienation looks and, similar to alienation, results in the ability to
think historically. According to Elin Diamond, alienation connotes
"looking-at-being-looked-at-ness."[45] Daphne Brooks specifies alienation
as a black tradition, coining the term "Afro-alienation acts," which
denotes how "the condition of alterity converts into cultural expressiveness
and a specific strategy of cultural performance. Afro-alienation recurs as a
trope that reflects and characterizes marginal cultural positions as well as a
tactic that the marginalized seized on and reordered in the self-making
process."[46] Similarly, dissonant black soundings require hearing the
call and response within the echo. The dissonance alerts the audience
to the players' awareness of the echoes within their screams, their moans,
and "the same patient humming ... of women, now, no men, only the
women ... strains of 'The Old Rugged Cross' ... and only the women and
the humming" (257). As indicated in the stage directions, Baraka offers
specific acoustic references for the sounds that emanate from the players,
from the infusion of the humming and gospel music to the "screaming
saxophone" that layers the "voices screaming" (257). The references in the
stage directions facilitate the dissonance. Similar to Brechtian alienation,
dissonance results in the ability to think historically, which requires
considering a woman in relation to her environment – a slave ship causes
heart-rending screams, wails, shrieks, moans, and cries that produce the
men and women aboard.[47] *Slave Ship* emphasizes that enslaved Africans
and their descendants marshal strategies to negotiate the acoustic alterity
resulting from the trans-Atlantic slave trade, creating polyphonic sounds
that require listening again. The condition of "moving through oceanic

space while 'suspended in time'" distills an acoustic legacy animated in
Slave Ship and made available to those who will hear it.[48]

Slave Ship consists of many sounds: drums' staccato, "the beat beat of
the darkness," "the mumble mumble rattle below," and "the drone of
terror," to name a few (252). Yet the "percussive sounds people make in
the hold of a ship" have different implications with regard to gender than
"old black women humming for three centuries." Even though the
published version of *Slave Ship* seems to codify the gender specificity of
the soundings, the 1969 production evidences that the pageant form leaves
room for alternative renderings. One could imagine men joining in the
humming to challenge the gendering of the sound. The melodic calming
humming creates a temporal incongruity that the pageant must manage
against the inscription of gendered sound.

Therefore, it is fitting to consider not only Lincoln and Coleman as
points of reference for the acoustic generation genealogy *Slave Ship* enacts
but also free jazz more generally. The markers of free jazz include
improvisation and unexpected shifts in tempo and chords and no predetermined harmonic structure. Free jazz constantly shifts the point of
departure and as a result beginnings and endings become blurred. The
formal characteristics of free jazz intersect with those of Baraka's pageant
in their fluidity. William J. Harris explains the characteristics of free
jazz thus:

free jazz is rooted in the African American audio past; that is, more specifically, it
is rooted in the shouts of the black church and the hollers of the field, sounds
saturated with the history of slavery. Furthermore, from its inception to the
present, extramusical sounds, such as shouts, screams, and grunts, have been
associated with the black musical tradition; in fact, they have been an integral
part of that tradition, from the anonymous singers of the spirituals to James
Brown to Albert Ayler to almost any contemporary black pop singer. In essence,
the music is a contemporary way into African American history and tradition,
into ethnic identity through sound and form, into what Baraka has called "the
changing same," that cultural continuity that persists in changing forms; what
Eliot calls "the present moment of the past."[49]

Harris, who focuses on the way free jazz informs Baraka's poetry, calls
attention to it as a mechanism for recuperation. If we understand the
scream, the shout, and the holler as echoes, however, we must also
contend with the persistent cleaving of loss with revelation. Even as the
sounds echo what came before, their very nature as echoes calls attention
to a partiality that coexists within an act of invention. *Slave Ship* alters
what we understand as coming before and therefore demonstrates how the

ongoing reproduction of the pageant (through publication and staging) situates the present as an active agent of what we know as the past.

Temporal negotiations specify the scream heard throughout *Slave Ship* and drive the action of *Joe Turner's Come and Gone*. In the same way that captivity interrupted the temporal progression of Loomis' life (placing him outside of time), the Middle Passage as depicted in both dramatic works represents a site of violence and temporal disruption. I probe the essential relationship between the representation of the Middle Passage that ends act 1 of Wilson's play and the climactic bloodletting scene that ends the play, asserting that read together they not only comment on Loomis' ability to enact self-repair but also imply a reparative strategy for the losses suffered due to slavery. Keeping in mind that many scholars (e.g., Shannon, Richards, and Elam) have considered the importance of the final bloodletting scene of Wilson's play, I contend that Loomis' revelation hinges on his ability to confront the losses of the Middle Passage and subsequently his own.

While the image of the bones people in act 1 causes Loomis to feel a profound division, as though "the world's busting half in two," the traumatic vision enacts revelation, which enables him to transcend the physical limitations that hold him in a state of limbo for most of the play (55). The scene begins with Seth and Bertha Holly and their boarders, sans Loomis, eating Sunday dinner. Upon completion of dinner they decide to perform the juba. According to the stage directions, "*The Juba is reminiscent of the Ring Shouts of the African slaves. It is a call and response dance*" (52). Similarly to the way enslaved Africans in the United States performed the dance after it migrated from Africa to the Caribbean and then to the United States, the play scripts the call and response nature of the juba between the participants and the percussive sounds that hand clapping and stomping make. Brenda Dixon Gottschild calls the US version of the dance "Pattin' Juba" and describes it as "foot tapping, hand clapping, and thigh slapping, all in precise rhythm."[50] Black dance scholars Jacqui Malone and Lynne Fauley Emery agree the dance qualifies as an African retention that expressed certain secular attributes when performed in the United States. Therefore, Wilson's direction, "*It should be as African as possible*," particularizes the performance of the dance and highlights his incorporation of its genealogy in the performance (52). His direction reflects what Diedrich, Gates, and Pedersen call a "Middle Passage sensibility" that "emerges not as a clean break between past and present but as a spatial continuum between Africa and the Americas."[51]

Adding to the spatial continuum produced through the dance, Wilson's call for the ritual reenactment also produces a temporal disruption. While Seth strives to figure himself as a modern subject, distancing himself from Bynum's spiritual practices at the beginning of the play, he participates in the pleasurable cultural ritual that situates the participants in a liminal temporal space. According to Victor Turner, "all rituals of any length and complexity represent passage from one position, constellation, or domain of structure to another. In this regard they may be said to possess 'temporal structure' and to be dominated by the notion of time."[52] Pattin' Juba creates another kind of feedback loop that situates the time of the play in intimate collaboration with what came before and what is yet to come.

Wilson's use of stage directions as spaces to historicize the body recalls Baraka's alienating directives – locating the player's body as "loaded with its own history and that of the character."[53] For example, Baraka calls for "slaves doing an old-new dance" (255) and "people in the slave ship in Miracles'/Temptations' dancing line. Some doing African dance. Some doing new Boogaloo" (258). The anachronistic mixing of forms aboard Baraka's slave ship and in Wilson's boarding house forms a cultural oscillation that weaves back and forth from old to new, Africa to the US, the past to the present. Yet while Wilson draws his literary audience's attention to a geographical connection that exceeds the dancers' and characters' bodies, Baraka foregrounds a temporal one. Read collaboratively, the dancing exemplifies the capacity of black performance to resituate black people in time and space. The dancing functions as rites of recuperation and restoration, drawing from the past as they create something new in the present.

For instance, as the juba moved from the Caribbean to the United States it became a competitive secular dance, instead of "a sacred polyrhythmic African step dance."[54] Nevertheless, its deployment in *Joe Turner* revives its ritualized function and establishes the vacillating line between life and death that the dance negotiates. In *Tell My Horse* (1938), Zora Neale Hurston describes the juba being performed in a wake she observed while conducting anthropological research in Haiti. Quoting Harold Courlander, Lynne Fauley Emery describes a practice of last rites that Courlander witnessed in Haiti: "nine or ten days following the burial of a dead person, there are more rites in his honor, and more dancing. On the habitation of the family there will be dancing of the Juba or Martinique, which is specifically reserved for such occasions."[55] Intended to honor and please the dead, the juba emphasizes the continuity of life and death, the persistent presence of the dead among the living. While Wilson's stage direction does not point to West African belief systems, he does call for the dance to be "*as African as possible*," which I interpret as a part of the syncretic spirituality expressed throughout the cycle. Wilson's use of the juba implies the continuity of life in death in West African belief systems and the principal result of Jesus Christ transcending death – the disciples gaining access to the Holy Ghost. He writes, "*The words can be improvised, but should include some mention of the Holy Ghost. In the middle of the dance Herald Loomis enters*" (52). The evocation of the Holy Ghost centralizes the idea of life after death while locating the practice within the tenets of an African-influenced Christianity. Writing about the play, Sandra Richards makes clear that African rituals and customs underpin the performances enacted in these episodes: "Yoruba gods sometimes wear the costumes of Catholic saints and fraternize with indigenous deities in order to remain in communication with their peoples shipped into the 'new' world of the Americas."[56] The flexibility of African cosmology does not undercut its influence in the play. As Sandra Shannon points out, "Wilson's motive for writing this disturbing story of spiritual and cultural alienation is that 'somewhere, sometime in the course of the play, the audience will discover these are African people. They're Black Americans; they speak English but their world view is African.'"[57]

Similarly, *Slave Ship* positions the singing and dancing as a negotiation of West African and US beliefs systems, specifically Yoruba and Christianity. At one moment the characters call for Yoruba gods and the next they sing spirituals or gospel songs. As in *Joe Turner's Come and Gone*, the syncretism underpins the representation of resurrection. Distinctively, *Slave Ship* locates the ability to transcend death in the acoustic realm rather than the visual one central to *Joe Turner's Come and Gone*. Directly preceding the revolutionary stand that ends the pageant, the stage directions call for "Ommmmm sound, mixed with sounds of slave ship, saxophone and drums. Sounds of people thrown against each other, now as if trying, all, to rise, pick up. Sounds of people picking up. Like dead people rising. And against that, the same sounds of slave ship" (257). Similarly to Baraka's earlier use of simile, the specification "Like dead people rising" creates absence and ambiguity where substance and clarity might more normally appear. Why depict the transmutation of resurrection and insurrection, primarily visual events, through sound?

Baraka's pageant deconstructs race by shrouding bodies in darkness and focusing on the power of sound. He locates the prototypical performance of the freedom drive in the sound of mass resurrection, which combines humming, drumming, and the screaming saxophone. The patient "Ommmmm" of the singers mixes with the persistent percussion and the urgent horn to resound a mood of prolonged and perpetual urgency. Although critics have noted the divisive nature of the 1969 production of *Slave Ship*, the staging offers a model of collectivity that does not necessarily depend on physical markers of race.[58] Moreover, the sounding that *Slave Ship* calls for precipitates the climactic scene of revolt and results in the death of the disembodied white voice. In the same way that the play offers models of black sound separate from but perhaps related to black people, it distinguishes the white voice as separate from but perhaps related to white people.

Throughout *Slave Ship* white laughter echoes from men on the slave ship which transforms to a disembodied voice of a plantation owner and then again into an unspecified man in power. By the end of the pageant all of the characters, save the Preacher figure, confront the white voice, who reasons, "you haha can't touch me . . . you scared of me, niggers. I'm God. You cain't kill white Jesus God. I got long blond blow-hair. I don't even need to wear a wig. You love the way I look. You want to look like me. You love me. You want me. Please. I'm good. I'm kind. I'll give you anything you want. I'm white Jesus savior right god pay you money nigger me is good god please . . ." (259). The self-referential nature of the comments calls attention to players' ability to question the investments of the characters, similarly to Suzan-Lori Parks' dramaturgy in her Lincoln plays. While *Slave Ship*, *Joe Turner's Come and Gone*, and Parks' Lincoln plays critique the regulatory norms that degrade black people, the dramas also call attention to the self-regulating phenomenon that must be killed in the pageant and in Wilson's play. Through the death of the white voice, the characters free themselves from the ideals that haunt them. A disembodied voice articulates standards of beauty and clarifies that whiteness as an ideal stands at a critical distance from all who seek it. The final scene of the pageant unburdens cast and audience alike, as does the final scene of *Joe Turner's Come and Gone*.

Wilson's play negotiates the imposition of Christianity on many enslaved Africans as it calls for one of the religion's fundamental principles, the transcendence of death. The singing, shouting, drumming, and dancing, central to the performance of the juba in the play, provokes Loomis to immediately question the authority being given to God, especially considering his experiences in captivity. How does the African-infused Christian performance recall his captivity? Moreover, how does his persistent homelessness and lack of place fit into the worldview his housemates celebrate? How does his lack of kin and place in the world situate him as a walking dead or render him what Orlando Patterson calls "socially dead?"[59] *Joe Turner's Come and Gone* renders Loomis socially unrecognizable to himself and therefore to anyone else. Although he claims to be a deacon, Seth asks, "Do he look like a deacon to you?" when he enters the boarding house (20). Hearing everyone chanting and witnessing the dancing of the juba further alienates Loomis, causing him to rant, "You all sitting up here singing about the Holy Ghost. What's so holy about the Holy Ghost?" (52). He demands that they explain how he fits into their model of transcendence. Instead of presenting Loomis with a straightforward linear answer, the play calls for the juba to usher in a trance-like state in which he sees the bones people.

Collapsed on the floor, Loomis recounts the movement of the bones people from walking on water to sinking down in the water, being washed onto the shore, obtaining flesh, and walking down the road. Each portion of the vision stands in for the journey Loomis must take. His testimony draws attention to the Middle Passage as "the birth canal that spawned the tribe" and "the death canal in which 'the African died to what was and to what could have been.'"[60] The first image marks a resistance to the rupture and dislocation slavery caused. The bones defy physics, rising up and walking across the water. Instead of sinking down and accepting defeat, the image suggests opposition embedded in the material remains of enslaved African Americans. The bones' rebellion against the natural order creates a mandate for the transformative vision as a whole.

As Loomis continues to recall the scene, Bynum stewarding Loomis' vision, suddenly tragedy strikes, the bones sink down. Bynum asks, "Sunk down like anybody else?" and Loomis explains, "When they sink down they made a big splash and this here wave come up." In the vision, the sinking of the bones may seem to represent a disastrous turn. When read in light of the history of the trans-Atlantic slave trade, however, the submergence of the bones marks a culmination of an effort to resist slavery. The water overcomes the bones, but the bones people render the forces of slavery impotent. Stephanie Smallwood clarifies:

in precolonial West African cultures (and many other premodern systems of belief), death was understood to engender a leave-taking of the most profound sort. Through the soul's departure from the body and migration to the realm of the ancestors, death entailed a change that resulted not in disconnection or disappearance but rather in its antithesis: a new kind of connection in the form of ancestral involvement in the life of kin and community. In this sense, the departure and displacement of the dead produced migrations that sustained connection, by carrying the soul of the deceased to the realm of the ancestors and returning the personality of the deceased to the realm of the living, reincarnated in the body of a newborn. Death thereby preserved and indeed strengthened an unbroken continuity. Indeed, such circularity was central to many precolonial African conceptualizations of time.[61]

The circularity that Smallwood attributes to West African cultures' perception of life explains why Loomis' vision does not end with the bones sinking down but continues. He imagines a life for the bones people after the water overtakes them. Although Loomis does not immediately recognize the power of his vision, the movement when considered from beginning to end represents an insurgent and determined ancestral spirit that lives within him.

The nature of the spirit, as Loomis will find, requires that he understand it and move past it. In that way, the resurrection central to Loomis' prophetic vision recalls Toni Morrison's eponymous character, Beloved, rising from the dead. In Morrison's Pulitzer Prize-winning novel, "A fully dressed woman walk[s] out of the water" (50). Beloved, the daughter of the protagonist, Sethe, returns from the dead, the "dark" "hot" place where she lay cramped in the fetal position (75). Beloved, who dies at the hands of her mother, must return to find out why her mother left her to die. Sethe summons Beloved through the water and across a bridge to atone for her choice to kill her child instead of allowing her to fall victim to the fugitive slave laws, the physical abuses of her former owner, schoolteacher, and the sexual ones of his nephews. Beloved's return, similarly to Loomis' vision of the bones people, signals a transformation in Sethe's life. Unlike the ghosts that haunt Loomis, however, Sethe must contend with an insatiable ghost. Sethe learns, as does Loomis, that she qualifies as the only sufficient sacrifice to exorcise the ghost. She must die and be reborn in order to give up the ghost. While Loomis makes it successfully to the other side of his journey, Sethe does not. I would like to submit that the architecture of each piece facilitates the character's ability, or lack thereof, to inhabit a state of repair in the midst of ghostly despair.

Joe Turner's Come and Gone introduces the imagery of the City of Bones, which Wilson depicts more fully in *Gem of the Ocean* (2003). In Wilson's cycle as in Baraka's pageant, the site of the trauma becomes the space for redemption. *Gem of the Ocean*, which represents the first decade of the twentieth century and precedes *Joe Turner's Come and Gone* in Wilson's chronicle of the twentieth century, describes a city in the sea created by the bones people, the City of Bones. Small in landmass, "only a half mile by a half mile," Esther Tyler, the spiritual leader of the Hill District (the setting of all but one of the plays in Wilson's cycle) and central character in *Gem of the Ocean*, describes the City of Bones to Citizen Barlow, a young man who has come to her to be "cleaned," to have his soul washed:

> Pearly white bones. All the buildings and everything is made of bones ... That's the center of the world. In time it will all come to light. The people made a kingdom out of nothing. They were the people that didn't make it across the water. They sat down right there. They say, "Let's make kingdom. Let's make a city of bones." The people got a burning tongue, Mr. Citizen. Their mouths are on fire with song. That water can't put it out. That song is powerful. It rise up and come across the water. Ten thousand tongues and ten thousand chariots coming across the water. They on their way.[62]

Aunt Esther informs Citizen of the centrality of the city, reorienting his geographical perspective at the same time as she imposes an epistemological lesson. After emphasizing the stunning quality of the remains, presumably human, used to create everything, she declares, "The people made a kingdom out of nothing." Her paradoxical comment emphasizes the overriding belief system of Americans in the US at the turn of the twentieth century. While the legacy of slavery deemed African Americans' primary worth to be as commodities, the role they played in building the infrastructure of the country contradicts their expendability. Similarly, even though an underwater city made of human remains of Africans in transit to the Americas may seem to be nothing, in Aunt Esther's estimation the city is a kingdom infused with a truth that will be brought "to light" and spill forth from the urgent "burning" tongues of the inhabitants. The insurmountable force of this message, which defies all the mandates of physical order, imbues this place with its healing power and transforms the grave-like Middle Passage into a memorial, a site of remembrance and renewal.

Morrison's novel could not possibly redeem the quintessential American house, Sweet Home, the plantation site of Sethe's objectification, rape, and beating. In the logic of subjectivity as self-possession, which relies on an understanding of materiality as static, Sweet Home, unlike Baraka's slave ship, is immutable. It exemplifies, as Samira Kawash argues, the fact that "the determination of both 'person' and 'property' – as shaped in and by the foundational distinction between subject possessing and object possessed – converge in the structure and substance of the house."[63] As residents of Sweet Home, the enslaved remain objects possessed, definitively excluded from the rights of possession, self or otherwise. Kawash suggests Baby Suggs' ownership of 124, a house on Bluestone Road, establishes her status as a free subject, no longer property and importantly able to own it. Alongside Kawash's critique, I would add that Baby Suggs' move to 124 enables a psychic reorientation expressed through the sermons that she delivers in a wooded Clearing. Her inhabitation of the Clearing, a space removed from her house, enables her to cultivate practices that coax 124 into becoming a home. And 124 also offers Sethe the possibility of finding an alternative configuration of home when she escapes to her mother-in-law's house. It promises some safety and reprieve for Sethe, her two sons, her "crawling- already baby girl," and her newborn daughter (178).

Although Baby Suggs occupies 124 and Sethe inherits permission to occupy it upon her mother-in-law's death, two whites, Mr. and Mrs. Bowdin, retain ownership of the house. Although "the house as property fulfills this promise of freedom many times over, serving as waystation for escaping slaves and as haven for Sethe and her children," Baby Suggs never owns the house.[64] The distinction between ownership and temporary guardianship points to a critical slippage in Kawash's argument and specifies the architectural politics of *Beloved*. Baby Suggs finds a space in-between that allows her to enjoy the shelter of a house and work toward the cohesion of a home. Within the strictures of US property laws, Baby Suggs never owns 124 and therefore Sethe has no right to inherit the property, including herself therein. Her escape from Sweet Home inaugurates a fugitive movement which is "stolen life, and its relation to law is reducible neither to simple interdiction nor bare transgression," to borrow a description from Moten.[65]

When Sethe takes up residence in 124 she remains a fugitive and her safety is short-lived. Not long after she arrives, her former owner, schoolteacher, with one of his nephews, the sheriff, and a slave catcher, tracks her to 124. Sethe "was squatting in the garden and when she saw them coming and recognized schoolteacher's hat, she heard wings. Little hummingbirds stuck their needle beaks right through her headcloth into her hair and beat their wings. And if she thought anything, it was No. No. Nono. Nonono. Simple. She just flew" (163). Fleet of foot and determined, the sound of wings sets Sethe in motion and exploits what "makes black social life ungovernable."[66] She ruptures the property laws that bind her and her children. So, Sethe "collected every bit of life she had made, all the parts of her that were precious and fine and beautiful, and carried, pushed, dragged them through the veil, out, away, over there where no one could hurt them. Over there. Outside this place, where they would be safe" (163). She flies to the shed, over there, outside this place, where they would be safe, to take the lives of her children and her own. (Un)fortunately, she does not finish the job. Schoolteacher finds her covered in blood holding Beloved's corpse and ready to kill her other daughter, Denver. In that moment, 124 transforms from a protected space to a "desolate and exposed" place, raw with the emotions of an infantile specter (163). Beloved will haunt 124 until Paul D, one of the Sweet Home men, a runaway slave, Sethe's friend, and eventually lover, drives her apparitional incarnation from the house.

Much like some utopic imaginings of Black Nationalism, which envision a repatriation of Africa's diasporic children, Sethe eventually interprets Beloved's embodied return as a material manifestation of the possibility of home. Although when the looming presence of schoolteacher pressures Sethe she adopts fugitive movements, she retains the fantasy that gives her the right to protect her property – in the persons of her children. Sethe's unlawful actions force the transfer of property; instead of reclaiming her and her children, schoolteacher allows Sethe to be sent to jail, which further alienates her from the status of propertied subject. Beloved's return solidifies Sethe's fugitive status as it locates the shed as a transgressive site. When Beloved returns as a physical form, the same shed in which she died transforms into the space in which she seduces Paul D. Beloved's return augments the shed, making it not only a site of violence and sacrifice but also an erotic one. The erotic quality of the shed weaves sexuality into the reparative project. While *Beloved* does not offer a model of healing in the characterization of Sethe, the architecture of the novel suggests that African American familial relationships based on the heterosexual coupling Sethe and Paul D engage in must negotiate the commodification and adherent shame of black sexuality. Morrison situates the vexed nature of black intimacy through the description of Sethe's ever-oozing milk-filled breasts that, like any other part of her reproductive anatomy, may be exploited at will. Her lack of agency, the inability to guard against anyone coming in her metaphorical or literal gates, shames her and her neighbors.

The shed serves as a site to locate the erotic origins of Sethe's shame and to connect it to the problematic conventions of the coupling that Sethe and Paul D attempt in 124. From the minute Paul D enters 124, he acts as a protector. He seeks to fill the role of patriarch by scaring away the ghost that resides in 124, coupling with Sethe, and taking "responsibility for her breasts [which], at last, was in somebody else's hands" (18). Paul D's ability to take on Sethe's burdens implies a structure of ownership that does not account for the debts she has yet to pay. Nor does it figure into their familial equation his outstanding balances. When the bill comes, as it always does, in the adult-sized body of Beloved, Sethe and Paul D both lack sufficient psychic currency to redeem each other or themselves. Instead, they settle for deferring their psychic debts.

When Paul D learns that Sethe killed one of her children in the shed, he confronts her and finally animalizes her, asserting, "you got two feet, Sethe, not four" (165). His willingness to deem her inhuman by counting her feet, the novel reveals, may have sprung from his desire to gain some distance from his youthful practice of bestiality "or the conviction that he was being observed through the ceiling? How fast he had moved from his shame to hers" (165). *Beloved* depicts displacement, on the part of either Paul D or Sethe, as a toxic psychic activity. Sethe cannot get out from under that feeling of guilt that alienates her from her neighbors; she remains essentially caged in 124 at the end of the novel. Her inability to leave the house that race built symbolically represents black people's state of imprisonment more broadly. By focusing on claiming the privileges of property ownership, Sethe loses sight of the importance of self-ownership, especially considering Baby Suggs' warning, "Yonder they do not love your flesh. They despise it. They don't love your eyes; they'd just as soon pick em out. No more do they love the skin on your back. Yonder they flay it ... *You* got to love it, *you!*" (88). When Sethe kills her crawling-already baby girl, she ruptures the structure of property central to slavery even as she replicates it by claiming her children as property. The use of erotic imagery in the shed specifies the particular burden black women must bear for having the *audacious* capacity to reproduce the capital of the enslaver. Perhaps if Paul D had found the courage to see in Sethe his own humanity he would have been able to enact some collaborative healing. Unfortunately the only truly collaborative partner that Sethe finds, her fellow "lawless outlaw" Amy Denver, the white girl that helps her give birth to Denver, only enables her to gain physical freedom (84). As *Beloved* poignantly acknowledges, "freeing yourself was one thing; claiming ownership of that freed self was another" (95).

REPAIR

Joe Turner's Come and Gone demonstrates the powerful implications of cultural performance, which plays a key role in causing Loomis to confront the memories and histories that hold him captive. In act II, Loomis discloses the reason for his entrapment and how it relates to his vision of the bones people in his second counseling session with Bynum.

As with his memory of the bones people, the pattern of call and response shapes this conversation (Figure 10). This encounter, however, Bynum crafts to evoke Loomis' revelation. Loomis enters Seth's boarding house and overhears Bynum singing a song about Joe Turner, the man who enslaved Loomis. The memories the song conjures anger Loomis and he insists that Bynum stop singing. Bynum acquiesces, but quickly forges into a subtle interrogation that reveals how much Bynum knows about Loomis, including that Loomis picked cotton for Joe Turner. Bynum claims, "I can tell from looking at you ... I can look at you, Mr. Loomis, and see you a man who done forgot his song. Forgot how to sing it ... That's why I can tell you one of Joe Turner's niggers, 'cause you forgot how to sing your song" (71). Bynum describes Loomis' loss of identity as his inability to "sing" his song. Although metaphorical, the imagery emphasizes the importance of embodied practice; it is not just that Loomis has forgotten his purpose, but that he has lost the ability to materialize it through action. Loomis, still unconvinced of Bynum's insight, reasons that he must have some type of physical marking that indicates his captivity. Eventually, Loomis recounts the circumstances of his kidnapping and forced labor. His narrative allows Bynum to explain that Joe Turner did not desire Loomis' labor, at least not primarily, but instead wanted what was essentially his. Although Joe Turner is not able to appropriate Loomis' song, his purpose in life, he does induce his social death. Quoting Orlando Patterson, Smallwood explains that "the slave, like the ancestor, is a 'liminal' being, one who is in society but cannot ever be fully of society ... [T]he slave ... lives on the margin between community and chaos, life and death, the sacred and the secular."[67] Loomis differs from those Smallwood describes who suffered the prolonged and, for many, interminable bondage of trans-Atlantic slavery. Nevertheless, the play places him on a continuum with the enslaved through his prophetic vision and his revelation at the end of this scene that Bynum is "one of them bones people." Loomis' moment of recognition makes room for the bones people to be intercessors for the perpetually lost African in America as well as enslaved Africans lost during the Middle Passage. Similarly to Loomis' vision (when he realizes the bones people are black), this moment of identification must quickly shift to action, represented in the vision as the bones people getting up and walking toward the road. The progression from vision to action also points to the way Loomis begins to seize his identity as he confronts his past. Through the mapping depicted in Wilson's play – from vision to action – a clear methodology of reparation emerges for the audience.

Figure 10 Actors Delroy Lindo and Ed Hall in *Joe Turner's Come and Gone*, January 1, 1988, directed by Lloyd Richards

The psychic repair Loomis desperately needs requires a wedding of consciousness and action that the play models through forms such as dancing the juba and singing the blues, which function as embodied modes of memory, consolation, and historical documentation. The vision of the Middle Passage in *Joe Turner's Come and Gone* reflects a form of reparation that reworks Melanie Klein's often-cited and useful meditations on psychic repair. Klein's work focuses primarily on the ability of a child to compensate for the real or imagined violence or ill will he or she has committed or wished on an object, what Klein calls the "bad object" that threatens him or her. In order to make reparations the child must engage in a creative process that atones for the violence done to the bad object.[68] Joshua Chambers-Letson elaborates: "Reparation, then, is not about a sublimation of past injury or a forgetting of guilt, so much as it is a coming to terms with the past as a means of putting oneself together, at least enough to be able to move into the future and possibility of love."[69] To move on, the child must make good the violence he or she has committed, or imagined committing. Therefore, within Klein's rubric the act of reparation is a self-motivated pursuit.

Usefully, Klein does extend her analysis beyond childhood development and ventures into an application of reparation as a social and historical process. She explains that the impetus for repair, the need to atone, comes from within the child and "merge[s] into the later drive to explore."[70] Klein clarifies the relationship between exploration and atonement, noting that "by finding new land the explorer gives something to the world at large and to a number of people in particular. In his pursuit the explorer actually gives expression to both aggression and the drive to reparation."[71] The idea of the explorer finding new land exemplifies how Loomis' journey to the Middle Passage may serve a communal function not only for the other characters in the play but also for the audience watching the play. When Loomis goes to the City of Bones he takes all of us with him; we achieve a surrogate benefit by way of his revelation that this place has a useful symbolic value necessary to the process of repair. The act of finding something new satisfies the need to repair even as it draws on the innate damaging violence. The commingling of such drives serves, in part, as a psychic explanation for acts of cruelty against native populations, conquest, and colonization. In terms of the colonial project, Klein clarifies: "The wished-for restoration, however, found full expression in repopulating the country with people of their own nationality. We can see that through the interest in exploring ... various impulses and emotions ... can be transferred to another sphere, far away from the original person."[72] Critics have questioned Klein's quick movement from a child's desire to adult motivations and from individual to collective action. While I recognize these reservations, I find the rationale for the progression of her argument compelling. Furthermore, my reference to Klein is to establish a point of departure. I appropriate her model to decipher how reparations function in Wilson's play and to suggest how *Joe Turner's Come and Gone* contributes to the discourse of African American reparations. Notably, Klein's analysis focuses on the individual's ability to make good real or fantasized violence. Her work considers to a far lesser extent how the object of the violence (the colonized, enslaved, or racialized individual) can assert a subject position and, in so doing, enact his or her own repair.

Reframing Klein's formulation from the perspective of the colonized allows theorization of reparation as decolonial and anti-racist practice. The July 2006 issue of the journal *Women & Performance* considers the implications for colonized subjects in Klein's scenario of reparative colonization. In the introduction to the volume, Joshua Chambers-Letson asserts, citing Frantz Fanon, that "the negotiation of guilt and the violence in the reparative process does not belong to the colonizer alone ... Which is to say that, anyone (both the perpetrator of gross violence and the victim) may perform reparation."[73] Chambers-Letson illuminates the agency that the psychoanalytic discourse concerning reparations allows for the subject of the violence. Similarly asserting the wronged individual's ability to repair himself, the cutting in the last scene of *Joe Turner's Come and Gone* demonstrates reparative action by drawing from the thick layers of meaning attached to racialized violence and the way violence also serves a reparative function in Christian typology, circum-Atlantic culture and spirituality, political action, and psychoanalytic discourse. Loomis' action allows him to flip the script written onto his body. As a result, he comes to terms with his personal and communal pasts as a means of putting himself together.

The climactic bloodletting, which melds word and deed, follows an exchange between Loomis and Martha in which he questions the efficacy of metaphorical action. For the past four years Loomis has thought Martha could save him. When she explains that she does not have the power to absolve him of his past pain and that the blood of Jesus is the means of salvation, Loomis questions the invocation of Christianity outside of historical particularity. He declares, "I been wading in the water" and "I been walking all over the River Jordan," which testifies to his knowledge of the fundamental Christian belief that Jesus died on the cross to remit the sins of man (93). For Christians, the offering of blood or animal flesh in the Old Testament reflected the ability to transform the spirit through a physical sacrifice. Since an animal offering could not atone completely for original sin, offerings had to be made repeatedly. The crucifixion mediated the persistent slippage created by the inability of an animal offering to pay the cost of original sin. Hebrews 9:12 explains: "Neither by blood of goats and calves, but by his own blood he entered in once into the holy place, having obtained eternal redemption for us." Jesus' death enacted the ultimate sacrifice precisely because he was able to transcend death. The power Christ holds for Christians is not only in death but also in his ability to rise again. Christ's ability to transcend death demonstrates the power to overcome the most profound type of loss. The spilling of Jesus' blood symbolizes atonement and sacrifice while, more importantly, it demonstrates the possibility for hope of transcendence. As previously mentioned, African Americans' investment in Christian typology did not eviscerate the African cultural resonances. "Spiritual faith in the afterlife beyond became a way of infusing Christianity with African rites as well as a methodology for surviving the overwhelming conditions of their existence."[74]

It is worthy of note that Loomis' investment in Martha as an intercessor for his redemption mirrors Sethe's desire for the reproduction of the black family through her relationship with Paul D, as well as the desire for heterosexual coupling as a remedy to despair alluded to in *Color Struck* and *A Raisin in the Sun*. In each example the collaboration fails when the actor seeks to defer her healing by focusing on curing a partner. The fruitful acts of collaboration require an intervention on the part of the collaborative party, even an uneasy and painful confrontation that forces the actor to change course. The final confrontation in *A Raisin in the Sun* between Mama and Walter Lee features this type of collaboration, as does the one in *Joe Turner's Come and Gone* between Loomis and Martha.

It is fitting, then, that in the final scene of the play Loomis' reaction to his estranged wife Martha functions as a performative because it requires the materialization of the body through the intertwining of Christian and racial discourse. In the final scene, Loomis returns with Zonia in tow to the space of transition – the boarding house – to confront Martha. Their conversation quickly evolves into a discussion of Loomis' agency when he realizes Bynum created a tie between Zonia and Martha. Loomis' years of wandering stem, in part, from his relationship with Zonia. Attempting to calm her husband, Martha asks Loomis to have faith, which Loomis perceives to indicate that he lacks self-sufficiency. Enraged, Loomis responds, "I been wading in the water. I been walking all over the River Jordan. I done been baptized with blood of the lamb and fire of the Holy Ghost ... My enemies all around me picking the flesh from my bones. I'm choking on my blood" (93). His enunciations of action do not enact themselves – he is not actually "wading in the water" – but serve to create his racialized body in time and space. The disturbing image of Loomis choking on his own blood recalls other references to the painful and persistent violence he is subject to as a black man living in America in the first decades of the twentieth century.

His comment demonstrates the utility of perfomatives, generally understood as words that enact actions, as in Austin's familiar depiction of the enunciation of "I do" in a wedding ceremony.[75] For Judith Butler the force of the performative lies in its ability "to undo the presumptive force of the heterosexual ceremonial."[76] Performance theorists following Austin (Butler, Elin Diamond, and Andrew Parker and Eve Kosofsky Sedgwick) demonstrate the ability of performatives to hold identities in place, primarily sexually based ones. Their theories of "the ways identities are constructed iteratively through complex citational processes" question the tension between the historically fueled force of iteration, including all of the regulatory laws speech acts call forth, and the visual presence of bodies.[77] If a woman with African ancestry appears white, does saying that she is so make it so? Or conversely and more to my point, does an African American man in the late nineteenth century or first decades of the twentieth century have the iterative power to announce his freedom? *Joe Turner's Come and Gone, Beloved,* and *Slave Ship* suggest not. They maintain that the materialization of a performative, particularly in racialized subjections, requires a transformation in appearance, whether through violence to the physical body or to the structures that frame the actor. In *Slave Ship,* an acoustic shift precipitated the emergence of the freed subjects who constituted their status through the repetition of "Rise, Rise, Rise" (258).

Joe Turner's Come and Gone advocates a violent recuperation of bodily authority. Yet even as African Americans reclaim blood rituals, they remain the object of brutality making the process of reclamation ambiguous at best. The model of biblical sacrifice becomes a social phenomenon in the United States in which black bodies serve as the sacrificial lambs. Hall charges: "Professor Bell, in his seminal text, *Race, Racism and American Law,* eloquently made the point that Black people in this society have been the 'involuntary sacrifice' to keep various groups of White united in this society, and to bring about a sense of equilibrium between competing political perspectives."[78] The complex web of violence as ritual, mode of social consolidation, and spiritual representation qualifies the act of bloodletting in Wilson's play. In a disjointed pattern of call and response, Loomis charges Martha to explain the use and implications of metaphysical transcendence in a society that authorizes his physical suffering. Martha's response, "blood makes you clean," resonates for Loomis but does not result in the conclusion she expects. Loomis slashes his chest as a method of self-purification, rejecting the symbolic quality of the blood Martha invokes. Furthermore, the play complicates the symbolic weight of the bloodshed by having Loomis then rub the blood over his face. As he washes himself with blood, Loomis participates in what Fanon calls the "cleansing force" of violence.[79] When Fanon discusses violence in *The Wretched of the Earth*, he refers to the fighting between the colonized and the colonizer. Although the circumstances are different – Loomis struggles to decolonize himself – Fanon's assertions serve a useful function because "Coming to consciousness is not a bloodless project and neither is reparation."[80] Whether the fracturing of bloodlines depicted in *Beloved* or Loomis' self-inflicted cutting, the material reconfiguration *Joe Turner's Come and Gone*, *Slave Ship*, and *Beloved* call for "flashes up in a moment of danger." Walter Benjamin explains, "The danger threatens both the content of the tradition and those who inherit it."[81] Collaborative confrontations provide the spark that enables Loomis to move past his fear and shift the content of American culture.

The spilling of blood that takes centerstage in *Slave Ship* features the sacrifice of a preacher figure in response to the death of a black baby. In ritualistic fashion, the shuffling black man with his hat in his hand becomes the Tomish slave that reports to the master that his fellow enslaved plan to revolt, and for his good efforts he receives a pork chop. The same figure becomes the black Preacher by the end of the play. Baraka's clear attack on the rhetoric of nonviolence in the person of Martin Luther King, Jr. and what appears as the black church's placation of white dominance heightens when a black man sits the "bloody corpse of a dead burned baby as if they had just taken the body from a blown-up church" in front of the Preacher (257). The placement of the dead baby momentarily halts the Preacher's babbling, but only for a moment. "Looking up at the 'person' he's Tomming before, then with his foot, tries to push baby's body behind him, grinning, and jeffing, all the time, showing teeth, and being 'dignified'" (257). In addition to implicating the black church in the violence black people suffered during the Civil

Rights Movement, the action also offers a class critique. The scene renders shameful the Preacher's attempt to act with dignity. He pays for this offense with his life.

In the final scene of the pageant, after the death of the White Voice all the characters begin to dance, inviting the audience to participate in the celebration. The stage directions call for the scene to turn into a party. As the party "reaches some loose improvisation" "somebody throws the preacher's head into center of floor, that is, after dancing starts for real" (259). Reminiscent of the cakewalking scene in *Color Struck*, the tragic fate of a central character has the potential to limit the pleasure and revelry of the dancing. The interruption of complacency draws the audience's attention to its own investments in the preacher figure. The pageant cultivates disdain for the preacher throughout; nonetheless, the beheading of the King-like figure is meant to shock the audience. Recall that Martin Luther King, Jr.'s assassination on April 4, 1968 resulted in riots throughout the US. The beheading of the preacher asserts the multiplicity and various allegiances of black people even as the final scene begs for collective revolt. The seeming contradiction points to the nagging flaw in models of revolution that feature displacement without accountability.

At the same time, I emphasize that *Joe Turner's Come and Gone* features internal collaborations that the literary one between Wilson and Baraka augments, in full recognition of Robin D.G. Kelley's critique of self-help ideology. Kelley suggests that self-help ideology does not account for the citizen's rights to make claims of the nation. He reminds us that "few African Americans nowadays express a sense of entitlement – that they have a right to state supports as taxpaying citizens. Rather, they see 'self-help' in terms of breaking dependency, getting out from under 'the white man.'"[82] *Joe Turner's Come and Gone* ends, in many ways as it began, with Loomis wandering. He does not expatriate himself, nor does he absolve Joe Turner of his wrongs. What he does do is find a way to "go on out the yard," to intervene in the materialization not of a defense against racialization – because, as Baby Suggs admonishes, "there ain't" one (244) – but an offense, a creative, confrontational, collaborative process.

The bloodletting in *Joe Turner's Come and Gone* also features the sacrifice of one body in the name of collectivity. The play establishes the performance of bloodletting as an act that attempts to repair the subject/object relations that sustained trans-Atlantic slavery and sustains racism in the Americas. As a result, Loomis' bloodletting qualifies as a circum-Atlantic performance.[83] The spilling of blood liberates

Loomis from dependency. *Joe Turner's Come and Gone* provides, through the introjection and successful management of the object, a route around the complicated subject/object relations typified by much of western thought, including psychoanalytic discourse. Loomis must act as his own sacrifice in order to assert and redeem forsaken histories and legacies. He transitions from the object of reparation to a subject performing repair, making the object and the subject one and the same.

The sacrifice in *Joe Turner's Come and Gone* recalls Richard's lynching in *Blues for Mister Charlie*. The staging of spectacles of violence animates the American theatrical tradition particularly in representations of race. I include in the American theatrical tradition the auctioning of slaves, minstrelsy, and lynching. Within this frame, as Hartman has shown, the blackness of the body does not appear a priori but must be made visible through rituals of display. While *Blues for Mister Charlie* metaphorically resurrects the dead protagonist to demonstrate the ways in which he continues to inform the actions and shape of his community after his death, *Joe Turner's Come and Gone* halts the force of racial formation through display by offering an alternative form of ritualized violence.

Joe Turner's Come and Gone, the fourth play in its cycle, establishes the ritual of bloodletting that establishes repetition/reproduction within Wilson's cycle. *Seven Guitars*, the play set in the 1940s and the seventh play in the cycle, and *King Hedley II*, set in the 1980s and the eighth in the cycle, feature blood rituals that specify the cycle's shape. In *King Hedley II*, the eponymous protagonist's choice at the end of the play to end the cycle of violence that plagues inner cities in the 1980s creates a historical detour that ruptures the chronological relationship between *Seven Guitars* and *King Hedley II* and enables a diachronic one among Wilson's 1980s play, *Joe Turner's Come and Gone* (1987), and *The Piano Lesson* (1990). In other words, *Seven Guitars* establishes a causal relationship with regard to social violence that the aphorism "an eye for an eye" encapsulates. Initially *King Hedley II*, which features some of the characters and their children from *Seven Guitars*, depicts an intensified expression of reciprocal violence. Yet, similarly to *Joe Turner's Come and Gone* and *The Piano Lesson*, *King Hedley II* disrupts the naturalized chain of aggression – if someone hits you, hit him back harder – by depicting King's refusal to enact vengeance. Through this detour, *King Hedley II* recoups the positive potential associated with the spilling of blood and specifies Wilson's historical model – the cycle. *King Hedley II* shows the redemptive power of sacrifice by harkening back to the spilling of blood in *Joe Turner's Come and Gone*, which bends the trajectory of the plays as a whole. Instead of a linear chronological trajectory from *Seven Guitars* (Wilson's seventh play) to *King Hedley II*, Wilson's eighth play *King Hedley II* picks up where *Joe Turner's Come and Gone* left off, circling back to the potential realized in one of Wilson's early works and reproducing the possibility to find some space in-between.[84]

Joe Turner's Come and Gone asserts the pressing need for black subjects to claim reparations for their losses as a part of a larger epistemological and spiritual shift. Indeed, as Saidiya Hartman has argued, "The limited means of redress available to the enslaved cannot compensate for the enormity of [their] loss; instead, redress is itself an articulation of loss and a longing for remedy and reparation."[85] *Joe Turner's Come and Gone* offers a model of how to mediate the longing Hartman describes, by refusing the idea that one can be given reparation and, instead, asserting that one must claim repair. In that way, Wilson's play provides stable yet uneven ground for Loomis to stand on. The sacrifice of blood, in the final scene of the play, reproduces fragmented and violent histories as it creates hope for life after the physical and symbolic death the trans-Atlantic slave trade and its aftermath caused. Loomis' revolutionary action and final declaration, "I'm standing! I'm standing. My legs stood up! I'm standing now!" draws its importance from the symbolic bond he has with enslaved African Americans and their descendants. When Loomis declares "I'm standing now!" he locates the spilling of his blood as a practice which enables him to incorporate traumatic personal and historical legacies that leave him nowhere and somewhere at the same time. As Loomis has found his starting place in the world, he must now continue to negotiate a path that, based on Wilson's cycle of plays, contains its very own barriers to progress. Nevertheless, Loomis now has the counter-memory of the City of Bones to act as a narrative that perpetually situates him in the world. The sense of dislocation central to Loomis' character also informs Suzan-Lori Parks' Lincoln plays. As demonstrated in the Overture, Parks makes use of the entire theater space, eschewing the restrictions of realism's fourth wall. The first act of *The America Play* features several monologues of direct address to the audience. *Topdog/Underdog* opens in a similar fashion, but Parks raises the ante in her second Lincoln play. *Topdog/Underdog* eliminates the space for the casual observer, demonstrating the collaborative nature of all meaning-making.

CHAPTER 7

Reconstitution

Suzan-Lori Parks' Topdog/Underdog

Suzan-Lori Parks' Pulitzer Prize-winning play *Topdog/Underdog* opens with Booth, one of the two characters, delivering the following lines while practicing his three-card monte routine:

Watch me close watch me close now: who-see-thuh-red-card-who-see-thuh-red-card? I-see-thuh-red-card. Thuh-red-card-is-thuh-winner. Pick-thuh-red-card-you-pick-uh-winner. Pick-uh-black-card-you-pick-uh-loser. Theres-thuh-loser, yeah, theres-thuh-black-card,theres-thuh-other-loser-and-theres-thuh-red-card, thuh-winner.
(*Rest*)
Watch me close watch me close now: 3-Card-throws-thuh-cards-lightning-fast. 3-Card-that's-me-and-Ima-last. Watch-me-throw-cause-here-I-go. One-good-pickll-get-you-in, 2-good-picks-and-you-gone-win. See-thuh-red-card-see-thuh-red-card-who-see-thuh-red-card?[1]

The first line of the play, "Watch me close watch me close now," establishes appearance as central to the work of the play. In order for Booth to succeed at throwing the cards, he must get the audience to *not* heed his command. Accompanying Booth's initial monologue, Parks scripts these stage directions: Booth's "*moves and accompanying patter are, for the most part, studied and awkward*" (5). At this point in the play, the audience does not know whether Booth's movements are intentionally or unintentionally "*studied and awkward.*" By instructing the audience members to "Watch me close watch me close now," Booth encourages them to trust their chances of winning and their acuity of vision. His inability to throw the cards, however, masterfully turns the scene from mesmerizing to comic.

The shift from definite to indefinite articles, from "thuh-winner" to "uh-winner," introduces a movement from the universal to the particular, which counterpoises an opposite shift in the text from the personal story of two brothers to a national American narrative. Drawing from an American history of hustlers, the success of Parks' protagonists, brothers

Lincoln and Booth, depends on their ability to create a break between what they say and what they do. Lincoln and Booth must convince the audience to not believe what it sees before its eyes and instead heed what they say. For example, as an Abraham Lincoln impersonator donning whiteface paint, Lincoln asks his audience to look past his racial difference so that he may keep his job at a local arcade in which he is assassinated on a daily basis. Booth spends his days in two activities that require a sleight of hand: shoplifting from stores and practicing three-card monte. Lincoln and Booth hustle to pay their bills. Even though Lincoln argues that his job at the arcade is legitimate, *Topdog/Underdog* suggests the deception at the heart of his performance qualifies the routine as a hustle. Following the historical narrative outlined by Jackson Lears in *Something for Nothing: Luck in America*, and the literary history established by Herman Melville's *The Confidence Man* (1857), Bert Williams and George Walker's *In Dahomey* (1902), and Ralph Ellison's *Invisible Man* (1952), the play aligns hustling with the constitution of the US.

The play intertwines the protagonists' personal narratives with the performances of their hustles and therefore suggests a relationship between Lincoln and Booth's familial history and a national narrative. Throughout the play, the brothers recall repeatedly that everyone in their lives, including their parents, lovers, and friends, abandoned them. Lincoln manages the loss of his loved ones by refusing to throw the cards. Booth responds to the persistent memories of abandonment by turning to Lincoln, a rehabilitated confidence man, for some tips on how to refine his three-card monte routine. Begrudgingly, Lincoln teaches Booth some of his skills. As Booth's proficiency in three-card monte increases so does his bravado. Booth eventually challenges Lincoln to a game. Lincoln, who reminds Booth you can never hustle a hustler, wins all of his brother's money, including Booth's share of their inheritance. Inevitably, as history dictates, Booth kills Lincoln. This is an American Play, so Lincoln must die. But in this national narrative revision, *Topdog/Underdog* complicates Lincoln's expected death by making Booth his brother.

Melding myths of family (sibling rivalry), nation (brotherhood), and race (brother as racial signifier), the play emphasizes an implicit ambiguity in Lincoln's and Booth's historical and social roles. One is never quite sure if either brother is telling the "truth." Further complicating matters, the brothers' names map the epistemological questions their identities raise onto a national narrative. In the play, Americanness is constituted through the intersection of competing identities, national, familial, and racial. In order to make their identities work, Lincoln and

Booth manipulate the process of identification. The performance of hustling represents the brothers' active manipulation of their appearance. Recall that in the Overture I described faking as a metonymic performance of black theatrical repair. As a kind of faking, hustling distorts the brothers' bodies and taps into individual desire to produce opacity. Hustling relies on appearance even as it causes the individual to appear. Therefore, by hustling the brothers actively participate in shaping their histories.

Individuals appear in response to familial, social, or historical demands. In *Topdog/Underdog* the social support necessary to provide symbolic validation to Lincoln and Booth has departed by the beginning of the play. The theme of abandonment sets the stage for the brothers to turn the "symbolic triumph of self-sameness" into a strategic performance.[2] Realizing the unavoidable gaps between themselves and their ideal image, Lincoln's and Booth's hustles function through personas that solicit validation. These performances, however, do not secure Lincoln and Booth; they satisfy the demands of the viewer. In *Racial Castration*, David Eng argues:

> Considering for a moment Lacan's *Four Fundamental Concepts of Psycho-Analysis* in light of his essay "The Mirror Stage," we come to understand that our psychic experience of the self-same body does not necessarily follow from our voluntary or self-willed identifications with the imago. On the contrary, any jubilant sense of identification with an external image hinges on collective social affirmation. In other words, it is only when the cumulative looks of others provide symbolic validation and social support that the subject can gain access to the desired image. Without this collective affirmation, the imago cannot be successfully mapped onto the bodily ego to produce any feeling of psychic triumph or self-sameness.[3]

Although Eng uses Lacan's theory of the mirror stage to analyze symbolic validation for Asian American men, I find it fitting to transpose his ideas, which I contend are fluid enough to apply to racialized bodies in general. The hustling in *Topdog/Underdog* affirms Eng's claim while it complicates the nature of "the cumulative looks of others." In order for the brothers to solicit collective affirmation from the audience and even from each other, they must aggressively conceal the physical ruptures that make the mapping of the imago onto their "bodily ego" incomplete. This chapter explores how Lincoln and Booth hustle to ensure the mapping even as they profit from the necessary slippage. As in *The America Play*, Parks' characters' appropriation of signature US styles transforms the body and disrupts the ease of identification.

Parks leverages the slippages inherent in identity throughout her work to turn the table on audiences and interrogate how watching in the theater parallels the quotidian experience of racial surveillance. She explains, "The most exciting thing about watching theater is that people are watching, and I think that's fascinating. That's why I get nervous when I go outside. There's so much watching going on. People are watching you, you are watching people. It's like over-stimulation. I think that is what theater's all about."[4] Although Parks does not grant racial specificity to her observation, her plays certainly do. In *Topdog/ Underdog*, marshaling Bertolt Brecht's famous alienation effect which she also deploys in *The Death of the Last Black Man in the Whole Entire World* (1989), Parks ingeniously wins her audience's confidence through her signature use of humor, including the familiar style of blackface, only to shine the spotlight on the audience by the end of the play. Parks' *Imperceptible Mutabilities in the Third Kingdom* (1986) and *Venus* (1996) employ a similar bait and switch although less stealthy. From her depiction of surveillance in *Imperceptible Mutabilities*, featuring a character named the Naturalist observing *Wild Kingdom*-style characters Molly and Charlene, to the stares actors and audiences produce in *Venus*, her play about Saartje Baartman, popularly known as the Venus Hottentot, Parks shocks her audiences, which serves to alienate them from the start. More jarring and difficult, the earlier plays did not have the same commercial success as *Topdog/Underdog* because they did not slyly lull their audiences into acceptance before shocking them into recognition. Instead of offering historical figures as in *Venus* and *The America Play*, *Topdog/Underdog* tells the story of two brothers who happen to be named Lincoln and Booth. Judging by the popularity of *A Raisin in the Sun* and August Wilson's *Fences* and *The Piano Lesson*, Broadway audiences find African American familial narratives more palatable than what they perceive as history lessons.[5] Adding to its accessibility, *Topdog/Underdog* simplifies Parks' previous depiction of identity formation in *Imperceptible Mutabilities*, depicting the characters' multiplicity through costume instead of multiple names for the same figure. The change enables her to produce a legible familial drama. She also uses the familial drama as a gateway to the traumatic histories explored in *Father Comes Home from the Wars (Parts 1, 8 & 9)* (2009) and *The Book of Grace* (2010). Although limited, *Topdog/Underdog* serves as an exemplar of the reparative potential of black performance because it foregrounds the sly power of performance to shift the gaze long enough to change history.

HUSTLING AS PERFORMATIVE MOTIF

Just like the national history recalled through their names, when the brothers perform at their best they are able to direct their diverse identifications toward a common goal. Being a black man, Lincoln (also known as Link) still has the ability to impersonate a white founding father; yet his performance does not eliminate the slippage between the two roles. Instead, it heightens the stakes of his identifications. By impersonating President Lincoln, Link questions the efficacy of racial categories and the national history that underpins them. Lincoln the brother calls attention to the racial strife that threatened the unity of the nation during Abraham Lincoln's presidency. As honest Abe, Link represents American history; at the same time, he embodies an identity as a black confidence man that threatens America. *Topdog/Underdog* revises the national narrative associated with Lincoln the president, insisting that a co-constitutive relationship exists between the self-made man, the man Parks calls the Foundling Father in *The America Play* (1994), Abraham Lincoln, and the confidence man.

I trace the performance of hustling through the embodiment of the hustler or confidence man in American literature and history. Examining cultural examples – Abraham Lincoln as the historical foil to the confidence man, Herman Melville's eponymous protagonist in *The Confidence Man*, and Ralph Ellison's Rinehart – I extrapolate the performative qualities of hustling that the confidence man and the self-made man exhibit. As historian Jackson Lears explains, certain types of hustling performed by the self-made man solidified America's hopes for itself, while other types performed by the confidence man undermined American identity:

The speculative confidence man is the hero of this tale – the man (almost always he is male) with his eye on the Main Chance rather than the Moral Imperative. The other narrative exalts a different sort of hero – a disciplined self-made man, whose success comes through careful cultivation of (implicitly Protestant) virtues in cooperation with a Providential plan. The first account implies a contingent universe where luck matters and admits that net worth may have nothing to do with moral worth. The second assumes a coherent universe where earthly rewards match ethical merits and suggests that Providence has ordered this world as well as the next. The self-made man has proven to be a far more influential culture hero than the confidence man. The secular version of Providence has resonated with some characteristically American presumptions. A providential sense of destiny could be expanded from individuals to groups and ultimately to nations – and to none more easily than the United States.[6]

The confidence man, as Herman Melville characterizes him in 1857, serves as the foil to the self-made man. This trickster figure demonstrates the short-comings of the Protestant work ethic and its associated "value." By revealing the unwritten rules, he demonstrates that no one is ever in total control. He relies on hope as he challenges the implicit reward of hard work.

The confidence man demonstrates the democratic process as the struggle between what America is and what it is to be. The act of demonstrating is the hustle. To hustle is to negotiate "absurdity while sustaining a vision of cosmic coherence."[7] A successful hustle depends on the manipulation of appearance, disrupts the ideals of entitlement, and challenges what is knowable. Therefore, the hustle as performative proto-type points to the negation of certain histories and narratives even as it models strategies for their recovery. Hustling therefore embodies the prototypical black performances of faking and digging up the past. The recuperation of history enabled by a turn to the performance of hustling requires an understanding of the psychic mechanisms that facili-tate knowing one history and covering over another, and the historical mandates that necessitate the appearance of certain histories and the disappearance of others.

Topdog/Underdog's symbolic engagement of American history through the lives of two brothers provides a social account of the psychic forces that drive individuals and communities. The play revises Freud's explica-tion of "the two instincts that move the world," by demonstrating the impact of identification on identity and therefore the social mandates on the instincts of love and death.[8] Situating the drives within social dynam-ics, the play sets them in productive tension necessitated by the individ-ual's need to appear before another. Harry J. Elam, Jr. suggests that the stage serves as an apt location to contemplate the relationship between death and appearance: "The live performance, paraphrasing Herbert Blau, is where we as audience, in the immediacy of theatrical space, witness the performer dying each night. The figure of death as unmarked presence lurks in the background, exists in the memory of the spectator, in the space of the theater."[9] *Topdog/Underdog* co-opts an American tale to call attention to the aggressiveness of death that constantly "lurks in the background." Death becomes a condition of the possibility of realizing and maintaining the appearance of the collective and individual imago.

Topdog/Underdog foreshadows Booth's expected assassination of Lincoln by depicting customers assassinating Lincoln every day at an arcade. The play reproduces the assassination of President Lincoln, shifting the historical focus from his life to his death. Concentrating on the performance of his death instead of the performance of him as a symbol of American democracy, the play subverts the cultural history surrounding the president from what is signified through him – American democracy – to the constant life-threatening tension underpinning that democracy. Therefore, the fact that Lincoln the brother plays Lincoln the president has particular significance. Abraham Lincoln holds iconic status in American culture, appearing on the penny and the five-dollar bill. As the Civil War president, Lincoln became a symbol of America and American democracy. Parks explains to the *New York Times* writer Joshua Wolf Shenk that "Lincoln is the closest thing we have to a mythic figure. In days of Greek drama, they had Apollo and Medea and Oedipus – these larger-than-life figures that walked the earth and spoke – and they turned them into plays. Shakespeare had kings and queens that he fashioned into his stories. Lincoln, to me is one of those."[10] Having a black man stage the reenactment of Lincoln's death repeatedly, the play draws attention to the bloody racial seams that attempt to hold history together. Parks astutely notes, "It's like Lincoln created an opening with that hole in his head … We've all passed through it into now, you know, like the eye of a needle. Everything that happens, from 1865 to today, has to pass through that wound."[11] The assassination of Lincoln created a physical opening parallel to the material rupture foreshadowed throughout the play but only felt in the final scene.

Lincoln is probably most well known for issuing the Emancipation Proclamation on January 1, 1863 and "freeing the slaves." As W.E.B. Du Bois asserts, however, the Emancipation Proclamation did not free the slaves. And although Lincoln is known for being a champion of democracy, the Civil War "has not to do with slaves, cried Congress, the President [Lincoln], and the Nation."[12] Du Bois explains this seeming contradiction thus: "the long-headed man with care-chiseled face who sat in the White House saw the inevitable, and emancipated the slaves of rebels on New Year's, 1863."[13] The Emancipation Proclamation only applied to slaves living in the Confederacy. The United States actually outlawed slavery on December 6, 1865 through the ratification of the Thirteenth Amendment.

The Civil War defined the historical period of Lincoln's presidency and positioned him as a cultural icon. In his speeches Lincoln mobilized the rhetoric of democracy, claiming in the Gettysburg Address "that this nation, under God, shall have a new birth of freedom – and that government of the people, by the people, for the people, shall not perish from the earth." Contextualizing Lincoln as a cultural icon, Lears writes,

"The universe envisioned by the evangelical rationalists was very much an all or nothing affair, filled with irreconcilable dualisms and baffling contrarieties ... Only Lincoln had the words to give that conflict tragic depth ... As the Civil War ended slavery and transformed the United States into a single nation, it also validated the cultural hegemony of evangelical rationality – the vision of a society whose inevitable progress was a part of a divine plan."[14] Embroiled in a battle set to rock America's democracy to the core, Lincoln led the Union Army to victory, enjoying the surrender of the Confederacy on April 9, 1865, five days before John Wilkes Booth assassinated him. Lincoln's ability to manage a resolution to the Civil War is read historically as evidence of the power and truth of democracy.

Topdog/Underdog does not focus, however, on Lincoln's ability to sim-ultaneously "give that conflict tragic depth" and mobilize the rhetoric of democracy. It focuses instead on Lincoln as a paradoxical historical figure. As Parks explains, "Can Lincoln be the Great Emancipator and a white supremacist? Hmmm. Yes. Both, both. I think both."[15] Parks' insight reveals a process of history predicated on the ability to overlook Lincoln as a white supremacist. By having a black man stage the reenactment of Lincoln's death, however, the play draws attention to the bloody seams that attempt to hold history together. Parks' first incarnation of Lincoln as the Foundling Father in *The America Play* disrupts the narrative of progress and instead provides the image of history as a hole. She scripts the play to be staged in *"A great hole. In the Middle of nowhere. The hole is an exact replica of the Great Hole of History."*[16] The Foundling Father, who "bore a strong resemblance to Abraham Lincoln," works as a gravedigger until he begins to impersonate "the Great Man."[17] His job transitions from burying remains to digging them up. The motif of digging recurs in Parks' novel *Getting Mother's Body* (2003) and points to an epistemological project at the heart of her work. In "Digging the Fo'fathers: Suzan-Lori Parks' histories," Debby Thompson represents digging as an aesthetic innovation in Parks' work. In terms of discovery, one might argue that the way Booth repeatedly berates Lincoln throughout the play functions as a mode of digging that results in the reproduction of the epistemologies of the brother's personal history and a national history.

The history materialized through the staging of Abraham Lincoln's death helped Parks to make some history of her own. Parks joined an elite group of American playwrights, winning the Pulitzer Prize for drama in 2002 for *Topdog/Underdog*. She also holds the distinction of being the first African American female to win the Pulitzer Prize for drama.[18]

Topdog/Underdog received praise from critics for its energy, freshness, and excitement. Ben Brantley of the *New York Times* claimed:

The two lonely, rowdy brothers who make up the entire cast of characters of Suzan-Lori Parks' thrilling comic drama give off more energy than the entire ensembles of "42nd Street," "The Lion King" and "The Graduate" combined . . . "Topdog/Underdog" now emerges as the most exciting new home-grown play to hit Broadway since Mr. Wolfe's production of Tony Kushner's "Angels in America." And it's blowing through the dusty lackluster theater season like the breeze of a long delayed spring.[19]

Critics claim the success of the play (the Pulitzer Prize and the movement from the Joseph Papp Public Theater after a successful run in 2001 to its Broadway premier at the Ambassador Theater) reflects Parks melding "a captivating narrative without sacrificing her high thematic ambitions."[20] The resonance of the play might also reflect what Parks describes as its consideration of our relationship to the past.[21]

SIBLING RIVALRY AS NATIONAL MEMORY

The structure – the tempo of the dialogue and the staging – of *Topdog/Underdog* mimics the slippage Lincoln's and Booth's multiple roles create. Embedding digressions in the *mise en scène*, *Topdog/Underdog* forestalls the foreboding threat evoked through the performance of multiple conflicting identities. The digressions serve to temporarily relieve the ambiguous tension embedded in Lincoln's and Booth's multiple roles, heightening the shock of the final death scene. Nevertheless, throughout the play the brothers' verbal altercations foreshadow Lincoln's death. Even the name of the play acknowledges their persistent rivalry. When Don Shewey, a reporter for the *New York Times*, asked about the name, Parks responded, "Topdog underdog! Sounds like two guys to me! They switch constantly. They're always trying to be the dominant person in the room. They always ask, 'Who the man? Who the man? I'm the man now! No, I'm the man!'"[22]

The brothers' rivalry reflects a long tradition of brotherly antagonism. From the biblical depictions of Cain and Abel to Sam Shepard's *True West* (1980), the idea of two brothers fighting, often for their parents' approval, has inspired many tales. As a black woman writer, Parks thickens the signifier "brother," highlighting the inherent multiplicity of the term. In the afterword to *Conjuring Black Women, Fiction, and Literary Tradition*, Hortense Spillers says "the work of black women's writing community not only redefines tradition, but also disarms it."[23] Similarly, Cheryl Wall's *Worrying the Line* explains how African American women writers often signify on literary tropes or historical narratives to challenge or reclaim lost genealogies and histories. The multilayered signifier "brother" connects Lincoln and Booth to a specific American history. At the same time, as black men Lincoln and Booth challenge American histories and cultural memories that exclude the multiple signification of brother.

Intertwining the trauma of their personal history with a national one, aligning, much as in *Color Struck*, personal loss with national loss, Lincoln and Booth strategically recall family memories to manipulate each other's actions and compensate for their perpetual state of melancholia. The brothers leverage their identities as siblings to enable and enhance their hustles for self-recognition and communal recognition. In one scene, Booth the younger brother recollects seeing their mother having an affair and ultimately abandoning them, to coerce Lincoln into teaching him how to throw the cards:

LINCOLN
BOOTH
LINCOLN
BOOTH
BOOTH You know what Mom told me when she was packing to leave? You was at school motherfucker you was at school. You got up that morning and sat down in yr regular place and read the cereal box while Dad read the sports section and Mom brought yr dick toast and then you got on the damn school bus cause you didnt have the sense to do nothing else you was so into yr own shit that you didnt have the sense to feel nothing else going on. I had the sense to go back cause I was feeling something going on man, I was feeling something changing. So I –
LINCOLN Cut school that day like you did almost every day –
BOOTH She was putting her stuff in bags. She had all them nice suitcases but she was putting her stuff in bags.
(*Rest*)
Packing up her shit. She told me to look out for you. I told her I was the little brother and the big brother should look out after the little brother. She just said it again. That I should look out for you. Yeah. So who gonna look out for me. Not like you care. Here I am interested in an economic opportunity, willing to work hard, willing to take risks and all you can say you shiteating motherfucking pathetic limpdick uncle tom, all you can tell me is how you dont do no more what I be wanting to do. Here I am trying to earn a living and you standing in my way. YOU STANDING IN MY WAY, LINK! (19)

The long pause that introduces this scene, communicated by the stacking of the speech prefixes on the page with no dialogue, intensifies the brothers' argument. The play imparts a foreboding quality to the dialogue through rests which Parks in her introduction defines as "a pause, a breather; make a transition" (2) and as spells. Parks writes that a spell "is a place where the figures experience their pure true simple state. While no action or stage business is necessary, directors should fill this moment as they best see fit" (2). Until the final sequence of the play, the viewer does not realize how little he or she understood about the figures' "pure true simple state." In the spells the director can either offer the viewer some physical evidence of what is to come or further elaborate the structural hustle the play performs, hiding the malice the brothers feel toward each other until the death scene. In the production of *Topdog/Underdog* at the Ambassador Theater, the director George C. Wolfe filled the spells with comic action. His choice tempered the intensity of the dialogue, which further magnified the stunning quality of the final death scene.

Moreover, in the Broadway production Mos Def portrayed Booth as a more volatile character than Lincoln. His aggression undermines his con and reinforces his status as impersonator, which the play introduces in the opening scene. The eruptions of anger point to his inability to come to terms with the loss of his mother, a violent effacement crystallized when "She was putting her stuff in bags. She had all them nice suitcases but she was putting her stuff in bags." Unlike the psychic trauma discussed in Chapter 5 that all subjects suffer at the loss of the mother, Booth's comment draws attention to the personal nature of the loss and the need for heightened modes of compensation.

In order to deal with maternal abandonment, which transforms to sexual abandonment in the second half of the play, Booth produces a narrative foregrounding his autonomy that he cannot sustain by himself; he needs an audience. He therefore creates (I use the word "creates" to draw attention to the brothers' dubious acts of self-willed production throughout the play) an identity that compensates for the loss of his mother through expressions of an exaggerated libido (he places himself in contrast to his "pathetic limpdick uncle tom" brother and in another scene asserts "Im hot. I need constant sexual release," 43). While in oedipalization in general the female sexual object takes the place of the lost maternal object, Booth's love interest Grace, whom he calls "Amazing Grace," must compensate for a psychic and spiritual loss (hence her name) that exceeds Freud's paradigm. Similarly to the ritualized mode of repair depicted in *Joe Turner's Come and Gone*, the familial loss Booth suffers requires rupture that occurs when he kills Grace (41). One might argue that at the end of *Joe Turner's Come and Gone* Loomis too kills "grace" in order to make room for his revolutionary practices. But unlike Loomis, Booth never moves beyond the need for collaborative performance and therefore crumbles in agony when he kills his brother at the end of the play. Unlike *Joe Turner's Come and Gone*, where the familial trauma results from white racism, Parks' play mirrors the national drama in the familial, creating ripples of trauma from the family to the nation. She creates a similar structure in *Father Comes Home from the Wars (Parts 1, 8 & 9)* and *The Book of Grace*, refusing to absolve anyone in her theater from wrongdoing. Her choice prevents Booth from achieving the self-sufficiency key to Loomis' final act and presents collaboration as inescapable.

Booth's recollection of maternal abandonment foregrounds his other coping strategy; besides substituting Grace for the lost maternal object, he lashes out at Lincoln. Booth focuses on the loss of their mother while Lincoln recalls their father leaving, making Booth more violent since he is more closely aligned with oedipalization and tied to a primary loss. Nevertheless, both brothers create identities to compensate for their familial losses, but when circumstances threaten the plausibility of their performances, the characters become violent. Booth's aggressive language communicates the degree of his violation and the shortcomings of his strategies of repairing his status as foundling. He attempts to account for his loss through a revision of birth order that their mother allegedly authorized. Booth's inability to craft an assimilable identity suggests a critique of the status of the descendants of enslaved Africans in the US who suffer the loss of the national ideal and experience that loss as a particularly violent separation. The same subjects must experience the secondary loss of nation when, in Du Bois' words, they are refused with a glance. Dismissed at every turn, Booth refuses to let his brother deny him as well.

Booth's attempt to control Lincoln through verbal manipulation intensifies Lincoln's internal conflict and his rivalry with Booth. The younger brother accuses the older one of not acting like his brother, of not performing the designated role of older sibling by taking care of him. He suggests that Lincoln should "look out for him" by teaching him how to throw the cards. Booth attempts to persuade Lincoln, aggressively evoking their familial relationship. As the play clarifies, however, Lincoln's choice to forfeit one form of hustling for another transfers the tension from his social identity to his familial one. Lincoln decides to stop throwing the cards after someone shoots and kills his friend Lonny. He begins working at a local arcade, but quickly realizes the economic limitations of his choice.

Unlike Booth who fixates on the loss of their mother, Lincoln recalls losing their father, his friend Lonny, and his ex-wife Cookie. Lincoln imbues each of his losses with a queer affiliation that offsets his personal investment in any one object and sets his identity at a critical distance from the melancholic subject. For example, when Lonny dies Lincoln loses his "stickman," the member of the crew who "knows the game inside and out" (72). The designation "stickman" transforms the homosocial overtones of Lincoln's crew in general into a homosexual relationship between Lincoln and the stickman in particular that multiplies Lincoln's desire. While he appears to live with Booth because his sweet wife Cookie left him, purportedly after letting Booth sample her goodies, Lincoln's recollection of the roles his professional relationships play in his current circumstances offers another rationale for the break-up and subsequent displacement. Therefore, instead of creating ruptures in Lincoln's performance of multiple identities, his intimate losses serve to bolster his slippery performance.

Booth's practice of recalling painful childhood memories creates a tension between dialogue and action, which foreshadows Lincoln's death. Before Booth recalls their mother's hasty, haphazard abandonment, he appeals to his older brother, suggesting that they become a team.

BOOTH Yeah. Scheming and dreaming. No one throws the cards like you, Link. And with yr moves and my magic, and we get Grace and a girl for you to round out the posse. We'd be golden, bro! Am I right?
LINCOLN
LINCOLN
BOOTH Am I right?
LINCOLN I don't throw thuh cards, 3-card. I don't touch thuh cards no more. (19)

The two spells, one just for Lincoln and the other scripted for Lincoln and Booth, provide time onstage for the brothers to figure out how to respond to one another. In these moments, mirroring the ambiguity fundamental to their identification, their motivations remain unclear. The position of the brothers onstage in the moments when no dialogue takes place – the spells – demonstrates how gesture, comportment, and bodily proximity produce identifications.

Throughout the play Lincoln consistently refuses Booth's hurtful demands for partnership, claiming he has found a legitimate job. Yet when Lincoln loses his job he resorts to throwing the cards and hides, or pretends to hide, his choice from Booth. Lincoln enters the apartment after a successful day of hustling and does not notice, or does not seem to notice, Booth standing behind a screen. The stage directions specify that "*The room looks empty, as if neither brother is home. Lincoln comes in . . . Booth appears in the room. He was standing behind the screen, unseen all this time*" (82, 83). Upon entering the room, Lincoln begins to brag about the money he won as Booth looks on. When Booth appears, Lincoln quickly conceals his money. Booth, aware that his brother has betrayed him by throwing the cards again without him, challenges Lincoln to a game of three-card. The game leads to their final argument, the loss of Booth's inheritance to Lincoln, and Lincoln's death. Considering the characters' positions onstage, the viewer never knows whether Lincoln hustles Booth throughout the play – does Lincoln know Booth is in the room? – or whether Lincoln's hustling begins in the final scene once he starts throwing the cards. Is the stage direction "*unseen all this time*" written for the audience's benefit or the actors'?

The play foreshadows the final death scene as the brothers practice Lincoln's assassination. Convinced that his boss intends to replace him with a wax dummy, Lincoln, donning honest Abe's signature stovepipe hat, a fake beard, and whiteface makeup, persuades Booth to help him practice his act. Lincoln complains, "I don't wanna lose my job" (33). Booth counsels, "Then you gotta jazz up yr act. Elaborate yr moves, you know. You was always too stiff with it. You cant just sit there! Maybe, when they shoot you, you know, leap up flail yr arms then fall down and wiggle around and shit so they gotta shoot you more than once. Blam Blam Blam! Blam!" (34). *Topdog/Underdog* consistently presents Booth insistently directing Lincoln's actions. In this scene Lincoln solicits Booth's advice. Later on Booth asserts, "Look at me! I am the assassin! *I am Booth!!* Come on man this is life and death! Go all out! (*Lincoln goes all out*)" (50). Booth's chilling and prophetic line functions ostensibly in the service of helping Lincoln perfect his performance so that Lincoln can keep his job. Even though Lincoln lives in Booth's "home," Lincoln pays the bills. Booth needs Lincoln, but by directing Lincoln's actions, Booth establishes his essential role in the relationship. The bi-weekly paycheck Lincoln brings home helps to maintain the brothers' material needs, but Lincoln's performance also helps to establish a psychic relationship. Booth's insistence that Lincoln "Go all out," a line that echoes a command made in *The America Play*, qualifies Lincoln's performance as a matter of life and death both in the realm of the arcade and in terms of the brothers' relationship. Booth's constant need to control Lincoln through verbal manipulation and physical commands reflects Booth's need to repeatedly establish his position; he wants Lincoln to need him.

THREE-CARD MONTE AND THE DEATH DRIVE

The practice scene functions as a stunning example of repetition/reproduction. Not only does the repetition of the assassination (and three-card monte for that matter) serve to materialize Lincoln's and Booth's identities as hustlers, the scene also provides another life for *The America Play* and the history of Lincoln, building on the logic Freud elaborates in his description of the death drive. In a discussion of repetition, Freud is as unavoidable a figure as Melville and Ellison are in a discussion of the confidence men who feed into *Topdog/Underdog*. In 1930, with the publication of *Civilization and Its Discontents*, Freud claimed "hunger and love" as the two instincts that move the world.[24] Hunger denotes the need for somatic preservation, "preserving the individual," while love "strives after objects" and describes the need for psychic preservation. Love enables the ego to introject objects and grow. Freud had contemplated the function of the instincts, or drives, as early as the publication of "On Narcissism: An Introduction" (1914). He did not fully conceptualize aggression as the death drive until 1920 in *Beyond the Pleasure Principle*:

My next step was taken in *Beyond the Pleasure Principle* (1920), when the compulsion to repeat and the conservative character of the instinctual life first attracted my attention. Starting from speculations of the beginning of life and from biological parallels, I drew the conclusion that, besides the instinct to preserve living substance and to join it into ever larger units, there must exist another, contrary instinct seeking to dissolve those units and to bring them back to their primaeval, inorganic state. That is to say, as well as Eros there was an instinct of death.[25]

Freud indicates that understanding the compulsion to repeat enabled him to theorize the instinct of death. He explains in *Beyond the Pleasure Principle* how individuals repeat performative strategies to manage the psychic pain of loss.

Freud describes the fort/da game, a strategy that a child develops in response to his mother leaving. As I summarize in Chapter 1, Freud observed a "good" little boy who never cried when his mother left and who had an interesting habit of throwing his toys under his bed. When he threw the toys he would say "fort," the German word for "gone." Anyone who has spent time with a toddler would be familiar with this game. Often children sitting in a high-chair or any structure that limits their mobility throw their toys off the edge of the apparatus and then wait for someone to retrieve them. Freud noticed on another occasion that the child altered this game slightly by playing it with a yo-yo, a "wooden reel with a piece of string tied round it."[26]

What he did was to hold the reel by the string and very skillfully throw it over the edge of his curtained cot, so that it disappeared into it, at the same time uttering his expressive "o-o-o-o." He then pulled the reel out of the cot again by the string and hailed its reappearance with a joyful "da" ["there"]. This, then, was the complete game – *disappearance and return* [my emphasis]. As a rule one only witnessed its first act, which was repeated untiringly as a game in itself, though there is no doubt that the greater pleasure was attached to the second act.[27]

In developing the game with the wooden reel, the boy is able to control the return. The game that the boy plays enables him to cope with the painful history – his mother's leaving. The game is successful because it generates pleasure. The game, however, does not resolve the primary issue; it does not bring his mother back. Reading the fort/da episode as a performance suggests that individuals learn to manage psychic loss through creative behaviors that secure the individual but do not directly mourn the loss. Therefore, as discussed in Chapter 1, the individual must repeat the behavior, the game, over and over again.

Freud's description of fort/da introduces performance into his theorization of loss. The game addresses a personal and individual history. I read the repeated performances of three-card monte in *Topdog/Underdog* as a game Booth aggressively pursues to help him cope with abandonment. *Topdog/Underdog* moves beyond the theorization of personal histories, intertwining the repetition of the game of three-card monte with the repetition of the game of assassination played by Lincoln and willing patrons in the arcade. Lincoln not only repeats the game at the arcade, he also practices his performance at home. The game that he plays involves a community of actors and stages in explicit detail the national history that it attempts to resolve. In the fort/da game, the wooden reel stands in for the mother. In the arcade Lincoln stands in for Abe Lincoln. Both games are mimetic and therefore create a productive incompleteness. While the games cannot recreate the scenario of loss – the mother leaving or the assassination of Abraham Lincoln – the choices the players make point to the effects of the loss. Freud's observations on the compulsion to repeat establish the stakes of his performance: to quote Booth, "this is life and death!"

Even though Freud offers the example of the game to demonstrate the individual's pursuit of control, in order for the game to work the little boy must first create chaos. Freud describes the little boy's "disturbing" habit, before he develops the fort/da game, of "taking any small objects he could get hold of and throwing them away from him into a corner, under a bed, and so on." He claims that "hunting for his toys," presumably done by some adult, "and picking them up was often quite a business."[28] Instead of exhibiting his ability to control his toys, the little boy's initial reaction to his mother's departure models a pleasure generated through manipulation. While Freud attributes a greater pleasure to the child's ability to establish order through fort/da, the child's original game points to the aggression that Freud ultimately calls the death drive.

As we have seen, Freud describes the competing instincts that drive humans toward cultivating civilization and the equally powerful instincts that push humans toward destruction. Following from his analysis, conducted midway between the two World Wars, he concludes, "civilization is a process in the service of Eros, whose purpose is to combine single human individuals, and after that families, then races, peoples and nations, into one great unity, the unity of mankind."[29] Freud did not suggest in 1930 that the aggressive tendencies of the death drive disappeared in the service of civilization. Managing the competing forces of Eros and death, the individual learns to direct the aggressiveness associated with the death drive inward instead of outward. In *Beyond the Pleasure Principle*, the little boy learns to turn the aggression he feels toward his mother for leaving toward an object that becomes an extension of him. Through the string the boy becomes connected to the wooden reel. The pleasure the little boy feels after he masters the return of the reel displaces the unpleasurable memory of his mother's departure, but the pleasure he feels does not eliminate the utility of aggression. In order for the little boy to feel the pleasure of the return of the reel, he must send it away.

Even though Freud represents aggressiveness as the largest threat to civilization in *Civilization and Its Discontents*, earlier he depicted the utilitarian property of aggression in "Reflections upon War and Death" (1915). As is normal in any time of war, in 1915 Freud was less interested in the unity of "races, peoples and nations" and more concerned with how states solidify themselves. The shift in his writing from 1915 to 1930, marked by the way he categorizes aggression in these two texts, reflects a political turn, not a theoretical lapse. In "Reflections upon War and Death," as in *Civilization and Its Discontents*, Freud claims that civilization suffers when aggression is turned outward through war. He maintains, however, that every stage of human development, including what he categorizes as the primitive instinctual aggressiveness of the death drive, persists even as groups move toward civilization. Therefore in moments of crisis, when the nation is threatened for example, war occurs as a "necessary regression," a return of the forgotten, a rememory.

The civilized state authorizes the aggressive tendencies of the death drive to be turned outward in the service of, and not apparently to the detriment of, civilization. Freud addresses the seeming contradiction between premising civilization on the "renunciation of instinctual satisfaction" and establishing the necessity of national solidification through war, by qualifying war as "temporary" regression: "Undoubtedly the influences of war are among the forces that can bring about such regression; therefore we need not deny adaptability for culture to all who are at the present time displaying uncivilized behaviour, and we may anticipate that the refinement of their instincts will be restored in times of peace."[30] Freud changes his focus from the human implications of war depicted in "Reflections upon War and Death" to the question of how civilization has grown and developed in *Civilization and Its Discontents*, but in both texts the channeling of the death drive remains a crucial mechanism for creating communities.

Topdog/Underdog poses a disarming revision to Freud's theory of the drives. The play depicts how American narratives emerge through strategic choices to conceal aggression. Although Freud maintains "one can suspect from this example that the two kinds of instincts seldom – perhaps never – appear in isolation from each other," he categorizes the struggle between Eros and death as fundamental to the evolution of civilization.[31] Instead of mapping the progression and regression of the death drive, *Topdog/Underdog* depicts the performances that filter the constant dialectical battle between Eros and death. The play suggests that individuals participate in performances that hide the constant struggle of the drives. The mastery of that performativity is measured by its ability to conceal. Moving from Freud's analysis, I am suggesting that *Topdog/Underdog* demonstrates the implications of the competing drives of life and death for understanding both personal and collective histories. Even though Lincoln and Booth consistently turn their aggressive tendencies inward, or at least partially inward, competing instincts informed by affects and social mandates are always, if not primarily, at play. The competition between the instincts constitutes the play, the brothers, and American historical memory.

CONFIDENCE MEN

The persona of confidence man raises questions about the daily psychic maintenance fulfilled through aggression. How would our conception of

American history change if the death drive emerges not as a temporary regression but instead as a constitutive aspect of the story? Freud asserts:

The phenomena of life could be explained from the concurrent or mutually opposing action of these two instincts. It was not easy, however, to demonstrate the activities of this supposed death instinct. The manifestations of Eros were conspicuous and noisy enough. It might be assumed that the death instinct operated silently within the organism towards its dissolution, but that of course was no proof. A more fruitful idea was that a portion of the instinct is diverted towards the external world and comes to light as an instinct of aggressiveness and destructiveness. In this way the instinct itself could be pressed into the service of Eros, in that the organism was destroying some other thing, whether animate or inanimate, instead of destroying its own self.[32]

Through his masquerade the confidence man undermines the fundamental assumption that by directing the instinct of aggressiveness outward "the organism was destroying some other thing, whether animate or inanimate, instead of destroying its own self." Complicating Freud's depiction of "self," the confidence man shows why the self needs to appear before the eyes of others. Instead of presenting a singular antagonism between self and other, the persona of the confidence man highlights the vital symbiosis between the subject and the onlooker. Since the actor does not have complete control over how he or she will appear, then he or she always runs the risk of destroying part of the self through the instinct of aggressiveness.

The confidence man is a useful prototype because his ambiguous identification corrects the general practice of identification. Melville's *The Confidence Man* takes place aboard a steamer *Fidèle* on April 1, departing from St. Louis, Missouri bound for New Orleans, Louisiana. The novel depicts a set of interactions between passengers on the ship and the confidence man. Critics widely disagree on the identity of the confidence man. He has been called unknowable or ambiguous, the devil, Christ, a trickster god, both God and the devil, and a man. The confidence man appears in the first scene of Melville's novel and is described as "a man in cream-colours ... His cheek was fair, his chin downy, his hair flaxen, his hat a white fur one, with a long fleecy nap ... He was unaccompanied by friends ... he was, in the extremest sense of the word, a stranger."[33] The stranger's facade, actions, and disability – he "was not alone dumb, but also deaf" – set him apart from the other passengers on the ship.[34] In the opening scene a group of passengers, including the stranger, gather around a wanted sign that offers a reward for "the capture of a mysterious imposter, supposed to have arrived recently from the East;

quite an original genius in his vocation, as would appear, though wherein his originality consisted was not clearly given."[35] The description of the stranger and the pursuit of the imposter, coupled with the impending reward, establish the "goals" of the novel.

The Confidence Man creates its first metaphorical cue through the juxtaposition of the stranger, who Carolyn L. Karcher argues is "described in terms similar to the apocalyptic Christ,"[36] and "the placard nigh the captain's office," announcing the reward for the imposter.[37] *The Confidence Man*, however, significantly distinguishes the stranger from Christ as described in Revelations by making him dumb. Revelations describes Christ's voice as "the sound of many waters." Alienating the voice, the stranger creates a distance between himself and the message. In order to communicate with the crowd, he begins to write notes which read "Charity thinketh no evil," "Charity suffereth long, and is kind," "Charity endureth all things," Charity never faileth."[38] In the Bible, Paul writes the epistle 1 Corinthians to the church to instill principles for action. The stranger's appropriation of biblical language (1 Corinthians 13:4–8) foregrounds the manipulation of charity throughout the novel. Similarly to the trust Booth attempts to command with his encouraging "Watch me close watch me close now," the stranger's references to charity cause him to appear wholly unthreatening. Moreover, just as Booth attempts to avert the attention of his imagined audience, commanding "Watch me close watch me close now," a sly reproduction, Melville's confidence man will corrupt the charity he draws attention to in the opening scene.

Although many critics have argued that the confidence man takes on many guises throughout the novel, if one takes seriously Karcher's compelling claim that "this Christlike stranger initiates" the confidence man's masquerade, then this initial performance inflects each subsequent performance. Thinking in terms of America's racial politics, perhaps the most pertinent incarnation of the confidence man, in terms of appearance, occurs when he takes on his second guise as Black Guinea. Black Guinea is described thus:

not the least attractive object, for a time, was a grotesque negro cripple, in towcloth attire and an old coal sifter of a tambourine in his hand, who, owing to something wrong about his legs, was, in effect, cut down to the stature of a Newfoundland dog; his knotted black fleece and good-natured, honest black face rubbing against the upper part of people's thighs as he made shift to shuffle about, making music, such as it was, and raising a smile even from the gravest.[39]

As Karcher explains, the description of Black Guinea in towcloth creates an image associated with slavery. Coupled with his spatial position, "cut down to the stature of a Newfoundland dog," Guinea pleases the white passengers by "rubbing against the upper part of people's thighs," and thus participating in a sexual fantasy his location authorizes. As Karcher asserts, "he indulges the sexual fantasies these respectable whites project on the Negro, and titillates their repressed lusts."[40] Nevertheless, the confidence man as Guinea cannot evoke even paltry monetary remuneration from the crowd until he actively performs the role of a grinning dog-like invalid. In order to garner favor, he must affirm the association of denigration with blackness, the joke being that his first and, I am suggesting, primary incarnation situates the constitution of whiteness in relationship to the grinning dog-like invalid. Associating Guinea with a dog, a familiar association for black people more generally, the novel deploys animality to delineate a representational space in which the human abides.

In order to induce the crowd's charity, Guinea must participate in a specific performance that not only solidifies their identification of him, but also confirms certain aspects of the onlookers' identity:

now and then he would pause, throwing back his head and opening his mouth like an elephant for tossed apples at a menagerie; when, making space before him, people would have a bout at a strange sort of pitch penny game, the cripple's mouth being at once target and purse, and he hailing each expertly caught copper with a cracked bravura from his tambourine. To be the subject of almsgiving is trying, and to feel in duty bound to appear cheerfully grateful under the trial, must be still more so; but whatever his secret emotions, he swallowed them, while still retaining each copper this side of the esophagus. And nearly always he grinned, and only once or twice did he wince, which was when certain coins, tossed by more playful almoners, came inconveniently nigh to his teeth, an accident whose unwelcomeness was not unedged by the circumstances that the pennies thus thrown proved buttons.[41]

Guinea supplements what he appears to be by also acting like an animal. Only then do the passengers deem him worthy of their charity. He still must pay a price for their benevolence. Fighting not to choke or wince in pain from the projectiles aimed at his mouth, Guinea "always grinned." Placing the scene in a historical context, Susan M. Ryan explains, "This representation of charitable giving as purchased entertainment, as public humiliation, and (indirectly) as hired fellatio was atypical, to say the least, in the era's discourses on benevolence."[42] The scene's descriptive uniqueness draws attention to the metaphorical import culled through the performance of "purchased entertainment, as public humiliation, and (indirectly) as hired fellatio" by a stranger who first appears in the novel as a white man. The hyper-realism of the scene uncovers the passengers' thirst to solidify their racial superiority, while the placement of the scene reveals race as a floating signifier that undermines the passengers' best efforts.

The racial ambiguity attached to the game of fetch moves the implications of the performance away from Guinea's identity to the way the crowd identifies him while playing the "game." As Karcher explains, "a 'grinning negro' beggar ... will play a major role in exposing the cant of his fellow pilgrims' millennial aspirations,"[43] a mode of identification that Parks' late twentieth-century audience might share. Through the game the passengers perform their superiority and secure Guinea's position as subhuman. The necessity to participate in performances that authenticate whiteness demonstrates the gripping anxiety felt about the category. The passengers' participation in the game acknowledges the limitations of physical characteristics as definitive signs of race. In order to authenticate Guinea's "black face" the passengers played along. "We cannot fully understand Black Guinea's role in *The Confidence-Man*, however, without realizing that he embodies the enslaved black man not merely as America's chief victim, but also as her apocalyptic nemesis," Karcher explains, and goes on to say, "Guinea ... is a victim-turned-inquisitor."[44]

The passengers' willingness to interact with Guinea during the game exposes how race straddles the boundaries of performance and ontology. The performativity of race prevents the passengers from affecting Guinea's identity through their identifications. Race becomes a stubborn signifier that seems to avoid concealment through performance. In the same moment that the passengers use Guinea to secure their "millennial aspirations," Guinea's racialized hustle highlights the limitations of their authority. While Ryan primarily reads Guinea as a victim, I contend, following on from Karcher's criticism, that his racial ambiguity interrupts the appearance of the passengers' whiteness, and instead demonstrates how every act of identification reads back onto the identity of the participant and the viewer.

The multiple personas Melville's confidence man assumes for the remainder of the novel pressure the idea of American exceptionalism and create a space to question the racial implications of America's idealized self-made man. The slipperiness of the confidence man's race calls to mind the contemporary practice of minstrelsy and how Bert Williams and George Walker's *In Dahomey* positions this racial masquerade as a hustle. The comic duo Williams and Walker rose to national prominence through playing the roles of Shylock Homestead (Williams) and Rareback Pinkerton (Walker). The novelty of its all-black cast successfully markets the protean musical, which features Williams and Walker on a mission to return a family treasure to its owner. In their pursuit, they travel from Boston to Florida to Dahomey. While the entire musical "plays with the boundaries of racial categories," I am primarily interested in how the opening scene establishes hustling as a performative practice that interrupts the materialization of race.[45]

The opening scene takes place in front of an "Intelligence Office," foregrounding mystery and "the theme of espionage hovering provocatively in the backdrop."[46] Just as the opening scene of *Topdog/Underdog* and the sign nigh the captain's office in *The Confidence Man* seek to lure the spectator in with the promise of cooperation and privileged information, the nineteenth-century version of what amounts to an infomercial that begins *In Dahomey* elaborates what the drama means by "Intelligence." Dr. Straight, "in name only" according to the characters, like the Foundling Father is a "fakir."[47] He peddles the cream "Oblicuticus" and the tonic "Straightaline," which can "immediately transform" "any dark skin son or daughter of the genus Africanus" "into an Apollo or Cleopatra with a hirsute appendage worthy of a Greek goddess."[48] His malapropism winks at the history of minstrelsy, while the staging of a satisfied customer convincingly deforms racial embodiment. His customer has "kinky" hair on one side and "silky straight hair" on the other. One side of the face displays "the bronze of nature" while the other "the peachlike complexion."[49] Notably, the desired complexion renders the idealized customer racially ambiguous, suggesting the space in between, the site of trickery, as the desired social body. "Rather perversely, at this moment, instead of becoming 'white,' the Oblicuticus consumer becomes something beyond or strangely outside of – perhaps even signifying on – whiteness."[50] In *The Confidence Man*, Guinea's previous embodiment of whiteness nods ever so slightly toward incorporating minstrelsy within the genealogy of trickery, and so too does Dr. Straight's sales pitch. *In Dahomey* reveals US black theatricality as a confidence game that black performance deforms. The possibilities of black performance, as I have shown, preoccupy black playwrights throughout the twentieth century and spark the interest of novelists.

The Confidence Man draws attention to the way race creates a visual matrix that orients the historical gaze; *Invisible Man* highlights strategies an individual covered with the discourse of blackness can enact to participate actively in history. In *Invisible Man*, the unnamed protagonist discovers the political potential of manipulating one's appearance,

through the chance juxtaposition of an encounter with Jack, the leader
of the Brotherhood (the organization that employs the protagonist), and
an introduction to the character Rinehart. As Ralph Ellison explains,
"Masking is a play upon possibility and ours is a society in which
possibilities are many. When American life is most American it is apt to
be most theatrical."[51] Ellison positions the theatrical as the *sine qua non* of
American culture in general. Following Ellison's assertion, and Toni
Morrison's analysis of the Africanist presence in American culture in
Playing in the Dark, one could argue that when American culture is at
its most anxious it is apt to resurrect black theatricality.

The protagonist's argumentative encounter with Jack unavoidably
anticipates his introduction to Rinehart. Feeling "confused and listless,"
the protagonist goes to meet with the leaders of the Brotherhood to
discuss a rally. The scene dramatizes an intense debate over what qualifies
as evidence warranting political action. Already feeling the tension before
he entered the room, the protagonist coyly responds to the accusations
and questions of the leaders of the Brotherhood. And just as the protagonist shifts the momentum of the conversation by evoking his race as an
irrefutable category of knowledge, Jack disrupts the primacy of physical
evidence:

suddenly something seemed to erupt out of his face. You're seeing things,
I thought, hearing it strike sharply against the table and roll as his arm shot
out and snatched an object the size of a large marble and dropped it, plop! into
his glass ... I stared at the glass ... and there on the bottom of the glass lay an
eye. A glass eye ... I looked from his face to the glass, thinking, he's disem-
boweled himself just in order to confound me ... And the others had known it all
along. They aren't even surprised. I stared at the eye, aware of Jack pacing up and
down, shouting.[52]

By revealing his inability to see out of one eye, Jack compels the protagonist
to consider how appearance relates to the presumptions and desires of the
viewer. Jack's violent act disorients the protagonist, creating a momentary
sense of chaos, which prepares the protagonist to see "the personification of
chaos" and understand how Rinehart represents America and change.

The protagonist leaves his meeting with the leaders of the Brotherhood
feeling beaten and dejected because they have upset the imperative of
biological certainty. In order to avoid anyone he knows recognizing him,
he adopts a disguise. Instead of creating anonymity, however, his slight
changes to his appearance create false recognition. As he walks down the
street, several different people think he is a man named Rinehart. In each
encounter the protagonist as Rinehart serves a different function for his

audience. His masquerade evokes pleasure, fear, and amazement, while it also leads him to question, "could he be all of them: Rine the runner and Rine the gambler and Rine the briber and Rine the lover and Rinehart the Reverend? Could he himself be both rind and heart? What is real anyway? ... His world was possibility and he knew it."[53] The protagonist's experiences as Rinehart help him to understand the political risks of presenting a fixed appearance when one does not exist. "Rine the rascal was at home" because he knew "the truth was always a lie," just as Jack's political vision had seemed like a lie after the protagonist attended the rally. Jack, however, reestablished the acuity of his political vision by revealing the limits of his physical vision, which he had concealed with his glass eye. The protagonist's masquerade closely follows the exposure of the glass eye, and through this proximity Rinehart moves the tradition of the confidence man. The scenes turn the protagonist's digression into a powerful redirection of political possibility. *Invisible Man* uncovers the echo of exposure in each act of concealment.

Jack's aggressiveness does not destroy the protagonist; rather, it leads to growth. Rinehart's existence, as the exposure of Jack's eye continually mirrors, exposes the possibilities of chaos, which are covered over in Freud's fort/da scenario. As Jack disarms the protagonist, he teaches him the art of manipulation. Similarly, when the little boy Freud describes throws his toys, he runs the risk of not seeing their return, but he also creates the possibility that someone else will return them. Equipped with sharper vision, the protagonist begins to realize the advantage of taking a strategic departure from history structured through cosmic coherence. The break Jack's performance enacts signals a choice to conceal his personal history, and it allows the protagonist to see invisibility as a choice.

Extending the critique of the self-made man that his constitutive counterpart the confidence man necessitates, Parks resurrects the man she names the Foundling Father. In *Topdog/Underdog*, as the brothers practice Lincoln's death scene, Lincoln reveals why certain regressions become part of the larger historical narrative and others remain invisible. The movement that Freud describes from civilization to national narrative delineates which stories are repeatedly told. Therefore, even though the competing drives are always functioning, *Topdog/Underdog* demonstrates how the eruptions of the death drive transform from repetitions (always functioning and informing the individual's behavior) to regressions (events that impact the status of the social organization). Lincoln's final attempt to refine his performance as honest Abe reveals the necessary regressions his practice produces. He asks Booth:

LINCOLN Whatdoyathink?
BOOTH I dunno, man. Something about it. I dunno. It was looking too real or
    something.
LINCOLN They don't want it looking too real. I'd scare the customers. Then I'd
    be out for sure. Yr trying to get me fired.
BOOTH Im trying to help. Cross my heart.
LINCOLN People are funny about they Lincoln shit. Its historical. People like
    they historical shit in a certain way. They like it to unfold the way they
    folded it up. Neatly like a book. Not raggedy and bloody and screaming.
    You trying to get me fired.
    (*Rest*)
    I am uh brother playing Lincoln. Its uh stretch for anyones imagination.
    And it aint easy for me neither. Every day I put on that shit, I leave my own
    shit at the door and I put on that shit and I go out there and I make it work.
    I make it look easy but its hard. That shit is hard. But it works. Cause I work
    it. And you trying to get me fired.
    (*Rest*) (48–51)

As Lincoln notes, authenticity emerges as a primary concern in his performance. His ability to play Lincoln relies upon the patrons' desire for history
presented in a certain way. The maintenance of national histories requires
that Lincoln portray a repeating progression, one that unfolds the way the
customers folded it up. Therefore, in each performative regression Lincoln
must conceal the aggressive, raggedy, bloody, screaming seams of the story.
In an attempt to not call attention to how hard it is to make this national
narrative work, Lincoln masks the material inconsistencies that mark each
performance as a deliberate reproduction and not a necessary historical
repetition. The historical repetition tends toward concealment, while the
reproduction tends toward exposure. In each reenactment, Lincoln remakes
the myth, but the process of mapping must remain unseen.

    Moreover, he's a brother, a black man, playing Lincoln. The duality
of "brother" points to the added racial performance necessitated by
Lincoln's role as a black man who must wear whiteface to play honest
Abe. Lincoln's ability to participate in the national story creates a bitter
historical irony and requires that he conceal his racial status. Lincoln's
use of whiteface evokes minstrelsy, which, Glenda Carpio argues, Parks
uses "to underscore the ways that the very medium in which she works
has been complicit in making black suffering into spectacle."[54] The
display of black bodies cannot be separated from the deformation
made possible through black performance. Therefore, the screaming
that Lincoln emotes as he tries to make it work, and the wailing that
Brazil mimics in *The America Play*, exist within a continuum of black

sound demarcated by the mo'nin of the lynching victim discussed in Chapter 5 and the screams heard aboard the slave ship analyzed in Chapter 6. "At the same time, [Parks] makes those minstrel features abstract and unfamiliar and turns them into vehicles for remembering and honoring the dead. Thus, while Parks creates comedy by inverting, juxtaposing, and otherwise de-familiarizing the features of minstrelsy, she uses that comedy as a counterpoint to highlight the tragic aspects of her drama."[55] Hence, Parks' signature dark comedy draws from the tragedy that is Lincoln making his performance work, which requires that he assimilate seamlessly the historical legacy of black men in the United States, as well as the current social status of black men, into his performance. The impossibility of such a move blackens up the performance and creates the same rippling effect as Booth's recollections of abandonment. Nevertheless, Lincoln covers up with whiteface in an attempt to "make it work." And it works. 'Cause he works it. Despite the psychic death he dies everyday at work. A death made material through his performance.

The cost to black men of incorporating themselves into the national narrative is not the only interesting aspect of Lincoln's role as a brother playing Lincoln. What I find even more fascinating is the coupling of him consistently turning the death drive inward with a historical rupture, Abraham Lincoln's assassination, which although it occurred only once, must be performed as a part of the national narrative over and over again. The constructed ordering of the return to the story of Abe Lincoln the president and the simultaneous disavowal of the repeated death of Lincoln the brother suggests how the multilayered function of the death drive corresponds to the movement from historical event to national narrative, from repetition to reproduction. Lincoln's performance undermines who he is; it does violence to his ego, and therefore reflects a willed internalization of the death drive even as it mimics Abe Lincoln's death.

Lincoln's performance is "uh stretch for anyones imagination" because it embodies a fundamental break in Freud's conceptualization of the death drive. Even though Freud concedes to momentary displays of uncivilized behavior, he maintains "we may anticipate that the refinement of their instincts will be restored in times of peace." Yet as *Topdog/Underdog* depicts, the instinct to turn the aggressive tendencies of the death drive outward, whether on the part of the white patrons in the arcade or in Booth's verbal and ultimately physical assault, is a part of the performative practices that maintain this national narrative.

WATCH CLOSELY

The multiple roles the brothers must play significantly contribute to the final outcome, as the play's ability to shock demonstrates the efficacy of Lincoln's and Booth's performances. The shock of Lincoln's death generates questions about the relationship between one's identity and the appearance of another. One could easily dismiss the competition between the brothers throughout the play as sibling rivalry. And even when Booth challenges Lincoln to a game of three-card monte after he discovers Lincoln "was out throwing" behind his back, the stakes do not appear to be life and death (96). The play challenges these assumptions, asserting that the individual's appearance is always a matter of life and death.

Nevertheless, Booth had admonished Lincoln early on to "go all out." So with Booth's five hundred dollar inheritance at stake, Lincoln begins to throw the cards (Figure 11). Lincoln commands, "Lean in close and watch me now: who see thuh black card who see thuh black card I see thuh black card black cards thuh winner pick thuh black card that's thuh winner pick thuh red card that's thuh loser pick thuh other red card thats thuh other loser pick thuh black card you pick thuh winner. Watch me as I throw thuh cards. Here we go" (101). Lincoln's patter repeats the list of instructions, heard again and again throughout the play, advising the mark to look. Nevertheless, Lincoln admonishes Booth "This is for real now," implying the elevated stakes of their interaction and the implicit inversion of the instruction "Watch me now." Drawing Booth into the game, Lincoln demonstrates the danger his multiple roles create. He asks, "You think we're really brothers?" (101). Booth, baffled, responds "Huh?" (101). Lincoln the master confidence man continues, "I know we *brothers*, but is we really brothers, you know, blood brothers or not, you and me, whatduhyathink?" (102). Lincoln's patter builds Booth's confidence, and then his question undermines it. Booth, now distracted, responds "I think we're brothers" (102). By questioning their lineage Lincoln calls attention to each of their conflicting roles and the work required to mask the slippage. Lincoln should not hustle Booth, but he does, asking "You think we're really brothers?" Having disarmed Booth, Lincoln encourages, "Go head man, wheres thuh deuce? (*In a flash Booth points out a card.*) ... (*The 2 brothers lock eyes. Lincoln turns over the card that Booth selected and Booth, in a desperate break of concentration, glances down to see that he has chosen the wrong card*)" (102). Lincoln's questions give him a strategic advantage. The paradox of being a brother playing

Figure 11 Actors Jeffrey Wright and Mos Def in *Topdog/Underdog*, Ambassador Theatre, Broadway, April 7 to August 11, 2002, directed by George C. Wolfe

Lincoln transforms into being a brother preying on Booth. Leveraging the slippage embedded in his identity, Lincoln gives Booth license to play a different role.

The historical imperative made material in the play is chilling and informative. Humiliated, disoriented, and betrayed, Booth attacks Lincoln; grabbing him he points a gun at his neck. Before Lincoln can reason with

Booth, Booth shoots and Lincoln slumps to the floor. As Parks argues, "There's a relationship with the past, an important one ... But I think to focus on that relationship and de-emphasize the relationship with the person right in the room with you is the great mistake of American culture and the mistake of history. We have to deal with what's happening right now."[56] When Lincoln hustles Booth in the final scene of the play, he opens up chaotic possibilities that Booth instantly forecloses by killing Lincoln. Lincoln's act forces Booth to confront the betrayal of their parents and necessitates that Booth step outside of their traumatic past to face the man in the room. Unfortunately, for Booth to plunge outside what he understands as his family history requires that he reconsider the one relationship he knows to be true. Booth would rather lose Lincoln than lose him as a brother. This is an American play, so Lincoln must die. And like the death of his namesake, his death draws into question the unfinished legacy of Lincoln the president and uncovers, for those who have watched closely, another means of passing through the hole left by Lincoln.

Epilogue: black movements

Tarell Alvin McCraney's In the Red and Brown Water

Tarell Alvin McCraney's *In the Red and Brown Water*, the first play in the *Brother/Sister Plays* trilogy, begins "like a chant or a moan."[1] In the Public Theater production (2009) you hear the central character Oya's "(sharp breath out) Ah!" and then the chorus of characters puzzles over her death (12).[2] With few observations and fewer answers, Oya (Kianné Muschett) confirms, "Oya in the air Oya ..." (12). Similarly to *Blues for Mister Charlie*, the play begins with a dead central figure and revolves around figuring out what caused her demise. The play depicts a sequence of Oya's dreams deferred. Oya defers attending a college called State on a track and field scholarship to care for her ailing mother Mama Moja who dies a few months later. Although she runs like the wind, State does not offer her a scholarship for the next academic year. After her mother dies, Oya begins dating Shango (Sterling K. Brown) and yearns for a life with him. Unfortunately that dream must too be deferred; Oya is infertile and unable to consummate her relationship with Shango through the birth of a child, the prize signifier of adulthood in her community. Oya settles for another man, Ogun Size (Marc Damon Johnson), who provides stability but no passion. She longs for a child and spends most of her life sitting on the porch waiting. When she learns, however, that another woman in the neighborhood is expecting Shango's child, she cuts off her ear and bleeds to death, fulfilling the only event in a sequence of deferred desire.

Although McCraney's plays focus on deferred dreams, his career has not experienced postponement, boasting what many theater critics mark as a dream emergence in New York and London. The second play in the trilogy, *The Brothers Size*, was first produced as a part of Public Theater's Under the Radar Festival in January 2007, and months later premiered in London at the Young Vic to critical acclaim. McCraney's distinctive style, unparalleled at least in recent history, his rocket-like launch to stardom, and his youth (born October 17, 1980) have made him a media darling. Besides receiving numerous awards, including a Royal Shakespeare

Company/Warwick International Playwriting Residency, London's *Evening Standard* Award (for most promising playwright), a National Endowment for the Arts Outstanding New American Play Award, and the inaugural *New York Times* Outstanding Playwright Award, the young playwright has been lauded effusively by the theater world. According to theater critic Randy Gener, "one quick Google search brings up results that make him seem like the Second Coming: 'one of the most exciting and distinctive young playwrights to have emerged in many years' (Oskar Eustis), 'one of the most startling new voices to emerge in American theatre' (Emily Mann), 'actually kind of a miracle' (Mark Russell), 'the new Shakespeare' (Afrodiziak.com) and – my favorite – 'the sexiest writer in town' (*Evening Standard*)."[3] He is well worth the hype, according to *New York Times* chief theater critic Ben Brantley, who asserts, "Watching [*The Brother/Sister Plays*] you experience the excited wonder that comes from witnessing something rare in the theater: a new, authentically original vision. It's what people must have felt during productions of the early works of Eugene O'Neill in the 1920s or of Sam Shepard in the 1960's."[4] McCraney's ability to sample from traditions as diverse as Yoruba cosmology, Federico García Lorca's *Yerma*, the sounds of Motown, and hip-hop, as well as to signify on the theatrical innovation of Zora Neale Hurston in his use of bawdy comedy and folk traditions, August Wilson in his syncretism and resistance to teleology, and Suzan-Lori Parks in his formal conventions, advances black theater in a new and exciting direction.

Stunning indeed, *In the Red and Brown Water*, the most ritualistic play of the trilogy, foregrounds McCraney's ability to render the unfamiliar familiar and the mundane strange. Straightforward and familiar, Oya's story of loss and self-sacrifice takes a dramatic turn through the use of Yoruba cosmology. If Oya is restricted to the mandates of physical embodiment in a person whose life begins at birth and ends decades later at death, and is confined to being in one place at one time, then it is irrefutable that her infertility is her downfall. Yet Oya is a mythic figure who is dead at the beginning of the play and nonetheless present in the air, and while she never leaves her hometown of San Pere, Louisiana (a fictional town), she serves as a symbolic figure of diaspora connected to the scattering of black people that slavery causes. Other figures in the play (Elegba, Mama Moja, and Aunt Elegua) also transcend time and place, creating a "cyclic reality" tied to the inflections of Yoruba cosmology.[5] The characters have names of Yoruba deities, including Elegba, also known as Elegua (the messenger, trickster, guardian of the crossroads, and spirit of chaos), Ogun (the spirit of iron, war, technology, and transformation), and Shango (the spirit of kingship and thunder and lightning).[6] The play, through its mythical characters, setting, staging of ritual, and spoken stage directions, places the body, place, and time on the move in order to extend the life of black performance.

The African American Theatrical Body has offered several examples of the way physical movement (a gesture or a dance) reveals the constitution of bodies and places. From Ethiopia's veiling, rendering her opaque, to Richard Henry's ghosting, severing him from his most prodigious part, from migration's impact on the interpretation of the Youngers' cramped apartment to the role singing plays in understanding the suffocating quarters of Baraka's slave ship, black performance disrupts the static materiality of objects. Instead of summarizing my argument that performance renders the black theatrical body flexible and therefore radically alters conceptions of bodies and places, I want to initiate a focused reading of a twenty-first-century African American play – McCraney's *In the Red and Brown Water* – that foregrounds how black performance moves through bodies, places, and time and in that motion extends black political movements. Because McCraney's play takes up the question of performance's relationship to time, a question that haunts many of the plays explored here, this analysis enables future considerations of African American theater's role in black freedom movements.

Depictions of death and life after death (physical and social) recur in black literary and cultural representations, including *The America Play, The Star of Ethiopia, Blues for Mister Charlie,* and *Joe Turner's Come and Gone.* Similarly, *In the Red and Brown Water* depicts Oya continuing to live in the air after bleeding to death from a self-inflicted wound to the head. Like the uncanny chill created by a whisper along your neck, Oya (named for the Yoruba goddess of wind, storms, thunder and lighting, and rage, and mother of the dead) remains present in the play and arguably in the trilogy, which ends with the threat of a hurricane of the magnitude of Katrina. "For the Yorùbá, death is not the annihilation of being. It is simply a rite of passage, a transition from human to divine essence."[7] Although Oya does not recur throughout the trilogy as some other characters do, she arguably gains momentum and force, threatening communal destruction to avenge her social deaths and physical one. Through death, Oya flies from a state of oppression to menacing freedom. Individually productive, her liberation also sparks the metaphorical kindling that brings forth familial relationships that transcend death. Much like Joseph Roach's description of effigies, which he argues "provide communities with a method of perpetuating themselves through specially nominated mediums or surrogates," Oya's act of self-sacrifice demonstrates the relationship between embodied and political movements, altering her body to extend the life of the performance.[8]

Oya's self-initiated rite of passage repeats other such ritualized inaugural events with a difference that reproduces the insurgent force of black performance. Throughout this book I use the term reproduction to describe the process of historical construction and recuperation that black performance enacts in the African American theater. While the term serves to situate this book in ongoing debates within performance studies, it also, more importantly, emphasizes the political stakes of the argument. Building on Fred Moten's groundbreaking work, I have argued that black performance shapes history by reproducing psychic and material traces, keeping in mind the debates concerning the ontology of performance that continue to circulate in response to Peggy Phelan's claim that "performance in a strict ontological sense is nonreproductive."[9] She further enunciates the inevitable end of performance: "Performance cannot be saved, recorded, documented, or otherwise participate in the circulation of representations of representation."[10] Analyzing the implications of Phelan's findings for Latin American studies, Diana Taylor offers an alternative understanding of performance. She suggests that we look at "the flip side of performance's ontology, at what Derrida has called its 'hauntology.'"[11] The ghostly trace Taylor ascribes to performance corresponds with Joseph Roach's depiction of the mutually constitutive intertwining of performance in history and memory. As such, I find Roach's and Taylor's explications of performance useful to the theorization of its manifestations in conjunction with the modifier "black." Black performance challenges the notion that once completed an event should and will remain in the past. The force that drives black performance belongs to a cyclic history that asserts itself in and through the body of the actor, reconfiguring the shape of that body, the location of the event, and the moment in time. While acting as sites of memory, black performances call for an engagement with traumatic events in the past so that those events do not need to be rehashed but, instead, may be incorporated into history. Exemplary of the way black performance works through traumatic history, the communal disavowal of Oya due to her inability to physically reproduce creates the opportunity for her to rupture the alignment of women's production with physical reproduction, and, much like Du Bois' Ethiopia, offer revolutionary action as an alternative. Through the physical cut she performs on her body, she produces a historical cut that rearranges lines of descent.

The play communicates the force of Oya's action through the ritualized remembrance of her sacrifice in the choric scenes of the play. Therefore, instead of focusing solely on Oya's ritualized death in the final scene of the play, I want to consider the relationship between her mutilation and the staging of her floating in the air – a performance of her uninhibited desire. The gentle caresses of Shango's fingers along Oya's ear promise her erotic fulfillment that he supplies in each encounter with her. Shango too finds satisfaction in their intimacy, but it does not keep him from "stepping out on" Oya or meriting Aunt Elegua's designation as a "freak" (54). The assignation "freak" is not necessarily an indictment in the language of the play, but Aunt Elegua specifies, "this boy got a wickedness in his / Stance, a driving in his pants / What a good girl doing with somebody like him" (54). The uneven exchange of desire between Shango and Oya damages Oya and therefore qualifies as a problem. In the final scene of the play, Oya gives Shango her ear – the object of his erotic desire – and through her act of benevolence frees herself from a system of disproportionate desire. The play represents this freedom in the choric scenes that feature Oya floating.

Lying on her back suspended in the air by a metal tub also used as a drum, Oya waves her arms and legs to simulate levitation. Her floating in the 2009 Public Theater production of the play renders Oya immune to Shango's touch and to the unfulfilled yearnings of her body to produce a child. Oya's floating draws attention to the often dangerous and some-times deadly pursuit of freedom by black people in the Americas; a pursuit that links life in what the play calls the "distant present" to the now of the theatrical production (10). Oya's floating demonstrates the temporal unrest at the heart of what might be best described by the phrase "black movements." I define black movements as embodied actions (i.e., floating) that further political movements (i.e., the pursuit of black women's bodily freedom) that in turn rearrange time and space. Black movements, then, can be seen as political practices but not ones whose duration can be measured solely in quantifiable, serial time. Rather, black movements reshape temporalities in order to reorganize the social and cultural fields that facilitate the social and physical deaths of black people.

The play opens with a prologue that establishes the choric tableaux that will structure the drama. Much like Parks' remix of ancient Greek dramaturgy, McCraney's chorus provides the disparate opinions of com-munity members, articulating the anticipated questions and assertions of the theater audience. The chorus generates the hushed local intimacy that Toni Morrison produces in the beginning of *The Bluest Eye* with the phrase "Quiet as it's kept" and the larger than life expansiveness that Nobel Prize-winning African playwright Wole Soyinka calls "cosmic entirety."[12] Harkening back to the all-encompassing scope of all theater according to Soyinka, *In the Red and Brown Water* creates a fusion between the heavens and the earth through the shifts among realism, choric breaks, and dreamscape. Yet it is in the choric breaks and Elegba's dreamy prophetic monologues that the characters' powers manifest themselves. These ruptures integrate the metaphysical into the quotidian and the future into the present. References to the gods elevate the battle against deferred dreaming to mythic proportions, highlighting the importance of systems of desire and hope. The play critiques Oya's inability to locate an alternative object of desire that does not depend on heteronormativity, while it dramatizes an alternative rite of passage for black women outside of physical reproduction. Through the ritualized reenactment of Oya's death staged as her floating, the play "disrupt[s] the idealization of the nuclear family and the cultural logic of sexual citizenship as lodged in 'normative' sexuality."[13]

The 2009 production opens with a man and a woman dressed in white walking out onto a bare stage, save a few buckets and tubs, with buckets in their hands. Music fills the air while the man walks forward and pours his bucket as blue light spills onto the floor. The electric and sky blue liquid light consumes the entire stage floor, turning land into water in the first few pulse beats of the play. The woman, Oya, remains upstage and the man begins to chant a song that the chorus, dressed in white and cream colors, echoes back to the call he makes as it marches down the aisle of the theater with buckets in hand. The chorus surrounds Oya and throws its water buckets at her. She moves to centerstage and white light illuminates her. As the chorus begins to discuss what befell Oya, she lies on her bucket and lifts her legs in the air to simulate floating. She holds her ear and whispers "Oya in the air Oya," "A breeze over Oya," "Oya ... Oya ..." as the others talk (12). The cacophony of sound, minimalist staging, references to water, and monochromatic costumes establish *In the Red and Brown Water* as ritual drama, "a cleansing, binding, communal, recreative force," according to Soyinka.[14] Paul Carter Harrison further specifies black theater in general as "the ritual reenactment of black experience."[15] While Soyinka locates ritual as central to the origins of all theater even if it is absent in contemporary works, Harrison excludes any dramatic form that does not include ritual reenactment from the category of theater. While I do not draw as strict a demarcation as Harrison, his assertion points to the essential role of ritual in black culture and the way it serves as a fundamental mode of meaning-making through performance. In McCraney's plays ritual enables the characters to craft liberatory dreams.

Oya killed herself because she couldn't have a baby. She cut off her ear, severing her zone of erotic pleasure, and gave it to Shango, freeing herself of the burden of desire. In the moment of self-sacrifice she also freed herself to commune with her ancestral namesake and become one with the air. Her ability to reorient herself comes through the sacrifice of her body, similar to that of Herald Loomis, and it enables the play to rupture time and comment on the way temporality limits our conception of the political potential of performance. Which is to say, performance moves through bodies, across spaces, and among times to activate the force of the fourth stage. "Commonly recognized in most African metaphysics are the three worlds ... the world of the ancestor, the living and the unborn. Less understood or explored is the fourth stage, the dark continuum of transition where occurs the inter-transmutation of essence-ideal and materiality. It houses the ultimate expression of the cosmic will."[16] Soyinka locates cosmic will as the particular province of African drama, which distinguishes the political power of the theatrical tradition. Similar to the drama Soyinka describes, *In the Red and Brown Water* depicts the process of moving through the fourth stage of transition because the space of transition helps to cultivate revolutionary performances. The moments of ritualized rupture in the play, Oya floating and Elegba prophesying, fill black freedom practices with ancient and yet unborn power.

Although drawing from other diasporic traditions, McCraney aspires toward a distinct form of African American drama that emphasizes the transformative power of performance to change the body, geographical locations, and time itself. Although the names of his characters clearly reference Yoruba deities, he laments, "The hard part is to keep people from talking about the West African cosmology of my plays ... Yes, you can trace the myths to Africa, but that's not how I learned them. The *orisha* stories I learned are American myths, not West African stories."[17] A native of Miami-Dade County, Florida, he insists on the syncretism of African American culture; he recalls seeing Yemayá (Yoruba goddess of the ocean and motherhood, known as the protector of children) for the first time "not on an urn from West Africa – it was in a painting of the Virgin Mary in the middle of Miami, and she was black."[18] In an adamant fashion, McCraney cultivates a resistance to teleology that animates the playful flow of associations in his theater and enables a "lushly streetwise mélange of homespun stories and ritual modes" that Gener calls "accessible and shimmeringly theatrical."[19] His theater, much like that of Parks, questions the process of inheritance – passing down of information, history, or performance from one generation to the next – and, instead, uses performances to interject the present in the past. The temporal interruption extends the life of black performance.

Through the performance of floating in the air and on the water, McCraney develops a mode of African American theater that activates political power in dispersal. McCraney aligns scattering with omnipresence, interwining the materiality of Oya's body with the air and the water. Therefore, the scatterings of black people that resulted from the trans-Atlantic slave trade and Hurricane Katrina, to name just two incidents in a long history of black people's displacement, serve as occasions that enable her repair. Oya suffers from the pain of deferred dreaming, but the play suggests that the source of her longing has as much to do with social forces outside of her control as her investment in objects of desire that lock her in place. McCraney disrupts the male-dominated imagery of the trickster figure, splitting the role into two characters, Elegba, a young boy, and Aunt Elegua, an older woman. Both have voracious sexual appetites and encourage Oya to consider alternative means of satisfying her desire besides heterosexual coupling and reproduction. At one point, Elegba invites Oya to join a threesome with him and a local deejay, Egungun, suggesting "You been looking, right? You came to see. / Maybe this what you looking for ... Maybe this fix whats broke" (113). The master lyricist, Elegba, spits game (a vernacular term for courting) so fluidly one almost mistakes the aggressive sexual advance for a gentle romantic suggestion. McCraney creates line breaks that ensure the musicality of the dialogue and the charisma of Elegba's character. Unmoved by the seductive ballad-like offer, Oya does not accept. Nevertheless, Elegba is the figure whom the trilogy reproduces, becoming the central character Marcus in the third play. Oya must lose her materiality in order to activate the subversive potential of her performance, while Esu elusively slips from Elegba to Aunt Elegua to Marcus throughout the plays. A secondary character remarks of Elegba's youthful body and yet uncanny presence, "You know that ain't no boy / This little motherfucker has been here before!" (58). His ability to transform his body recalls the trickster figures discussed in Chapter 7 as it marks a departure in that Esu participates in an intergenerational substitution in the person of a timeless figure.

Elegba's strange familiarity bolsters another characteristic of McCraney's dramaturgy, the spoken stage directions. Also a technique used in Parks' theater, in McCraney's vernacular-driven, hip-hop-inflected prose the spoken stage directions draw audience members in instead of, as in Parks' usage, creating a Brechtian sense of alienation. The direct address, often delivered with a wink and a smile in the 2009 production, renders the audience complicit. Linguistically the play communicates mutuality through the repetition of a phrase of inevitability: "How could they not?" (29). How could the audience not laugh at Aunt Elegua's and Elegba's erotic signifying in act 1, scene 9, or notice Oya bleeding as she runs around the track in act 1, scene 3. The play mocks social mandates that ensure certain responses even as it creates a tone that facilitates uncritical looking. The mockery of the very state of being that the play encourages its audience members to inhabit creates sympathy for Oya as it marks the stunning courage expressed in moments of departure from social mandates.

With a sleight of hand, the play directs the audience through indirection and capitalizes on its use of African retentions in local contexts to create a twenty-first-century ritual theater that has much in common with Soyinka's and Wilson's twentieth-century ones. Soyinka's theater sought to revise tragedy in spiritual terms that mine the power of temporal fluidity. Harry J. Elam, Jr. persuasively argues that Wilson "refigures African American spirituality, fusing the African with the American in a distinct form that celebrates a sense of spiritual self-definition and inner self-determination, a secular, sacred, and visual expression of 'song.'"[20] McCraney marshals a similar pantheon of traditions, but his drama, unlike Wilson's, has the distinctive flavor of the American south and foregrounds the struggles of queer community members.

Wilson alludes to Ogun, one of the central figures in Yoruba theater, through the characterization of Loomis in *Joe Turner's Come and Gone*. In the Yoruba tradition, Ogun performs the archetypal act of overcoming by transcending the fourth stage through an act of sheer will. He moves through the transitional fourth stage, which Soyinka describes as the "chthonic realm," "the immeasurable gulf of transition," and the "home of the tragic spirit."[21] Ogun, according to Soyinka, "plunged" into the immeasurable gulf bound for disintegration but "resists the final step towards complete annihilation."[22] Elam explains, "Ogun performed a symbolic act that reaffirmed the power of the human will to overcome" and therefore functions as the prototypical tragic figure.[23] Although a central figure throughout McCraney's trilogy, none of the plays focuses on Ogun. Rather, they appropriate his mighty will and assign it to other figures, including Oya. Giving Oya the power to resist annihilation even in the face of a deferred rite of passage transforms the theater into a space where queer theatrical bodies affirm the power of the human will to overcome.

As in *Joe Turner's Come and Gone*, McCraney's play foregrounds in-between spaces as productive ones through Oya's airy location and the setting of the play. It is set in the government housing projects of San Pere, in the distant present, although the opening scene could take place anywhere and in the 2009 production seems to be set in the middle of a body of water. The references to water take on two connotations in the trilogy: the trans-Atlantic slave trade and the floods that devastated the Gulf Coast in 2005. McCraney first staged *In the Red and Brown Water* in 2006, just months after Hurricane Katrina hit the Gulf Coast. While the prologue does not call for the lighting or staging presented in the 2009 production (in fact the play calls for Oya to lie down on the ground), the director Tina Landau evokes a contemporary context that the play and the trilogy affirm, while it harkens back to an initiating site of racial dispersal. *In the Red and Brown Water*, borrowing from August Wilson's rich theater legacy, describes those lost in the Middle Passage as the bones people.

Recounting a dream to Oya's mother Mama Moja, Elegba reveals a prophetic vision that contextualizes the prologue. As the messenger begins to describe his dream, the stage is bathed in blue light except for Mama Moja and Elegba who are centerstage and covered in white light. Elegba recalls:

> It's always about the water, my dreams . . .
> I walk on the bottom on
> The floor of the waters and they's these people
> Walk alongside me but they all bones and they
> Click the bone people, they talk in the click.
> I say, "Where yall going?" And they say, "Just
> Walking for a while." I say, "Don't you want
> To go home . . ." They say, "When we walk there, it
> Wasn't there no more." I feel bad for them . . .
> Then they click and I come up on the mud part,
> Like they send me to the land part, and I'm
> Sitting there waiting 'cause I know they want
> Me to wait I wait there looking and on
> Top of the waters is Oya.   (22–23)

Known by several different names ("Esu-Elegbara in Nigeria and Legba among the Fon in Benin . . . Exú in Brazil, Echu-Elegua in Cuba, Papa Legba (pronounced La-Bas) in the pantheon of the loa of Vaudou of Haiti, and Papa La Bas in the loa of Hoodoo in the United States"),[24] the messenger figure, Elegba, has access to the space-in-between, the crossroads, the fourth stage. Henry Louis Gates, Jr. explains, "Esu is the guardian of the crossroads ... master of that elusive, mystical barrier that separates the divine world from the profane."[25] His ability to cross over enables him to commune with other transitional spirits, including the mythical bones people, those lost in the Middle Passage. Strikingly, during his commiseration with the homeless bones people, whom he recognizes but distinguishes himself from by going "up on the mud part," he sees Oya floating. For the second time – the first is the prologue – Oya floats in the middle of a scene of liminality. Her bodily suspension transforms into erotic desire as Elegba describes her: "Oya girl floating on top of the water, / Looking up towards the sky with no clothes / She hardly got no clothes on and she got her legs / Wide ... And she holding he head on the side with her / Hand like something ailing her. / But from her legs blood coming down and its making the pond / Red" (23). Elegba situates Oya in proximity to the bones people and through that proximity seems to create a visual link that joins the social trauma of Oya's infertility to the physical violence of the trans-Atlantic slave trade. Yet he does not describe the spilling of enslaved Africans' blood; instead he depicts the bones people on the move. Moreover, he insists "she / Ain't in pain Mama Moja she ain't in / No pain it look like just laying on top of / That water. Brown skin in the red water" (23). Oya's ease belies the traumatic connotation of middle passages and suggests that her ability to inhabit the liminal space provides some comfort that she cannot access in the present.

Many artists, including Kara Walker in *After the Deluge*, the Classical Theater of Harlem in their 2007 production of *Waiting for Godot*, and Spike Lee in his documentary film *When the Levees Broke: A Requiem in Four Acts*, have linked the devastation of the twenty-first-century disaster to the trans-Atlantic slave trade, but McCraney does not indict the government or whiteness for the failures that enabled the destruction in 2005. Instead he focuses on the cultural rituals that sustain the community imagined in the play, and links them to a long history of insurgent power. His play suggests that the movement from place to place depicted in *A Raisin in the Sun* does not ameliorate the displacement racialized homelessness causes and instead offers a retreat to a temporal underground, a fourth stage where freedom practices circulate. Performance enables an active engagement with the past that transforms not only what will be but also what was.

The transformation focuses on interrupting the finality of death. In act 1, scene 4 the play depicts dying through movement, drumming, and chanting. Mama Moja is called out to her porch where Oya finds her. In the "near distance" (37) she hears "death calling" (38). The sound of death is Aunt Elegua singing, "Gonna lay down my burdens ... Down by the riverside" (38). In the 2009 production, as Aunt Elegua sings she holds a drum that emits light and leads the chorus, which sings behind her with hands outstretched. Mama Moja takes the drum and starts singing, "I ain't going to study war no more," before she announces her death, saying "Mama Moja moves / To lay her cross down" and Oya replies, "Oya sees it." Mama affirms, "How could she not?" (39). The inexorability of death that forces Mama to, in word and deed, "leave this world" – with a gasp she trembles, crosses her arms over her chest while kneeling, and curls over – does not prevent her from joining the chorus and speaking from the world of the ancestors in act I, scene II. Aunt Elegua leads the chorus, which performs the function of "chthonic reflections (or memory)," reconstituting Oya's narrative to usher in her transition.[26]

Similarly to Bynum in his role of surrogate in *Joe Turner's Come and Gone*, Aunt Elegua and Elegba play critical roles at the crossroads, but ultimately Oya, like Loomis, must find her own voice. On the night when Oya learns that Shango betrayed her, impregnating one of her neighbors, Oya greets him and tells him she has a present for him "so he remembers [her] in his new life and times!" (122). Oya returns to the stage holding the side of her head, the former space of erotic connection. In the final scene as Shango greets her he reaches out to touch her right ear, but Oya's hand blocks his advance. Now that this erogenous zone is inaccessible, Shango must focus on what else Oya has to offer. "In the other hand, her left ... / Oya gives it to Shango. / I do this in remembrance of you ... / I wished I could make a part of me / To give you but I had to take what's / Already there ... Just give you what I got. / Oya bleeds, down her right hand" (123–24). In this misguided act of mutilation, Oya not only disfigures herself as a sacrifice for her insufficiency, she also reconfigures the body as a zone of possibility. Locating the site of her pleasure and removing it as an act of sacrifice results in the unlikely opportunity for, according to Elegba, the closing of all her wounds (124). The ritual act of cutting not only problematically affirms her insufficiency, it also severs her tie to a mode of desire that places her in a perpetual state of deferment. Now freed of the burden of heteronormative desire, Oya moves freely in the air. Serving as a cautionary tale that ushers in an otherworldly force, Oya performs her own rites of passage; a young black woman's act of self-fashioning black freedom movements.

Notes

OVERTURE: RITES OF REPARATION

1 Diana Taylor, *The Archive and the Repertoire: Performing Cultural Memory in the Americas* (Durham, NC: Duke University Press, 2003), 13.

2 Suzan-Lori Parks, *The America Play and Other Works* (New York: Theatre Communications Group, 1995), 159. Further references are to this edition and are cited parenthetically.

3 Richard Schechner, *Between Theater and Anthropology* (Philadelphia: University of Pennsylvania Press, 1985), 36; Ngugi wa Thiong'o, *Penpoints, Gunpoints, and Dreams: Towards a Critical Theory of the Arts and the State in Africa* (Oxford: Clarendon Press, 1998), 5.

4 Tavia Nyong'o, *The Amalgamation Waltz* (Minneapolis: University of Minnesota Press, 2009), 1.

5 See Madhu Dubey, *Signs and Cities: Black Literary Postmodernism* (University of Chicago Press, 2003); E. Patrick Johnson, *Appropriating Blackness: Performance and the Politics of Authenticity* (Durham, NC: Duke University Press, 2003); and Marty Favor, *Authentic Blackness: The Folk in the New Negro Renaissance* (Durham, NC: Duke University Press, 1999).

6 In *Bodies that Matter: On the Discursive Limits of "Sex"* (New York: Routledge, 1993) Judith Butler interrogates what functions as the limit to deconstructive models of performance that suggest identity categories (race, class, gender) develop out of repeated citational practices that precede the subject. Instead of conceding that these practices emerge in response to bodies, Butler contends that the practices serve to "constitute the materiality of bodies and, more specifically, to materialize the body's sex" (2). Through social, cultural, and economic modes of regulation the body perpetually becomes sexed. Therefore, the body's materiality may not be thought of as existing in excess of discourse, but should be considered as appearing by way of it.

7 See Taylor, *The Archive and the Repertoire*; Daphne A. Brooks, *Bodies in Dissent: Spectacular Performances of Race and Freedom, 1850–1910* (Durham, NC: Duke University Press, 2006), 9–10; and Saidiya V. Hartman, *Scenes of Subjection: Terror, Slavery, and Self-Making in Nineteenth-Century America* (Oxford University Press, 1997).

8 Suzan-Lori Parks, "Possession," *The America Play and Other Works*, 5.

9 Harry J. Elam, Jr. and Michele Elam, "Blood Debt: Reparations in Langston Hughes's *Mulatto*," *Theatre Journal*, 61 (March 2009), 85–103 (103).

10 Stephen Best and Saidiya Hartman, "Fugitive Justice," *Representations*, 92 (autumn 2005), 1–15 (4).

11 *Ibid.*, 5.

12 *Ibid.*

13 Elam, Jr. and Elam, "Blood Debt," 103.

14 Taylor, *The Archive and the Repertoire*, xvii.

15 Glenda R. Carpio, *Laughing Fit to Kill: Black Humor in the Fictions of Slavery* (Oxford University Press, 2008), 194.

16 Quoted in Thelma Gordon, introduction to Thelma Gordon, Hamza Walker *et al.* (eds.), *Freestyle* (New York: The Studio Museum in Harlem, 2001), 14.

17 Some of the first exhibits of people of the Americas occurred when Columbus returned to Spain in 1493 with an Arawak he "discovered."

18 Some of the most eminent scholars of black culture have considered performance as central to blackness. Cedric Robinson theorizes the revolutionary character of black culture in *Black Marxism: The Making of the Black Radical Tradition* (London: Zed; Totawa, NJ: Biblio Distribution Center, 1983) and offers models of performance as evidence of this insurgent impulse. He clarifies: "The evidence of the tradition's persistence and ideological vitality among the Black slave masses was to be found not only in the rebellions and the underground but as well in the shouts, the spirituals, the sermons, and the very textual body of Black Christianity" (311). Robinson's examples, and Hartman's groundbreaking analysis in *Scenes of Subjection* of black subjectivity formation through subjection, depend on the dynamics of display. In terms of twentieth-century manifestations of black performance, Fred Moten locates an acoustic materiality that emanated from the scenes of subjection Hartman describes and that works to institute the sound of the tradition Robinson delineates. The sounds that echo throughout Moten's *In the Break: The Aesthetics of the Black Radical Tradition* (Minneapolis: University of Minnesota Press, 2003) necessarily belong to a history of revolutionary action that emerged in response to degrading and dehumanizing images of black people. That twinned history disallows reading Bert Williams' performance in *In Dahomey*, for example, as that of either a trickster or a clown and necessitates considering the insistent mutuality of the roles. Throughout the twentieth century, authors, including Ralph Ellison and Suzan-Lori Parks, battle continually the trickster–clown dyad. Ellison and Parks deploy the figure of the trickster to create productive ambiguities.

19 See Moten, *In the Break*.

20 In Freud's rendering, the primal scene, in which the child witnesses his parents having sex, traumatizes the child. He subsequently creates psychic mechanisms to compensate for the trauma. See Sigmund Freud, *The Case of the Wolf-man: From the History of an Infantile Neurosis* (San Francisco: Arion Press, 1993).

21 In *The America Play*, Suzan-Lori Parks depicts the central character transforming a hole into a whole. I use the parentheses around the "w" in the word "whole" to call attention to the ghostly presence of the hole therein.

22 Frederick Douglass, *The Narrative of the Life of Frederick Douglass, an American Slave, Written by Himself* (Boston: Bedford Books of St. Martin's Press, 1993; first published in 1845), 75.

23 See John Stauffer, *Giants: The Parallel Lives of Frederick Douglass and Abraham Lincoln* (New York: Twelve, 2008).

24 See the introduction to Daphne A. Brooks, *Bodies in Dissent*, for a detailed analysis of William Wells Brown's *The Escape* and its implications for insurgent strategies of black performance.

25 Eleanor W. Traylor, "Two Afro-American Contributions to Dramatic Form," in Errol Hill (ed.), *The Theater of Black Americans: A Collection of Critical Essays* (New York: Applause, 1987), 45–60 (47).

26 Many theorists have positioned Frederick Douglass as a kind of forefather of the African American literary tradition. See Robert Stepto, *From Behind the Veil: A Study of Afro-American Narrative* (Urbana: University of Illinois Press, 1979); Houston A. Baker, *Blues, Ideology, and Afro-American Literature: A Vernacular Theory* (University of Chicago Press, 1984); William A. Andrews, *To Tell a Free Story: The First Century of Afro-American Autobiography, 1760–1865* (Urbana: University of Illinois Press, 1986); and Deborah E. McDowell, "In the First Place: Making Frederick Douglass and the Afro-American Narrative Tradition," in William A. Andrews (ed.), *African American Autobiography: A Collection of Critical Essays* (Englewood Cliffs, NJ: Prentice Hall, 1993), 36–58.

27 Hartman, *Scenes of Subjection*, 4; Moten, *In the Break*, 5.

28 Suzan-Lori Parks and Liz Diamond, "Doo-a-Diddly-Dit-Dit: An Interview" (interview by Steven Drukman), *TDR*, 39 (autumn 1995), 56–75.

29 See Douglass, *Narrative*, 2–3.

30 Hortense Spillers, "Mama's Baby, Papa's Maybe: An American Grammar Book," in *Black, White, and in Color: Essays on American Literature and Culture* (University of Chicago Press, 2003), 228.

31 Moten, *In the Break*, 5.

32 In performance theory, one of the most often-quoted definitions of performance, Richard Schechner's "performance is any twice-behaved behavior," situates repetition at the center. Additionally, James Snead's "Repetition as a Figure of Black Culture," in Henry Louis Gates, Jr. (ed.), *Black Literature and Literary Theory* (New York: Methuen, 1984), explains the importance of repetition in terms of black studies.

33 See Henry Louis Gates, Jr., *The Signifying Monkey: A Theory of African American Literary Criticism* (Oxford University Press, 1988); and Suzan-Lori Parks, "From Elements of Style," *The America Play and Other Works*.

34 As Andrew Parker and Eve Kosofsky Sedgwick elucidate in their "Introduction" to Parker and Sedgwick (eds.), *Performativity and Performance* (New York: Routledge, 1995), 1–18, the question of when is saying something doing

something reaches back to Genesis, Plato, and Aristotle. The hallmark modern rendering of the question occurs in J.L. Austin's *How to do Things with Words*, ed. J.O. Urmson and Mariana Sbisà (Cambridge, MA: Harvard University Press, 1962). Parker and Sedgwick explain that "performativity has enabled a powerful appreciation of the ways identities are constructed iteratively through complex citational processes." They reason, therefore, that performance studies as a discipline emerges at the crossroads of philosophical and theatrical studies of performativity and its uses (2–3). See also Judith Butler's *Excitable Speech: A Politics of the Performative* (New York: Routledge, 1997), which distinguishes between illocutionary and perlocutionary performatives, noting that "the perlocutionary … leads to certain effects that are not the same as the speech act itself" (3).

35 Some of the critics who have found psychoanalytic theory useful to ethnic studies include Gwen Bergner, *Taboo Subjects* (Minneapolis: University of Minnesota Press, 2005); Anne Anlin Cheng, *The Melancholy of Race: Psychoanalysis, Assimilation, and Hidden Grief* (Oxford University Press, 2001); David Eng, *Racial Castration: Managing Masculinity in Asian America* (Durham, NC: Duke University Press, 2001); Barbara Johnson, *The Feminist Difference: Literature, Psychoanalysis, Race, and Gender* (Cambridge, MA: Harvard University Press, 1998); Christopher Lane (ed.), *The Psychoanalysis of Race* (New York: Columbia University Press, 1998); Dana Luciano, "Passing Shadows: Melancholic Nationality and Black Critical Publicity in Pauline E. Hopkins's *Of One Blood*," in David Eng and David Kazanjian (eds.), *Loss: The Politics of Mourning* (Berkeley: University of California Press, 2003); Ann Pellegrini, *Performance Anxieties: Staging Psychoanalysis, Staging Race* (New York: Routledge, 1997); Kalpana Seshadri-Crooks, *Desiring Whiteness: A Lacanian Analysis of Race* (London; New York: Routledge, 2000); Kaja Silverman, *The Acoustic Mirror: The Female Voice in Psychoanalysis and Cinema* (Bloomington: Indiana University Press, 1988); Hortense Spillers, *Black, White, and in Color*; Claudia Tate, *Psychoanalysis and Black Novels: Desire and the Protocols of Race* (Oxford University Press, 1998); and Jean Walton, *Fair Sex, Savage Dreams: Race, Psychoanalysis, Sexual Difference* (Durham, NC: Duke University Press, 2001).

36 Hortense Spillers, "'All the Things You Could Be By Now, If Sigmund Freud's Wife Was Your Mother': Psychoanalysis and Race," *Black, White, and in Color*, 386.

37 Nicolas Abraham and Maria Torok, *The Shell and the Kernel: Renewals of Psychoanalysis*, vol. 1 (University of Chicago Press, 1994), 8–9.

38 Most studies of African American drama focus on plays written after *A Raisin in the Sun*. Although Daphne A. Brooks' *Bodies in Dissent* and David Krasner's *Resistance, Parody, and Double Consciousness in African American Theatre, 1895–1910* (New York: St. Martin's Press, 1997) and *A Beautiful Pageant: African American Theatre, Drama, and Performance in the Harlem Renaissance, 1910–1927* (New York: Palgrave Macmillan, 2002) stand as important

exceptions, *The African American Theatrical Body* uniquely delineates a theoretical argument for twentieth-century African American drama.

39 See Taylor, *The Archive and the Repertoire*; and Daphne A. Brooks, *Bodies in Dissent*.

1 REPETITION/REPRODUCTION: THE DNA OF BLACK EXPRESSIVE CULTURE

1 Richard Zoglin, "Theater: Raisin and the Rapper," *Time* (May 10, 2004), www.time.com/time/magazine/article/0,9171,994156,00.html (accessed October 17, 2009).

2 Joseph Roach, *Cities of the Dead: Circum-Atlantic Performance* (New York: Columbia University Press, 1996), 2.

3 *Ibid.*

4 Misty Brown, "Kenny Leon Directs 'A Raisin in the Sun' on Broadway," *Washington Informer*, 40 (July 7, 2004), 25.

5 *Ibid.*

6 Anna Deavere Smith, "Two Visions of Love, Family and Race across the Generations," *New York Times* (May 29, 2004),www.nytimes.com/2004/05/29/theater/two-visions-of-love-family-and-race-across-the-generations.html (accessed October 17, 2009).

7 Marvin Carlson, *The Haunted Stage: The Theatre as Memory Machine* (Ann Arbor: University of Michigan Press, 2001), 69.

8 For decades critics have debated the artistic merit and social import of *A Raisin in the Sun*. Most critics agree that the play qualifies as a classic American drama. Over the years, however, different aspects of the play have evoked discussion. Most of the criticism focuses on how the play engages family dynamics (economics, marriage, motherhood, fatherhood, and sibling rivalry) or social dynamics (integration and freedom). Investigation of the implications of the family and social dynamics in the play informs my work; nevertheless, I approach those concerns by investigating how the Younger family's apartment acts as a physical representation of many of the themes of the play but ultimately cannot consolidate the Youngers' driving desire for freedom. Doris E. Abrahamson's chapter on *A Raisin in the Sun*, in *Negro Playwrights in the American Theater, 1925–1959* (New York: Columbia University Press, 1969), situates the play as a part of 1950s American drama, focusing on critics' reception of it, its function as a mechanism for protest, and its artistic value. In "Lorraine Hansberry as Ironist: A Reappraisal of *A Raisin in the Sun*," *Journal of Black Studies*, 4 (March 1974), 237–47, Lloyd W. Brown offers an aesthetic analysis of the play based on the debate which emerged during the 1960s about representations of integration. Brown questions "the tendency, for one reason or another, to isolate questions of structure or technique from those of social or racial significance" (238). Anne Cheney argues in "Measure Him Right: *A Raisin in the Sun*," *Lorraine Hansberry* (Boston, MA: Twayne, 1984) that it is a play that tells the truth about people;

it is "a quiet celebration of the black family, the importance of African roots, the equality of women, the vulnerability of marriage, the true value of money, the survival of the individual, and the nature of man's dreams ... a universal representation of all people's hopes, fears, and dreams" (55). Considering the categorization of Amiri Baraka and Ed Bullins as militant playwrights, Margaret B. Wilkerson argues in "The Sighted Eyes and Feeling Heart of Lorraine Hansberry," *Black American Literature Forum*, 17 (spring 1983), 8–13, that Hansberry's drama reflected a militancy of its own, while it also served to usher in the art of the Black Arts Movement. Similarly, scholars writing in the last two decades have worked to refute the claim that *A Raisin in the Sun* is an integrationalist play, and therefore dated and no longer important. In *"A Raisin in the Sun," Hansberry's Drama: Commitment and Perplexity* (Urbana: University of Illinois Press, 1991), Steven R. Carter asserts that critics misread the play when they claim it was written for white Americans. He goes on to claim that integration is not the main concern of the play. Instead, he argues the play focuses on the differing beliefs and desires of three generations of an American family; "the test that the Youngers face is of their willingness to take potentially fatal risks to get out of an intolerable situation and to force change upon an oppressive system" (22). Y.S. Sharadha agrees that *A Raisin in the Sun* qualifies as a classic piece of American drama because it explores universal human struggles. In *"A Raisin in the Sun:* Quest for African American Identity and Universality," *Black Women's Writing: Quest for Identity in the Plays of Lorraine Hansberry and Ntozake Shange* (London: Sangam Books, 1998), Sharadha claims that the play asks "what kind of conviction and commitment it takes to bring hope out of hopelessness, courage out of fear, and idealism out of fatalism" (29).

9 Felicia R. Lee, "Deferred Dreams that Resonate Across Decades," *New York Times* (February 17, 2008), AR19.

10 Langston Hughes, *The Selected Poems of Langston Hughes* (New York: Vintage Books, 1990), 268.

11 Imamu Amiri Baraka, "Sweet Lorraine," *The LeRoi Jones/Amiri Baraka Reader*, ed. William J. Harris (New York: Thunder's Mouth Press, 1991).

12 Throughout the book I use the term black performance instead of African American performance to draw attention to the ways the performances build on and draw from embodied action throughout the world. Although all the plays I discuss are written by African Americans and therefore qualify as African American drama, I consider the performances as part of an international network of production.

13 Quoted in Doris E. Abrahamson, *Negro Playwrights*, 239.

14 Lorraine Hansberry, *A Raisin in the Sun* (New York: Vintage Books, 1994; first published 1959), 144. Further references are to this edition and will be cited parenthetically.

15 Anon., "Cinema: Acute Ghettoitis," *Time* (March 31, 1961), www.time.com/time/magazine/article/0,9171,872215,00.html (accessed October 17, 2009).

16 In a letter published in *Time*, www.time.com/time/magazine/article/0,9171,895264-3,00.html (accessed October 17, 2009), Lorraine Hansberry

responds to the reviewer of her film: "Whoops – am afraid that TIME'S ever-diminishing pretenses to sophistication took yet another dip by way of its reviewer's baffling determination to employ ante-bellum terminology in his incoherent notation on the movie. I don't have any idea what 'Mammy' and 'blackface' adjectives have to do with reviewing a motion picture, but save your copy; it is believed, in some quarters of the world, that the Herrenvolk may rise again!"

17 Nina Simone, *I Put a Spell on You* (New York: Da Capo Press, 1991), 87.
18 Robin D.G. Kelley, *Freedom Dreams: The Black Radical Imagination* (Boston: Beacon Press, 2002), 58.
19 Ivy Wilson, "'Are You Man Enough?': Imagining Ethiopia and Transnational Black Masculinity," *Callaloo*, 33 (winter 2010), 265–77 (267).
20 *Ibid.*
21 Stephen Meyer, *As Long as They Don't Move Next Door: Segregation and Racial Conflict in American Neighborhoods* (Lanham, MD: Rowman & Littlefield, 2000), 121.
22 Sylvia Hood Washington, *Packing Them In: An Archaeology of Environmental Racism in Chicago, 1865–1954* (Lanham, MD: Lexington Books, 2005), 149.
23 *Ibid.*
24 Taylor, *The Archive and the Repertoire*, 36.
25 Toni Morrison, "Home," in Wahneema Lubiano (ed.), *The House that Race Built* (New York: Vintage, 1998), 3–12 (3, 4).
26 *Ibid.*, 3.
27 Eng, *Racial Castration*, 206.
28 Although primarily known in literary studies as a novel, *Native Son* was adapted for the stage and premiered at the St. James Theatre on Broadway, March 24, 1941.
29 Jacques Lacan, *The Four Fundamental Concepts of Psycho-analysis: The Seminar of Jacques Lacan*, ed. Jacques-Alain Miller, trans. Alan Sheridan (New York: W.W. Norton, 1988), 62.
30 Walter Benjamin, *Illuminations: Essays and Reflections* (New York: Schocken Books, 1988), 255.
31 Kimberly W. Benston, *Performing Blackness: Enactments of African-American Modernism* (London: Routledge, 2000), 11.
32 Una Chaudhuri, *Staging Place: The Geography of Modern Drama* (Ann Arbor: University of Michigan Press, 1997), 5.
33 *Ibid.*
34 Farah Jasmine Griffin, *"Who Set You Flowin'?": The African American Migration Narrative* (Oxford University Press, 1995), 8.
35 Gwendolyn Brooks, *Blacks* (Chicago: Third World Press, 1987), 70.
36 Judith Butler, *The Psychic Life of Power: Theories in Subjection* (Stanford University Press, 1997), 2.
37 Richard Wright, *Twelve Million Black Voices* (New York: Thunder's Mouth Press, 1941), 142.
38 W.E.B. Du Bois, "The Negro and the American Stage," *The Crisis* (June 1924), 56–57.

39 Barbara Freedman, *Staging the Gaze: Postmodernism, Psychoanalysis, and Shakespearean Comedy* (Ithaca, NY: Cornell University Press, 1991), 56.

2 RECUPERATING BLACK DIASPORIC HISTORY

1 Before 1915 *The Star of Ethiopia* would assume three different titles, shifting focus as Du Bois renamed it. When Du Bois first conceived the pageant it was called *The Jewel of Freedom: A Masque in Episodes.* In "*The Star of Ethiopia*: A Contribution toward the Development of Black Drama and Theater in the Harlem Renaissance," in Amritjit Singh, William S. Shiver, and Stanley Brodwin (eds.), *The Harlem Renaissance: Revaluations* (New York: Garland, 1989), Freda L. Scott contends that Du Bois began working on the pageant in 1911. The Du Bois papers (reel 87) contain evidence that supports her claim. David Levering Lewis, in *W.E.B. Du Bois*, 2 vols. (New York: H. Holt, 1993–2000), concurs: "Refining and enlarging the original 1911 draft (probably completed after the Races Congress), he transformed *The Star of Ethiopia* into a three-hour extravaganza in six episodes ..." (vol. 1, 460). In 1913 *The Jewel of Freedom* became *The People of Peoples and Their Gifts to Men.* The only anthologized versions of the pageant are of *The People of Peoples and Their Gifts to Men*, even though *The Oxford W.E.B. Du Bois Reader*, ed. Eric J. Sundquist (New York: Oxford University Press, 1996), and James V. Hatch and Ted Shine (eds.), *Black Theater, USA: Plays by African Americans* (New York: Free Press, 1996), have the 1913 version of the pageant listed as *The Star of Ethiopia.* The 1913 version was originally published in *The Crisis* in October. On October 9, 1915 the *Washington Bee* published the revised version named *The Star of Ethiopia.* Du Bois adds to the confusion surrounding the names of the various versions of the pageant(s) when he refers to the 1911 and 1913 texts as *The Star of Ethiopia* in "The Drama among Black Folk," an article published in *The Crisis* in 1916 following the Philadelphia production. Although Du Bois refers to these early versions as *The Star of Ethiopia*, the published versions and drafts of the pageant in the Du Bois papers suggest the character "Ethiopia" did not appear in the pageant until 1915. Therefore, it seems the pageant would only fittingly adopt the title *The Star of Ethiopia* at that time. The 1915 version, which appeared before thousands of spectators in 1916 and 1925, focuses on the shape of history and has Ethiopia guiding the action. A centralization of the narrative around the character Ethiopia accompanies this shift in emphasis. Further references to *The Star of Ethiopia* will be cited parenthetically. I reference the 1913 version published in *The Oxford W.E.B. Du Bois Reader* (ox), the 1915 version published in the *Washington Bee*, October 9, 1915, 1 and 6 (wb), and a version found in the Du Bois papers (pa), and also use the description of the pageant printed in the December 1915 edition of *The Crisis*, and the October 23, 1915 edition of the *Washington Bee*.

2 W.E.B. Du Bois, "The Drama Among Black Folk," *The Crisis* (August 1916), 171. Further references will be cited parenthetically in the text as da.

3 Prior to the 1915 production, the October 9, 1915 edition of the *Washington Bee* reports that the pageant stages 1,000 years of the history of the Negro Race. The October 23, 1915 edition of the *Washington Bee* reports that the pageant presents 10,000 years of history.

4 In their "Introduction" to Barbara McCaskill and Caroline Gebhard (eds.), *Post-Bellum, Pre-Harlem: African American Literature and Culture, 1877–1919* (New York University Press, 2006), 1–14, McCaskill and Gebhard explain the competing names used to describe the period in the African American literary tradition between Reconstruction and World War I. Charles Waddell Chesnutt first described the period as "Post-Bellum–Pre-Harlem" in an essay of that name, in *Stories, Novels & Essays* (New York: Library of America, 2002), 906–12.

5 Leon F. Litwack, "Hellhounds," in James Allen *et al.*, *Without Sanctuary: Lynching Photography in America* (Sante Fe , NM: Twin Palms, 2000), 8–37 (13–14).

6 Taylor, *The Archive and the Repertoire*, 13.

7 Orlando Patterson, *Rituals of Blood: Consequences of Slavery in Two American Centuries* (New York: Civitas/Counterpoint, 1998), 242.

8 See Eric Lott, *Love and Theft: Blackface Minstrelsy and the American Working Class* (Oxford University Press, 1993).

9 Daphne A. Brooks, *Bodies in Dissent*, 29.

10 Tate, *Psychoanalysis and Black Novels*, 49.

11 *Ibid.*

12 Angelina Weld Grimké, *Rachel*, in Kathy Perkins and Judith L. Stephens (eds.), *Strange Fruit: Plays on Lynching by American Women* (Bloomington: Indiana University Press, 1998), 27–78 (42).

13 Alys Eve Weinbaum, *Wayward Reproductions: Genealogies of Race and Nation in Transatlantic Modern Thought* (Durham, NC: Duke University Press, 2004), 23.

14 Koritha A. Mitchell, "Anti-Lynching Plays: Angelina Weld Grimké, Alice Dunbar-Nelson, and the Evolution of African American Drama," in Barbara McCaskill and Caroline Gebhard (eds.), *Post-Bellum, Pre-Harlem: African American Literature and Culture 1877–1919* (New York University Press, 2006), 210–30 (218).

15 See *ibid.* for more information about the production history of anti-lynching drama in the early twentieth century.

16 Susan Gilman, *Blood Talk: American Race Melodrama and the Culture of the Occult* (University of Chicago Press, 2003), 10.

17 In her "Introduction" to Du Bois' *Dark Princess* (New York: Harcourt, 1995; first published 1928), Claudia Tate comments on Du Bois' use of the black Christ. She writes, "For were it not for the figure of the black Christ, allusions to oppression, and the personification of freedom, respectively in "The Riddle of the Sphinx," "The Princess of the Hither Isles," and "Children of the Moon," for example, his readers probably would not have been able to connect the passion in these works to racial propaganda" (52).

18 Spillers, "Mama's Baby," *Black, White, and in Color*, 203.

19 *Ibid.*, 209.

20 Hortense Spillers, "Moving On Down the Line: Variations on the African-American Sermon," *Black, White, and in Color*, 273.

21 Arnold Rampersad, "W.E.B. Du Bois as a Man of Literature," *American Literature*, 51 (March 1979), 50–68 (51).

22 W.E.B. Du Bois, "Criteria of Negro Art," *Oxford W.E.B. Du Bois Reader*, 324–28 (328).

23 In "*The Star of Ethiopia*" Scott argues that Du Bois saw drama "as an instrument of instruction and enlightenment, and as a valuable weapon in the black cultural and political propaganda arsenal" (257). She maintains that his production of *The Star of Ethiopia* evidences his support of black drama during the Harlem Renaissance and serves to inspire a renewed interest in black theatre during that period.

24 W.E.B. Du Bois, "Three Expositions," *The Crisis* (October 1913), 297.

25 W.E.B. Du Bois, "The Star of Ethiopia," *The Crisis* (December 1915), 91–92 (91).

26 *Ibid.*, 91–92.

27 Naima Prevots, *American Pageantry: A Movement for Art and Democracy* (Ann Arbor: UMI Research Press, 1990), 5.

28 David Glassberg, *American Historical Pageantry: The Uses of Tradition in the Early Twentieth Century* (Chapel Hill: University of North Carolina Press, 1990), 105.

29 Gilman, *Blood Talk*, 7.

30 See Michelle Ann Stephens, *Black Empire: The Masculine Global Imaginary of Caribbean Intellectuals in the United States, 1914–1962* (Durham, NC: Duke University Press, 2005), 114; and Monica L. Miller, *Slaves to Fashion: Black Dandyism and the Styling of Black Diasporic Identity* (Durham, NC: Duke University Press, 2009), 184–85.

31 Glassberg, *American Historical Pageantry*, 128.

32 Prevots, *American Pageantry*, 31.

33 Errol G. Hill and James V. Hatch, *A History of African American Theatre* (New York: Cambridge University Press, 2003), 136.

34 Four African American pageants, following *The Star of Ethiopia*, are contained in Willis Richardson (ed.), *Plays and Pageants from the Life of the Negro* (Washington, DC: Associated Publishers, 1930).

35 Gilman, *Blood Talk*, 160.

36 See Evelyn Brooks Higginbotham, *Righteous Discontent: The Women's Movement in the Black Baptist Church, 1880–1920* (Cambridge, MA: Harvard University Press, 1993).

37 W.E.B. Du Bois, "A Pageant," *The Crisis* (September 1915), 230–31.

38 Glassberg, *American Historical Pageantry*, 133.

39 Anon., "The Great Pageant," *Washington Bee* (October 23, 1915), 1, 6.

40 See Eileen Southern, *The Music of Black Americans: A History* (New York: W.W. Norton, 1997), 274.

41 In *African American Theatre: An Historical and Critical Analysis* (Cambridge University Press, 1994), Samuel Hay states that Wesley, Terrell, and Howard University theater professor, Montgomery Gregory, acted in the Washington, DC production, which he misdates as 1913 (195).

42 Du Bois, "The Star of Ethiopia," 93.

43 *Ibid.*

44 I borrow the imagery of the veil being like a theater curtain from Eric J. Sundquist, *To Wake the Nations: Race in the Making of American Literature* (Cambridge, MA: Harvard University Press, 1993), 580.

45 Brent Hayes Edwards, *The Practice of Diaspora: Literature, Translation, and the Rise of Black Internationalism* (Cambridge, MA: Harvard University Press, 2003), 2.

46 W.E.B. Du Bois, "World War and the Color Line," *The Crisis* (November 1914), 28.

47 W.E.B. Du Bois, "The Color Line Belts the World," *W.E.B. Du Bois: A Reader*, ed. David Levering Lewis (New York: H. Holt, 1995), 42–43 (42).

48 W.E.B. Du Bois, *The Negro* (Mineola, NY: Dover Publications, 2001), 5.

49 Susan Gilman, in *Blood Talk*, considers Du Bois' penchant for self-citation.

50 See Nah Dove, "African Womanism: An Afrocentric Theory," *Journal of Black Studies*, 28 (May 1998), 515–39 (532).

51 Anon., "The Great Pageant," 6.

52 Oyèrónké Oyěwùmi, "Visualizing the Body: Western Theories and African Subjects," *The Invention of Women: Making an African Sense of Western Gender Discourses* (Minneapolis: University of Minnesota Press, 1997), 2.

53 Joseph Roach, *Cities of the Dead: Circum-Atlantic Performance* (New York: Columbia University Press, 1996), 41.

54 Daphne A. Brooks, *Bodies in Dissent*, 322.

55 *Ibid.*

56 *Ibid.*, 323.

57 Pauline Hopkins, *Of One Blood* (New York: Washington Square Press, 2004; first published serially 1902–03), 73.

58 *Ibid.*

59 Luciano, "Passing Shadows," 166.

60 Fred Moten, "The Case of Blackness," *Criticism*, 50 (2008), 177–218 (205).

61 Daphne A. Brooks, *Bodies in Dissent*, 331.

62 Jayna Brown, *Babylon Girls: Black Women Performers and the Shaping of the Modern* (Durham, NC: Duke University Press, 2008), 182.

63 Daphne A. Brooks, *Bodies in Dissent*, 332–33; Jayna Brown, *Babylon Girls*, 182; Krasner, *Beautiful Pageant*, 65–67. See also P. Gabrielle Foreman, *Activist Sentiments: Reading Black Women in the Nineteenth Century* (Urbana: University of Illinois Press, 2009), 73–80.

64 Luciano, "Passing Shadows," 149–50.

65 *Ibid.*, 149.

66 *Ibid.*, 151.

67 Daphne A. Brooks, *Bodies in Dissent*, 283.

68 Aida Overton Walker, "Colored Men and Women on the American Stage," *Colored American Magazine* (October 1905), 574.

69 See Krasner, *Beautiful Pageant,* 55–70.

70 Shelby Steele, "Notes on Ritual in the New Black Theater," in Errol Hill (ed.), *The Theater of Black Americans* (New York: Applause, 1987), 30–44 (31).

71 Moten, *In the Break,* 1.

72 Paul Gilroy, *The Black Atlantic: Modernity and Double Consciousness* (Cambridge, MA: Harvard University Press, 1993), 68.

73 G.W.F. Hegel, *Phenomenology of Spirit,* trans. A.V. Miller (Oxford University Press, 1977), 115.

74 Sandra Adell, *Double-Consciousness/Double Bind: Theoretical Issues in Twentieth-Century Black Literature* (Urbana: University of Illinois Press, 1994), 16.

75 Anthony Bogues, *Empire of Liberty: Power, Desire, and Freedom* (Hanover, NH: Dartmouth College Press, 2010), 113.

76 Gilroy, *Black Atlantic,* 53–54.

77 Paul Gilroy suggests, "It *matters* little, at this point, whether this 'second sight' is a true privilege rather than some sort of disability," since he is primarily concerned with locating Du Bois' intervention within the modernist discourse on Africa (*Black Atlantic,* 134). In *Race Men* (Cambridge, MA: Harvard University Press, 1998), Hazel Carby contends that "While double-consciousness is, indeed, a product of the articulation between race and nation, I would argue that we need to revise our understanding of how this double-consciousness works in order to understand how gender is an ever-present, though under-acknowledged, factor in theory" (37).

78 Sandra Adell locates *The Souls of Black Folk* within the tradition of western philosophy. She contends that previous scholars' attempts, namely Robert Stepto's and Henry Louis Gates', to present *The Souls of Black Folk* as an alternative to western thought are flawed. In the first chapter of *Race Men,* "The Souls of Black Men," Carby has a greatly different agenda. She performs a feminist reading of *The Souls of Black Folk* to try to locate the ways that language, even written by a speaker who professes to promote women's rights, can reaffirm male privilege. In "W.E.B. Du Bois as a Hegelian," in David G. Sansing (ed.), *What Was Freedom's Price* (Jackson: University Press of Mississippi, 1978), Joel Williamson, similarly to both Adell and Carby, considers Hegel's influence on Du Bois. Finally, the first chapter of Part II of Shamoon Zamir's *Dark Voices* takes up the question of Hegel's influence on Du Bois by focusing on the concept of double consciousness. In the second chapter of Part II, "A Prosody of Those Dark Voices," Zamir argues that encounters with the past via the spirituals Du Bois hears throughout his travels profoundly shape his consciousness.

79 W.E.B. Du Bois, *The Souls of Black Folk* (New York: Barnes and Noble Classics, 2003; first published 1903), 9.

80 *Ibid.,* 8.

81 *Ibid.,* 7.

82 *Ibid.,* 9.

83 Snead, "Repetition," 62–63.
84 Weinbaum, *Wayward Reproductions*, 5.
85 Patterson, *Rituals of Blood*, 175.
86 Gilman, *Blood Talk*, 195.
87 Douglass, *Narrative*, 42.
88 *Ibid.*, 46–47.
89 Moten, *In the Break*, 16.
90 *Ibid.*, 5.
91 Butler, *Psychic Life of Power*, 13.
92 Spillers, "Mama's Baby," *Black, White, and in Color*, 228.

3 REENACTING THE HARLEM RENAISSANCE

1 Cheryl Wall, "On Freedom and the Will to Adorn: Debating Aesthetics and/ as Ideology in African American Literature," in George Levine (ed.), *Aesthetics and Ideology* (New Brunswick, NJ: Rutgers University Press, 1994), 283–303 (288).
2 I will use the term "New Negro," most readily associated with Alain Locke's anthology, to reference the imagined emerging African American citizen Locke describes, and the cultural history the identity signifies.
3 George Walker, "The Negro on the American Stage," *Colored American Magazine* (October 1906), 243–48 (243).
4 Daphne A. Brooks, *Bodies in Dissent*, 270.
5 Hortense Spillers, "Notes on an Alternative Model – Neither/Nor," *Black, White, and in Color*, 302.
6 Cherene Sherrard-Johnson, *Portraits of the New Negro Woman: Visual and Literary Culture in the Harlem Renaissance* (New Brunswick, NJ: Rutgers University Press, 2007), 38.
7 *Ibid.*, 10.
8 *Ibid.*
9 Pearlie Mae Fisher-Peters, in *The Assertive Woman in Zora Neale Hurston's Fiction, Folklore, and Drama* (New York: Garland; Taylor & Francis, 1997), and Lynda Marion Hill, in *Social Rituals and the Verbal Art of Zora Neale Hurston* (Washington, DC: Howard University Press, 1996), note the play's "melodrama" as one of its fundamental flaws. One important exception to the depictions of *Color Struck* as melodramatic is "Migration, Fragmentation, and Identity: Zora Neale Hurston's *Color Struck* and the Geography of the Harlem Renaissance," *Theatre Journal*, 53 (2001), 533–50, in which David Krasner argues, "Analyzing Hurston's play, *Color Struck* reveals some of the tragic and devastating implications of the Great Migration" (534).
10 Zora Neale Hurston, *Color Struck*, in Wallace Thurman, Langston Hughes, Zora Neale Hurston, Gwendolyn Bennett, Aaron Douglas, Richard Bruce and John Davis (eds.), *Fire* (Westport, CT: Negro Universities Press, 1970; first published 1926), 7–14 (7). Further references are to this edition and will be cited parenthetically.

11 Cheryl Wall, *Women of the Harlem Renaissance* (Bloomington: Indiana University Press, 1995), 140.

12 Zora Neale Hurston, "Characteristics of Negro Expression," in Angelyn Mitchell (ed.), *Within the Circle: An Anthology of African American Literary Criticism from the Harlem Renaissance to the Present* (Durham, NC: Duke University Press, 1994), 79–94 (81).

13 *Ibid.*, 79.

14 *Ibid.*

15 I borrow the paradigm of celebration and struggle from Cheryl Wall, "On Freedom."

16 Elin Diamond, "Deploying/Destroying the Primitivist Body in Hurston and Brecht," in Alan Ackerman and Martin Puchner (eds.), *Against Theatre: Creative Destructions on the Modernist Stage* (New York: Palgrave Macmillan, 2006), 112–32 (121).

17 Henry Louis Gates, Jr., "The Trope of the New Negro and the Reconstruction of the Image of the Black," *Representations*, 24 (fall 1988), 129–55 (132).

18 Locke, *The New Negro* (New York: Touchstone, 1997; first published 1925), 11.

19 Gates, "Trope of the New Negro," 147.

20 Locke, *The New Negro*, 4.

21 Nannie H. Burroughs, "Not Color, but Character," *Voice of the Negro* (July 1904), 277–80 (279).

22 See Foreman, *Activist Sentiments*.

23 Addie Hunton, "Negro Womanhood Defended," *Voice of the Negro* (July 1904), 280–82 (281).

24 Higginbotham, "The Politics of Respectability," *Righteous Discontent*, 196.

25 Locke, *The New Negro*, 11.

26 Wallace Thurman, *The Blacker the Berry* (New York: Scribner, 1996; first published 1929), 28.

27 *Ibid.*, 21.

28 *Ibid.*, 146.

29 William Wells Brown, *Clotel; or, the President's Daughter*, in Henry Louis Gates, Jr. and Nellie Y. McKay (eds.), *The Norton Anthology of African American Literature*, 2nd edn. (New York: W.W. Norton, 2004), 325–45 (329).

30 Langston Hughes, *Mulatto*, in *The Collected Works of Langston Hughes*, vol. V: *The Plays to 1942: Mulatto to The Sun Do Move*, ed. Leslie Catherine Sanders and Nancy Johnson (Columbia: University of Missouri Press, 2002), 17–50 (30, 34).

31 *Ibid.*, 33.

32 Leigh Anne Duck's "'Go there tuh *know* there': Zora Neale Hurston and the Chronotope of the Folk," *American Literary History*, 13 (summer 2001), 265–94, refutes the claim that Hurston's characters exist outside of time. Duck explains the competing interpretation of the folk in Hurston's work.

33 Wall, *Women of the Harlem Renaissance*, 32.

34 Gilman, *Blood Talk*, 4.

35 *Ibid.*, 16.

36 *Ibid.*, 4.

37 Sandra L. Richards, "Writing the Absent Potential Drama, Performance, and the Canon of African-American Literature," in Andrew Parker and Eve Kosofsky Sedgwick (eds.), *Performativity and Performance* (New York: Routledge, 1995), 64–88 (77).

38 Toni Morrison, *Playing in the Dark: Whiteness and the Literary Imagination* (New York: Vintage Books, 1993), 33.

39 Hurston, "Characteristics of Negro Expression," 79.

40 Du Bois, *The Souls of Black Folk*, 9.

41 Spillers, "Mama's Baby," *Black, White, and in Color*, 203.

42 Homi K. Bhabha, "On Mimicry and Man: The Ambivalence of Colonial Discourse," *The Location of Culture* (New York: Routledge, 1994), 89.

43 Sundquist, *To Wake the Nations*, 277.

44 Daphne A. Brooks, *Bodies in Dissent*, 270.

45 David Krasner, "Rewriting the Body: Aida Overton Walker and the Social Formation of Cakewalking," *Theatre Survey*, 37 (November 1996), 67–92 (69–70).

46 Brooke Baldwin, "The Cakewalk: A Study in Stereotype and Reality," *Journal of Social History*, 15 (winter 1981), 205–18 (213).

47 Walker, "The Negro on the American Stage," 248.

48 Brooke Baldwin, "The Cakewalk," 213.

49 Krasner, "Rewriting the Body," 67.

50 Daphne A. Brooks, *Bodies in Dissent*, 272.

51 Hurston, "Characteristics of Negro Expression," 86.

52 In "Rewriting the Body" Krasner explains that "Walker appealed to this new social group (America's *nouveau riche*) as a bona fide cakewalker who had taught the dance to British royalty; in dancing the cakewalk, American whites vicariously associated themselves with aristocracy." As he goes on to explain, "Cultural identification with blacks within the white elite supplied motivation for whites eager to explore black cultural experiences as an excavation into the exotic world of what they thought of as the inferior, but fascinating, Other" (79).

53 *Ibid.*

54 Jayna Brown, *Babylon Girls*, 146.

55 In *Black Dance* (Woodstock, NY: Overlook Press, 1990), Edward Thorpe explains, "beginning as a West African tribal ceremony, the dance (the cakewalk) continued through the Afro-Caribbean Ring Shouts to plantation competition dances, and ended up as a dance craze not only featured in Broadway shows but also in ballroom competitions around the world" (58). Although Hurston situates it as an internal communal activity in the play, the fact that most people could probably recognize the dance as a part of a wider cultural display supports my claim that a political dynamic exists in *Color Struck*.

56 David Eng and Shinhee Han, "A Dialogue on Racial Melancholia," in David Eng and David Kazanjian (eds.), *Loss: The Politics of Mourning* (Berkeley: University of California Press, 2003), 344.

57 *Ibid.*, 344.

58 Luciano, "Passing Shadows," 149.

59 See Shannon Steen, "Melancholy Bodies: Racial Subjectivity and Whiteness in O'Neill's *The Emperor Jones*," *Theatre Journal*, 52 (October 2000), 339–59, for a consideration of how whiteness functions as a social fantasy that produces the loss associated with melancholia.

60 Sigmund Freud, "Mourning and Melancholia," in *Standard Edition*, vol. XIV, 237–58 (245).

61 Eng and Han, "Dialogue on Racial Melancholia," 344.

62 Freud, "Mourning and Melancholia," 246, 245.

63 *Ibid.*

64 Diamond, "Deploying/Destroying the Primitivist Body," 128.

65 I borrow from Nicolas Abraham and Maria Torok's definitions of "introjection" and "incorporation." In "Mourning *or* Melancholia: Introjection *versus* Incorporation," in *The Shell and the Kernel*, they explain that "Incorporation denotes a fantasy, introjection a process ... Incorporation is the refusal to reclaim as our own the part of ourselves that we placed in what we lost; incorporation is the refusal to acknowledge the full import of the loss, a loss that, if recognized as such, would effectively transform us ... incorporation is the refusal to introject loss ... Sandor Ferenczi, the inventor of both the term and the concept, defined 'introjection' as the process of broadening the ego" (126–27).

66 Cheng, *Melancholy of Race*, 127–28.

67 Morrison, "Home," 5.

68 On opacity, see Daphne A. Brooks, *Bodies in Dissent*, 8.

69 Foreman, *Activist Sentiments*, 77.

70 Hazel Carby, "Introduction," in Frances E.W. Harper, *Iola Leroy, or, Shadows Uplifted* (Boston: Beacon Press, 1987), ix–xxvi (xxi–xxii).

71 Locke, *The New Negro*, xxvi.

4 RESISTING SHAME AND OFFERING PRAISE AND WORSHIP

1 Langston Hughes, *Tambourines to Glory*, in *Five Plays by Langston Hughes*, ed. Webster Smalley (Bloomington: Indiana University Press, 1968), 183–258 (193). Further references to the play and to Hughes' prefatory note are to this edition unless otherwise indicated and will be cited parenthetically. The first version of *Tambourines to Glory* was written in 1956. The play debuted in New York in 1963 and was first published in that year. Other versions of the play include: New Haven, CT: Beinecke Rare Book and Manuscript Library, Yale University: Langston Hughes Papers (JWJ MSS 26): "Old Version" (abbreviated OV); "Version IV" (abbreviated IV); and "After Westport."

2 Henry Louis Gates, Jr., *The Signifying Monkey: A Theory of African American Literary Criticism* (Oxford University Press, 1988), 107; Carpio, *Laughing Fit to Kill*, 21.

3 Mikhail Bakhtin, "Discourse Typology in Prose," in Ladislav Matejka and Krystyna Pomorska (eds.), *Readings in Russian Poetics: Formalist and Structuralist Views* (Cambridge, MA: MIT Press, 1971), 176–96 (185).

4 Gates, *Signifying Monkey*, 110.

5 Gerald L. Davis, *I Got the Word in Me and I Can Sing It, You Know: A Study of the Performed African American Sermon* (Philadelphia: University of Pennsylvania Press, 1985), 6.

6 Wallace Best, "'The Spirit of the Holy Ghost is a Male Spirit': African American Preaching Women and the Paradoxes of Gender," in R. Marie Griffin and Barbara Dianne Savage (eds.), *Women and Religion in the African Diaspora: Knowledge, Power, and Performance* (Baltimore, MD: Johns Hopkins University Press, 2006), 101–27 (126).

7 Leslie Catherine Sanders, "'I've Wrestled With Them All My Life': Langston Hughes' *Tambourines to Glory*," *Black American Literature Forum*, 25 (spring 1991), 63–72 (66–67).

8 Henry H. Mitchell, *Black Preaching* (Philadelphia: J.B. Lippincott, 1970), 25.

9 Leslie Catherine Sanders, *The Development of Black Theatre in America: From Shadows to Selves* (Baton Rouge: Louisiana State University Press, 1988), 115, 116.

10 Leslie Catherine Sanders, "'Also Own the Theatre': Representation in the Comedies of Langston Hughes," *Langston Hughes Review*, 11 (spring 1992), 6–13 (11).

11 Susan Bennett, *Theatre Audiences: A Theory of Production and Reception* (New York: Routledge, 1990), 104.

12 Henry Louis Gates, Jr., "The Chitlin Circuit," in Harry J. Elam, Jr. and David Krasner (eds.), *African American Performance and Theater History: A Critical Reader* (Oxford University Press, 2001), 132–48 (142).

13 Carpio, *Laughing Fit to Kill*, 75.

14 Toni Morrison, *The Bluest Eye* (New York: Plume, 1994; first published 1970), 17.

15 Langston Hughes, *Angelo Herndon Jones*, in *The Collected Works of Langston Hughes*, vol. v: *The Plays to 1942: Mulatto to The Sun Do Move*, ed. Leslie Catherine Sanders and Nancy Johnson (Columbia: University of Missouri Press, 2002), 184–95 (193).

16 *Ibid.*

17 Ralph Ellison, *Invisible Man* (New York: Vintage International, 1995), 267. Further references are to this edition and will be cited parenthetically.

18 See Joseph Adamson and Hilary Clark, "Introduction: Shame, Affect, Writing," in Adamson and Clark (eds.), *Scenes of Shame: Psychoanalysis, Shame, and Writing* (Albany: State University of New York Press, 1998), 1–34 (2); and Donald Nathanson, "A Timetable for Shame," in Nathanson (ed.), *The Many Faces of Shame* (New York: Guilford Press, 1987), 1–63 (33).

19 J. Brooks Bouson, *Quiet as It's Kept: Shame, Trauma, and Race in the Novels of Toni Morrison* (Albany: State University of New York Press, 2000), 78, 85.
20 *Ibid.*, 14.
21 Judith Halberstam, "Shame and White Gay Masculinity," *Social Text*, 23 (fall–winter 2005), 219–33 (225).
22 Morrison, *The Bluest Eye*, 83.
23 In *Beloved* (New York: Plume, 1988), Toni Morrison offers an example of the way spiritual practice functions to resist the shame and hatred associated with blackness. The well-known scene that recounts Baby Suggs preaching in the clearing supports my claim that practices of African American spirituality functioned to contest racism (86–89). Further references are to this edition and will be cited parenthetically.
24 Bouson, *Quiet as It's Kept*, 16.
25 Spillers, "Moving On Down the Line," *Black, White, and in Color*, 254.
26 Nathanson, "Timetable for Shame," 4.
27 Spillers, "Moving On Down the Line," *Black, White, and in Color*, 263.
28 Langston Hughes, "Down Under in Harlem," in Gerald Early (ed.), *Speech & Power: The African-American Essay and its Cultural Content from Polemics to Pulpit*, vol. 1 (Hopewell, NJ: Ecco Press, 1992), 92–94 (93).
29 *Ibid.*
30 Arnold Rampersad, *The Life of Langston Hughes*, 2 vols. (Oxford University Press, 2002), vol. II, 322.
31 *Ibid.*
32 Spillers, "Moving On Down the Line," *Black, White, and in Color*, 253.
33 *Ibid.*, 252.
34 *Ibid.*, 254.
35 Foreman, *Activist Sentiments*, 77.
36 Cornel West, *Prophesy Deliverance!: An Afro-American Revolutionary Christianity*, 2nd edn. (Philadelphia: Westminster Press, 2002), 15.
37 *Ibid.*, 16.
38 Carpio, *Laughing Fit to Kill*, 6.
39 Gilman, *Blood Talk*, 16.
40 Atlanta, GA: Emory University Manuscript, Archives, and Rare Book Library: Louise Thompson Patterson Papers: MS 869, Box 18, folder 26: Langston Hughes, "Concerning Good-bye, Christ."
41 *Ibid.*
42 Langston Hughes, "The Negro Artist and the Racial Mountain," in Angelyn Mitchell (ed.), *Within the Circle: An Anthology of African American Literary Criticism from the Harlem Renaissance to the Present* (Durham, NC: Duke University Press, 1994), 51–59 (59).
43 Rampersad, *Life of Langston Hughes*, vol. 1, 64.
44 Gerald L. Davis, *I Got the Word in Me*, 46.
45 Spillers, "Moving On Down the Line," *Black, White, and in Color*, 258.
46 Lewis Nicholas, "Poems to Play: Langston Hughes Describes the Genesis of His 'Tambourines to Glory,'" *New York Times* (October 27, 1963), 115.

47 Farah Jasmine Griffin, *"Who Set You Flowin'?"*, 63.
48 Spillers, "Moving On Down the Line," *Black, White, and in Color*, 254.
49 *Ibid.*, 263.
50 Rampersad, *Life of Langston Hughes*, vol. ii, 370.
51 *Ibid.*

5 RESISTING DEATH: THE BLUES BRAVADO OF A GHOST

1 James Baldwin, *Blues for Mister Charlie* (New York: Vintage International, 1995; first published 1964), 2. Further references are to this edition and will be cited parenthetically.
2 In "Unspeakable Things Unspoken: The Afro-American Presence in American Literature," *Michigan Quarterly Review*, 28 (winter 1989), 1–34, Toni Morrison calls this presence "the ghost in the machine" (11). The phrase was coined by Gilbert Ryle.
3 Jacqueline Goldsby's *A Spectacular Secret: Lynching in American Life and Literature* (University of Chicago Press, 2006) offers a model of "reading history *out* of literary texts instead of *into* them." She considers "accounts of lynching's 'life' – its formation, meaning, and significance as a social practice – that identify the material and psychic forces in addition to racism that allowed the violence to remained unchecked" (4). I too am interested in the psychic forces that *Blues for Mister Charlie* reveals and argue that the play situates those forces as a primary obstacle to the Civil Rights Movement.
4 See Alice Rayner, *Ghosts: Death's Double and the Phenomena of Theatre* (Minneapolis: University of Minnesota Press, 2006), xix.
5 *Ibid.*
6 Marvin Carlson, *The Haunted Stage: The Theatre as Memory Machine* (Ann Arbor: University of Michigan Press, 2001), 17.
7 Alexander Weheliye, *Phonographies: Grooves in Sonic Afro-Modernity* (Durham, NC: Duke University Press, 2005), 93.
8 Ellison, *Invisible Man*, 581.
9 James Baldwin, *Amen Corner* (New York: Vintage International, 1998; first published 1968), xvi.
10 Karla F.C. Holloway, *Passed On: African American Mourning Stories* (Durham, NC: Duke University Press, 2002), 61.
11 In Gayl Jones' novel *Corregidora* (Boston: Beacon Press, 1986), Cat, a secondary character, categorizes the voice of the main character, Ursa, as a voice that sounds like she "been through something" (44). I appropriate Jones' phrase to describe Holiday's voice.
12 Abraham and Torok, *The Shell and the Kernel*, 8.
13 Michel Foucault, *Discipline and Punish: The Birth of the Prison* (New York: Vintage Books, 1995), 49.
14 Elizabeth Alexander, "'Can you be BLACK and look at this': Reading the Rodney King Video(s)," in Thelma Gordon (ed.), *Black Male: Representations*

of Masculinity in Contemporary American Art (New York: Whitney Museum of American Art, 1994), 91–110 (102).

15 Goldsby, *Spectacular Secret*, 5.

16 Moten, *In the Break*, 196.

17 Harry J. Elam, Jr., "Reality Check," in Janelle G. Reinelt and Joseph R. Roach (eds.), *Critical Theory and Performance*, rev. and enlarged edn. (Ann Arbor: University of Michigan Press, 2007), 173–90 (173).

18 Goldsby, *Spectacular Secret*, 297.

19 Hanover, NH: Dartmouth College: Rauner Special Collections Library: ANTA Theater playbill, June 29, 1964.

20 Goldsby, *Spectacular Secret*, 304.

21 Hartman, *Scenes of Subjection*, 4.

22 Ashraf Rushdy, "Exquisite Corpse," *Transition*, 9.3 (2000), 70–77 (72).

23 Morrison, *Playing in the Dark*, xii.

24 Sigmund Freud, "The Unconscious," *Standard Edition*, vol. xiv, 166–204 (166).

25 *Ibid.*

26 J. Laplanche and J.-B. Pontalis, *The Language of Psychoanalysis*, trans. Donald Nicholson-Smith (New York: W.W. Norton, 1973), 474.

27 Eng, *Racial Castration*, 126.

28 Sigmund Freud, "Some Psychical Consequences of the Anatomical Distinction Between the Sexes," *Standard Edition*, vol. xix, 241–60 (252).

29 Sigmund Freud, "The 'Uncanny,'" *Standard Edition*, vol. xvii, 217–56 (220).

30 In the lynching scene described in Jean Toomer's "Blood-Burning Moon," in *Cane* (New York: Liveright, 1975; first published 1923), a "Ghost of a yell" emanates from the yelling mob (36).

31 Spillers, "Mama's Baby," *Black, White, and in Color*, 203.

32 Rushdy, "Exquisite Corpse," 77.

33 Kathy Perkins, "Introduction," in Perkins (ed.), *Black Female Playwrights: An Anthology of Plays before 1950* (Bloomington: Indiana University Press, 1990), 1–18 (9, 10).

34 See Goldsby, *A Spectacular Secret*; and Koritha A. Mitchell, "Anti-Lynching Plays."

35 Nicholas K. Davis, "Go Tell It on the Stage: *Blues for Mister Charlie* as Dialectical Drama," *Journal of American Drama and Theatre*, 17 (spring 2005), 30–42 (33, 34).

36 Robert Brustein, "Everybody's Protest Play," *The New Republic* (May 16, 1964), 35.

37 Rayner, *Ghosts*, xv.

38 Anon., "Maybe You Can Save 'Blues for Mr. Charlie,'" *New Pittsburgh Courier*, 5 (May 30, 1964), 7.

39 Ralph Ellison, "Richard Wright's Blues," *Shadow and Act* (New York: Vintage International, 1964), 78–79.

40 Farah Jasmine Griffin, *"Who Set You Flowin'?"*, 25–26.

41 *Ibid.*, 26.

42 Toomer, "Blood-Burning Moon," 30.
43 *Ibid.*, 33.
44 *Ibid.*
45 *Ibid.*, 36.
46 *Ibid.*
47 Moten, *In the Break*, 196.
48 *Ibid.*
49 *Ibid.*, 201.
50 Amiri Baraka, "African Slaves/American Slaves: Their Music," *LeRoi Jones/ Amiri Baraka Reader*, 21.
51 Cheryl Wall, *Worrying the Line: Black Women Writers, Lineage, and Literary Tradition* (Chapel Hill: University of North Carolina Press, 2005), 118.
52 The ANTA Theater became the Virginia Theater in 1981 and the August Wilson Theatre in 2006.
53 Martin Gansberg, "James Baldwin Turns to Broadway with a Play about Our Times," *New York Times* (April 19, 1964), XI.
54 Silverman, *Acoustic Mirror*, 1.
55 *Ibid.*, 17.
56 *Ibid.*, 26.
57 *Ibid.*, 17.
58 Sigmund Freud, "Fetishism," *Standard Edition*, vol. XXI, 152–57 (152–53).
59 Eng, *Racial Castration*, 2.
60 Freud, "Fetishism," 153.
61 Harvcy Young, *Embodying Black Experience: Stillness, Critical Memory, and the Black Body* (Ann Arbor: University of Michigan Press, 2010), 179.
62 Eng, *Racial Castration*, 2.
63 *Ibid.*
64 Silverman, *Acoustic Mirror*, 81.
65 Moten, *In the Break*, 195.
66 *Ibid.*, 196.
67 Silverman, *Acoustic Mirror*, 26.
68 Paul Griffin, "James Baldwin's Confrontation with Racist Terror in the American South: Psychoneurosis in 'Going to Meet the Man,'" *Journal of Black Studies*, 32 (May 2002), 506–27 (509).
69 James Baldwin, "Going to Meet the Man," *Going to Meet the Man* (New York: Vintage, 1995; first published 1965), 249.
70 *Ibid.*, 232.
71 *Ibid.*, 239, 248, 249.
72 Toni Morrison, "The Site of Memory," in William Zinsser (ed.), *Inventing the Truth: The Art and Craft of Memoir* (Boston: Houghton Mifflin, 1987), 103–24 (III).
73 *Ibid.*
74 *Ibid.*
75 Kalamu ya Salaam, "James Baldwin: Looking towards the Eighties," in Fred L. Standley and Nancy V. Burt (eds.), *Critical Essays on James Baldwin* (Boston: G.K. Hall, 1988), 35–42 (36).

76 *Ibid.*, 37.
77 Baldwin quoted in Gansberg, "James Baldwin."
78 Quoted in Daryl C. Dance, "You Can't Go Home Again: James Baldwin and the South," in Fred L. Standley and Nancy V. Burt (eds.), *Critical Essays on James Baldwin* (Boston: G.K. Hall), 54–61 (55).
79 Quoted *ibid.*
80 Barbara Christian, "'Somebody Forgot to Tell Somebody Something': African-American Women's Historical Novels," in Joanne M. Braxton and Andree Nicola McLaughlin (eds.), *Wild Women in the Whirlwind: Afra-American Culture and the Contemporary Literary Renaissance* (New Brunswick, NJ: Rutgers University Press, 1990), 326–41 (333).
81 Baldwin quoted in Dance, "You Can't Go Home Again," 61.
82 James Baldwin, "Here Be Dragons," in Rudolph P. Byrd and Beverly Guy-Sheftall (eds.), *Traps: African American Men on Gender and Sexuality* (Bloomington: Indiana University Press, 2001; first published as "Freaks and the American Ideal of Manhood," in *Playboy*, January 1985), 208–18 (208).
83 James Baldwin, "The Fire Next Time," *Collected Essays*, ed. Toni Morrison (New York: Library of America, 1988), 326–47 (347).
84 Sigmund Freud, *An Outline of Psycho-Analysis*, ed. James Strachey (New York: W.W. Norton, 1969), 21.
85 Albert Murray, *Stomping the Blues* (New York: McGraw-Hill, 1976), 99.
86 Angela Davis, *Blues Legacies and Black Feminism: Gertrude "Ma" Rainey, Bessie Smith, and Billie Holiday* (New York: Pantheon Books, 1998), 10.
87 Avery F. Gordon, *Ghostly Matters: Haunting and the Sociological Imagination* (Minneapolis: University of Minnesota Press, 1997), 184.

6 RITUALS OF REPAIR

1 August Wilson, *Joe Turner's Come and Gone* (New York: Plume, 1988), 72. Further references are to this edition and will be cited parenthetically.
2 Harry J. Elam, Jr., in *The Past as Present in the Drama of August Wilson* (Ann Arbor: University of Michigan Press, 2006), argues that "In Wilson's (w)righting, the domestic becomes a site that is both problematic and enabling for female characters. While Jill Dolan has argued that the genre of realism is 'a conservative force that reproduces and reinforces dominant culture relationships,' Wilson's dramatic structure with its rituals, musicality, and lyricism defies certain conventions of domestic realism even as it works within other constraints of the genre" (89).
3 David Hall, "The Spirit of Reparation," *Boston College Third World Law Journal*, 24 (2004), 1–12 (6).
4 For example, Jerry Gafio Watts argues, in *Amiri Baraka: The Politics and Art of a Black Intellectual* (New York University Press, 2001), that "While we can remain skeptical about assigning to any single event or person the responsibility for launching a national arts movement, we must recognize that Baraka was a pioneer and leader in this [the Black Arts Movement] endeavor" (171).

5 See August Wilson, *The Ground on Which I Stand* (New York: Theatre Communications Group, 1996), 20.

6 See Amiri Baraka, "Black Liberation/Socialist Revolution," *Daggers and Javelins: Essays, 1974–1979* (New York: Morrow, 1984), 88–101.

7 Amiri Baraka, "Black Power & Jesse Jackson II," *LeRoi Jones/Amiri Baraka Reader*, 467.

8 In a 1994 essay entitled "The Black Arts Movement," in *LeRoi Jones/Amiri Baraka Reader*, he explains, "Except that whatever else the most sensitive of us was doing, what remained is what was the deepest hunger in our souls, the urge to democracy, to self determination, the understanding that no matter how much we might be 'recognized' or 'accepted' or even lionized as artists &c., we were still somehow burdened with the disorienting realization of alienation" (497).

9 Amiri Baraka, "*Black Fire*: A New Introduction," in Amiri Baraka and Larry Neal (eds.), *Black Fire: An Anthology of Afro-American Writing* (Baltimore: Black Classic Press, 2007; first published 1968), xvii–xx (xvii).

10 Elam, Jr., *Past as Present*, 217.

11 August Wilson, *The Ground on Which I Stand*, 13–14.

12 Amiri Baraka, "Malcolm as Ideology," *LeRoi Jones/Amiri Baraka Reader*, 515. See also Baraka, "The Legacy of Malcolm X, and the Coming of the Black Nation," *LeRoi Jones/Amiri Baraka Reader*.

13 María Josefina Saldaña-Portillo, *The Revolutionary Imagination in the Americas and the Age of Development* (Durham, NC: Duke University Press, 2003).

14 Baraka, "Malcolm as Ideology," *LeRoi Jones/Amiri Baraka Reader*, 516.

15 Maria Diedrich, Henry Louis Gates, Jr., and Carl Pedersen, "The Middle Passage between History and Fiction: Introductory Remarks," in Diedrich, Gates, Jr., and Pedersen (eds.), *Black Imagination and the Middle Passage* (New York: Oxford University Press, 1999), 5–20 (7).

16 Soyica Diggs Colbert, "A Pedagogical Approach to Understanding Rioting as Revolutionary Action in Alice Childress's *Wine in the Wilderness*," *Theatre Topics*, 19 (March 2009), 77–85 (79).

17 See Harry J. Elam, Jr., *Taking It to the Streets: The Social Protest Theater of Luis Valdez and Amiri Baraka* (Ann Arbor: University of Michigan Press, 2001), 77; Forster Hirsch, "*Slave Ship* by LeRoi Jones," *Educational Theatre Journal*, 22 (March 1970), 102–03; and Dan Isaac, "The Death of the Proscenium Stage," *Antioch Review* (summer 1971), 246.

18 Walter Benjamin, "On the Concept of History," *Selected Writings*, vol. IV: *1938–1940*, ed. Howard Eiland and Michael Jennings, trans. Edmund Jephcott *et al.* (Cambridge, MA: Harvard University Press, 2003), 389–400 (392).

19 Weheliye, *Phonographies*, 79.

20 Ellison, *Invisible Man*, 6.

21 In an article for the *New York Times* (March 10, 1991), sec. 2.5, 17, entitled "How to Write a Play Like August Wilson" that was adapted from a talk Wilson gave at the Poetry Center in Manhattan in 1991, Wilson explains, "In terms of influence on my work, I have what I call my four B's: Romare

Bearden; Imamu Amiri Baraka, the writer; Jorge Luis Borges, the Argentine short-story writer; and the biggest B of all: the blues. I don't play an instrument. I don't know any musical terms. And I don't know anything about music. But I have a very good ear and I'm a good listener. And I listen mostly to the blues. I have been variously influenced by them and also by the 2,000 or some poets I have read. I have not been, per se, influenced by playwrights or any writers other than that. Some of the black writers I read. For instance, I read Ralph Ellison's "Invisible Man" when I was 14. I guess I've been influenced by him. I've certainly been inspired by examples like that."

22 August Wilson, "Preface," *Three Plays* (University of Pittsburgh Press, 1991), vii–xiv (ix).

23 August Wilson, "August Wilson" (interview by David Savran), in Jackson R. Byer and Mary C. Hartig (eds.), *Conversations with August Wilson* (Jackson: University of Mississippi Press, 2006), 19–37 (23).

24 August Wilson, "August Wilson Explains His Dramatic Vision: An Interview" (interview by Sandra Shannon), in *Conversations with August Wilson*, 118–54 (146).

25 I owe this insight to conversations generated by the New England Black Scholars Collective (NEBSC).

26 *Oxford English Dictionary*, online edition (Oxford University Press) (accessed January 12, 2010).

27 Amiri Baraka, *Slave Ship*, in William B. Branch (ed.), *Crosswinds: An Anthology of Black Dramatists in the Diaspora* (Bloomington: Indiana University Press, 1993), 250–59 (251). Further references are to this edition and will be cited parenthetically.

28 Isaac, "Death of the Proscenium Stage," 246; and Hirsch, "*Slave Ship* by LeRoi Jones," 102.

29 Elam, Jr., *Taking It to the Streets*, 78.

30 Isaac, "Death of the Proscenium Stage," 246.

31 Du Bois, *The Souls of Black Folk*, 9.

32 José Esteban Muñoz, "Feeling Brown: Ethnicity and Affect in Ricardo Bracho's *The Sweetest Hangover (and Other STDs)*," *Theater Journal*, 52 (March 2000), 67–79 (70).

33 The 1969 Chelsea Theater production emphasized the visual markers most readily associated with race. In a review of the pageant, Foster Hirsch charges that "To black spectators, I think Jones wants to enforce a sense of solidarity through suffering and victimization, past and present. At the end, the actors shake hands with the black members of the audience, and invite them to dance: there is a terrific sense of pride and fierce determination, and the kind of superhuman energy which heralds the dawn of a new era" ("*Slave Ship* by LeRoi Jones," 102).

34 Kimberly W. Benston, *Baraka: The Renegade and the Mask* (New Haven, CT: Yale University Press, 1976), 244. See also Clive Barnes, "The Theater: New LeRoi Jones Play," *New York Times* (November 22, 1969), 46.

35 Weinbaum, *Wayward Reproductions*, 23.

36 Amiri Baraka, *The Autobiography of LeRoi Jones* (Chicago: Lawrence Hill Books, 1984), xiii.

37 Moten, *In the Break*, 99.

38 *Ibid.*

39 Wilson, "August Wilson Explains His Dramatic Vision," 134.

40 Patrick Healy, "Race an Issue in Wilson Play, and its Production," *New York Times* (April 23, 2009), A1.

41 Moten, *In the Break*, 99.

42 *Ibid.*

43 Critics and reviewers of the 1969 Chelsea Theater production of *Slave Ship* have noted similar experiences of feeling uncomfortable and cramped and experiencing suffering and shame. See Hirsch, "*Slave Ship* by LeRoi Jones"; Barnes, "New LeRoi Jones Play"; Benston, *Baraka*; and Elam, Jr., *Taking It to the Streets*.

44 (Amiri Baraka as) LeRoi Jones, *Black Music* (New York: Da Capo Press, 1998; first published 1968), 15.

45 Elin Diamond, *Unmaking Mimesis* (New York: Routledge, 1997), 52.

46 Daphne A. Brooks, *Bodies in Dissent*, 4.

47 See Bertolt Brecht, "A Short Organum for the Theatre," *Brecht on Theatre: The Development of an Aesthetic*, ed. and trans. John Willett (New York: Hill and Wang, 1991), 179–208.

48 Daphne A. Brooks, *Bodies in Dissent*, 5.

49 William J. Harris, "'How you Sound??': Amiri Baraka Writes Free Jazz," in Robert G. O'Meally, Brent Hayes Edwards, and Farah Jasmine Griffin (eds.), *Uptown Conversation: The New Jazz Studies* (New York: Columbia University Press, 2004), 312–25 (313).

50 Brenda Dixon Gottschild, *The Black Dancing Body: A Geography from Coon to Cool* (New York: Palgrave Macmillan, 2003), 110.

51 Diedrich, Gates, Jr., and Pedersen, "Middle Passage between History and Fiction," 8.

52 Victor Turner, *Dramas, Fields, and Metaphors: Symbolic Action in Human Society* (Ithaca, NY: Cornell University Press, 1974), 238.

53 Diamond, *Unmaking Mimesis*, 52.

54 Mary L. Bogumil, "'Tomorrow Never Comes': Songs of Cultural Identity in August Wilson's *Joe Turner's Come and Gone*," *Theatre Journal*, 46 (December 1994), 463–76 (465).

55 Lynne Fauley Emery, *Black Dance from 1619 to Today* (Hightstown, NJ: Princeton Book Company, 1988), 44.

56 Sandra L. Richards, "Yoruba Gods on the American Stage: August Wilson's *Joe Turner's Come and Gone*," in John Conteh-Morgan and Tejumola Olaniyan (eds.), *African Drama and Performance* (Bloomington: Indiana University Press, 2004), 94–106 (103).

57 Sandra Shannon, *The Dramatic Vision of August Wilson* (Washington, DC: Howard University Press, 1995), 126.

58 Hirsch, "*Slave Ship* by LeRoi Jones."
59 Patterson, *Rituals of Blood*, 28.
60 Saidiya V. Hartman, *Lose Your Mother: A Journey along the Atlantic Slave Route* (New York: Farrar, Straus and Giroux, 2007), 103.
61 Stephanie E. Smallwood, *Saltwater Slavery: A Middle Passage from African to American Diaspora* (Cambridge, MA: Harvard University Press, 2007), 58–59.
62 August Wilson, *Gem of the Ocean* (New York: Theatre Communications Group, 2006), 53.
63 Samira Kawash, "Haunted Houses, Sinking Ships: Race, Architecture, and Identity in *Beloved* and *Middle Passage*," *New Centennial Review*, 1 (winter 2001), 67–86 (74).
64 *Ibid.*, 73.
65 Moten, "Case of Blackness," 179.
66 *Ibid.*
67 Smallwood, *Saltwater Slavery*, 59.
68 Melanie Klein, *Love, Guilt and Reparation & Other Works, 1921–1945* (London: Hogarth Press, 1975), 336.
69 Joshua Chambers-Letson, "Reparative Feminisms, Repairing Feminism – Reparation, Postcolonial Violence, and Feminism," *Women and Performance*, 16 (July 2006), 169–90 (173).
70 Klein, *Love, Guilt and Reparation*, 334.
71 *Ibid.*
72 *Ibid.*
73 Chambers-Letson, "Reparative Feminisms," 176.
74 Elam, Jr., *Past as Present*, 170.
75 Austin, *How to Do Things with Words*, 5–6.
76 Butler, *Bodies that Matter*, 224–25.
77 Parker and Sedgwick, "Introduction," 2.
78 Hall, "Spirit of Reparation," 10.
79 Frantz Fanon, *The Wretched of the Earth* (New York: Grove Press, 1963), 51.
80 Chambers-Letson, "Reparative Feminisms," 177.
81 Benjamin, "On the Concept of History," 391.
82 Robin D.G. Kelley, *Yo' Mama's Disfunktional!* (Boston: Beacon Press, 1997), 81.
83 See Elam, Jr., *Past as Present*; Paul Carter Harrison, "August Wilson's Blues Poetic," in Wilson, *Three Plays*, 291–317; and Kim Pereira, *August Wilson and the African-American Odyssey* (Urbana: University of Illinois Press, 1995).
84 I discuss the implications of the detour in Wilson's cycle in terms of *King Hedley II* in "If We Must Die: Violence as History Lesson in *Seven Guitars* and *King Hedley II*," in Alan Nadel (ed.), *August Wilson: Completing the Cycle* (University of Iowa Press, 2010), 71–96.
85 Hartman, *Scenes of Subjection*, 63.

7 RECONSTITUTION

1 Suzan-Lori Parks, *Topdog/Underdog* (New York: Theatre Communications Group, 1999), 5. Further references are to this edition and will be cited parenthetically.

2 Eng, *Racial Castration*, 115.

3 *Ibid.*

4 Suzan Lori-Parks, "Interview with Suzan-Lori Parks" (interview by Shelby Jiggetts), *Callaloo*, 19 (spring 1996), 309–17 (313).

5 See Charles Isherwood, "Theatrical Stumbles of Historic Proportions," *New York Times* (December 12, 2010), AR1.

6 Jackson Lears, *Something for Nothing: Luck in America* (New York: Penguin, 2003), 3.

7 *Ibid.*, 9.

8 Sigmund Freud, *Civilization and Its Discontents*, ed. and trans. James Strachey (New York: W.W. Norton, 1989), 75.

9 Elam, Jr., *Past as Present*, 197.

10 Joshua Wolf Shenk, "Beyond a Black-and-White Lincoln," *New York Times* (April 7, 2002), 2.6.

11 *Ibid.*

12 Du Bois, *The Souls of Black Folk*, 17.

13 *Ibid.*, 18.

14 Lears, *Something for Nothing*, 103.

15 Shenk, "Beyond a Black-and-White Lincoln," 6.

16 Parks, *The America Play and Other Works*, 159.

17 *Ibid.*, 159.

18 *Topdog/Underdog* not only has the honor of being the first play written by an African American to win a Pulitzer Prize, it also holds the chilling distinction of winning the prize the same year that "The New York Times won a record seven Pulitzer Prizes . . . including six for its coverage of Sept. 11, its victims, its causes and its aftermath, all transformative events in the modern history of the United States." Felicity Barringer, in her article "Pulitzers focus on Sept. 11, and the Times Wins 7," *New York Times* (April 9, 2002), A1, juxtaposes description of Parks' award and others on page B4 with the infamous images of September 11, 2001 and its aftermath, including one of the North Tower of the World Trade Center beginning to collapse, on page B5. September 11 certainly did not inspire Parks' *Topdog/Underdog*, nor are there any references to the war on terrorism in the play. Yet the position of the play in the layout of the newspaper next to the collapsing North Tower calls attention to how America changed that day. September 11 and its aftermath did not create *Topdog/Underdog*, but it does inform the reception of the play.

19 Ben Brantley, "Not to Worry, Mr. Lincoln, It's Just a Con Game," *New York Times* (April 8, 2002), E1.

20 *Ibid.*

21 Robin Fin, "Hip-hopping Along, from Brooklyn to Broadway," *New York Times* (April 19, 2002), B2.

22 Don Shewey, "This Time the Shock is Her Turn Toward Naturalism," *New York Times* (July 22, 2001), AR4.

23 Hortense Spillers, "Afterword," in Hortense Spillers and Marjorie Pryse (eds.), *Conjuring Black Women, Fiction, and Literary Tradition* (Bloomington: Indiana University Press, 1985), 249–61 (251).

24 Freud, *Civilization and Its Discontents*, 75.

25 *Ibid.*, 77.

26 Sigmund Freud, *Beyond the Pleasure Principle*, ed. and trans. James Strachey (New York: W.W. Norton, 1961), 14.

27 *Ibid.*

28 *Ibid.*, 13.

29 *Ibid.*, 81.

30 Sigmund Freud, "Reflections upon War and Death," *Character and Culture*, ed. Philip Rieff (New York: Collier Books, 1963), 119.

31 Freud, *Civilization and Its Discontents*, 78.

32 *Ibid.*

33 Herman Melville, *The Confidence Man* (New York: Prometheus Books, 1995; first published 1857), 22.

34 *Ibid.*, 19.

35 *Ibid.*

36 Carolyn L. Karcher, *Shadow over the Promised Land: Slavery, Race, and Violence in Melville's America* (Baton Rouge: Louisiana State University Press, 1980), 187.

37 Melville, *The Confidence Man*, 19.

38 *Ibid.*, 20–21.

39 *Ibid.*, 26.

40 Karcher, *Shadow over the Promised Land*, 200.

41 Melville, *The Confidence Man*, 28.

42 Susan M. Ryan, "Misgivings: Melville, Race and the Ambiguities of Benevolence," *American Literary History*, 12 (winter 2000), 685–712 (688).

43 Karcher, *Shadow over the Promised Land*, 194.

44 *Ibid.*, 195.

45 Daphne A. Brooks, *Bodies in Dissent*, 229.

46 *Ibid.*, 227.

47 Jesse A. Shipp, Will Marion Cook, and Paul Laurence Dunbar, *In Dahomey*, in James V. Hatch and Ted Shine (eds.), *Black Theater, USA: Plays by African Americans* (New York: Free Press, 1996), 63–85 (66).

48 *Ibid.*

49 *Ibid.*, 67.

50 Daphne A. Brooks, *Bodies in Dissent*, 230.

51 Ralph Ellison, *Shadow and Act* (New York: Vintage International, 1995), 54.

52 Ellison, *Invisible Man*, 474.

53 *Ibid.*, 498, 499–500.

54 Carpio, *Laughing Fit to Kill*, 206.

55 *Ibid.*

56 Shenk, "Beyond a Black-and-White Lincoln," 6.

EPILOGUE: BLACK MOVEMENTS

1 Tarell Alvin McCraney, *The Brother/Sister Plays* (New York: Theatre Communications Group, 2010), 11. Further references are to this edition and will be cited parenthetically.

2 See the December 13, 2009 Public Theater production of *In the Red and Brown Water*, recorded by the Theatre on Film and Tape Archive, in the Billy Rose Theatre Collection, New York Public Library for the Performing Arts (call no: NCOV 3570).

3 Randy Gener, "Dreaming in Yoruba Land," *American Theatre*, 26 (September 2009), 24–27, 81–82 (82).

4 Ben Brantley, "Lives in the Bayou Tap All Realism of Dreams," *New York Times* (November 18, 2009) www.theater.nytimes.com/2009/11/18/theater/reviews/ 18brother.html?adxnnl=18adxnnl=1309935437-Lz47q4v/vqcrCw2HMKgpsg (accessed December 31, 2010).

5 Wole Soyinka, *Myth, Literature and the African World* (Cambridge University Press, 1976), 10.

6 See Ina J. Fandrich, "Yorùbá Influences on Haitian Vodou and New Orleans Voodoo," *Journal of Black Studies*, 37 (May 2007), 775–91 (784).

7 Benedict M. Ibitokun, *African Drama and the Yorùbá World-View* (Ibadan, Nigeria: Ibadan University Press, 1995), 21.

8 Roach, *Cities of the Dead*, 36.

9 Peggy Phelan, *Unmarked: The Politics of Performance* (New York: Routledge, 1993), 146.

10 *Ibid.*

11 Taylor, *The Archive and the Repertoire*, 142.

12 Morrison, *The Bluest Eye*, n.p.; Soyinka, *Myth, Literature and the African World*, 2.

13 E. Patrick Johnson, *Appropriating Blackness*, 77.

14 Soyinka, *Myth, Literature and the African World*, 4.

15 Paul Carter Harrison, "Praise/Word," in Paul Carter Harrison, Victor Leo Walker II, and Gus Edwards (eds.), *Black Theatre: Ritual Performance in the African Diaspora* (Philadelphia: Temple University Press, 2002), 1–10 (4).

16 Soyinka, *Myth, Literature and the African World*, 26.

17 McCraney quoted in Gener, "Dreaming in Yoruba Land," 26.

18 *Ibid.*

19 *Ibid.*

20 Elam, Jr., *Past as Present*, 171.

21 Soyinka, *Myth, Literature and the African World*, 142, 148, 149.

22 *Ibid.*, 142, 143.

23 Elam, *Past as Present*, 171.

24 Gates, Jr., *Signifying Monkey*, 5.

25 *Ibid.*, 6.

26 Soyinka, *Myth, Literature and the African World*, 143.

Bibliography

ARCHIVAL SOURCES

ATLANTA, GA: EMORY UNIVERSITY MANUSCRIPT, ARCHIVES, AND RARE BOOK LIBRARY

Louise Thompson Patterson Papers: MS 869, Box 18, folder 26: Langston Hughes, "Concerning Good-bye, Christ."

HANOVER, NH: RAUNER SPECIAL COLLECTIONS LIBRARY, DARTMOUTH COLLEGE

ANTA Theater playbill, June 29, 1964.

NEW HAVEN, CT: BEINECKE RARE BOOK AND MANUSCRIPT LIBRARY, YALE UNIVERSITY: LANGSTON HUGHES PAPERS (JWJ MSS 26)

"After Westport"
"Old Version"
"Version IV"

NEW YORK: BILLY ROSE THEATRE COLLECTION, NEW YORK PUBLIC LIBRARY FOR THE PERFORMING ARTS

Hansberry, Lorraine. *A Raisin in the Sun* [videorecording], directed by Kenny Leon. Theatre on Film and Tape Archive. Call no: NCOV 2867.

McCraney, Tarell Alvin. *In the Red and Brown Water* [videorecording], Public Theater, directed by Tina Landau. Theatre on Film and Tape Archive. Call no: NCOV 3570.

Parks, Suzan-Lori. *The America Play* [videorecording], Yale Repertory Theatre, directed by Liz Diamond. Theatre on Film and Tape Archive. Call no: NCOV 1646.

Topdog/Underdog [videorecording], Joseph Papp Public Theater, directed by George C. Wolfe. Call no: NCOV 2535.

Wilson, August. *Joe Turner's Come and Gone* [videorecording], Lincoln Center Theater, directed by Bartlett Sher. Theatre on Film and Tape Archive. Call no: NCOV 3541.

PUBLISHED WORKS

Abraham, Nicolas, and Maria Torok. *The Shell and the Kernel: Renewals of Psychoanalysis*, vol. 1 (University of Chicago Press, 1994).

Abrahamson, Doris E. *Negro Playwrights in the American Theater, 1925–1959* (New York: Columbia University Press, 1969).

Adamson, Joseph, and Hilary Clark. "Introduction: Shame, Affect, Writing," in Adamson and Clark (eds.), *Scenes of Shame: Psychoanalysis, Shame, and Writing* (Albany: State University of New York Press, 1998), 1–34.

Adell, Sandra. *Double-Consciousness/Double Bind: Theoretical Issues in Twentieth-Century Black Literature* (Urbana: University of Illinois Press, 1994).

Alexander, Elizabeth. "'Can you be BLACK and look at this': Reading the Rodney King Video(s)," in Thelma Gordon (ed.), *Black Male: Representations of Masculinity in Contemporary American Art* (New York: Whitney Museum of American Art, 1994), 91–110.

Andrews, William A. *To Tell a Free Story: The First Century of Afro-American Autobiography, 1760–1865* (Urbana: University of Illinois Press, 1986).

Anon. "Cinema: Acute Ghettoitis," *Time* (March 31, 1961), www.time.com/time/magazine/article/0,9171,872215,00.html (accessed October 17, 2009).

"The Great Pageant," *Washington Bee* (October 23, 1915), 1, 6.

"Maybe You Can Save 'Blues for Mr. Charlie,'" *New Pittsburgh Courier*, 5 (May 30, 1964), 7.

Austin, J. L. *How to Do Things with Words*, ed. J. O. Urmson and Mariana Sbisà (Cambridge, MA: Harvard University Press, 1962).

Baker, Houston A. *Blues, Ideology, and Afro-American Literature: A Vernacular Theory* (University of Chicago Press, 1984).

Bakhtin, Mikhail. "Discourse Typology in Prose," in Ladislav Matejka and Krystyna Pomorska (eds.), *Readings in Russian Poetics: Formalist and Structuralist Views* (Cambridge, MA: MIT Press, 1971), 176–96.

Baldwin, Brooke. "The Cakewalk: A Study in Stereotype and Reality," *Journal of Social History*, 15 (winter 1981), 205–18.

Baldwin, James. *Amen Corner* (New York: Vintage International, 1998; first published 1968).

Blues for Mister Charlie (New York: Vintage International, 1995; first published 1964).

"The Fire Next Time," *Collected Essays*, ed. Toni Morrison (New York: Library of America, 1988), 326–47.

Going to Meet the Man (New York: Vintage International, 1995; first published 1965).

"Here Be Dragons," in Rudolph P. Byrd and Beverly Guy-Sheftall (eds.), *Traps: African American Men on Gender and Sexuality* (Bloomington:

Indiana University Press, 2001; first published as "Freaks and the American Ideal of Manhood," in *Playboy*, January 1985), 208–18.

Baraka, (Imamu) Amiri. *The Autobiography of LeRoi Jones* (Chicago: Lawrence Hill Books, 1984).

"*Black Fire*: A New Introduction," in Amiri Baraka and Larry Neal (eds.), *Black Fire: An Anthology of Afro-American Writing* (Baltimore: Black Classic Press, 2007; first published 1968), xvii–xx.

"Black Liberation/Socialist Revolution," *Daggers and Javelins: Essays, 1974– 1979* (New York: Morrow, 1984), 88–101.

(as LeRoi Jones.) *Black Music* (New York: Da Capo Press, 1998; first published 1968).

The LeRoi Jones/Amiri Baraka Reader, ed. William J. Harris (New York: Thunder's Mouth Press, 1991).

Slave Ship, in William B. Branch (ed.), *Crosswinds: An Anthology of Black Dramatists in the Diaspora* (Bloomington: Indiana University Press, 1993), 250–59.

Barnes, Clive. "The Theater: New LeRoi Jones Play," *New York Times* (November 22, 1969), 46.

Barringer, Felicity. "Pulitzers Focus on Sept. 11, and the Times Wins 7," *New York Times* (April 9, 2002), A1.

Benjamin, Walter. *Illuminations: Essays and Reflections* (New York: Schocken Books, 1988).

"On the Concept of History," *Selected Writings*, vol. IV: *1938–1940*, ed. Howard Eiland and Michael Jennings, trans. Edmund Jephcott *et al.* (Cambridge, MA: Harvard University Press, 2003), 389–400.

Bennett, Susan. *Theatre Audiences: A Theory of Production and Reception* (New York: Routledge, 1990).

Benston, Kimberly W. *Baraka: The Renegade and the Mask* (New Haven, CT: Yale University Press, 1976), 244.

Performing Blackness: Enactments of African-American Modernism (London: Routledge, 2000).

Bergner, Gwen. *Taboo Subjects* (Minneapolis: University of Minnesota Press, 2005).

Best, Stephen, and Saidiya Hartman. "Fugitive Justice," *Representations*, 92 (autumn 2005), 1–15.

Best, Wallace. "'The Spirit of the Holy Ghost is a Male Spirit': African American Preaching Women and the Paradoxes of Gender," in R. Marie Griffin and Barbara Dianne Savage (eds.), *Women and Religion in the African Diaspora: Knowledge, Power, and Performance* (Baltimore, MD: Johns Hopkins University Press, 2006), 101–27.

Bhabha, Homi K. *The Location of Culture* (New York: Routledge, 1994).

Bogues, Anthony. *Empire of Liberty: Power, Desire, and Freedom* (Hanover, NH: Dartmouth College Press, 2010).

Bogumil, Mary L. "'Tomorrow Never Comes': Songs of Cultural Identity in August Wilson's *Joe Turner's Come and Gone*," *Theatre Journal*, 46 (December 1994), 463–76.

Bouson, J. Brooks. *Quiet as It's Kept: Shame, Trauma, and Race in the Novels of Toni Morrison* (Albany: State University of New York Press, 2000).

Brantley, Ben. "Lives in the Bayou Tap All Realism of Dreams," *New York Times* (November 18, 2009), www.theater.nytimes.com/2009/11/18/theater/reviews/18brother.html?adxnnl=18adxnnl=1309935437-Lz47q4v/vqcrCw2HMKgpsg (accessed December 31, 2010).

"Not to Worry, Mr. Lincoln, It's Just a Con Game," *New York Times* (April 8, 2002), EI.

Brecht, Bertolt. "A Short Organum for the Theatre," *Brecht on Theatre: The Development of an Aesthetic*, ed. and trans. John Willett (New York: Hill and Wang, 1991), 179–208.

Brooks, Daphne A. *Bodies in Dissent: Spectacular Performances of Race and Freedom, 1850–1910* (Durham, NC: Duke University Press, 2006).

Brooks, Gwendolyn. *Blacks* (Chicago: Third World Press, 1987).

Brown, Jayna. *Babylon Girls: Black Women Performers and the Shaping of the Modern* (Durham, NC: Duke University Press, 2008).

Brown, Lloyd W. "Lorraine Hansberry as Ironist: A Reappraisal of *A Raisin in the Sun*," *Journal of Black Studies*, 4 (March 1974), 237–47.

Brown, Misty. "Kenny Leon Directs 'A Raisin in the Sun' on Broadway," *Washington Informer*, 40 (July 7, 2004), 25.

Brown, William Wells. *Clotel; or, the President's Daughter*, in Henry Louis Gates, Jr. and Nellie Y. McKay (eds.), *The Norton Anthology of African American Literature*, 2nd edn. (New York: W.W. Norton, 2004), 325–45.

Brustein, Robert. "Everybody's Protest Play," *The New Republic* (May 16, 1964), 35.

Burroughs, Nannie H. "Not Color, but Character," *Voice of the Negro* (July 1904), 277–80.

Butler, Judith. *Bodies that Matter: On the Discursive Limits of "Sex"* (New York: Routledge, 1993).

Excitable Speech: A Politics of the Performative (New York: Routledge, 1997).

The Psychic Life of Power: Theories in Subjection (Stanford University Press, 1997).

Carby, Hazel. "Introduction," in Frances E. W. Harper, *Iola Leroy, or, Shadows Uplifted* (Boston: Beacon Press, 1987), ix–xxvi.

Race Men (Cambridge, MA: Harvard University Press, 1998).

Carlson, Marvin. *The Haunted Stage: The Theatre as Memory Machine* (Ann Arbor: University of Michigan Press, 2001).

Carpio, Glenda R. *Laughing Fit to Kill: Black Humor in the Fictions of Slavery* (Oxford University Press, 2008).

Carter, Steven R. *Hansberry's Drama: Commitment and Perplexity* (Urbana: University of Illinois Press, 1991).

Chambers-Letson, Joshua. "Reparative Feminisms, Repairing Feminism – Reparation, Postcolonial Violence, and Feminism," *Women and Performance*, 16 (July 2006), 169–90.

Chaudhuri, Una. *Staging Place: The Geography of Modern Drama* (Ann Arbor: University of Michigan Press, 1997).

Cheney, Anne. *Lorraine Hansberry* (Boston: Twayne, 1984).

Cheng, Anne Anlin. *The Melancholy of Race: Psychoanalysis, Assimilation, and Hidden Grief* (Oxford University Press, 2001).

Chesnutt, Charles Waddell. "Post Bellum–Pre Harlem," *Stories, Novels & Essays* (New York: Library of America, 2002), 906–12.

Christian, Barbara. "'Somebody Forgot to Tell Somebody Something': African-American Women's Historical Novels," in Joanne M. Braxton and Andree Nicola McLaughlin (eds.), *Wild Women in the Whirlwind: Afra-American Culture and the Contemporary Literary Renaissance* (New Brunswick, NJ: Rutgers University Press, 1990), 326–41.

Colbert, Soyica Diggs. "If We Must Die: Violence as History Lesson in *Seven Guitars* and *King Hedley II*," in Alan Nadel (ed.), *August Wilson: Completing the Cycle* (University of Iowa Press, 2010), 71–96.

"A Pedagogical Approach to Understanding Rioting as Revolutionary Action in Alice Childress's *Wine in the Wilderness*," *Theatre Topics*, 19 (March 2009), 77–85.

Dance, Daryl C. "You Can't Go Home Again: James Baldwin and the South," in Fred L. Standley and Nancy V. Burt (eds.), *Critical Essays on James Baldwin* (Boston: G.K. Hall), 54–61.

Davis, Angela. *Blues Legacies and Black Feminism: Gertrude "Ma" Rainey, Bessie Smith, and Billie Holiday* (New York: Pantheon Books, 1998).

Davis, Gerald L. *I Got the Word in Me and I Can Sing It, You Know: A Study of the Performed African American Sermon* (Philadelphia: University of Pennsylvania Press, 1985).

Davis, Nicholas K. "Go Tell It on the Stage: *Blues for Mister Charlie* as Dialectical Drama," *Journal of American Drama and Theatre*, 17 (spring 2005), 30–42.

Diamond, Elin. "Deploying/Destroying the Primitivist Body in Hurston and Brecht," in Alan Ackerman and Martin Puchner (eds.), *Against Theatre: Creative Destructions on the Modernist Stage* (New York: Palgrave Macmillan, 2006), 112–32.

Unmaking Mimesis (New York: Routledge, 1997).

Diedrich, Maria, Henry Louis Gates, Jr., and Carl Pendersen. "The Middle Passage between History and Fiction," in Diedrich, Gates, Jr., and Pedersen, (eds.), *Black Imagination and the Middle Passage* (New York: Oxford University Press, 1999), 5–20.

Douglass, Frederick. *The Narrative of the Life of Frederick Douglass, an American Slave, Written by Himself* (Boston: Bedford Books of St. Martin's Press, 1993; first published 1845).

Dove, Nah. "African Womanism: An Afrocentric Theory," *Journal of Black Studies*, 28 (May 1998), 515–39.

Dubey, Madhu. *Signs and Cities: Black Literary Postmodernism* (University of Chicago Press, 2003).

Du Bois, W.E.B. "The Color Line Belts the World," *W.E.B. Du Bois: A Reader*, ed. David Levering Lewis (New York: H. Holt, 1995), 42–43.

"Criteria of Negro Art," *The Oxford W.E.B. Du Bois Reader*, ed. Eric J. Sundquist (Oxford University Press, 1996), 324–28.

Dark Princess, with an introduction by Claudia Tate (New York: Harcourt, 1995; first published 1928).

"The Drama among Black Folk," *The Crisis* (August 1916), 171.

Dusk of Dawn: An Essay toward an Autobiography of a Race Concept (New York: Schocken Books, 1968).

The Negro (Mineola, NY: Dover Publications, 2001).

"The Negro and the American Stage," *The Crisis* (June 1924), 56–57.

"A Pageant," *The Crisis* (September 1915), 230–31.

"The Pageant," *The Crisis* (May 1916), 28–29.

The People of Peoples and Their Gifts to Men, in *The Crisis* (November 1913), 339–41.

The Souls of Black Folk (New York: Barnes and Noble Classics, 2003; first published 1903).

"The Star of Ethiopia," *The Crisis* (December 1915), 90–94.

The Star of Ethiopia, in *The Oxford W.E.B. Du Bois Reader*, ed. Eric Sundquist (New York: Oxford University Press, 1996), 305–10.

The Star of Ethiopia, in *The Papers of W.E.B. Du Bois*, Reel 87, 1521 (Sanford, NC: Microfilming Corporation of America, 1980).

The Star of Ethiopia, in *Washington Bee* (October 9, 1915), 1, 6.

"Three Expositions," *The Crisis* (October 1913), 297.

The World and Africa: An Inquiry into the Part which Africa Has Played in World History (New York: International Publishers, 1996).

"World War and the Color Line," *The Crisis* (November 1914), 28.

Duck, Leigh Anne. "'Go there tuh *know* there': Zora Neale Hurston and the Chronotope of the Folk," *American Literary History*, 13 (summer 2001), 265–94.

Edwards, Brent Hayes. *The Practice of Diaspora: Literature, Translation, and the Rise of Black Internationalism* (Cambridge, MA: Harvard University Press, 2003).

Elam, Jr., Harry J. *The Past as Present in the Drama of August Wilson* (Ann Arbor: University of Michigan Press, 2006).

"Reality Check," in Janelle G. Reinelt and Joseph R. Roach (eds.), *Critical Theory and Performance*, rev. and enlarged edn. (Ann Arbor: University of Michigan Press, 2007), 173–90.

Taking It to the Streets: The Social Protest Theater of Luis Valdez and Amiri Baraka (Ann Arbor: University of Michigan Press, 2001).

and Michele Elam. "Blood Debt: Reparations in Langston Hughes's *Mulatto*," *Theatre Journal*, 61 (March 2009), 85–103.

Ellison, Ralph. *Invisible Man* (New York: Vintage International, 1995).

Shadow and Act (New York: Vintage International, 1995).

Emery, Lynne Fauley. *Black Dance from 1619 to Today* (Hightstown, NJ: Princeton Book Company, 1988).

Eng, David. *Racial Castration: Managing Masculinity in Asian America* (Durham, NC: Duke University Press, 2001).

and Shinhee Han. "A Dialogue on Racial Melancholia," in David Eng and David Kazanjian (eds.), *Loss: The Politics of Mourning* (Berkeley: University of California Press, 2003).

Fandrich, Ina J. "Yorùbá Influences on Haitian Vodou and New Orleans Voodoo," *Journal of Black Studies*, 37 (May 2007), 775–91.

Fanon, Frantz. *The Wretched of the Earth* (New York: Grove Press, 1963).

Favor, Marty. *Authentic Blackness: The Folk in the New Negro Renaissance* (Durham, NC: Duke University Press, 1999).

Fin, Robin. "Hip-hopping Along, from Brooklyn to Broadway," *New York Times* (April 19, 2002), B2.

Fisher-Peters, Pearlie Mae. *The Assertive Woman in Zora Neale Hurston's Fiction, Folklore, and Drama* (New York: Garland; Taylor & Francis, 1997).

Foreman, P. Gabrielle. *Activist Sentiments: Reading Black Women in the Nineteenth Century* (Urbana: University of Illinois Press, 2009).

Foucault, Michel. *Discipline and Punish: The Birth of the Prison* (New York: Vintage Books, 1995).

Freedman, Barbara. *Staging the Gaze: Postmodernism, Psychoanalysis, and Shakespearean Comedy* (Ithaca, NY: Cornell University Press, 1991).

Freud, Sigmund. *Beyond the Pleasure Principle*, ed. and trans. James Strachey (London: W.W. Norton, 1961).

The Case of the Wolf-man: From the History of an Infantile Neurosis (San Francisco: Arion Press, 1993).

Civilization and Its Discontents, ed. and trans. James Strachey (London: W.W. Norton, 1989).

"Fetishism," *Standard Edition*, vol. xxi, 152–57.

"Mourning and Melancholia," *Standard Edition*, vol. xiv, 237–58.

An Outline of Psycho-Analysis, ed. and trans. James Strachey (New York: W.W. Norton, 1969).

"Reflections upon War and Death," *Character and Culture*, ed. Philip Rieff (New York: Collier Books, 1963), 107–33.

"Some Psychical Consequences of the Anatomical Distinction Between the Sexes," *Standard Edition*, vol. xix, 241–60.

The Standard Edition of the Complete Psychological Works of Sigmund Freud, gen. ed. James Strachey (London: Hogarth Press and the Institute of Psycho-analysis, 1953–74).

"The 'UnCanny,'" *Standard Edition*, vol. xvii, 217–56.

"The Unconscious," *Standard Edition*, vol. xiv, 166–204.

Gansberg, Martin. "James Baldwin Turns to Broadway with a Play about Our Times," *New York Times* (April 19, 1964), xi.

Gates, Jr., Henry Louis. "The Chitlin Circuit," in Harry J. Elam, Jr. and David Krasner (eds.), *African American Performance and Theater History: A Critical Reader* (Oxford University Press, 2001), 132–48.

The Signifying Monkey: A Theory of African American Literary Criticism (Oxford University Press, 1988).

"The Trope of the New Negro and the Reconstruction of the Image of the Black," *Representations*, 24 (fall 1988), 129–55.

Gener, Randy. "Dreaming in Yoruba Land," *American Theatre*, 26 (September 2009), 24–27, 81–82.

Gilman, Susan. *Blood Talk: American Race Melodrama and the Culture of the Occult* (University of Chicago Press, 2003).

Gilroy, Paul. *The Black Atlantic: Modernity and Double Consciousness* (Cambridge, MA: Harvard University Press, 1993).

Glassberg, David. *American Historical Pageantry: The Uses of Tradition in the Early Twentieth Century* (Chapel Hill: University of North Carolina Press, 1990).

Goldsby, Jacqueline. *A Spectacular Secret: Lynching in American Life and Literature* (University of Chicago Press, 2006).

Gordon, Avery F. *Ghostly Matters: Haunting and the Sociological Imagination* (Minneapolis: University of Minnesota Press, 1997).

Gordon, Thelma, and Hamza Walker *et al.* (eds.). *Freestyle* (New York: The Studio Museum in Harlem, 2001).

Gottschild, Brenda Dixon. *The Black Dancing Body: A Geography from Coon to Cool* (New York: Palgrave Macmillan, 2003).

Griffin, Farah Jasmine. *"Who Set You Flowin'?": The African American Migration Narrative* (Oxford University Press, 1995).

Griffin, Paul. "James Baldwin's Confrontation with Racist Terror in the American South: Psychoneurosis in 'Going to Meet the Man,'" *Journal of Black Studies*, 32 (May 2002), 506–27.

Grimké, Angelina Weld. *Rachel*, in Kathy Perkins and Judith L. Stephens (eds.), *Strange Fruit: Plays on Lynching by American Women* (Bloomington: Indiana University Press, 1998), 27–78.

Halberstam, Judith. "Shame and White Gay Masculinity," *Social Text*, 23 (fall–winter 2005), 219–33.

Hall, David. "The Spirit of Reparation," *Boston College Third World Law Journal*, 24 (2004), 1–12.

Hansberry, Lorraine. *A Raisin in the Sun* (New York: Vintage Books, 1994; first published 1959).

Harris, William J. "'How you Sound??': Amiri Baraka Writes Free Jazz," in Robert G. O'Meally, Brent Hayes Edwards, and Farah Jasmine Griffin (eds.), *Uptown Conversation: The New Jazz Studies* (New York: Columbia University Press, 2004), 312–25.

Harrison, Paul Carter. "August Wilson's Blues Poetic," in August Wilson, *Three Plays* (University of Pittsburgh Press, 1991), 291–317.

"Praise/Word," in Paul Carter Harrison, Victor Leo Walker II, and Gus Edwards (eds.), *Black Theatre: Ritual Performance in the African Diaspora* (Philadelphia: Temple University Press, 2002), 1–10.

Hartman, Saidiya V. *Lose Your Mother: A Journey along the Atlantic Slave Route* (New York: Farrar, Straus and Giroux, 2007).

Scenes of Subjection: Terror, Slavery, and Self-Making in Nineteenth-Century America (Oxford University Press, 1997).

Hatch, James V., and Ted Shine (eds.). *Black Theater, USA: Plays by African Americans* (New York: Free Press, 1996).

Hay, Samuel. *African American Theatre: An Historical and Critical Analysis* (Cambridge University Press, 1994).

Healy, Patrick. "Race an Issue in Wilson Play, and its Production," *New York Times* (April 23, 2009), A1.

Hegel, G. W. F. *Phenomenology of Spirit*, trans. A. V. Miller (Oxford University Press, 1977).

Higginbotham, Evelyn Brooks. *Righteous Discontent: The Women's Movement in the Black Baptist Church, 1880–1920* (Cambridge, MA: Harvard University Press, 1993).

Hill, Errol G., and James V. Hatch. *A History of African American Theatre* (New York: Cambridge University Press, 2003).

Hill, Lynda Marion. *Social Rituals and the Verbal Art of Zora Neale Hurston* (Washington, DC: Howard University Press, 1996).

Hirsch, Foster. "*Slave Ship* by LeRoi Jones," *Educational Theatre Journal*, 22 (March 1970), 102–03.

Holloway, Karla F. C. *Passed On: African American Mourning Stories* (Durham, NC: Duke University Press, 2002).

Hopkins, Pauline. *Of One Blood* (New York: Washington Square Press, 2004; first published serially 1902–03).

Hughes, Langston. *Angelo Herndon Jones*, in *The Collected Works of Langston Hughes*, vol. v: *The Plays to 1942:* Mulatto *to* The Sun Do Move, ed. Leslie Catherine Sanders and Nancy Johnson (Columbia: University of Missouri Press, 2002), 184–95.

"Down Under in Harlem," in Gerald Early (ed.), *Speech & Power: The African-American Essay and its Cultural Content from Polemics to Pulpit*, vol. 1 (Hopewell, NJ: Ecco Press, 1992), 92–94.

Mulatto, in *The Collected Works of Langston Hughes*, vol. v: *The Plays to 1942:* Mulatto *to* The Sun Do Move, ed. Leslie Catherine Sanders and Nancy Johnson (Columbia: University of Missouri Press, 2002), 17–50.

"The Negro Artist and the Racial Mountain," in Angelyn Mitchell (ed.), *Within the Circle: An Anthology of African American Literary Criticism from the Harlem Renaissance to the Present* (Durham, NC: Duke University Press, 1994), 51–59.

The Selected Poems of Langston Hughes (New York: Vintage Books, 1990).

Tambourines to Glory, in *Five Plays by Langston Hughes*, ed. Webster Smalley (Bloomington: Indiana University Press, 1968; first published 1963), 183–258.

Hunton, Addie. "Negro Womanhood Defended," *The Voice of the Negro* (July 1904), 280–82.

Hurston, Zora Neale. "Characteristics of Negro Expression," in Angelyn Mitchell (ed.), *Within the Circle: An Anthology of African American Literary Criticism from the Harlem Renaissance to the Present* (Durham, NC: Duke University Press, 1994), 79–94.

Color Struck, in Wallace Thurman, Langston Hughes, Zora Neale Hurston, Gwendolyn Bennett, Aaron Douglas, Richard Bruce, and John Davis (eds.), *Fire* (Westport, CT: Negro Universities Press, 1970; first published 1926), 7–14.

Ibitokun, Benedict M. *African Drama and the Yorùbá World-View* (Ibadan, Nigeria: Ibadan University Press, 1995).

Isaac, Dan. "The Death of the Proscenium Stage," *Antioch Review* (summer 1971), 246.

Isherwood, Charles. "Theatrical Stumbles of Historic Proportions," *New York Times* (December 12, 2010), AR1.

Johnson, Barbara. *The Feminist Difference: Literature, Psychoanalysis, Race, and Gender* (Cambridge, MA: Harvard University Press, 1998).

Johnson, E. Patrick. *Appropriating Blackness: Performance and the Politics of Authenticity* (Durham, NC: Duke University Press, 2003).

Jones, Gayl. *Corregidora* (Boston: Beacon Press, 1986).

Jones, LeRoi. *See* Baraka, (Imamu) Amiri.

Karcher, Carolyn L. *Shadow over the Promised Land: Slavery, Race, and Violence in Melville's America* (Baton Rouge: Louisiana State University Press, 1980).

Kawash, Samira. "Haunted Houses, Sinking Ships: Race, Architecture, and Identity in Beloved and Middle Passage," *New Centennial Review*, 1 (winter 2001), 67–86.

Kelley, Robin D. G. *Freedom Dreams: The Black Radical Imagination* (Boston: Beacon Press, 2002).

Yo' Mama's Disfunktional! (Boston: Beacon Press, 1997).

Klein, Melanie. *Love, Guilt and Reparation & Other Works, 1921–1945* (London: Hogarth Press, 1975).

Krasner, David. *A Beautiful Pageant: African American Theatre, Drama, and Performance in the Harlem Renaissance, 1910–1927* (New York: Palgrave Macmillan, 2002).

"Migration, Fragmentation, and Identity: Zora Neale Hurston's *Color Struck* and the Geography of the Harlem Renaissance," *Theatre Journal*, 53 (December 2001), 533–50.

"'The Pageant is the Thing': Black Nationalism and *The Star of Ethiopia*," in Jeffrey C. Mason and Ellen Gainor (eds.), *Performing America: Cultural Nationalism in American Theater* (Ann Arbor: University of Michigan Press, 1998).

Resistance, Parody, and Double Consciousness in African American Theatre, 1895–1910 (New York: St. Martin's Press, 1997).

"Rewriting the Body: Aida Overton Walker and the Social Formation of Cakewalking," *Theatre Survey*, 37 (November 1996), 67–92.

Lacan, Jacques. *The Four Fundamental Concepts of Psycho-analysis: The Seminar of Jacques Lacan*, ed. Jacques-Alain Miller, trans. Alan Sheridan (New York: W.W. Norton, 1988).

Lane, Christopher (ed.). *The Psychoanalysis of Race* (New York: Columbia University Press, 1998).

Laplanche, J., and J. -B. Pontalis. *The Language of Psychoanalysis*, trans. Donald Nicholson-Smith (New York: W.W. Norton, 1973).

Lears, Jackson. *Something for Nothing: Luck in America* (New York: Penguin, 2003).

Lee, Felicia R. "Deferred Dreams that Resonate Across Decades," *New York Times* (February 17, 2008), AR 19.

Lewis, David Levering. *W.E.B. Du Bois*, 2 vols. (New York: H. Holt, 1993–2000).

Litwack, Leon F. "Hellhounds," in James Allen *et al.*, *Without Sanctuary: Lynching Photography in America* (Sante Fe, NM: Twin Palms, 2000), 8–37.

Locke, Alain. *The New Negro* (New York: Touchstone, 1997; first published 1925).

Lott, Eric. *Love and Theft: Blackface Minstrelsy and the American Working Class* (Oxford University Press, 1993).

Luciano, Dana. "Passing Shadows: Melancholic Nationality and Black Critical Publicity in Pauline E. Hopkins' *Of One Blood*," in David Eng and David Kazanjian (eds.), *Loss: The Politics of Mourning* (Berkeley: University of California Press, 2003), 148–87.

McCaskill, Barbara, and Caroline Gebhard. "Introduction," in McCaskill and Gebhard (eds.), *Post-Bellum, Pre-Harlem: African American Literature and Culture, 1877–1919* (New York University Press, 2006), 1–14.

McCraney, Tarell Alvin. *The Brother/Sister Plays* (New York: Theatre Communications Group, 2010).

McDowell, Deborah E. "In the First Place: Making Frederick Douglass and the Afro-American Narrative Tradition," in William L. Andrews (ed.), *African American Autobiography: A Collection of Critical Essays* (Englewood Cliffs, NJ: Prentice Hall, 1993), 36–58.

McLaren, Joseph. "From Protest to Soul Fest: Langston Hughes' Gospel Plays," *Langston Hughes Review*, 15 (spring 1988), 49–61.

Melville, Herman. *The Confidence Man* (New York: Prometheus Books, 1995; first published 1857).

Meyer, Stephen. *As Long as They Don't Move Next Door: Segregation and Racial Conflict in American Neighborhoods* (Lanham, MD: Rowman & Littlefield, 2000).

Miller, Monica L. *Slaves to Fashion: Black Dandyism and the Styling of Black Diasporic Identity* (Durham, NC: Duke University Press, 2009).

Mitchell, Henry H. *Black Preaching* (Philadelphia: J.B. Lippincott, 1970).

Mitchell, Koritha A. "Anti-Lynching Plays: Angelina Weld Grimké, Alice Dunbar-Nelson, and the Evolution of African American Drama," in Barbara McCaskill and Caroline Gebhard (eds.), *Post-Bellum, Pre-Harlem: African American Literature and Culture, 1877–1919* (New York University Press, 2006), 210–30.

Morrison, Toni. *Beloved* (New York: Plume, 1988).

The Bluest Eye (New York: Plume, 1994; first published 1970).

"Home," in Wahneema Lubiano (ed.), *The House that Race Built* (New York: Vintage, 1998), 3–12.

Playing in the Dark: Whiteness and the Literary Imagination (New York: Vintage Books, 1993).

"The Site of Memory," in William Zinsser (ed.), *Inventing the Truth: The Art and Craft of Memoir* (Boston: Houghton Mifflin, 1987), 103–24.

"Unspeakable Things Unspoken: The Afro-American Presence in American Literature," *Michigan Quarterly Review*, 28 (winter 1989), 1–34.

Moten, Fred. "The Case of Blackness," *Criticism*, 50 (spring 2008), 177–218.

In the Break: The Aesthetics of the Black Radical Tradition (Minneapolis: University of Minnesota Press, 2003).

Muñoz, José Esteban. "Feeling Brown: Ethnicity and Affect in Ricardo Bracho's *The Sweetest Hangover (and Other STDs)*," *Theater Journal*, 52 (March 2000), 67–79.

Murray, Albert. *Stomping the Blues* (New York: McGraw-Hill, 1976).

Nathanson, Donald. "A Timetable for Shame," in Nathanson (ed.), *The Many Faces of Shame* (New York: Guilford Press, 1987), 1–63.

Nicholas, Lewis. "Poems to Play: Langston Hughes Describes the Genesis of His 'Tambourines to Glory,'" *New York Times* (October 27, 1963), 115.

Nyong'o, Tavia. *The Amalgamation Waltz* (Minneapolis: University of Minnesota Press, 2009).

Oyěwùmi, Oyèrónké. "Visualizing the Body: Western Theories and African Subjects," *The Invention of Women: Making an African Sense of Western Gender Discourses* (Minneapolis: University of Minnesota Press, 1997).

Parker, Andrew, and Eve Kosofsky Sedgwick. "Introduction," in Parker and Kosofsky (eds.), *Performativity and Performance* (New York: Routledge, 1995), 1–18.

Parks, Suzan-Lori. *The America Play and Other Works* (New York: Theatre Communications Group, 1995).

"Interview with Suzan-Lori Parks" (interview by Shelby Jiggetts), *Callaloo*, 19 (spring 1996), 309–17.

Topdog/Underdog (New York: Theatre Communications Group, 1999).

and Liz Diamond. "Doo-a-Diddly-Dit-Dit: An Interview" (interview by Steven Drukman), *TDR*, 39 (autumn 1995), 56–75.

Patterson, Orlando. *Rituals of Blood: Consequences of Slavery in Two American Centuries* (New York: Civitas/Counterpoint, 1998).

Pellegrini, Ann. *Performance Anxieties: Staging Psychoanalysis, Staging Race* (New York: Routledge, 1997).

Perkins, Kathy. "Introduction," in Perkins (ed.), *Black Female Playwrights: An Anthology of Plays before 1950* (Bloomington: Indiana University Press, 1990), 1–18.

Phelan, Peggy. *Unmarked: The Politics of Performance* (Routledge: New York, 1993).

Prevots, Naima. *American Pageantry: A Movement for Art and Democracy* (Ann Arbor: UMI Research Press, 1990).

Rampersad, Arnold. *The Life of Langston Hughes*, 2 vols. (Oxford University Press, 2002).

"W.E.B. Du Bois as a Man of Literature," *American Literature*, 51 (March 1979), 50–68.

Rayner, Alice. *Ghosts: Death's Double and the Phenomena of Theatre* (Minneapolis: University of Minnesota Press, 2006).

Richards, Sandra L. "Writing the Absent Potential Drama, Performance, and the Canon of African-American Literature," in Andrew Parker and Eve Kosofsky Sedgwick (eds.), *Performativity and Performance* (New York: Routledge, 1995), 64–88.

"Yoruba Gods on the American Stage: August Wilson's *Joe Turner's Come and Gone*," in John Conteh-Morgan and Tejumola Olaniyan (eds.), *African Drama and Performance* (Bloomington: Indiana University Press, 2004), 94–106.

Richardson, Willis (ed.). *Plays and Pageants from the Life of the Negro* (Washington, DC: Associated Publishers, 1930).

Roach, Joseph. *Cities of the Dead: Circum-Atlantic Performance* (New York: Columbia University Press, 1996).

Robinson, Cedric. *Black Marxism: The Making of the Black Radical Tradition* (London: Zed; Totawa, NJ: Biblio Distribution Center, 1983).

Rushdy, Ashraf. "Exquisite Corpse," *Transition*, 9.3 (2000), 70–77.

Ryan, Susan M. "Misgivings: Melville, Race and the Ambiguities of Benevolence," *American Literary History*, 12 (winter 2000), 685–712.

Salaam, Kalamu ya. "James Baldwin: Looking towards the Eighties," in Fred L. Standley and Nancy V. Burt (eds.), *Critical Essays on James Baldwin* (Boston: G.K. Hall, 1988), 35–42.

Saldaña-Portillo, María Josefina. *The Revolutionary Imagination in the Americas and the Age of Development* (Durham, NC: Duke University Press, 2003).

Sanders, Leslie Catherine. "'Also Own the Theatre': Representation in the Comedies of Langston Hughes," *Langston Hughes Review*, 11 (spring 1992), 6–13.

The Development of Black Theatre in America: From Shadows to Selves (Baton Rouge: Louisiana State University Press, 1988).

"'I've Wrestled With Them All My Life': Langston Hughes' *Tambourines to Glory*," *Black American Literature Forum*, 25 (spring 1991), 63–72.

Schechner, Richard. *Between Theater and Anthropology* (Philadelphia: University of Pennsylvania Press, 1985).

Scott, Freda L. "*The Star of Ethiopia*: A Contribution toward the Development of Black Drama and Theater in the Harlem Renaissance," in Amritjit Singh, William S. Shiver, and Stanley Brodwin (eds.), *The Harlem Renaissance: Revaluations* (New York: Garland, 1989).

Seshadri-Crooks, Kalpana. *Desiring Whiteness: A Lacanian Analysis of Race* (London; New York: Routledge, 2000).

Shannon, Sandra. *The Dramatic Vision of August Wilson* (Washington, DC: Howard University Press, 1995).

Sharadha, Y. S. *Black Women's Writing: Quest for Identity in the Plays of Lorraine Hansberry and Ntozake Shange* (London: Sangam Books, 1998).

Shenk, Joshua Wolf. "Beyond a Black-and-White Lincoln," *New York Times* (April 7, 2002), 2.6.

Sherrard-Johnson, Cherene. *Portraits of the New Negro Woman: Visual and Literary Culture in the Harlem Renaissance* (New Brunswick, NJ: Rutgers University Press, 2007).

Shewey, Don. "This Time the Shock is Her Turn Toward Naturalism," *New York Times* (July 22, 2001), AR4.

Shipp, Jesse A., Will Marion Cook, and Paul Laurence Dunbar. *In Dahomey*, in Hatch and Shine (eds.), 63–85.

Silverman, Kaja. *The Acoustic Mirror: The Female Voice in Psychoanalysis and Cinema* (Bloomington: Indiana University Press, 1988).

Simone, Nina. *I Put a Spell on You* (New York: Da Capo Press, 1991).

Smallwood, Stephanie E. *Saltwater Slavery: A Middle Passage from African to American Diaspora* (Cambridge, MA: Harvard University Press, 2007).

Smith, Anna Deavere. "Two Visions of Love, Family and Race across the Generations," *New York Times* (May 29, 2004), www.nytimes.com/2004/05/29/theater/two-visions-of-love-family-and-race-across-the-generations.html (accessed October 17, 2009).

Snead, James. "Repetition as a Figure of Black Culture," in Henry Louis Gates, Jr. (ed.), *Black Literature and Literary Theory* (New York: Methuen, 1984).

Southern, Eileen. *The Music of Black Americans: A History* (New York: W.W. Norton, 1997).

Soyinka, Wole. *Myth, Literature and the African World* (Cambridge University Press, 1976).

Spillers, Hortense. "Afterword," in Hortense Spillers and Marjorie Pryse (eds.), *Conjuring Black Women, Fiction, and Literary Tradition*, (Bloomington: Indiana University Press, 1985), 249–61.

    Black, White, and in Color: Essays on American Literature and Culture (University of Chicago Press, 2003).

Stauffer, John. *Giants: The Parallel Lives of Frederick Douglass and Abraham Lincoln* (New York: Twelve, 2008).

Steele, Shelby. "Notes on Ritual in the New Black Theater," in Errol Hill (ed.), *The Theater of Black Americans* (New York: Applause, 1987), 30–44.

Steen, Shannon. "Melancholy Bodies: Racial Subjectivity and Whiteness in O'Neill's *The Emperor Jones*," *Theatre Journal*, 52 (October 2000), 339–59.

Stephens, Michelle Ann. *Black Empire: The Masculine Global Imaginary of Caribbean Intellectuals in the United States, 1914–1962* (Durham, NC: Duke University Press, 2005).

Stepto, Robert. *From Behind the Veil: A Study of Afro-American Narrative* (Urbana: University of Illinois Press, 1979).

Sundquist, Eric J. *To Wake the Nations: Race in the Making of American Literature* (Cambridge, MA: Harvard University Press, 1993).

Tate, Claudia. *Psychoanalysis and Black Novels: Desire and the Protocols of Race* (Oxford University Press, 1998).

Taylor, Diana. *The Archive and the Repertoire: Performing Cultural Memory in the Americas* (Durham, NC: Duke University Press, 2003).

Thiong'o, Ngugi wa. *Penpoints, Gunpoints, and Dreams: Towards a Critical Theory of the Arts and the State in Africa* (Oxford: Clarendon Press, 1998).

Thorpe, Edward. *Black Dance* (Woodstock, NY: Overlook Press, 1990).

Thurman, Wallace. *The Blacker the Berry* (New York: Scribner, 1996; first published 1929).

Toomer, Jean. *Cane* (New York: Liveright, 1975; first published 1923).

Traylor, Eleanor W. "Two Afro-American Contributions to Dramatic Form," in Errol Hill (ed.), *The Theater of Black Americans: A Collection of Critical Essays* (New York: Applause, 1987), 45–60.

Turner, Victor. *Dramas, Fields, and Metaphors: Symbolic Action in Human Society* (Ithaca, NY: Cornell University Press, 1974).

Walker, Aida Overton. "Colored Men and Women on the American Stage," *Colored American Magazine* (October 1905), 574.

Walker, George. "The Negro on the American Stage," *Colored American Magazine* (October 1906), 243–48.

Wall, Cheryl. "On Freedom and the Will to Adorn: Debating Aesthetics and/ as Ideology in African American Literature," in George Levine (ed.), *Aesthetics and Ideology* (New Brunswick, NJ: Rutgers University Press, 1994), 283–303.

Women of the Harlem Renaissance (Bloomington: Indiana University Press, 1995).

Worrying the Line: Black Women Writers, Lineage, and Literary Tradition (Chapel Hill: University of North Carolina Press, 2005).

Walton, Jean. *Fair Sex, Savage Dreams: Race, Psychoanalysis, Sexual Difference* (Durham, NC: Duke University Press, 2001).

Washington, Sylvia Hood. *Packing Them In: An Archaeology of Environmental Racism in Chicago, 1865–1954* (Lanham, MD: Lexington Books, 2005).

Watts, Jerry Gafio. *Amiri Baraka: The Politics and Art of a Black Intellectual* (New York University Press, 2001).

Weheliye, Alexander. *Phonographies: Grooves in Sonic Afro-Modernity* (Durham, NC: Duke University Press, 2005).

Weinbaum, Alys Eve. *Wayward Reproductions: Genealogies of Race and Nation in Transatlantic Modern Thought* (Durham, NC: Duke University Press, 2004).

West, Cornel. *Prophesy Deliverance!: An Afro-American Revolutionary Christianity*, 2nd edn. (Philadelphia: Westminster Press, 2002).

Wilkerson, Margaret B. "The Sighted Eyes and Feeling Heart of Lorraine Hansberry," *Black American Literature Forum*, 17 (spring 1983), 8–13.

Williamson, Joel. "W.E.B. Du Bois as a Hegelian," in David G. Sansing (ed.), *What Was Freedom's Price* (Jackson: University Press of Mississippi, 1978).

Wilson, August. "August Wilson" (interview by David Savran), in Jackson R. Byer and Mary C. Hartig (eds.), *Conversations with August Wilson* (Jackson: University of Mississippi Press, 2006), 19–37.

"August Wilson Explains His Dramatic Vision: An Interview" (interview by Sandra Shannon), in Jackson R. Byer and Mary C. Hartig (eds.), *Conversations with August Wilson* (Jackson: University of Mississippi Press, 2006), 118–54.

Gem of the Ocean (New York: Theatre Communications Group, 2006).

The Ground on Which I Stand (New York: Theatre Communications Group, 1996).

"How to Write a Play Like August Wilson," *New York Times* (March 10, 1991), sec. 2.5, 17.

Joe Turner's Come and Gone (New York: Plume, 1988).

"Preface," in *Three Plays* (University of Pittsburgh Press, 1991), vii–xiv.

Wilson, Ivy. "'Are You Man Enough?': Imagining Ethiopia and Transnational Black Masculinity," *Callaloo*, 33 (winter 2010), 265–77.

Wright, Richard. *Twelve Million Black Voices* (New York: Thunder's Mouth Press, 1941).

Young, Harvey. *Embodying Black Experience: Stillness, Critical Memory, and the Black Body* (Ann Arbor: University of Michigan Press, 2010).

Zamir, Shamoon. *Dark Voices: W.E.B. Du Bois and American Thought, 1888–1903* (University of Chicago Press, 1995).

Zoglin, Richard. "Theater: Raisin and the Rapper," *Time* (May 10, 2004), www.time.com/time/magazine/article/0,9171,994156,00.html (accessed October 17, 2009).

Index

Lightning Source UK Ltd.
Milton Keynes UK
UKHW022120271222
414250UK00032B/882